THE LONG WAR

THE
LONG WAR

Judy Kutulas

The Intellectual

People's Front and

Anti-Stalinism,

1930–1940

DUKE UNIVERSITY PRESS | Durham and London 1995

© 1995 Duke University Press

All rights reserved

Printed in the United States on

acid-free paper ∞

Designed by Cherie H. Westmoreland

Typeset by Keystone Typesetting, Inc.

Library of Congress Cataloging-in-Publication Data

appear on the last printed page of this book.

To my parents,

John and Alexandra Kutulas

CONTENTS

Contents

ACKNOWLEDGMENTS

As one does with any long-term project, I have accrued a fair number of debts along the way. This work began as a dissertation at the University of California at Los Angeles under the direction of Richard Weiss and Robert Dallek. Both gave generously of their time in reading over the work and in offering valuable criticism. I would especially like to thank Richard Weiss for his friendship, support and useful advice over the years.

The research was accomplished through a number of grants and fellowships, both pre- and post-doctorate, including a Carey McWilliams fellowship, a Newberry Library short-term fellowship, a National Endowment for the Humanities travel grant, and an American Council of Learned Societies grant. St. Olaf College provided time off to facilitate writing.

Libraries and archives have been generous in sending materials through the mails, particularly when poverty and two pregnancies limited my ability to travel extensively. Librarians at the University of Washington, University of Oregon, Smith College, the Franklin D. Roosevelt Library, Harvard University, Yale University, Radcliffe College, Syracuse University, Southern Illinois University, and the University of Maryland dispatched small sheaves of photocopies that aided my work.

Acknowledgments

x   Many librarians and archivists have been helpful in my quest for
ever more obscure material. The interlibrary loan staffs at UCLA, St.
Olaf College, the University of California at Irvine, and the University
of Virginia found just about everything I ever asked for. Archivists at
the Newberry Library, the Hoover Archives, the New York Public Library, the Library of Congress, the University of California at Berkeley,
the Stanford University Library, the Bancroft Library, the Tamiment
Library, the Wisconsin State Historical Society, and the Mudd Library
at Princeton answered many questions and many unusual requests.

One of the most exciting aspects of working in "recent" history is
the availability of a special kind of source: participants. I would like to
thank the following for their valuable interviews or letters: Michael
Blankfort, Mrs. James Burnham, Hal Draper, Theodore Draper, Louis
Filler, Emanuel Geltman, Sidney Hook, Alfred Kazin, George Novack,
and William Phillips. I would especially like to thank Malcolm Cowley, whose patience with a graduate student seemed unlimited.

Numerous people have improved my reading of the 1930s. Michael
Furmanovsky shares my interest in the left and has listened to me spin
many theories. Avital Bloch writes on the next generation of intellectuals, the neoconservatives; she has helped me link the 1930s with
later decades. Mark Kleinman has been a great resource on the Americans for Democratic Action and the 1950s more generally. Harvey
Klehr, Alan Wald, and Daniel Aaron each helped a junior scholar find
her way. Barbara Foley was, conveniently, at the Newberry the same
time as I. I like to hope we both benefited from the experience; I certainly know I did. Members of the History Department at St. Olaf College, both past and present, have read parts of this manuscript and
commented upon them. Jim Farrell's advice was especially valuable
and I appreciate the time he took to provide critiques of several parts of
the manuscript. A summer seminar on American intellectual history
sponsored by the National Endowment for the Humanities under the
direction of John Patrick Diggins helped me sharpen my sense of myself within the broader field of history and introduced me to several
other academics whose interests overlap my own. Art Casciato and
Alan Filreis gave this manuscript several thorough readings for Duke
University Press. Their comments were invaluable. Lawrence Malley
of Duke Press waited patiently through multiple drafts until I got it
right and his successor, Rachel Toor, helped shepherd it through the
final steps of the publication process. Pam Morrison of Duke has answered *many* questions.

Other colleagues have provided the moral support necessary to get through a long project. Jill Watts, Monte Kugel, Chip Hixson, Jackie Braitman, Dolores Peters, Jeane DeLaney, Mary Titus, Gary DeKrey, and Sarah and Robert Entenmann have not read this manuscript, but they have listened to me complain about it and taken me out for coffee when things have gone wrong. My parents, John and Alexandra Kutulas, and my three sisters, Janet and Nikki Kutulas and Sandra Perez, are puzzled by why this has taken so long, but have been very supportive nonetheless. Michael Fitzgerald has extended his scholarly help as a historian and his moral support and logistical help as a spouse and if I grow any more sentimental about his contributions, he will edit me. My sons, Alex and Nate, have not aided in the completion of this manuscript at all and have, in fact, often hindered it; but I love them dearly for it.

ABBREVIATIONS USED IN THE TEXT

ACCF	American Committee for Cultural Freedom
ACLU	American Civil Liberties Union
ACDIF	American Committee for Democracy and Intellectual Freedom
ACDLT	American Committee for the Defense of Leon Trotsky
ADA	Americans for Democratic Action
AFT	American Federation of Teachers
AIF	American Intellectuals for Freedom
AJC	American Jewish Committee
ALPD	American League for Peace and Democracy
ALWF	American League against War and Fascism
ASU	American Student Union
AWP	American Workers Party
CCF	Committee for Cultural Freedom
CIO	Congress of Industrial Organizations
CLA	Communist League of America
CPA	Communist Political Association
CPUSA	Communist Party, U.S.A.
ECLC	Emergency Civil Liberties Committee
FSU	Friends of the Soviet Union
HUAC	House UnAmerican Activities Committee

ILD	International Labor Defense
JRCS	John Reed Clubs
KAOWC	Keep America Out of War Committee
LAW	League of American Writers
LID	League for Industrial Democracy
MPDC	Motion Picture Democratic Committee
NAACP	National Association for the Advancement of Colored People
NCDPP	National Committee for the Defense of Political Prisoners
NPLD	Non-Partisan Labor Defense
SPUSA	Socialist Party, U.S.A.
SWP	Socialist Workers Party
UDA	Union for Democratic Action
WP	Workers Party
WPA	Works Progress Administration

THE LONG WAR

Instead of Communists, fellow travelers, liberals and radicals in one lump, the reality of the period lay in its battles.—Harold Rosenberg, "Couch Liberalism and the Guilty Past"

When Lillian Hellman died in 1984 she left unsettled a 2.25 million dollar libel suit against Mary McCarthy. The suit, which included Dick Cavett and the PBS affiliate producing his television show, alleged that McCarthy defamed Hellman by calling her "a bad writer and dishonest writer"[1] on national television. To the outsider, McCarthy's accusations and Hellman's response seem exaggerated and uncivil. Scholars of the 1930s, however, immediately recognize the episode as part of a longer feud among American intellectuals. Hellman and McCarthy fought to legitimate two very different left-wing pasts. Hellman was part of the People's Front, a loose conglomeration of organizations shepherded by the American Communist Party in the 1930s in order to help defeat fascism. McCarthy opposed the Front. Hellman regarded her membership in front organizations as a political responsibility, a way an intellectual might join the battle against Hitler. McCarthy believed such partisanship threatened her status as a critical commentator. Their positions represented opposing sides in a long war waged among left-wing intellectuals in the 1930s and beyond.

Ever since the People's Front strategy ended in 1940, partisans, scholars, and activists alike have debated its accomplishments and failures. They have disagreed over what participants termed the "means" of politics rather than the "ends."[2] In the early half of the

1930s, the end they sought was some form of planned and collective economy, a goal embraced by virtually all intellectuals left of the New Deal. In the latter half of the decade, left intellectuals felt constrained enough by reality to scale down their expectations and redefine their goals. "Democracy," a term that would turn out to be as vague and loaded as "communism," "totalitarianism," "socialism," and "fascism," became their objective. Mustering consensus over abstract principles meant little, however, because the dispute over means completely obscured whatever shared values liberals and radicals had.

Liberals and radicals usually occupy rather different political orbits. Reformers promote evolutionary change complimentary to American democratic traditions. Radicals desire more far-reaching and dramatic change, often imagining that revolution is the only way to strip away the old society and usher in a new one. These differences frequently describe an unbridgeable gap; liberals and radicals do not generally get along. In the 1930s, however, some did. This was in part because of the existence and relative power of the American Communist Party. Paired groups of liberals and radicals formed alliances defined by their conflicting evaluations of the cpusa and the role it should play in the process of social transformation. These alliances emerged because the American Communist Party relied on the cooperation of noncommunists to further its goals. Front politics drew noncommunists into the Communists' "movement culture"[3] so that they might share in the Communists' larger vision without having to participate in the more problematic parts of vanguard party membership. Communists gained access to a broader community, but did not have to worry about the rectitude of people often unsuited to the discipline of a vanguard party. The benefits thus were supposed to be reciprocal. But some left-wing intellectuals thought front politics immoral. Rather than everyone benefiting, they argued, Communists gained disproportionately, deliberately manipulating the larger community for their own ends. By 1937, the intellectual left was divided into two warring camps, one focused on the People's Front and a second one opposing it.

Once that happened, joining or refusing to join fronts became political acts that communicated a host of symbolic meanings. A few intellectuals were oblivious to this reality, moving in or out of fronts on their own merit. Most, however, recognized the figurative dimension of their choices. Favoring the People's Front meant choosing Stalin as the lesser of two evils. It also connoted an intellectual ideal that was practical, active, and, hopefully, relevant to the masses. Opposing the People's Front meant rejecting the very idea that a lesser of two evils could be a moral choice. It also stood for an intellectual style that was pure, detached, and critical. Subscribing to a journal, signing a manifesto, joining—or refusing to join—an organization, or endorsing a cause became shorthand methods of expressing one's position within these extremes.

No political debate exists in a vacuum. Advocates of the People's Front and their opponents competed for status and power as they fought over the Front, the cpusa, and Stalin. Being a "good" intellectual might be intrinsically satisfying, but intellectuals also expected external recognition for their efforts. In a just universe, "good" intellectuals would reap certain personal advantages: the respect of their peers, a wider audience, the ability to function as intellectuals, and the financial wherewithal to do so. During the Depression, those material aspects of success or, conversely, the costs of failure, became increasingly significant. Yet some would prosper and others would fail. The side that won the debate over front politics stood a far better chance than the other of gaining access to the perquisites of status.

Such success is generally elusive, but in the 1930s it was especially so. The Depression economy narrowed opportunities. The polarization of the community created by front politics limited the scope of one's audience. But no single factor so shaped the possibilities of individuals as their birthrights. Intellectuals traditionally mirrored the characteristics of the American middle class. The vast majority of the most famous intellectuals born before 1900 were white, Protestant, and liberal. Certainly there were Jewish, African American, and radical intellectuals, but their successes tended to remain within smaller circles. The generation of intellectuals who came of age just before or during the Depression were not like their older counterparts. They reflected a changed America, one marked by the diversity that industrialization wrought. Younger intellectuals were more likely to be the children of eastern and southern European immigrants. Many were Jewish or Catholic; many grew up poor. Most came from East Coast cities. On the whole, the younger generation opposed the People's Front and the older generation supported it, which meant the balance of forces was not especially even. Older, more established, and more traditional intellectuals would have had more power under any cir-

4 cumstances; but the Depression exacerbated the differences between the well-placed and the struggling. The fight for authority implicit in the fight over front politics pitted two generations against one another.

This aspect of the quarrel between the Front and its opposites often makes people uneasy. People are more willing to accept that bankers, factory workers, even politicians struggle for power. Moreover, since the matter had an ethnic dimension, commentators feel they must tread carefully or find themselves attributing particular characteristics to certain ethnic groups. But power is not an illegitimate goal of intellectuals. They need time and energy to refine their ideas and the opportunity to explain their thoughts to the larger world. This was really all the younger generation sought. There were few intellectual opportunists in the 1930s; but there were many people who felt they deserved the earmarks of intellectual success because they did their jobs well. The long war between anti-Stalinists and representatives of the People's Front was about right and wrong and how critics and creative people ought to relate to the society in which they lived; but it also marked an inevitable transition from generation to generation. It was only in its particulars, the values the next generation espoused and the psychic scars they carried, that the story is any different from that of other times.

Over the years, many people have written about those who supported the People's Front and the advocates of anti-Stalinism. Unfortunately, the lengthy historiography does not reveal as much about the period as about its chroniclers. The topic presents a number of methodological pitfalls. It is politically problematic; communism, as an issue, sensationalizes the story. It also invites reproofs and evasion. During the cold war, especially, some people found it politically advantageous to misrepresent their pasts. Evaluating what intellectuals say and write is difficult, for they can be glib or misleading. The biggest ideological pitfall, however, is that the moral judgments made by participants extend into the historiography, where they sometimes seem to become objective truth. The many memoirs of the period have entered the historical record in two incompatible ways, as primary and secondary texts. People who have much to gain or lose from the way historians evaluate what happened in the 1930s have not been content to let others write their histories, but have produced their own. Their renderings have blurred the lines between document and interpretation. The fight over the People's Front is perpetuated in its historiography, through what Alan Wald called "the politics of memory."[4]

The classic example of a work that straddles the fence is Eugene Lyons's *The Red Decade,* written in 1941.[5] Lyons intended to write a partisan book that was "frankly journalistic and polemic." A disillusioned admirer of the Soviet Union who suffered as his views changed, he had a very clear agenda in mind. His goal was to expose the communist "conspiracy" of the 1930s by revealing the ways the CPUSA used fronts to control various American institutions. Lyons was an extremist, but his book has not always been considered extreme. His interpretive framework seemed intuitively right to other anticommunists. Both Lyons and his intellectual audience felt persecuted by the People's Front, so it is hardly surprising that they believed in a massive conspiratorial apparatus of fronts manipulated by a cynical clique of Communists who meshed their activities with Stalin's changes of line. *The Red Decade* is a very useful document. But as a secondary source, it leaves much to be desired.

Lyons's work was but the first of scores of books written by the Front's many opponents, few of whom would claim to be his heirs. Lyons was an extremist full of conspiracy theories. However, his premise, that no intellectual could think freely while committed to the People's Front, had a wide currency amongst an otherwise politically diverse group of Front critics. Thus it was possible for Mary McCarthy, whose political perspective was otherwise light years apart from Lyons's, to be persuaded that Lillian Hellman had been a KGB operative; Hellman was, after all, an enthusiastic supporter of front politics and, logically, capable of such intellectual depravity.[6] Opponents of the Front ordered their world just as Lyons did his, by casting themselves as beleaguered but morally responsible individuals fighting against a much larger and unprincipled enemy. In considering the costs of a morally inverted universe, they noted that their enemies' double standard sanctioned the Moscow trials and the purges, fostering such an uncritical acceptance of communism that even as unscrupulous an anticommunist as Joseph McCarthy could gain a backlash following fifteen years later.[7]

Because of the potency of anticommunism as an ideology in the United States after World War II and the age gap between Front supporters and their critics, anti-Front memoirs received wide circulation and were respected as objective history rather than self-serving opinion. Postwar liberal anticommunism itself owed much to intellectuals who opposed the Front in the 1930s and made it their life's work to see that such an alignment of political forces never again occurred. People like Diana Trilling, Sidney Hook, and William Phillips became public "experts" by dint of their superior knowledge of the evils of communism and their claims of superior morality.[8] Their expertise enabled them to cross the historiographic line from unreliable eyewitnesses to judicious analysts and to triumph in the "autobiographical wars."[9] Their delineation of the forces at work in the 1930s, seemingly reinforced by the passage of time, prevailed for a considerable period and, to some extent, continues to prevail today.

Later historians and commentators accept almost without question anticommunists' conceptualization of the anti-Front side as the "better" one, to use William O'Neill's word, and the pro-Front one as immoral. O'Neill, whose *A Better World* focused on the period after 1939, suggested that those allied with the Front and its successors did not deserve to be considered real intellectuals: "To defend Stalinism was self-defeating, but, even worse, to set a bad example. And this was not simply unfortunate, a matter of leading innocents astray; it was to misconstrue a central purpose of the intelligentsia . . . When intellectuals, for whatever reasons, abandon their calling and join the zealots, they give up a role they alone can play."[10] The costs of such partisanship, he believes, were significant. Left intellectuals failed to create a true "*American* left, democratic, loyal, and with no compulsion to admire or emulate foreign tyrannies" which might have counterbalanced the worse excesses of the 1950s.[11] Paul Hollander argues in *Political Pilgrims* that intellectuals who used a separate standard to judge socialist societies denigrated their own in the process.[12] So too did they hurt innocent people, including their more scrupulous colleagues. This version of the 1930s intellectual left uncritically accepts the anticommunists' categories and premises, giving added nuance to a story that has, otherwise, changed rather little over time.[13]

This interpretation has not gone unchallenged, despite the occasional risks involved in articulating a very different version of what being a part of the Front meant. Defenders of the Front offer a more muted reckoning, as the title of Malcolm Cowley's memoir, "The Sense of Guilt,"[14] suggests. Cowley conceded that Stalinism was more dangerous than he believed at the time and acknowledged that his opponents were more astute in their evaluations of the Soviet Union. But he also felt that while he and other Front supporters might have underestimated Stalin's crimes, anticommunists became so obsessed with those crimes that they underestimated Hitler's. "Even after forty years, and even while trying to be completely fair about the time," he concluded, "I still cannot believe that the errors were equally distributed on the two sides." The same people Lyons attacked he saw as "good writer[s] and . . . honest m[e]n" trying to make reasonable choices in an imperfect world. Associating with the People's Front was, to them, nothing more than a practical vehicle for their antifascism and "the only sound policy . . . to check Hitler."

Cowley's comrades on the Front's barricades often remembered their pasts as grand gestures to defeat Hitler. The Moscow trials were deplorable, they admitted, but nothing they could change; many claimed they were scrupulously neutral on the matter publicly. If public neutrality was what it took to oppose Hitler, then so be it. In this construction, the people who faced political realities and accepted an imperfect deal with the CPUSA were courageous while their opponents were too wishy-washy to take a real stand at all. Thus, if Mary McCarthy thought Lillian Hellman's political affiliations prevented her from being a good intellectual, Hellman believed McCarthy's lack of commitment in the 1930s demonstrated a kind of intellectual timidity that allowed a Joseph McCarthy full scope.[15]

Intellectual historians sympathetic to the Front invoke many of these same arguments. They tread cautiously, conceding, as Cowley did, that the anticommunists were right about the Front's drawbacks, but counterbalance that admission by suggesting that intellectuals, especially literary intellectuals, had no power to influence political events anyway. Intentions were what really counted. Intellectuals felt strongly enough about fascism to mobilize, and that was to be applauded. Signing a few petitions or writing a few articles about civil liberties in the Soviet Union was hardly going to change the course of world history. Thus, Richard Pells argued, the intellectual People's Front was more important "as a cultural phenomenon than as a political strategy."[16] Its true achievements were individual. Intellectuals who tried "to change the world," Daniel Aaron concluded in *Writers on the Left*,[17] became more thoughtful and subtle in the process; they were better intellectuals because they learned to engage in political discourse and empathize with others. What mattered about the Front, then, was not its eventual failure so much as the experience itself.

These two versions of the 1930s, one derived from the value system of anticommunists and the other from one-time representatives of the People's Front, describe mirror universes where some intellectuals were "better" than others because they meant well, even if their pro-Sovietism or anticommunism occasionally got out of hand. There is no middle ground; in defending one version commentators almost automatically assume that the other is false, even deliberately so. Yet there are also differences. One view sees intellectuals as powerful moral arbiters whose failure to behave as intellectuals should was the cause of immense grief at home and abroad. The other sees intellectuals as dabblers whose somewhat naive political adventures had few real consequences but made them better people. For the next twenty years, the historiography of the 1930s was as fractious as the decade itself.

As the cold war climate weakened, scholars attempted to refocus the story of the 1930s in the hopes of breaking this impasse. They borrowed techniques from social historians, turning the same microscope others used on New England towns or steel workers' unions on intellectuals. The proliferation of intellectual biographies and group biographies written in the 1970s and 1980s give us a great deal of detail, sometimes reconstructing lives almost day-by-day. These studies avoid the categories that have so polarized the historiography of the 1930s intellectual left by showing that politics, intellectual ideals, and creativity were extremely complex and personal matters.

One of the earliest of these works was Frank Warren's *Liberals and Communism*.[18] As the title suggests, his subject was the larger segment of the 1930s left. But, as his subtitle, *The "Red Decade" Revisited*, indicated, he was not content to reiterate either of the established lines. Rather than using the dividing line of the People's Front, Warren placed his liberals on a continuum ranging from "fellow travelers" to "Russian sympathizers" to "anti-Communists." His chapters trace their varied responses to such crises as the Depression, the rise of fascism, the Spanish Civil War, and the Moscow trials. The texture of his work is different from others' and the result is at least more complex even if it is not fully freed of older assumptions. Warren takes on elements of the anticommunist and pro-Front positions, first condemning those who practiced front politics (presumably a blurring of his first two categories) for allowing "an atrophy of the[ir] critical function" in the 1930s, then blaming those who critiqued the Front for becoming "uncritical cheerleaders" of American society in the 1950s.

Still, Warren was among the first to move beyond the deadlock between anticommunists and Front defenders, offering a more nuanced
perspective by looking at a smaller segment of the intellectual left.

The logical extreme of this trend has been individual biographies of
phenomenal depth and detail which extend before and beyond the
1930s, but regard the 1930s experience as pivotal. The written record
left behind by most intellectual figures is extensive, especially when
augmented by new sources like FBI files and interviews. Piecing together records and extracting a narrative requires amazing patience
and dedication. Works like Elinor Langer's biography of Josephine
Herbst, Leonard Wilcox's of V. F. Calverton, and Townsend Ludington's of John Dos Passos[19] enable us to re-create the personal, political,
and intellectual forces that moved individuals. These biographies are
valuable resources. They are not, however, always suitable commentaries on the period. Although some, like Wilcox's work, examine the
larger intellectual community, others are strictly biographical, often
depicting quirky and unique individuals whose particular place in a
larger cosmos is not clearly fixed. No matter how scrupulously they are
written, the reader is inevitably drawn to the more sensational aspects
of life like marital problems, personal failings, and private anxieties.
Moreover, even at this most microcosmic of levels, many commentators still cannot escape the good Front/bad anticommunists or good
anticommunists/bad Front dichotomy.[20]

Taking the middle ground between the broader perspective of Warren and the very precise subject matter of the single-individual biographies, are a series of group biographies. These combine some of the advantages of both types of work. They are sufficiently broad to provide a
sense of some larger trends on the left; yet they are also nicely detailed.
Moreover, by tracing individuals' backgrounds and later lives, they
help to put the 1930s in context. Unfortunately, the subject of the
group biographies has been one segment of the community almost to
the exclusion of any other. The New York intellectuals—Marxists clus-
tered around the *Partisan Review* who were anti-Stalinist in the late
1930s and shifted gradually toward the center and, in some cases, the
far right—have become, in James Gilbert's trenchant phrase, "the new
burnt-over district of American cultural history."[21] Scholars are attracted to them for several reasons: their political odysseys are long
and interesting, they were influential, and their lives provide a springboard for those interested in their politics or their cultural critiques.

10   Consequently, the New York intellectuals have been elevated by the historiography to a status well beyond their actual place in 1930s America.

In the last half decade there have been four full-length books on the New York intellectuals, each offering a slightly different interpretation of their remarkable transformations. Alexander Bloom invokes a series of family metaphors in his *Prodigal Sons*,[22] suggesting that there was an inevitable maturation behind their transitions. Youthful exuberance and a desire to step outside their Jewish identities led young intellectuals to become radicals. With age came greater acceptance, both of the status quo and their Jewish heritages. The result was a collective shift to the center. Terry Cooney[23] takes more of a class tack, arguing that during the 1930s the New York intellectuals were "on the margin," as Irving Howe put it, gaining stature only after the Nazi-Soviet Pact of 1939. That stature made them more a part of the system than before. Money, mainstream jobs, and status softened their views. Neil Jumonville's *Critical Crossings*[24] addresses only the postwar period and concerns itself primarily with cultural issues. He argues that there was a consistency of intellectual style that gave form to the New York intellectuals' many changes. Alan Wald[25] examines a somewhat broader community of dissident Marxists and concludes that the New York intellectuals' failure to remain both Marxist and anti-Stalinist resulted from their unwillingness to join what he calls radical "counterinstitutions." Real political commitment to the labor movement and the Trotskyist sects provided a Marxist anchor for other, less well known intellectuals. All of these books have much to recommend them. Bloom and Cooney are certainly on target when they describe the New York intellectuals' trajectory. Jumonville's contention that a self-conception drove them more than any particular political issue gives us a better sense of the harmony and structure of their intellectual lives. And Wald's distinction between activists and more traditional intellectuals keeps us from stereotyping all dissidents as youthful radicals who got old and conservative simultaneously. Bloom, Cooney, Jumonville, and Wald do precisely what they set out to do, giving us a clear and comprehensible picture of one specific segment of the 1930s intellectual left.

But we now know so much about the New York intellectuals that they tend to loom larger in the historiography than they did in life.[26] By illuminating them so brightly, we lose sight of the rest of the community, their lives, expectations, and changes. Wald, Cooney, Bloom, and Jumonville do not exaggerate the role of the New York intellectuals in their individual works; however, the collective weight of what they write suggests that these were the people who mattered and who most influenced policy. Because these scholars are so successful at detailing life in the anti-Stalinist intelligentsia, it becomes harder to imagine the New York intellectuals' opponents and to credit them with the same sensitivity and depth. We cannot help but wonder why so many others did not see the world as the New York intellectuals did and why so many others supported a People's Front these clever men and women found so offensive.

The new historiography of the 1930s intellectual left fragments the past just as much as it enriches our knowledge of it. The plethora of group biographies of the New York intellectuals have drawn scholarly attention and resources away from the People's Front. This exacerbates a problem already extant in the literature, the unequal volume of information available on the two sides. From the beginning there has been far more written by and about anticommunists than intellectual Communists and their Front allies. Some of the reasons are obvious. Communists wrote for a more specialized audience and many preferred not to leave extensive paper trails for the government. As Wald himself noted, "the McCarthyite witch-hunt . . . forced a generation of writers to conceal, dissemble, and even to actually forget what they had gone through."[27] Anti-Stalinists tended to be younger and have lengthier careers in the public eye. Party intellectuals, stereotyped as posturing proletarians and shrill politicos, did not seem to offer much depth. The "new" historiography of the 1930s intellectual left renders the People's Front more invisible than anything else.

Only now are we starting to see a reversal of this trend. New literary analyses of the early 1930s suggest that we must reassess our assumptions about the Communist intelligentsia. Literary historians have long taken it for granted that cultural dicta were handed down from the Comintern along with political lines. But the new works on the proletarian culture show that older assumptions about "artists in uniform," to borrow Max Eastman's phrase, have remained unexamined for too long. James Murphy's study of the dissemination of aesthetics from the Russian Association of Proletarian Writers to American and German communists suggests that the "prolet cult" began as something quite unlike our stereotypes, only to be changed by a few writ-

12   ers.[28] Barbara Foley rejects "the standard view of 1930s literary radicalism" that portrays American writers "obliged to follow lockstep in
the tracks of Soviet cultural policy."[29] Alan Wald has proposed a new
agenda for our study of Communist literary figures, one that asks us
to look at them through lenses other than their political affiliation.[30]
James D. Bloom's portrait of Michael Gold and Joseph Freeman tells us
about two of the more significant thirties literary Communists, successfully demonstrating that their Party politics and literary ideals
were not contradictory categories.[31] Paula Rabinowitz's groundbreak-
ing book on the prolet cult and women writers draws upon postmod-
ernist literary analysis to show how women wrote themselves into a
form that was explicitly radical and implicitly masculine.[32] These literary histories supersede works like *Writers on the Left,* which treat
Party activism as a burden that provided benefits only once it was
thrust aside. They are just beginning to reexamine a field long ago
dismissed. Until recently, the strength of the "artists in uniform" metaphor has made scholars uninterested in intellectuals who seemed supremely unattractive and unrewarding subjects of study.

Curiously, the situation is reversed when it comes to general histories of 1930s radicalism. If literary historians have been more interested in anti-Front groupings, political scientists and social and political historians prefer to write about the American Communist Party.
There is one book on American Trotskyism, Constance Ashton Myers's
The Prophet's Army, a few books on the American Socialist Party, part
of a book on American Lovestoneites, and nothing on the American
Workers Party.[33] This is not to say that the history of the CPUSA has
been written from a sympathetic perspective. Anticommunism, either
directly or indirectly, dominated its historiography for a long time.
By the standards of the cold war, such books as Theodore Draper's
American Communism and Soviet Russia and Lewis Coser and Irving
Howe's *The American Communist Party: A Critical History*[34] were
considered moderate, but their authors assume, as Eugene Lyons and
Mary McCarthy did, that power within the Communist movement em-
anated only from the top down, that Stalin controlled the Comintern,
the Comintern controlled the CPUSA, and the CPUSA controlled the People's Front. This chain of command, most cold war era commentators
believed, shaped the movement far more decisively than any other
factor. That perception continues to affect the writing of Communist
Party history today. In one of the two more recent studies of the CPUSA

in the 1930s, *The Heyday of American Communism,* Harvey Klehr argues that the most relevant fact about the CPUSA was its complete obeisance to Moscow. "To pretend otherwise," he concludes, "is to misunderstand and distort the history of American Communism."[35] Klehr and earlier historians of the CPUSA suggest this institutional rooting doomed the American People's Front to failure. As Draper put it: "the Communist-style Popular Front did not and could not develop into an authentic American socialism or radicalism."[36]

A number of scholars have challenged this assumption. The revisionists argue that works like Klehr's are institutional histories that ignore the beliefs and expectations of the average Communist. Theirs is a history from the bottom up, often drawn from oral narratives. They question how far directives from the Comintern really percolated down into the rank-and-file and conclude that most in the Party's labor contingent knew little about Russia and were primarily interested in building a truly American movement. They see the undeniable input from Moscow as a jumping off place for a more creative, more homegrown set of policies. Fraser Ottanelli's *The Communist Party of the United States: From the Depression to World War II* shows "an intricate interaction" amongst American Communists, their leaders, and Moscow when it came to policy.[37] He attempts to substantiate the interpretation first offered by Mark Naison, Roy Rozenzweig, Gary Gerstle, and Paul Buhle, who see the Popular Front as "a crucial transition in the history of American radicalism" and view it as an ultimately failed opportunity for "individual communists . . . to act on their desires to root their radicalism in American soil."[38] Michael E. Brown has recently repositioned this debate between "orthodox" and "new" historians of American Communism, arguing that the "new" history reflects the impact of "a considerably expanded empirical field and a correspondingly different sense of what is involved in writing history." The "new" history of the CPUSA, then, is not merely a New Left history, but one informed by changing literary, sociological, anthropological, and political theories, by deconstruction, by gender issues, and by "consuming discourses of identity and otherness."[39]

It is difficult at this point to assess how much impact these developments will have on our conception of the intellectual People's Front. On the one hand we have literary canon-busters interested in reconsidering the cultural accomplishments of Party intellectuals. On the other, we have political and social historians reevaluating the sig-

14   nificance of the People's Front as a historical moment. Logically, these analyses would seem to fit together, but there is a piece missing, and that missing piece is how the intellectual People's Front functioned. The literary revisionism parallels the revisionist political analysis of the CPUSA without actually connecting the intellectual with the political.[40] If politicized intellectuals created art or wrote criticism that was subtle rather than strident and rooted in a more complex tradition than historians once believed, what can we conclude about their politics? Was the intellectual People's Front more like what Klehr and Draper imagined or what Murphy and Foley assume?

This study is an attempt to address such questions. In the last two decades there has been a virtual explosion of memoirs and secondary works on the 1930s left-wing intellectual community, but they are either about the literary or the political. Almost none of them considers the intersection of the two in the personae of intellectuals as a social group. Without that information, we can neither fully understand the cultural and critical products nor fully evaluate the nature of the People's Front. When Mary McCarthy denounced Lillian Hellman, she called her not just a bad writer, but a dishonest one as well. The implication was unmistakable; in McCarthy's eyes, Hellman was unfit to be an intellectual, unfit to command the resources she could, unfit to be respected by an interested public. Hellman's politics and whole concept of what good intellectuals were supposed to do made her a bad writer, a bad intellectual, and a bad human being. This study will consider what Hellman—and others like her—did that was so politically offensive to McCarthy—and others like her—that the two ultimately turned to the courts for vindication. It will show when, how, and why their views on the responsibilities and appropriate political comportment of intellectuals diverged and how both their views found institutional support in the 1930s. I will argue that the fights between them and between anti-Stalinists and supporters of the People's Front more generally were so heated that they led to a rupture between generations. In the process, the front mentality of the 1930s gave way to liberal anticommunism in the 1940s and 1950s.

This work challenges an unspoken but almost universal assumption about the 1930s, that there were no unreconcilable differences between Front supporters and critics. Most historians recognize conflict in the 1930s, but tend to believe it smooths out later on, when everyone worth mentioning ends up on the same side, as anticommunists, or at least no longer "Stalinists." Implicit in this interpretation is the corollary that any thoughtful person must eventually grow disillusioned of communism. Those who do not are simply written out of history as intellectually sterile Party mouthpieces. Since only the ultimately disillusioned counted, what was crucial was the timing, the particular milestones (Louis Fischer used the term "Kronstadts")[41] that caused individuals to lose their illusions about Soviet communism. Anti-Stalinists, most scholars would argue, reached their Kronstadts before those who supported the Front, creating temporary antagonisms the Nazi-Soviet Pact and the end of the People's Front eliminated. After that, the vast majority of intellectuals saw eye-to-eye on most matters, simply rehashing old battles out of sheer cantankerousness. But there was no real accord between the sides after 1940; as Hellman's lawsuit suggests, there was continued animosity between those who endorsed the Front—even after they lost their admiration for the Soviet Union and the CPUSA—and those who believed front politics immoral. The two sides were not at different evolutionary stages in the same disillusionment process. Their conflict continued and intensified after the Nazi-Soviet Pact because what they fought over was more profound than any single issue.

I will argue that the People's Front was not a gate through which the disillusioned would ultimately pass, but the manifestation of a particular set of values imperfectly connected with the older intellectual generation. In much the same way, anti-Stalinism represented a second set of values, one often more relevant to the younger generation, values that would transmute over the years but retain aspects of their original character. Rather than traveling the same road at different paces, these two groups of intellectuals were on a collision course because they both wanted the same things as individuals: power, status, and the respect of their peers. As the 1930s progressed, their senses of self sharpened, making conflict more inevitable. External matters, like the Spanish Civil War and the Moscow trials, continued to push them apart rather than bring them together. The more intellectuals parried, the more extreme their positions grew, until the events that should have brought them together, the Nazi-Soviet Pact and the Front's demise, actually pushed them further apart.

This brief sketch should suggest that the story of the intellectual left in the 1930s is one of continual skirmishes driving individuals to ex-

16   tremes. Their battles were fought in the coffeehouses, meeting rooms, editorial offices, and studio apartments that delineated their world and then communicated via statements, manifestos, and open letters. Intellectuals might well have considered their pens their mightiest weapons, but they were inveterate joiners who helped build and populate the League of American Writers, the American Committee for the Defense of Leon Trotsky, the John Reed Clubs, the Committee for Cultural Freedom, the Nonpartisan Labor Defense, the American Civil Liberties Union, the League of Professionals for Foster and Ford, numerous Spanish war relief agencies, the American League for Peace and Democracy, and the National Committee for the Defense of Political Prisoners. They regarded the editorial offices of literary and political magazines, *New Masses, The Nation, The New Republic, Modern Monthly,* the *Partisan Review,* and *Marxist Quarterly* as bastions of particular political perspectives. They took seriously manifestos and editorial lines and open letters, treating them as weapons. These were the arenas in which writers, critics, academics, and other intellectuals fought their battles. These are arenas relatively neglected by intellectual historians, who tend to assume that intellectuals were, by definition, solitary human beings. But 1930s intellectuals were political beings, who grouped together to maximize their impact and who valued collective political action.

This is not, then, a traditional literary or intellectual history, but a social history of intellectuals and their institutions. Their literary and intellectual concerns intrude on politics (and will here too), but it is not the literary expressions of politics that interest me as much as the institutions, manifestos, and political activities that they used to express themselves and to oppose one another. It is my hope that readers will come away from this book persuaded that there was more to the 1930s than a simple and ultimately resolved dispute about the Soviet Union and the American Communist Party. The intellectuals in this study were not merely abstract thinkers whose ideas—cultural and political—emerged in vacuums, but real human beings with expectations, experiences, and petty vendettas. They could not always be perfectly logical and perfectly objective. How they fused their personal imperfections with what they perceived as their critical intellectual roles is what this story is about.

Like other histories of intellectuals and the Depression, this one will not escape making political judgments. However, I hope that by looking at what happened in the 1930s as an interaction or process that changed all its participants I can at least articulate the motives of people I dislike or cannot respect. The purpose here is to ask how it was that individuals with the same set of social priorities ended up so divided and why they evolved in such different directions politically. The answers may not make some intellectuals any less heroes or villains in some readers' eyes; but they may make them more human.

ONE

"Leftbound Local":

The Lost Generation, Social

Activists, Communists, and

the Depression

The Depression drew a larger number of American intellectuals into politics; but most were already politicized in some sense by their experiences in the teens and twenties. It is sometimes difficult to see the continuities between the twenties and the thirties, however, because of all the myths about that "roaring" decade, many of them perpetuated by intellectuals themselves. Dozens of memoirs speak of a nonstop "merry-go-round"[1] of wild parties, exotic locales, and obscure cultural movements. Like many myths, this one had some truth to it, but perhaps more apt was Malcolm Cowley's word, "exiles," or Gertrude Stein's appellation, "the lost generation," to describe young middle-class intellectuals who came of age during World War I, for they spent their youth feeling alienated from authority and power, whether or not they actually were. As they later told their story, however, it was hedonism that moved them in the 1920s, not anxiety. And, when their country was in trouble, the story continued, they realized the error of their ways and "went left" in a "spontaneous and generous spirit" to help save it.[2] But the Depression did not mark the end of one clear-cut period of their lives and the beginning of another. Their post-1929 radicalization was tentative and incomplete and their 1920s experiences were never as effete as they imagined.

The typical 1920s intellectual had already traveled a great distance

from his or her beginnings long before the decade began. Most mainstream intellectuals back then came from genteel, conservative, small
town, middle-class, Protestant families. But because they were born
at a time of rapid change, both material and philosophical, there was
a great gap between them and their parents. The very circumstances
of their lives were technologically different thanks to telephones,
automobiles, bathtubs, and gas furnaces. More importantly, their con-
sciousnesses were shaped by a much less certain world than the one
their parents knew. Darwinism challenged older notions about religion and hierarchy. Marxism provided a new political and economic
perspective. The new disciplines of the social sciences sensitized educated people to cultural diversity and difference. The society they
faced—industrialized, urban, and filled with immigrants—was more
complex. The values handed down from their parents seemed badly
outmoded to the precocious younger generation.

   The full impact of the changes did not hit until these young people
reached college. Helen Lefkowitz Horowitz argued that before World
War I a rebel culture emerged at many universities. Its advocates rejected their families and the traditional college culture of sports and
organized activities in favor of a more intellectually engaging model.
Young people banded together to talk about suffrage, socialism, and
social problems, to work in settlement houses, and to read and discuss
literature. Such rebels found it hard to fit back into the parents' worlds.
College was, Malcolm Cowley believed, the first step in "a long process of deracination . . . making us homeless citizens of the world."[3]
Once out of their small midwestern or New England towns, few returned. They left, Henry F. May noted, "in a mood of excitement and
hope, not necessarily in a spirit of rejection."[4] Indeed, it was easy to
forget one's past when faced with intoxicating future possibilities.

   As members of this intellectual generation stepped into the wider
world, the social issues of the Progressive Era engaged many of
them. The Reverend John Haynes Holmes became an urban progressive, a settlement house worker, and a pacifist. Roger Baldwin also
worked in a settlement house, as did his one-time fiancée, Anna
Louise Strong. Freda Kirchwey joined the picket line during the New
York City shirtwaist strike while still at Barnard and supported Margaret Sanger's crusade for birth control.[5] Feminism particularly influenced female intellectuals of this generation. Inez Haynes Irwin,
Sara Bard Field (who left her children behind with a maid while she

campaigned for the vote in Oregon), Suzanne LaFollette, Agnes Smedley, Genevieve Taggard, and Kirchwey all campaigned for women's rights. Several male intellectuals were also ardent feminists, especially Floyd Dell and Max Eastman, whose sister, Crystal, was one of the country's better-known feminists. Progressivism and feminism introduced young people to a wider and more diverse America and taught them to question orthodoxy and build networks. Both gave intellectuals a head start on the 1930s.[6]

World War I was an important milestone in the maturation of young intellectuals. Some rushed off to fight, pumped full of Wilsonian idealism, and returned disillusioned. Others opposed the war and suffered because of it. War ended the period of domestic reform and fostered a new atmosphere, one intolerant of dissent. A handful of intellectuals were directly affected by wartime laws. The editors of *The Masses* went on trial for violating the Espionage Act of 1917. War's lesson was a bitter one for optimistic young people nurtured by progressive rhetoric and values: reform was only a temporary expedient pulled away by the powerful at whim. "Progress" was a complicated matter.[7]

After the war, many young intellectuals felt let down by their society. Some retrenched in smaller enclaves like Greenwich Village, Paris, and the South of France to escape what they perceived as the soulless existence of postwar America. They were "lost" in a world that seemed senseless, exiling themselves before the larger society exiled them. In his famous essay for *Civilization in the United States,* "The Literary Life," Van Wyck Brooks complained that there was no support for creative expression because Americans valued only what was "practical." Whatever spirit talented writers had quickly evaporated in such an atmosphere because "one must feel . . . that what one is doing *matters.*" By withdrawing, the so-called bohemians could maintain their critical élan; flouting cultural and social conventions became a way of expressing their dissatisfaction with American capitalism. "Society could never be changed by any effort of the will," Cowley remembered, so there was no sense tilting at windmills.[8]

It would be a mistake to see this retreat as stagnation, however. Intellectuals grew creatively during the 1920s. They tried out different forms and new ideas. They interacted with their European counterparts. Some wrote novels of social protest. Others experimented with dada, cubism, or expressionism, currents strong in Europe. Still others produced histories, literary criticism, plays, or poetry. They also grew as human beings, got married, had children, settled down. The process was not always an easy one. A number of intellectuals struggled with depression, alcoholism, or sexual problems. By the end of the decade, even they perceived their situation more ambiguously. The salons of Greenwich Village exerted less pull on them, and farms in upstate New York more. They were perhaps not as fully alienated from the world as they imagined.

Many, moreover, were not alienated at all. Some were merely unhappy with society as it existed and ready to change it. What distinguished them from the lost generation was their age (they were slightly older) and their social activism. Prewar social activists—ministers, social scientists, lawyers, and editors—generally stuck with their commitments after the war. They had a confidence that fiction writers and critics often lacked. Activism kept them fresh and made them optimistic. They were better grounded politically. Many successfully replaced the verities of the Victorian era with their own secular trinity: science, pragmatism, and rationality. Others embraced socialism. Still further to the left, the new Communist Party offered an agenda modeled on the Russian Revolution. What set these intellectuals apart from their less optimistic colleagues was not so much the specific politics they adopted as their willingness to risk direct political commitment at all. They demonstrated by their actions that they had a faith in the possibility of change.

Consciously or unconsciously, a fair percentage of those who were politically active intellectuals in the 1920s derived their ideas from a few critical thinkers. Charles Beard, Franz Boas, and Morris Raphael Cohen each had their advocates. But it was John Dewey who became "a leader among those eager to take part in social reorganization," as Robert Westbrook has noted. Dewey had great faith in "American democracy," but not as it existed in the 1920s. He envisioned a community constructed to "liberat[e] . . . individuals" from the tyranny of tradition, competition, waste, and selfishness. Liberating people, he argued, released "the greatest amount of human energy," the building block of social change. Maximizing human potential inevitably led to social progress. Individual wants and social good converged for Dewey at a point rationality and experimentation defined. Social engineering would improve the quality of Americans' lives. These reforms would rid America of the prudishness and superstition of the past while making the economy more efficient, the political process more accessible, and society more equitable.[9]

Science and experts were key to the process Dewey described. His ideal society trucked no compromise with tradition or superstition. It functioned according to observable laws. Social experts, people like himself, could help define and correct social ills. His was a reform agenda, even though the business climate was hostile to reform. Throughout the 1920s, social activists tied themselves to institutional bases like the American Civil Liberties Union, the National Association for the Advancement of Colored People, the International Committee for the Defense of Political Prisoners, and the National Women's Party. Although they measured their progress in small increments, their willingness to form, fund, and maintain agencies for change suggests they never succumbed to the lost generation's sense of impotence.

Not all social activists were so optimistic, however. Dewey's enthusiasm seemed misplaced to at least one other intellectual in the 1920s, Reinhold Niebuhr. Niebuhr scoffed at Dewey's belief in "man's essential goodness . . . [and] faith in human history." The sum of individual goals was not the larger social good. Thinking so was a "liberal illusion." Individual interests inevitably clashed, he insisted. Greed and conflict were just as likely outcomes as social harmony. Liberalism had no safeguards against such eventualities. Niebuhr's views differed considerably from Dewey's, but their remedies were similar. Niebuhr belonged to the Socialist Party, putting him politically to the left of Dewey, yet both favored government-mandated economic equity.[10] And, like other left-leaning intellectuals in the 1920s, both were opposed to the business-oriented economic structure of American society.

Whether they were as hopeful as Dewey or as gloomy as the lost generation, 1920s intellectuals had an impact on one another and the larger society. Despite their sense that they were unacknowledged and frivolous, writers discovered that critical creativity paid well and was popular. Americans liked to read about the foibles of the middle class and a culture without values. The alternative lifestyles of Greenwich Village rebels entertained them. A few members of the lost generation became nationally recognized celebrities. It was a bit difficult to maintain a sense of alienation when foundations offered you money and magazines bought what you wrote. New ideas trickled through educated society. Social critics disputed long-standing notions of Anglo-Saxon superiority, African American inferiority, social Darwinism, and manifest destiny. College professors, *The New Republic*'s editors, and Greenwich Village poets embraced sexual liberation, pro-union sentiment, pacifism, and vague socialism. The 1920s experience was not as bleak as members of the lost generation later painted it, though their dissatisfaction with the larger culture helped to unite them as a community.

There were, however, intellectuals who were more consistently marginalized by 1920s society. They were doubly invisible, distinguished both by their atraditional backgrounds and their political radicalism. Most radical intellectuals of the 1920s were neither middle class nor Protestant. They did not attend Yale or Princeton or have the money to spend a year or two in Paris. They could not travel in the same circles as most intellectuals, even bohemians. They lacked the connections, money, credentials, and experiences that would facilitate their admission into mainstream intellectual circles. Their association with the American Communist Party reinforced their distance from orthodox American society and the orthodox intellectual community. Before World War I, socialist intellectuals like Michael Gold, Joseph Freeman, and Bertram Wolfe found the boundaries between bohemia and radicalism far more flexible than after.[11] In the 1920s, circumstances pushed them into a small, self-contained radical world.

That world was very different from either the bohemia of the lost generation or the established institutions of social activism. In fact, the places radicals called home were often the targets of social activists' efforts. Radical intellectuals were ethnic, poor, and urban as a group. A substantial percentage were immigrants or the children of immigrants, particularly Eastern European Jews who relocated to New York City. Many were exposed early to radical politics, on the street, from their parents, in the pages of *Freiheit*. Like Michael Gold, they "blundered into"[12] the socialist movement and it moved them, but it also provided them with an avenue for their ambitions. Very few sons or daughters of working-class Jews became college professors, particularly in the age of quotas. But many such people led unions, organized protests, or wrote for *The Masses*. Radical intellectuals found that the radical subculture of the prewar years was conducive to literary and artistic expressions of politics. *The Masses* published many such political cartoons, stories, poems, and plays.[13] After the war and the Bolshevik Revolution, however, such an easy overlapping of politics and art became less tenable. Governmental harassment made radical politics a riskier occupation. The revolution in Russia reordered radical priori-

24 A Comparison of Subgroups within the Left Intellectual Community of the 1930s

	Trots.	Anti-Stal.	NY Ints.[a]	CPUSA	Progs.	Libs.
Number in Sample	27	42	21	90	102	52
Mean Birth Year	1906	1900	1908	1900	1895	1888
Religion						
Prot.	29.5%	26%	14%	44%	68.5%	79%
Jew.	55.5%	59.5%	81%	47%	21.5%	11%
Cath.	15%	12%	5%	7%	5%	6%
Unknown	0	2.5%	0	2%	5%	4%
Birthplace						
U.S./urban	70%	62%	81%	39%	38%	25%
(NYC)	(44%)	(43%)	(71%)	(23%)	(16%)	(12%)
U.S./small towns, rural	15%	19%	9.5%	41%	55%	63%
Foreign born	15%	19%	9.5%	17%	7%	10%
Unknown	0	0	0	3%	0	2%
Class Background						
Working	52%	31%	33.5%	33%	10%	6%
Middle	41%	55%	52.5%	50%	70.5%	73%
Upper	7%	7%	14%	7%	11.5%	13%
Unknown	0	7%	0	10%	8%	8%
College						
Attended	81%	91%	95%	74%	90%	81%
(CCNY)	(19%)	(24%)	(33%)	(10%)	(2%)	(4%)
Grad./prof. school	21.5%	42%	42%	26%	42.5%	44%
Ph.D.s	3%	14%	14%	9%	21.5%	21%
No college	15%	9%	5%	20%	10%	13%
Unknown	0	0	0	6%	0	6%
Career Type						
Journalism/essay-ists/analysts	22%	38%	28.5%	19%	29.5%	38%
Literary/creative	37%	36%	52.5%	48%	49%	35%
Academic	4%	19%	19%	9%	16.5%	13.5%
Activist	37%	7%	0	24%	5%	13.5%

[a] For purposes of comparisons, this category, the New York intellectuals, contains some members of 1930s Trotskyist and anti-Stalinist groups.

ties in the United States. The SPUSA split three ways, creating two new organizations pledged to the Bolshevik model of revolution in addition to the more evolutionary Socialists. Most of the more traditional left-wing intellectual community stayed with the Socialists. The less traditional intellectuals, people like Gold, Louis Fraina, and Jay Lovestone, went with one or the other communist organizations.[14] In the Communist Party or the Communist Labor Party (later fused into the modern CPUSA) their first responsibility was to nurture the movement; only in their spare time could they pursue their more private careers.

The Party's overriding need for committed and active members created tensions between its functionaries and radical intellectuals. The CPUSA valued volunteers more as members of the working class than as writers, artists, and thinkers. An anti-intellectual radical tradition already existed; the new party's small stature and desperate status exacerbated it. Gold recalled that in the old Industrial Workers of the World, "the word 'intellectual' became a synonym for the word 'bastard.'" "In the American Communist movement," he concluded, "there is some of this feeling as well." Gold certainly reinforced that bias with his "proletarian props" and "peppery" style. Party functionaries encouraged the belief that intellectual ambitions were invariably individual and, therefore, selfish, decadent, and elitist. "Lenin never drew cartoons," declared Robert Minor as he temporarily shelved his artistic career to become a Party activist. He might aspire to a leadership role, but those not willing to devote themselves wholly to the CPUSA were expected to serve it "in the ranks" as Joseph Freeman noted. Consigned to the bottom of the radical status hierarchy because the working class came first, intellectuals were expected to be "damned humble and damned disciplined."[15] Accepting these tensions was far easier in the abstract than on a day-to-day basis.

From John Reed on, a few CPUSA intellectuals questioned their status within the movement. Some found it hard to reconcile their concepts of what intellectuals did with the centralized structure of the CPUSA, which made top functionaries the keepers of Marxist orthodoxy. Some left the movement during the 1920s, including the American version of the "Left Opposition," James P. Cannon and other supporters of Leon Trotsky, and the "Right Opposition" or American exceptionalists, Lovestone, Wolfe, and Will Herberg.[16] Radical intellectuals broke with the American Communist Party for both philosophical and personal reasons. In either case, it was the Party's un-

26   willingness to tolerate dissent and heterodoxy that prompted their departures.

The burden of Party responsibilities was, indeed, often a hard one for intellectuals to shoulder. Functionaries demanded a heavy schedule of politically useful work. So too might they review an individual's work in progress, something even the most dedicated never quite accepted as necessary. Although the functionaries who negotiated between Party intellectuals and the leadership were themselves intellectuals, their primary loyalty was to the Party. Having made that choice, they were never totally sympathetic to those who still sought to be something different. When they wielded a red pencil for politic's sake, they gained more enemies than friends. Their power was not absolute, which in some ways made the whole process seem all the more irrational. "Higher authority," as Maurice Hindus once sarcastically called it, decided creative, artistic, or philosophical matters, or so it seemed to those who had to either learn to tolerate the system or leave.[17]

Life in the 1920s communist movement was such that Party intellectuals contributed little as theoreticians and had few opportunities for wider intellectual success. There were almost no spaces tailored to their dual interests. *The Liberator* and then *The New Masses* accepted their contributions and brought them in contact with other radicals. Neither magazine was Party controlled, however, and there were clashes between Party writers and other radical writers skeptical of those committed to the CPUSA. Michael Gold, who wrote for both periodicals, was often responsible, for he wanted to democratize them, one disgruntled *Liberator* coeditor complained, into "popular proletarian magazine[s], printing doggerel from lumberjacks and stevedores." Gold had a talent for intimidating noncommunists, who thought his "bombastic" manner was typical of Party connivance.[18] He dared to do what few other Communist intellectuals could, carry his politics into a wider sphere. His experiences showed that Party intellectuals faced two very real sets of barriers, Communist Party needs and noncommunists' stereotypes.

There were, however, issues that brought together Communist and noncommunist intellectuals. In the 1920s, the most important was the case of Nicola Sacco and Bartolomeo Vanzetti. Lost-generation writers like John Dos Passos and Dorothy Parker walked the picket line protesting their conviction. Liberal social activists like Dewey and Roger

Baldwin played an active part in their defense. And the CPUSA used its organizational base to raise funds and support for them. Many different intellectuals found the case significant; but even a shared interest in Sacco and Vanzetti's defense did not smooth over non-communists' doubts about the Party's sincerity. The CPUSA sent its International Labor Defense to help raise money for the Sacco and Vanzetti Defense Committee. The leaders of the Defense Committee saw the ILD coming and quickly ran the other way, figuring, probably rightly, that the Party expected to control the larger movement. Ultimately the Communists had to settle for working alongside middle-class intellectuals without being part of their prestigious institutional groupings.[19] The Communists confronted a long-term reality in the Sacco-Vanzetti case: the greater a cause's appeal, the greater the number of intellectuals whose support paralleled the CPUSA's, but the less able they were to shape any broader coalition.

Excluded though they were from the official Sacco and Vanzetti defense movement, the Communists gained, nevertheless, because the case sensitized intellectuals to a more overtly class-conscious point of view. It marked, Robert Morss Lovett believed, their initiation into the realities of "the class war in the United States." "No event since the War has so shaken the Liberal's belief in the working for equal justice of free institutions, in the application of intelligence to correct the short-comings of the system," he explained. Many traced their first real political awareness to the case. Others found it hard to retreat back to individual endeavors after being involved. Those who were most active in the protests, Dos Passos, Parker, John Howard Lawson, and others, had to confront the fact that their sincere involvement was not enough to save Sacco and Vanzetti. America seemed a more unpleasant place than ever and intellectuals more ineffectual than they suspected; yet once committed there seemed no turning back. "You try battering your head up against a stone wall," Dos Passos commented,[20] but he *would* try again, over and over. The case affected the way members of the lost generation looked at their society and encouraged some to think more about the value of concerted action against the system.

While some in the lost generation reconsidered their assumptions about their own social impotence after Sacco and Vanzetti, the radical intelligentsia faced a reckoning of its own. During the second half of the 1920s, the struggle for power in the Soviet Union affected the American Communist Party. Since the Comintern linked all national communist parties, events in the Soviet Union inevitably impacted them. The American movement, however, was particularly affected because of its peculiar circumstances. Three roughly equal factions were locked in an impasse for much of the decade, none with sufficient strength to defeat the other two. The best way any one could triumph over the two was by receiving endorsement from the Comintern, so each continually appealed to Moscow for legitimacy. Once Lenin died, leaders of all three factions had to predict which of the Old Bolsheviks would be his heir. Guessing wrong was tantamount to committing organizational suicide. For much of the 1920s, the American Communist Party adopted bland programs that would offend no potential victor in Moscow. By the late 1920s, the dispute amongst Lenin's successors resolved itself and American Communists had to deal with the consequences.[21]

The situation within the CPUSA so disturbed some Party intellectuals that they fled the movement. There was considerably more intellectual input in the prewar movement than the postwar Party. This turn of events bothered Louis Fraina, particularly since he had been a significant theorist with the prewar Socialist left wing. By the early 1920s, he was appalled to see that "the Russians [gave] . . . all the orders." The discomfort was not one-sided; the Comintern was concerned about his behavior, so sent him to Mexico to organize. Fraina was loyal enough to go, but quickly dismayed when he arrived, a communist in a country where most radicals were anarchists who spoke neither his native language, Italian, nor his adopted English. Surely he realized that he was sent because he was politically untrustworthy. Ultimately he grew frustrated and quietly left the Party. Several years later, he reentered the United States illegally, adopting as his new name the more Americanized Lewis Corey. Corey became an expert on Marxian economics, for while he lost interest in the American Communist Party he remained a Marxist. His quarrel was not with the theory, but the way it was used in the USSR and by the CPUSA.[22] He was perhaps the first of a phenomenon that would grow considerably during the 1930s, a Marxist opposition to the Party.

Max Eastman was another dissident Marxist and an early casualty of the leadership struggle in Moscow. He was one of the more prominent Marxists in Russia after Lenin's death (although he only belonged to the above-ground, legal branch of the Party, the Workers Party), so Trotsky passed him the key points of Lenin's deathbed repudiation of

Stalin, his *Testament*. Poor Eastman not only believed he had a brilliant journalistic scoop, but also a document of some importance to the CPUSA hierarchy. Party leaders did not want to embrace the *Testament*, however, for fear that if Stalin triumphed over Trotsky, they would be in an awkward position. Even Trotsky failed to come to his defense. Eastman denounced the American Communist Party as well as the Comintern for deflecting the true path of the revolution. "Since Lenin died," he warned, those who succeeded him "have established and solidified to an extremely dangerous degree a dictatorship of the officialdom within the Communist Party, entailing a separation of the party from the masses." The Workers Party made him "extinct," persona non grata to his former friends and comrades. But he continued to critique what he believed was the growing centralization of the Comintern nonetheless.[23] Like Fraina, he was concerned that Marxism had become something other than what Marx intended it to be.

The most obvious victims of the post-Lenin leadership struggle in the Soviet Union were the heads of the losing Party factions. As Stalin solidified his control of the Soviet Union, the CPUSA stalemate was likewise resolved, leaving behind a trail of dissident Marxists with strong negative feelings about the organization. James P. Cannon learned of Trotsky's program by accident while he was in Moscow on Party business. He was impressed, but kept quiet until he returned to the United States and talked to others. His strong suit in the CPUSA was his organizational skill, so when he left the Party in 1928 he was already fortified by a small clique and his own newspaper, *The Militant*. Cannon's first assumption was that all he had built was temporary, that the Party hierarchy would see the error of its ways and come around to the Trotskyist perspective. In the meantime, his Communist League of America (Opposition) would serve as a propaganda agency separate from the CPUSA but part of the Comintern. Cannon's sudden enthusiasm for Trotsky blinded him to the realities of radical politics; there was no likelihood the CPUSA would support Trotsky while the Comintern supported Stalin. Communist functionaries turned on Cannon with a vengeance and dispatched workers to beat up CLA members in the streets. He eventually concluded that these "dog days" could not continue, so in 1933 he broke with the Comintern and made the CLA its own entity, the first real rival to the CPUSA.[24]

Small though it was, the CLA had several important advantages. One was Cannon's organizing ability. Another was that theory had to be at

30   the center of its identity; hence, the CLA was attractive to intellectuals and would-be intellectuals. The most impressive of them was Max Shachtman. Shachtman's background was typical of many radical intellectuals. One of a cadre Cannon dubbed the "City College boys," he was well-educated and ambitious, but poorer and more marginal than the members of the lost generation. Shachtman was a Jew whose family fled Russia for the United States shortly after his birth. He grew up on the Lower East Side of New York City, watching his father, a tailor, participate in both union and radical activities. He started at the City College of New York at the age of sixteen, dropping out as the radical movement exercised its allure. He wrote for *The Liberator* in the early 1920s, but slowly soured on the CPUSA because "the initiative and independence of the rank and file party member were being stifled." Shachtman would become an inspiring figure to radical young people, especially those who came out of similar backgrounds.[25] He was a pivotal figure as the Marxist opposition began to coalesce as an intellectual body.

One year after the American Trotskyist faction first asserted itself, a second splinter group emerged from the American movement. Cannon's departure upset the balance of factions, forcing the leaders of the remaining two into competition. Jay Lovestone and Bertram Wolfe represented the numerically larger group, but they were suspect to Stalin and that cost them their claim to orthodoxy. Like Fraina, they were uncomfortable with the idea that all nations would follow the Bolshevik path to socialism. Breaking down capitalism in the United States, where it was strong and reinforced by imperialism, they argued, would be much harder than in Russia, where capitalism almost did not exist. The degree of independence they wanted for the CPUSA was unacceptable to Stalin, who saw his ability to control the international movement as a way of reinforcing his power at home. Moreover, Stalin interpreted their line as an offshoot of Nikolai Bukharin's, another of his rivals for power. When Lovestone and his faction appealed to Stalin for leniency, he showed them the door. The experience was a hard lesson in Comintern power politics that the Lovestoneites never forgot. Like Cannon, Lovestone had the experience and the desire to build a rival organization to challenge the CPUSA. And, like the CLA, the Lovestoneite faction, by virtue of its self-identified interest in Marxist theory, attracted intellectuals.[26] By 1929 the American Communist Party had thus resolved its three-way tie for control but only by expelling representatives of two of the three competing factions. Along with the dissidents who left the Party on their own, they constituted a potential threat to the CPUSA, a well-spoken, reasoned, theoretically motivated Marxist opposition vying for some measure of radical respectability.

As it changed so many other things, so too did the Depression have a profound impact on American intellectuals. At one level, that impact was personal. Nearly all faced the prosaic tasks of survival in a world with fewer paying jobs. The older and more mainstream intellectuals fared better financially, of course, but also seemed more psychologically vulnerable to the Depression. Younger intellectuals and would-be intellectuals, especially those of college age, felt the economic downturn most dramatically of all. The Depression made freelancing, once attractive because it offered the most freedom, less manageable, even for the most prominent. At the top of the new pyramid of desirable intellectual jobs were the steady ones, editors' positions at publishers or journals. Established intellectuals usually held those plums and few willingly relinquished them during hard times. Teaching jobs had slightly lower status because they were less secure, tied up valuable time, and paid less well. They also required some graduate training and many were restricted against Jews. For the younger generation, particularly, this latter fact was a concern. Those without credentials or status devoted a large proportion of their time to the constant round of part-time teaching jobs, book reviews that paid by the word, and endless applications for fellowship money. Worst of all was the prospect of having to do other work, to temporarily subordinate the life intellectuals claimed for themselves to their more urgent needs. Finding ways to survive was not a very glamorous part of the intellectual's job, but it was a very real part nonetheless.[27]

The situation was especially bad for radical intellectuals and those outside the power structure, two categories that often overlapped. Intellectual Communists obviously had to work, but their employment prospects were very limited. There was always Party work, and more of it during bad times, but much of that was unpaid "duty" work. The larger intellectual arena was more problematic. "There is only one job I have had in the past ten years outside of the Communist movement," Liston Oak lamented in a 1937 letter detailing the trouble he had breaking out of the Party's literary marketplace. Roger Baldwin told the

32 Dies Committee on UnAmerican Activities in 1939 that in its whole history the ACLU, which stood for equality of opportunity, employed only one Party member. Many young radicals sought the comfort of familiar terrain—Party youth groups and the radical and Jewish press— because they could not penetrate more traditional intellectual en- claves.[28] To such people, middle-class intellectuals often seemed like obstacles to their success rather than allies in their struggles.

While the Depression made the intellectual's life considerably more difficult, it also brought with it a new sense of optimism. It was strangely reassuring to know that capitalism failed people in the end, that business got its comeuppance, and that adversity united Ameri- cans. As Granville Hicks recalled:

> We—I mean vaguely the intellectuals—had for the most part been opposed all through the twenties to the status quo, to what we thought of as a busi- ness civilization, but in the period business had been so strong that our criticism seemed futile. We were somewhere on the sidelines, snickering at this and thumbing our noses at that, while the men of power paid no atten- tion. Now, however, for the first time we felt that we could—and must—take responsibility.

Liberals and radicals alike recognized that change was likely. With business repudiated by the Crash, new forces would be called upon to shape American society. The 1930s seemed a new beginning for intel- lectuals, a time "of hope."[29]

Liberal social scientists and philosophers were perhaps best situ- ated to address the economic questions raised by the Depression. They had a history of social activism and a clear sense of their goals. One was to protect civil liberties and individual rights, a traditionally lib- eral idea. But as "collectivists," they wanted to rationalize the econ- omy, bringing in experts to eliminate waste, to streamline, to plan. The League for Independent Political Action, founded in 1929 by John Dewey and other liberal advocates of Thorstein Veblen and Edward Bellamy, included in its minimum program national planning, na- tionalization of the banks, farm cooperatives, and public ownership of railroads and other basic industries. With their institutional experi- ence and clear agenda, liberals were prepared. Their mission was to sacrifice capitalism in order to preserve liberalism, a divorce they be- lieved both possible and necessary.[30]

Members of the lost generation rejected that basic premise because capitalism was "doomed" and liberalism "bankrupt." The divorce that

1920s social activists proposed seemed unworkable. "Liberalism," one *New Republic* editorial commented, ". . . is certainly not the right name for the views of those who see no hope of permanency for economic individualism or capitalism."[31] But if lost-generation intellectuals did not consider themselves liberals, what exactly were they? The 1930s liberals, curiously, were far more likely than they to be members of the Socialist Party, for the lost generation found the socialist moniker almost as unattractive as the liberal one. Matthew Josephson, following Norman Thomas's 1932 presidential campaign on the Socialist Party ticket for *The New Republic,* complained that he was "all sweetness-and-light, an American liberal Protestant, not a real socialist; . . . he is weak, personally and politically." Diana Trilling recalled thinking the SPUSA "cowardly and ineffectual." Theodore Dreiser believed that everything the Socialists undertook was a "dismal failure." John Dos Passos likened the SPUSA to "near beer," tantalizing, but without the kick of real alcohol. It was "not a radical party at all," Heywood Broun suggested,[32] and that, as far as many intellectuals were concerned, put it in the same unappealing category as liberalism.

Lost-generation intellectuals were so busy reacting to the words *socialist* and *liberal* that they failed to really look at the programs beneath the labels. Had they looked, they might have discovered that their own vague notions of transforming capitalism into "something else"[33] were not all that different from either 1930s-style liberalism or socialism. Yet the label they preferred, in a tentative, imperfect, cautious, and unofficial way, was more radical. "I cannot help calling myself a communist," Lewis Mumford told Van Wyck Brooks in 1932, "for that points to the fundamental demand: but I am certainly post-Marxist," whatever that designation implied. While they thought they "wanted what the Communists wanted," what most attracted such people to the CPUSA was its boldness rather than its specific programs. Many had romantic fantasies about being Communists, which briefly liberated them from their isolation, fears, and inertia. Malcolm Cowley recalled that the attraction of the CPUSA was that it "seemed capable of supplying the moral qualities that writers had missed in a bourgeois society: the comradship in struggle, the self-imposed discipline, the ultimate purpose, . . . the opportunity for heroism." The Communist Party represented all that was noble and quixotic for many otherwise liberal intellectuals in 1930, but only if they could enjoy the thrills of Party life vicariously and without all the drudge work.[34]

Thus, while the CPUSA offered "something . . . [to] take hold of," as

34 Sherwood Anderson described it, the Depression brought no great influx of intellectuals into the organization. Their dreams of becoming self-sacrificing, decisive, and purposeful cogs in the Communist Party machine hit the implacable reality of what the organization was really like: "rigid instead of resilient," F. O. Matthiessen noted. It lived up to none of their fantasies. It was steeped in "parochialism" and ingrown, *The Nation* suggested, and its recruiters spoke in "incomprehensible jargon . . . [that] frightened away potential members." Despite their glorious ideals, Party leaders engaged in "petty squabbles and riots." The chimeric vision of the steely Marxist-activist was hard to reconcile with an organization noncommunist intellectuals found provincial, inflexible, and occasionally violent.[35]

Communism captured the lost generation's hearts but not their minds, so while they rarely joined the Party, they had great trouble forgiving themselves for lacking the courage to try. "As far as logic goes, I ought to be a Communist," Broun confessed, conveniently forgetting his qualms about the organization. Matthew Josephson joked that he was "not virtuous enough to be a communist," which hit the nail right on the head. Those who did not join often attributed their hesitation to a failure of will. Their ideal Communists were self-sacrificing; but *they* were consumed with selfish fears. Newton Arvin, for example, worried that becoming a Party member would cut off his "means of support," and he told Granville Hicks, "There is something quite unreal in trying to be a Communist and an English professor in a ladies' seminary [he taught at Smith College] . . . at the same time." Robert Cantwell feared that even regular contributions to *The New Masses* would "imperil . . . most of my income." William Carlos Williams could not picture a poet as a Communist, and since he was a poet, joining the Party would be "a false position."[36] The many misgivings intellectuals voiced about fitting their lives into the CPUSA's mold were not a sign of weakness so much as difference. They had legitimate reasons for holding back; they had no business being Communists.

For one thing, while they pledged themselves to Marxism, their understanding of the theory was jumbled and incomplete, based on a few key concepts in oversimplified form. Few actually read Marx. "So help me," Carey McWilliams confessed many years later, "I never finished *Das Kapital*." Michael Blankfort abandoned his attempt and instead read "a lot of popularizations." These people did not see their unfamiliarity with Marx's writings as a drawback because Marxism,

Kenneth Rexroth later recalled, "was something you dug." Those who did absorb the classics were usually critical. The whole of Marxist theory was "as unsound as it is cocky and self-confident," Lewis Mumford wrote. Certainly Marx's goals made sense to left-leaning intellectuals, but his methods did not. They seemed mechanistic and violent. "Dictatorships tend to perpetuate themselves," Sherwood Eddy suggested in response to the idea that the socialist state would simply wither away. Lost-generation intellectuals extracted no theoretical whole from Marxism, but used it piecemeal, taking what made sense to them while jettisoning what disturbed them. Their Marxism was, in Theodore Dreiser's telling phrase, "a very liberal thing."[37]

Another obstacle standing between radicalizing intellectuals and Party membership was their inability to imagine themselves as Communists. Their view of the CPUSA was stereotyped and negative. Party life was "too straitjacketed," Blankfort recalled; it defined your politics, your friendships, and your priorities. It would surely hurt your reputation. Intellectuals worried that upon joining the CPUSA they would be forced to produce formulaic propaganda of little real value. Meyer Levin remembered watching "one mediocrity after another puffed into temporary literary eminence by the comrades." "Talent," he concluded, "was a secondary consideration." For Cowley, Communist intellectuals seemed to lead simply miserable lives: "After testing them in a variety of humble tasks, such as selling *The Daily Worker* on street corners and getting up at five in the morning to push leaflets under tenement doors, it [the Party] wanted them to take vows, not of chastity, but of poverty and utter obedience."[38]

The solution, Edmund Wilson suggested, was to circumvent the Party's drawbacks by "tak[ing] communism away from the communists." His 1931 "Appeal to Progressives" called upon people like Cowley, Levin, and Blankfort to look beyond the CPUSA and use Marxism for their own purposes. Intellectuals were "deeply stirred" by Wilson's article, but did not follow his advice. However imperfect the CPUSA seemed, they could not imagine themselves striking out without it. They were too unsure of change, too unwilling to risk failure, and too afraid that the level of political commitment necessary to lead a movement jeopardized their ability to be intellectuals. So, ironically, they adopted the name Wilson gave them, "progressives," and altered its meaning to express their dependence on the Communist movement. "Progressivism" stood for a place between liberalism and radicalism where intellectuals were willing to work alongside the CPUSA for certain shared ends. Progressives did not take communism away from the communists, but tried to work out compromises with the CPUSA.[39]

Progressives and liberals divided in the early 1930s over Wilson's terms and its connotations. Liberals continued to think of themselves as "liberals," despite the negative reputation attached to the word. They were sure enough of their own place within the cosmos to recognize that they would not be comfortable pretending to be Marxists. Often better versed in the specifics of Marxism than the progressives who never made it through *Kapital,* they were not impressed by what they learned. They considered Marxism a relic of an earlier era, a "mystical faith" better suited to nineteenth-century Europe than to twentieth-century America. Marxian dialectics were anathema to them, clashing with their rationalist, pragmatic, and scientific values. "It is a curious sort of science which announces . . . that its conclusions are final and unalterable," Elmer Davis observed. The dialectic allowed Marxists to pursue their goals, John Dewey warned, without considering how those goals were achieved. But "means," he concluded, "cannot be divorced from the end"; science was consistent with democracy, a dictatorship of the proletariat was not.[40]

Liberals had no romantic illusions about the Communist Party or the sovietized United States they assumed the Communists wanted. A communist America was not as bad a prospect as total anarchy would be, Davis thought, but "far worse than our present situation." Even John Chamberlain, who repudiated any form of patched-up capitalism, had serious doubts about what the CPUSA might do to the country. He thought the Party illogical, unscientific, and lacking when it came to humanitarian issues. "The communist idea that only communists are 'scientific' and know the truth," Charles Beard told Herbert Solow, "has always seemed merely absurd to me."[41] Given these attitudes, it was clear that liberals would not be in a mood to work with the CPUSA. As for their progressive colleagues, time would tell, for their doubts about the CPUSA could only be assuaged if the Party was flexible enough to accommodate their desires.

In 1930 the abstract likelihood of Communists and progressives working together seemed small. The American Communist Party's Third Period line defined an isolated movement with little room for middle-class intellectuals. The Comintern directed the American party to concentrate on mobilizing the working class via organizations already tied to the CPUSA. Any other union, political faction, or party, from the Socialist Party to the German American Bund, was a manifestation of social fascism, and all social fascism was equally fascist. The Third Period enabled Stalin to consolidate power in the Soviet Union against a truculent Right Opposition. It was not designed to assist Depression-era American Communists. What they might fashion out of the Third Period line was entirely their responsibility.

Despite its foreign beginnings, American Communists tailored the Third Period to American conditions during the first years of the Depression. Party organizers put together councils of the unemployed, led marches protesting homelessness, and started rent strikes. These were modest beginnings, however. Considering the magnitude of the economic crisis, most commentators agreed that the CPUSA made surprisingly little headway. Part of the problem was the wasted energy devoted to sectarian battles. Communists fought Trotskyists, Socialists, dual unionists. They felt compelled to justify collectivization and other Soviet policies. Not only did they achieve little, but their record seemed very uneven to those on the outside. "I liked their readiness to act," Richard Wright remembered of the Communists, "but they seemed lost in folly, wandering in a fantasy."[42]

Along with political instruction, American Communists also accepted cultural guidance from abroad. The creative adjunct to the Third Period was known as the proletarian culture, or prolet cult. Precisely what distinguished a proletarian work from any other is difficult to assert with authority. As Barbara Foley has successfully demonstrated, the prolet cult—or at least proletarian literature—was defined by different people at different times according to different criteria, including "authorship, audience, subject matter, and political perspective." What made a text, painting, dance, play, or piece of criticism proletarian might be who created it, who it was created for, what it was about, or its message, depending on circumstance, medium, or time frame. The prolet cult, in short, was considerably more diverse than traditional analyses suggest. Its point was not to portray heroic workers who had sudden communist epiphanies, but to enable radicalized intellectuals to bring their politics into the creative or critical process. Communist intellectuals struggled to articulate differences between what they did and what other intellectuals did so that they

38   might give meaning to their perceived uniqueness. Their goal, never
fully defined or realized, was to create a distinctive radical culture.[43]
When they fell short of this goal, the international movement's literary
branch, the International Bureau of Revolutionary Literature, provided additional guidance in the form of a ten-point cultural critique at
its Second World Plenum in Kharkov in 1930.

Traditionally, the Kharkov conference has been regarded as a turning point in literary Communist history, the first serious intrusion
of the international communist movement into the affairs of American intellectuals. Today, however, its impact is more debated. Harvey
Klehr uses words like "directives" to suggest that American representatives were simply handed an artistic program. Foley argues the ten
points were suggestions that Americans "took seriously" and acted
upon. James Murphy distinguishes between Kharkov's influence on
"literary policies" and its lack of impact "over aesthetic theory." It is
simplistic to see the ten-point Kharkov document as a set of orders. It is
clear from firsthand reports from Kharkov and the presence of non-
Party writers there that the conference was a conference and nothing
more.[44] Yet it is equally hard to imagine that American Communists
would do anything less than "take seriously" and adjust their cultural
program in accordance with the ten-point critique. The real question
raised by Kharkov was not how much control over the CPUSA's cultural
line did the Comintern claim, but, rather, how much creativity did
American Communist intellectuals show in response to the International Bureau of Revolutionary Literature's advice.

The Kharkov document suggested where American Communists
had been most and least effective at constructing a politicized culture.
One strength was the attempt to reach the people closest to Michael
Gold's heart: "lumberjacks, hoboes, miners, clerks, sectionhands, ma-
chinists, harvesthands, waiters." One weakness was the traditional
organ used by the Party's established intelligentsia, *The New Masses,*
which the International Union of Revolutionary Writers considered
too conservative and pitched at too broad an audience. Most of the
advice delivered at Kharkov concerned building a culture both revolutionary and proletarian, although CPUSA intellectuals were also encouraged to "win . . . over the radicalized intellectuals" whatever their
class background. In constructing such a culture, American Communists drew on many already existing tendencies, styles, and forums.
"Throughout history," Joseph Freeman told *The New Masses'* reader-

ship, "art has had social roots, has been 'propaganda.'" Certainly there
were precedents in the socially conscious and realistic novels produced by older generations of writers and in Gold's 1920s work. And
there was carryover in terms of where this new culture might be expressed. The prolet cult's many forums already existed as alternatives
to the more mainstream culture. The Provincetown Players and the
New Playwrights Theater pioneered new theatrical techniques in the
1920s. The Red Dancers, formed in 1928, explicitly embraced the revolutionary themes their leader, Ruth Segal, had incorporated in her per-
formances since the early 1920s. *The New Masses,* although much
maligned, was read by more intellectuals than any other radical journal. But there were also discontinuities. Alfred Kazin remembered that
while the 1920s' most prestigious authors were "rebels from 'good'
families, . . . writers now came from anywhere." What they wrote was
sometimes not all that different from what had come before, yet sometimes different on several simultaneous levels. The most important
venue for the prolet cult was the one singled out for praise in the
Kharkov points, the John Reed Clubs, which were initially formed on
an ad hoc basis because younger working-class writers felt *The New
Masses* ignored their needs.[45] Building on these beginnings, Communist intellectuals sought to remake culture.

Spurred on by the Kharkov advice, Communist intellectuals took
their most visible advocate of the prolet cult, Michael Gold, and put
him center stage. It was not a popular decision, either within or outside the movement. He was reputed to be intolerant, opinionated, and
hopelessly infatuated with a romanticized image of himself as a proletarian. Most of his colleagues thought he lacked integrity. Among
noncommunists, Gold was seen as proof that joining the CPUSA inevitably compromised one's cultural standards. Communists believed he
was personally undisciplined and opportunistic. Dell resigned from
The New Masses' staff on account of Gold, alleging that he was "lazy,
disorderly, and too much given to sponging on other people." Gold's
reputation, "as a bully and a vulgarian," as one of his literary biographers characterized him, guaranteed that there was bound to be controversy as soon as he gained stature. Still, Gold had his audience.
"I came from that class Mike Gold extolled," Joseph North recalled,
". . . [he] was Isaiah to me."[46] He represented both the possibilities and
limits of the Third Period line and its cultural corollary.

Like Gold, the John Reed Clubs also benefited from the Kharkov

40   conference. From a single New York City club in 1929, they blossomed
to some thirty clubs with 1,200 members a few years later, many with
their own literary magazines. The JRCS were a perfect example of
the complexities of the prolet cult. Party intellectuals could not take
credit for them, nor were they fashioned after the Kharkov conference.
Rather, the first Reed Club was a spontaneous creation by young writers and artists with nowhere to go. For a while they tried meeting at
The New Masses' offices, but the staff there treated them badly and
they decided to find their own office and organize themselves. They
pledged themselves "to the development of a cultural movement dedicated to advancing the interests of the working class." The initial popularity of the JRCS took the CPUSA by surprise, but their quick growth
and the endorsement accorded them by the International Bureau of
Revolutionary Literature prompted Party functionaries to nurture
them.[47]

Support for the Reed Clubs was perhaps the most successful of the
Kharkov recommendations. The clubs were vital and attractive. Even
skeptics took notice. After visiting the Chicago club, Richard Wright
declared himself "impressed by the scope and seriousness of its activities . . . The members were fervent, democratic, restless, eager, self-
sacrificing." Kenneth Rexroth recalled that "there was a great deal of
ferment" in the JRCS, an atmosphere of excitement that attracted writers, even those "who had been very antagonistic to the Communist
Party until then." One reason for this level of enthusiasm was that the
Reed Clubs filled a need satisfiable nowhere else. Here was the only
place young day laborers, bricklayers, and factory workers might be
taken seriously as writers. Here they might meet others with the same
political agendas. For artists, the JRCS offered "one of the few outlets for
social or political expression in art."[48] Young people joined eagerly,
attended meetings regularly, discussed intensely, and created as much
as their time allowed. Their enthusiasm was contagious; middle-class
writers and artists were also interested in the Reed Clubs. Their popularity demonstrated that the Kharkov suggestions were worthy of serious consideration by the CPUSA.

The overall goal recommended at Kharkov, supported by Michael
Gold and practiced in the JRCS, was best summarized by the JRCS'
motto, "Art Is a Class Weapon." The goal of the creative process was, in
Paula Rabinowitz's phrase, to build a "political alliance" between a
creator and his or her audience. While many noncommunists dis-

missed the prolet cult as crude propaganda, advocates saw a fusion of form and content that would produce poems, plays, stories, and paintings that were artistically sound and politically significant. The prolet cult did not reject standards; it redefined them. The revolution would create a new aesthetic. Until that time, what was politically useful might not qualify as great art to everyone; but the art that was a class weapon would reach those it should. If the bourgeoisie was repulsed, it just demonstrated that the advocates of the new cultural line had done their job well. The prolet cult was supposed to be as controversial as Gold himself.[49]

And it was. Beyond the CPUSA's intellectual cadre, its impact was uneven. Liberals evinced the most hostility toward it. The prolet cult devalued them as intellectuals, left them feeling "alienated," and caused several to lose all confidence in themselves as intellectuals. Bessie Breuer attributed her writer's block to fears that younger readers considered her work "a dead thing." Arthur Davidson Ficke preferred "the silences" to "the yoke" of propaganda. "Doubtless I shall seem to you very old-fashioned and middle-class," he told two younger writers. Often liberals did not fully understand the scope of the prolet cult, but considered it a bunch of badly written stories about tramps, union organizers, and farm laborers. They neither recognized nor accepted the theory behind it, especially the notion of inevitable class conflict. Therefore, "art as a class weapon" seemed only "hasty, crude, . . . inevitably narrow," as Louis Adamic argued. He could not even imagine workers reading what Party intellectuals wrote. Liberals stood up for the older cultural values with as much vehemence as they stood by the liberal political label.[50]

Progressives, on the other hand, were predisposed toward the prolet cult because of their admiration for the CPUSA. Yet they too often had trouble understanding it. Like liberals, they did not always see it as a revolutionary culture, but more narrowly as stories, poems, and paintings about workers. Stripped of its political intent, however, it became very like the naturalism popular earlier in the century. Sherwood Anderson, for example, greeted all the ballyhoo about the prolet cult with puzzlement. "What in hell," he wondered, "has Dreiser been doing all his life?" Even though they did not understand the prolet cult, progressives were quickly influenced by certain—generally less political—aspects of it, particularly its interest in working-class subjects and its gritty details of life. Some experimented with new ways of presenting material, borrowing the staccato style of reporters to give works of fiction a realistic flavor. Others introduced new subjects and new themes in their works. Anderson visited southern mills; Malcolm Cowley followed the rout of the Bonus Marchers; Edmund Wilson and James Rorty toured the country.[51] Immersions into things working class, however, only rarely produced in noncommunists that political engagement so central to the prolet cult. Many progressives helped themselves to the Party's cultural ideology just as they used Marxist theory, in bits and pieces. As it reached the wider intellectual community, its revolutionary content was diluted.

There were, however, additional obstacles for middle-class intellectuals interested in the prolet cult, and chief among them was their class status. If art was to be a class weapon, middle-class intellectuals might well be conceived of as enemies. The place of the intellectual was ambiguous; but the militancy of some of the prolet cult's advocates was enough to intimidate many. To them it seemed that almost by definition the new culture would marginalize those with little familiarity to revolutionary ideals or the working class. Why would they want to shift their focus and write "bad working-class novels?" Cowley wondered. There seemed to be more that middle-aged, middle-class intellectuals would lose than gain from the prolet cult.[52] Since the Kharkov points offered conflicting advice on that score and American Communist Party functionaries had little interest in the intellectual community, Communist intellectuals had no real consensus about the place of the prolet cult in a broader cultural world.[53]

Traditionally, the Party had little use for noncommunist intellectuals unless their reputations were good enough to enhance support for Communist causes. Party functionaries created front groups to mediate between noncommunists and the CPUSA. Fronts bypassed debates about compromising or diluting values to widen support by placing any interaction between Communists and noncommunists on a businesslike basis. They defined a common ground, a limited end which all their members endorsed. Party people provided the skills necessary to manage the cause, often serving behind the scenes. Progressives provided the more acquiescent membership. While Party intellectuals, as we shall see, grappled with the conflicting cultural implications of the prolet cult, organizers of fronts felt no such immediate hesitations. Jack Conroy and Clara Weatherwax might produce according to the Party canon, but far more Americans had heard of

Sherwood Anderson and Ernest Hemingway. The names and reputations of famous middle-class intellectuals thus became a valuable
commodity. Progressive enthusiasm about the CPUSA promised fronts
a good crop of noncommunists. Their level of intimidation likewise
hinted at their relative cooperation. Fronts seemed to offer many advantages to Party functionaries and few drawbacks. They would soon
discover otherwise.[54]

The front formula was in place long before the Depression, as the
function of the Friends of the Soviet Union well illustrates. Soviet-
American friendship societies dated back to 1921 and liberal attempts
to provide famine aid. In 1927, the international organization Friends
of the Soviet Union formed with an American affiliate. The visit of a
group of Russian aviators in 1929 helped popularize it and bring in
new members. Early on, the FSU promoted regularization of relations
between the two nations. Later, it mainly served to generate favorable
public opinion of the USSR. The FSU published a glossy monthly journal beginning in 1931, *Soviet Russia Today,* which presented a fluffy
Life Magazine view of the Soviet Union.[55] The FSU also organized tours
and sent union delegations to the new socialist paradise. Originally,
most of the tours were for workers, but increasingly the FSU sponsored
better-known guests in the hopes of recruiting articulate pro-Soviet
spokespersons. Its emissaries worked hard to ensure that these tourists
had the best possible experiences and made sure that they did not
"meet the wrong people and come back with the wrong ideas." From
the day a famous intellectual announced his or her intention of visiting
the USSR, the red carpet treatment began, including a bon voyage
party. The coddling was so predictable that it sometimes had the opposite effect, prompting visitors to ponder whether or not they saw only
Potemkin Villages.[56] FSU's propaganda attempts were often so clumsy
that most took its pronouncements with more than a grain of salt. Yet
its views "closely approximated the Communist Party"[57] and it introduced intellectuals to the rudiments and etiquette of front activities.

As intellectuals became more politically active, front groups prolif-
erated. One of the most successful was the National Committee for the
Defense of Political Prisoners. It was initially organized by noncommunists but quickly connected to a better-controlled front, the International Labor Defense. Yet officially it was "an independent organization of writers, artists, teachers, architects and men and women in
kindred professions" committed "to defend all persons prosecuted

44 or persecuted on charges basically political or economic in nature."
Compared to other fronts, the NCDPP was unusually active; it sent delegations into strike-torn Harlan County, the Pennsylvania coal fields,
and elsewhere, it organized forums, and it produced a book. Members
thus had to be prepared to commit themselves with more than just
words. From both the Party and nonParty perspective, the NCDPP was
successful. But greater involvement by noncommunists also created at
least the potential for conflict.[58]

The NCDPP gave middle-class intellectuals the opportunity to fulfill
their revolutionary fantasies, putting themselves smack in the middle
of a struggle without having to perform the more mundane tasks of
Party organizing. The two delegations of writers who went into Kentucky, for instance, confronted all of the evils of capitalism firsthand,
including the techniques authorities used against the union. "We were
kidnapped and forcibly ejected from the state," Liston Oak reported to
The New Republic. Waldo Frank's account suggested the dramatic impact of the experience in more detail:

> We found the lobby [of the hotel where the second delegation stayed] filled
> with armed men who ordered us to leave town . . . Each of us was hustled to
> his or her own room and ordered to pack. Then we were loaded into auto-
> mobiles. Taub [Alan Taub, ILD attorney] and I were placed in the same car, as
> they had picked us for special punishment. They drove us toward the Ten-
> nessee line . . . When we reached the State line they forced us out of the cars
> and turned off the lights. Somebody struck me on the head with a heavy
> instrument. They flashed the lights on and I could see Taub's face was
> covered with blood. They all laughed and said "Well, you two fellows have
> been fighting."

Frank came away from Harlan County with "a scalp wound, a slight
concussion of the brain, and a shock at the mendacity and treachery of
man." The NCDPP gained not just plenty of publicity but a new convert
to the cause. He did not join the CPUSA, but after his visit to Kentucky
he was much more inclined to be an active worker on its behalf.[59]

Frank's experience was unusual; others had more mixed motives
for joining the NCDPP and their experiences made them either more
cynical about class warfare or less optimistic. Diana Trilling's motives for volunteering at NCDPP headquarters were entirely selfish; she
needed to get out of the house during a period of increasing psychological dysfunction. Doing "the women's work of revolution" failed to

engage her much and she suspected that another office worker was a CP "monitor."[60] Those NCDPP members who left the office were often no more excited than Trilling. Talking with "average" Americans proved discouraging. Farmers and miners blamed themselves for their economic failures and were not especially interested in radical parties. After a tour of farming communities, Granville Hicks concluded that "a little violence did not mean that the farmers were ripe for revolution." Nor did a visit from well-known writers end the strikes or improve conditions. Edmund Wilson went to Harlan County with Frank but had a very different experience. It was, he conceded, "very interesting—though I don't know that it did much for the miners." Sherwood Anderson had a similar reaction, suggesting that the romantic notions some intellectuals had about helping the working class fight against injustice did not survive closer scrutiny. Responding to an invitation to speak to striking miners, he admitted to "a queer guilty feeling just now [1931] about taking any part in pulling people out on strike. We go and stir them up. Out they come and presently get licked. Then we go comfortably off." What Anderson recognized was that intellectuals could not really affect the lives of the poor, unless they were willing "to go live with them."[61] The NCDPP, while inarguably successful in drawing middle-class intellectuals into the fray and radicalizing them, did not turn them into Communists.

The interaction, moreover, bred suspicion on both sides. Party functionaries tried to control fronts because they did not trust their allies. Some noncommunists scrutinized every front action for evidence of Communist treachery. Progressives were often the least of the Party faction's worries. They were far more inclined to be trusting than the few liberals or dissident Marxists in front groups. Liberals, for example, fought to keep the International Labor Defense from overtaking the Sacco and Vanzetti Defense Committee.[62] A similar scenario played itself out during the Scottsboro case when the ILD again insisted upon sole control of the defendants' case. The NAACP expected to make an equal contribution to the Scottsboro defense, but would not work through the Communists. The result was "an acute quarrel . . . between the radicals and all the rest." Neither side would give up, hampering both organizations' work. "The double defense," Wilson concluded, "makes things harder."[63] The higher the stakes appeared to be, the greater the potential for conflict between Communists and noncommunists. An ineffectual front like the Friends of the Soviet Union

46 could publish pictures of rosy-cheeked peasant girls that did not offend very many people; but an organization committed to action, like the NCDPP, found its members disagreeing about the mechanics of the struggle. Party intellectuals had few expectations about their middle-class cohorts, not wishing to convert them so much as enlist their aid. Even such a modest goal, though, could not be easily met.

However shattering the Depression was as an event, it did not facilitate any great union between Communists and noncommunists. Despite the alleged radicalization of the intellectual community, there was no great run on Party headquarters for membership blanks. Nor was the prolet cult initially received with great enthusiasm, understanding, or support. While analysts might argue over the success or failure of the Third Period as a recruitment tool during a time of potential mass enrollment, intellectuals were outside any enrollment schemes. Neither the Third Period nor the prolet cult had much to offer middle-class intellectuals, but neither was designed for that purpose. The fronts made a good beginning in building trust; but the number of intellectuals willing to actively participate in fronts was small. Most were no more interested in a career in the Communist Party than the Communist hierarchy was interested in having them. The Depression altered the circumstances of intellectuals' lives and their political agendas without substantially altering the relationship between them and the CPUSA.

The Depression did have one important impact on intellectuals' opinions of communism; it heightened their interest in the Soviet Union. As they watched their own country slide into depression, they became more interested in economic matters and the Soviet "experiment" caught their attention. Their enthusiasm for the policies of Stalin, however, did not mean that they endorsed Marxist theory. Rather, they appreciated what Maurice Hindus called the "arithmetical results"[64] of national planning. Many understood Bolshevism about as well as they understood the prolet cult, with similar results. The conclusions they reached about the reasons for Russian success and the application of Soviet programs in the United States appalled and horrified the CPUSA. But for noncommunist intellectuals, it was far easier to be enthusiastic about Russian communism than its American counterpart. It seemed dynamic, unambiguously scientific, and, best of all, far away.

Long before the Depression, a steady stream of liberal intellectuals visited the new Soviet Union and found it "enormously invigorating." "Russia is stirring," columnist Dorothy Thompson reported to husband Sinclair Lewis back in the states. In the 1920s the comparison with their own society also worked to Russia's advantage. If America seemed stagnant and decadent, the Russian people faced enormous hardships with a marvelous sense of greater purpose. "One has the impression," John Dewey recorded, "of movement, vitality, energy."[65] Liberals envisioned a kind of new pioneer society reconstructed by experts, but with the support of a citizenry eager for change. Its most attractive feature was the spirit that the revolution unleashed.

Liberals explained the great positive energy they so admired not as a function of Bolshevism, which Dewey thought was "secondary," but as a release from the burdens of tsarism. They characterized the Russian autocracy as brutal, backward, repressive, and superstitious. Postrevolutionary society, by contrast, embraced "the familiar democratic ideals . . . of liberty, equality and brotherhood." Such virtues were the hallmarks of liberalism rather than Marxian socialism, and it was a liberal revolution rather than a Bolshevik one that many thought was the real story in Russia. Reinhold Niebuhr concluded that "the tremendous energy which the new Russia is unfolding is, in one of its aspects at least, not the product of communism at all, but simply the vigor of an emancipated people who are standing upright for the first time in the dignity of a new freedom." Liberal visitors to the USSR imprinted their own ideals onto the Russian Revolution, figuring that the values they so cherished were bound to overwhelm any more transitory Marxist theories.[66]

The first years of Bolshevik rule reinforced their assumptions. The Bolsheviks' educational reforms, health care system, commitment to sexual equality and birth control, and government support for the arts endorsed rather than challenged liberal beliefs. Such programs seemed scientific, rational, innovative, in a word, liberal. The mild socialism of the New Economic Policy likewise mollified many liberals about what socialism would actually mean in practice. Yet the Bolshevik leaders made 1920s liberals uneasy and they were inclined to view the government as a force that worked against reason and popular desire rather than promoting those virtues. "Which will win [the people or the Bolsheviks]," Dewey wondered, articulating a dichotomy no Marxist would imagine, ". . . is impossible to say." Wil-

48   liam Henry Chamberlin, on the other hand, was quite certain "of the
ultimate victory of the democratic forces. . . . Time is unmistakably on
their side."[67]

The first pilgrims to the "new" Russia confirmed that even if time
was on the side of democracy, the Bolsheviks were a force to be feared.
John Dos Passos remembered experiencing "jitters" during his 1928
tour. Joseph Wood Krutch felt "the watchful eyes of the servants of the
police state" everywhere. So did John Haynes Holmes, who noted that
people seemed afraid to express their opinions for fear of reprisals.
Oswald Garrison Villard described "a complete denial of political liberty, of the right to dissent and to oppose, yes, even to hold conflicting
economic opinions in plain view." He worried that the Bolsheviks'
class dictatorship might overwhelm the "human side" of the revolution.[68] If science and rationality were to prevail in the Soviet Union,
liberals concluded, it would not be because of the Bolsheviks, but
despite them.

The Depression and the first of the Soviets' Five Year Plans changed
liberals' thinking about the government in Russia, but, once again, not
in a way Communists would find very edifying. Middle-class intellectuals no longer saw the Bolsheviks as a negative force; they stopped
seeing them as Bolsheviks. Both liberals and progressives chose to
interpret the Five Year Plans as a departure from Marxist theory in the
name of practicality. "The Kremlin has finally emerged from the fog of
ideological discussion," New York *Times* correspondent Walter Duranty proclaimed. While such a conclusion might seem unwarranted,
it reflected Americans' preoccupation with their own situation. Liberals and progressives used American standards to evaluate the Five
Year Plans. Compared to the Hoover administration's clumsy attempts
to deal with the economic crisis without substantially rethinking
capitalism, the Five Year Plans seemed overwhelmingly practical,
pragmatic, sensible, even scientific. "Everything moves here," Louis
Fischer reported from the Soviet Union. "Life, the air, people are dynamic. When I watch these recently unsealed reservoirs of energy I am
sometimes carried away and think that nothing is impossible in the
Soviet Union." George Counts spoke of villages remade, productivity
that doubled and tripled, labor problems solved, costs cut, and living
standards on the rise. This was the kind of practical accomplishment
that struck progressives as eminently sensible. Those who directed it,
they reasoned, were motivated by logic, not dogma.[69]

The practical bent of the Five Year Plans reflected well on Joseph Stalin while detracting from Leon Trotsky's prestige, although, in general, noncommunists in the early 1930s were not very interested in what they regarded as *Bolsheviki* factional feuds. While Marxists debated the theoretical positions of the two figures, progressives measured them by what they accomplished. Stalin was a success and Trotsky a failure at Bolshevik politics, Michael Blankfort recalled, and that made a big difference. So too was Stalin pushing the Soviet Union into the twentieth century. Trotsky, on the other hand, seemed ideologically rigid and afraid of action. He was an impressive intellectual, Jerome Davis explained, and his type of person was useful during the revolutionary period. When it was time to actually build socialism in Russia, Stalin's personal qualities—"courage, will-power, maneuvering talents, political organizing ability, and primitive tenacity"—better suited the country. Even his crudeness, Fischer thought, appealed to a people who were themselves crude.[70] Noncommunist intellectuals admired Stalin and disliked Trotsky, but their conclusions about the two Bolsheviks were not based on the kinds of theoretical debates that pitted Stalinist against Trotskyist.

Communist Party intellectuals followed the implementation of the Five Year Plans even more avidly than progressives. Given the Russia worship that permeated the CPUSA, their conclusions were predictable: the Plans were the perfect embodiment of Marxist theory and Stalin the brilliant pragmatist who put theory into practice. "The Bolsheviks may be hard," Joseph Freeman explained, "they may make mistakes— but they are building a better world." Communists accepted violence and class inequalities, two facets of revolutionary Russia that distressed liberals, as necessary features of the new regime's evolution. Sending people to Siberia, Michael Gold once noted in a statement that greatly offended Oswald Garrison Villard, was petty "flea-bite violence." As the Soviet Union progressed toward Marx's communist ideal, Communist Party intellectuals credited Stalin with industrializing, nationalizing, and collectivizing. So too did they endorse the official Comintern condemnation of Leon Trotsky. Nothing suggests, though, that they felt constrained by these pronouncements. Rather, they sincerely believed that Stalin was good for Soviet society and Trotsky, more interested in his own reputation than the success of his homeland, bad.[71]

Non-Party Marxists had a more conditional response to the accom-

50   plishments of the Russian Revolution. They credited Lenin with putting the USSR on the right path toward socialism and saw Stalin as a
potential interloper who might deflect the revolution. Dissident Marxists admired Lenin for the same reason noncommunists preferred Stalin to Trotsky—he seemed to put good sense ahead of theory. According to Max Eastman, one of the most devout of the Leninists, what
made Lenin great was his pragmatism. He was "an engineer, not a
prophet," whose revolution represented a victory over Marxian meta-
physics. His was "the attitude of a practical artisan who is doing work
and doing it scientifically." When compared to Lenin, Stalin did not
measure up as a realist, but neither did Trotsky. Edmund Wilson concluded that Lenin "cared nothing about power for its own sake," while
Stalin gloried in creating a cult for himself that "has nothing to do with
Marxism." Yet Wilson had a grudging respect for Stalin's ability to
accomplish things. So too did most other American Marxists (Trotskyists excepted) even when Stalin personally offended them. His grasp
of realities and the power to turn theory into plants, farm communes,
and industrial statistics outweighed his less attractive edges, at least
initially.[72]

More than any other factor, then, it was the juxtaposition of the
Depression and the Five Year Plans that produced a mainly positive
intellectual response to the Soviet Union in 1930 and 1931. Stalin
seemed able to chart a course toward industrialization and to provide
jobs for people. Trotsky lived in exile and wrote theoretical tracts.
These facts spoke volumes to American intellectuals, Communists
and noncommunists alike. By the same token, the Soviet economy
climbed while the American economy seemed to collapse. Surely this
suggested that the Soviets were doing something right and the Americans something wrong. The Soviet success story reflected well on the
CPUSA, but resulted in no groundswell of intellectual commitment to
the Party. Communism abroad was exciting; Communism at home was
far more intimidating.

In 1932, the editors of *The New Republic,* having heard so many
rumors about the emergence of a new radical intelligentsia, confessed
that all the talk led them to imagine that "thousands of writers together, each with his portable typewriter, had boarded an express train
for Moscow and points left." Upon closer examination, however, they
concluded that while intellectuals had indeed caught the train left, it
was a "leftbound local" and not a "Red Express." Intellectuals ap-

proved of communism, which they conceived as an economic system, 51
but not Communism; a "capitalized Communist," the editorial explained, ". . . is a different matter entirely."[73] The gap between communism and Communism limited the Party's inroads into the larger social
intelligentsia and defined exactly how far left most intellectuals were
willing to go.

TWO

"The Disinherited":

The Emergence of a Left-wing

Opposition, 1932–1935

In 1941, Michael Gold offered a rather fanciful version of what happened when intellectuals confronted the Depression: "The depression had stripped all of the literary world of its cherished philosophies. Freudianism, pessimism, Bohemianism, Joyceism, Humanism, even the fuzzy 'democracy' of the midwest school—all proved inadequate. They could not explain the great crash, or show a way out. But Marxism did explain, and did offer a fighting hope."[1] The leftward trend was more complex than Gold's Party perspective allowed. Intellectuals found their literary and political beliefs challenged by the Depression. Some found Marxism intriguing as well. But they were decidedly dubious of the merits of joining the CPUSA. Wooing intellectuals was not a goal all Communists, or Communist intellectuals, shared. In the course of even minimally pursuing that goal, moreover, the Party made enemies. By the middle of the decade it faced a shadow movement of intellectuals opposed from the left who threatened its status as the radical establishment.

Cultural programs were not matters of particular concern to the CPUSA's national leadership. The Party's intellectual cadre was self-governing, for the most part, although hardly democratic. "Political commissars"—Alexander Trachtenberg was perhaps the most famous—oversaw the community, adopting the same centralized and hierarchical structure as elsewhere in the organization. Theirs was an impossible task, for they had to be alternatively sympathetic and directive. They made decisions, defined larger goals, and generally tried to keep the sometimes unruly intelligentsia in hand.

There was a finely graduated scale of intellectual devotion to the CPUSA. Intellectual functionaries represented one end. Trachtenberg had no career beyond the CPUSA and his job within it was overseeing others. He handled International Publishers and served as the voice of Party authority in several front groups. Next to Trachtenberg were activists like Robert Minor and Joseph North who had some role within the hierarchy (Minor was briefly the CP's head) and wrote mainly for Party organs. They blended their responsibilities as intellectuals and Communists and did not mind that others regarded them as cultural spokespersons for the movement. The further intellectuals moved away from the end of the spectrum occupied by Trachtenberg, Minor, and North, the more likely they were to see themselves in an adversarial relationship with the Party hierarchy. It was not always easy to devise strategies to straddle the great divide between CPUSA organs and popular ones. Some became almost literally split personalities, like Kyle Crichton, who used his own name to write for *Colliers* and a pen name, Robert Forsythe, at *The New Masses*. At the far end of the scale were those who "went Left because they wanted careers and power,"[2] a fanciful notion considering the Party's reputation. Those who joined the CPUSA for personal gain rarely lasted very long in the organization.

Although there was no objective reason why joining the Party would render incompatible an intellectual's creative priorities and the movement's political needs, many Communist intellectuals felt those tensions, and the larger community simply assumed they existed. Part of the reason for the stereotype was the certainty with which the CPUSA made pronouncements and laid down its line. Such attitudes seemed to contradict the intellectual process. New Party member Alvah Bessie, for example, noted that he was automatically "leery of the intellectual communists"[3] because they expressed their political opinions so easily that they undermined their reputations as critical thinkers. Joining the CPUSA thus did not signal the end of an intellectual's suspicion of politically motivated culture but, often, the beginning. Probably no Party intellectual consistently grappled with the notion of a divided self more than Joseph Freeman. Freeman wanted to be truthful as a writer; yet he also strove to be a good Party member. Writing truthfully, though, always seemed to violate the Party line, and being a good Party member meant he had to put dogma above truth. When he published *An American Testament,* Party function-aries found subversive ideas in the text. No less an authority than Earl Browder asked him to "stop the circulation of the book, then do good work." If Freeman met these requirements, "all will be forgotten," Browder promised, so Freeman sacrificed his own popularity for the sake of the Party and asked his publisher to stop promoting the book. A year later, his essay on "Our Literary Heritage" got him in trouble again. Minor and Trachtenberg thought it contradicted the Party's cultural line. This time Freeman "tore up the galleys and called the whole project off."[4] His experience was unusual, but every Party intellectual's worst nightmare. It did not necessarily follow that a good Marxist intellectual made a good Communist. The discipline required by the movement could inspire creative individuals or offend them.

Party intellectuals wore two hats. Within the organization, they helped reify ideas formulated elsewhere. The Party line came from Moscow, was fine-tuned at the highest levels of the American CP, and then, most commentators would agree, reshaped by grass-roots activists. Intellectuals were part of that grass-roots effort to make the Third Period and the prolet cult relevant to American realities.[5] Beyond the organization was a larger creative community, offering different possibilities. Here was an audience to be engaged as intellectuals and radicals. Here was a place where CPUSA writers, thinkers, and critics might gain recognition as intellectuals while spreading the good word. What Party intellectuals did paralleled the tasks of union organizers and those Communists who worked with the unemployed; they reached out to the sympathetic in the hopes of expanding their influence. In the cultural realm, this meant finding some way of embracing the Granville Hickses and Malcolm Cowleys on the fringes of the organization, who were interested, middle class, but not yet ready to fully commit themselves to Party discipline.

Over time, the prolet cult became more interesting to middle-class intellectuals as it evolved and as interpretations of who might produce it became more generous. The new culture always posed a dilemma for intellectuals. If, as was popularly assumed, proletarians wrote and painted its masterpieces, would they not eventually cease to be proletarians and become, instead, intellectuals? As Floyd Dell sarcastically pointed out, even "Comrade Mike [Gold] is a literary man, an intellectual, and a member of the salaried middle class." Gold at least had the experience of being poor and second-generation immigrant. Those without working-class backgrounds felt very uncomfortable about participating in a movement called the prolet cult. Edwin Seaver suggested one way around these dilemmas, arguing that "it is not the class origin of the writer which is the determining factor [in the prolet cult], but his present class loyalties." All intellectuals became, then, "allies of the working class" if they chose to be, whatever their backgrounds. Hicks replaced the widely misused phrase "proletarian writers" with "revolutionary writers," substituting what Barbara Foley calls "the criterion of perspective" for that of authorship. Gold resurrected an old hero, John Reed, Harvard educated but a "common soldier of the cause," to illustrate the new role, which required only that intellectuals be politically committed and put those commitments ahead of their personal success. By 1935, experimentation and exploration had made the prolet cult something more sophisticated than the stereotypes and the slogans suggested.[6]

The gradually expanding definition of who might create a revolutionary culture benefited some and threatened others. Younger would-be intellectuals often loved the prolet cult, especially those with fierce pride about their working-class roots and deep commitments to radicalism. The Third Period's cultural corollary enabled them to fuse their intellectual aspirations and political concerns in a particularly satisfying manner. It also gave their careers a boost. The John Reed Clubs usually limited their membership to the working class. Yet, as forums, they offered wide exposure, particularly through such publications as the *Partisan Review*. Many younger radical intellectuals had a vested interest in preserving a definition of the prolet cult more class-based than revolutionary.[7]

The Reed Clubs became the center of one of the most sustained battles between advocates of a broader definition of the prolet cult and those who preferred to leave matters as they were. The JRCs were so successful that Party functionaries flocked to them. Some ran local clubs as sanctuaries of political rectitude, forcing all members to join the Party while padding out the ranks with activists of dubious talents. At the First National Conference of JRCs, held in 1932, delegates complained about the cultural commissars who hovered anxiously and made sure they produced acceptable work. Joseph Freeman wondered why they were there in the first place. "The JRC must be rid of elements who do not properly belong there," he told the convention, "who are not writers, artists or worker-intellectuals." At stake was not just who ran the Reed Clubs, but each creative person's integrity. Functionaries "are not responsible to the traditions of ideas," he explained. Joshua Kunitz agreed with Freeman; the Reed Clubs needed leaders "who talk to us in our own language, intellectual language." The looming presence of the functionaries in the JRCS served as a sometimes bitter reminder of the low regard in which the Party held intellectuals. They made cultural decisions while writers had to perform all kinds of nonliterary tasks. Freeman felt hamstrung. "Party writers must be given time to *write*," he proclaimed. But the functionaries remained, and as late as 1934 JRC members were asked to organize writers' unions and perform "mass work."[8]

Younger Party intellectuals, in particular, challenged Freeman and the other advocates of a looser definition of the prolet cult. When Michael Gold proposed that the JRCS "bring in forces that can help the movement," they cried foul. Without restrictions to keep the clubs pure, proletarian, and small, younger intellectuals feared they would become playgrounds for already established writers and artists. Harry Carlisle protested "the conciliatory attitude of Mike Gold toward middle class intellectuals." Oakley Johnson insisted that the Reed Clubs' connections to the Party were not a "handicap" but an advantage. Kenneth Rexroth argued that the JRC was not "an organization to bring in big names." In the end, the JRCS' 1932 draft manifesto allowed that "allies from the disillusioned middle-class intelligentsia are to be welcomed," but affirmed that "of primary importance at this stage is the development of the revolutionary culture of the working class itself." Moreover, if one of the goals of the Reed Clubs was to "fight against the influence of middle-class ideas in the work of revolutionary writers and artists,"[9] they hardly seemed like very hospitable places for the Edmund Wilsons or Malcolm Cowleys of the world. Younger intellectuals prevailed, but not necessarily because they won any ideological debate. Rather, functionaries preferred not to tinker with success and the JRCS had an international reputation among communists along with the interest of the outside intellectual community.

At the Party's unofficial cultural organ, *The New Masses,* a similar battle raged. But the Reed Clubs prospered despite their limited clientele; *The New Masses* did not. Although more and more intellectuals considered themselves radical in the early 1930s, fewer and fewer read—or bought—the journal. By mid-1933, it was "near collapse," its editorial atmosphere "gloomy," its offerings "thin, dull," and its line so predictable as to be "monotonous." Asked to evaluate the "crisis" at the magazine for Party leaders, Freeman concluded that it lacked "central direction." Much of the blame lay with editor Gold, who, according to his staff, "got all the glory while they did all the dirty work." Staff morale was low because of Gold, the generally "shabby treatment," and the excessive demands "'for the good of the cause.'" Staffers wanted a more "collective editorship." Poor Freeman, himself following orders, tried to turn the situation around at *The New Masses,* well knowing that "I would be blamed for the end result."[10]

Freeman wanted to produce a magazine that would be attractive to a broader segment of intellectuals. Gold likewise endorsed the view that *The New Masses* should become "more popular, more lively," and less visibly CP. Yet to facilitate that goal he had to forfeit his sole editorial control, which hardly made him happy. The editorial board that replaced him had representatives from many perspectives, including a young proletarian, Granville Hicks as literary editor, and an economist. On "the political end" of the magazine, Freeman expanded coverage but employed a wider circle of analysts to alleviate complaints that *New Masses* parroted the Party line. Freeman worked very hard to satisfy conflicting interests, including those who wanted "a magazine for the middle-classes" and those who thought *The New Masses* "too remote from Party life." What he thought he created was a compromise, "a Communist magazine FOR the middle-classes."[11]

For a while, he believed the publication would turn around: "Comrades [Stanley] Burnshaw and [Bruce] Minton assured me I was an asset on the magazine. An esprit de corps seemed to be developing, I fancied." Ultimately, however, he could not bring together the disparate forces associated with the publication. Gold sulked and "ceased to come to the office." Freeman invited him to write a regular column, but the board of editors vetoed the idea because "his writings did not meet the high standards of *The New Masses.*" The old-timers ignored the new people, whether close to the Party or not. Freeman's recruits complained "that they were treated by certain staff members with arrogance" and not given space in the magazine. About the only real change in *The New Masses* in 1933 was that it switched from a monthly to a weekly format, a move that suggested not any increased readership so much as increased Party financial support. Freeman was blamed for failing to turn around the journal and recalled that "in a most uncomradely manner I was asked to resign."[12] *The New Masses* did not become a more respectable or popular cultural magazine in 1933 and remained in a precarious position.

Freeman failed because he ran headlong into several interlocking problems endemic to the Communist Party's cultural movement in the early 1930s. One was the struggle between the prolet cult narrowly defined versus more loosely constructed. When he tried to bring in nonParty contributors, those already on staff felt threatened. Yet they were also mindful that their reputations were at stake, which was why Gold could write a regular column in *The Daily Worker* but not *The New Masses*. The former publication was for factory workers; intellectuals, however, read the latter. Staff members also protected their status by resisting the incursion of newer contributors onto the editorial board. Their unwillingness to accord the younger writers and artists who gathered at *The New Masses*' offices any respect had, remember, been the impetus behind the Reed Clubs. Once the JRCs acquired their own literary magazines, *The New Masses* staff saw little reason to give young proletarians access to "their" journal as well.[13] Functionaries wanted to improve *The New Masses*' reputation, but lacked faith in Freeman's ability to make wise political choices. They questioned nearly every one of his recommendations. Ultimately, they were unwilling to take the risks involved to change the situation. Freeman was neither the first nor the last Party intellectual unable to find a middle ground between radical purity and popular success.

The more practical solution to some of the problems Freeman faced was to leave alone such Party bastions as *The New Masses* and the Reed Clubs and use other venues to reach the radicalizing middle class. Front groups threatened neither Party intellectuals nor progressives, since their relationships were symbiotic. Intellectual functionaries could short-circuit debates about the meaning of a proletarian culture, building alternatives that defined the prolet cult more expansively while protecting the more explicitly proletarian Reed Clubs. One of the reasons *The New Masses* stagnated was that intellectual functionaries increasingly transferred their energies elsewhere, trying to make the fronts viable. If their efforts allowed them to avoid the philosophical and professional complaints Party intellectuals raised about working with noncommunists elsewhere, so too did they introduce them to a whole new set of problems.

The League of Professionals for Foster and Ford, for example, promoted the Party's presidential and vice-presidential candidates in the 1932 election, but barely made it through the election intact. Fifty-three "responsible intellectual workers" publicly declared their support for "the frankly revolutionary Communist Party." The League counted on progressive support. Yet many progressives wavered. Lewis Mumford sent the group's manifesto to a friend, noting his own reservations, but assuring him it was "worth signing." Several months later, however, he reneged; "I find it impossible to 'support' the Communist ticket," he told two other friends. John Dos Passos confessed, "I havent [sic] enough confidence in the C.P. to give it a blanket endorsement." Dos Passos and Mumford had a different concept of their role in radical politics than Waldo Frank, who likely disagreed with bits and pieces of the manifesto but was more anxious to make a statement of protest against the status quo. "Use my name," he urged Malcolm Cowley, "in sending out appeals for other signatures."[14] By election time, the League of Professionals for Foster and Ford had amassed an impressive roster of well-known intellectuals who, like Frank, understood that their names were more important to the fronts than their full endorsement of front actions.

The League of Professionals suggests how intellectual front politics were supposed to work. Big-name intellectuals endorsed the platform because they wanted to add their voices in favor of radical change. A gentle Party presence handled the more routine details of the organization and harnessed progressives' unfocused radical élan. There were no flamboyant functionaries in the League, just other "professionals" who happened to be Communists. The manifesto itself proved that harmony was possible, so long as everyone performed his or her assigned tasks. Progressives wrote the rough draft, expecting to "be supervised, in effect censored by the Communist Party's experts in ideology." The text then went to Party headquarters, where it emerged "with a preamble written in heavy Marxist jargon" and the instruction that certain Party programs be incorporated into it. The initial authors made cosmetic changes to improve readability.[15] This was precisely the kind of interaction the Party's intellectual cadre encouraged. The Party contribution was accepted, took place quietly, and was cheerfully accommodated. Party people sought out middle-class writers "to try to find out just what these guys think ought to be done with the LPG, and also to talk to them a little bit about the Party." Middle-class

60   writers, "being too busy," could leave the day-to-day operation of the
      League to others.[16] There were not many progressives willing to join
      early fronts, but those who did presumably gained what they wanted
      from them and caused the organizations little trouble.

      Trouble in the early fronts came from another source, young Marx-
      ists who rejected the CPUSA. There was no real place in the fronts for
      such people since they refused to be gracious about the Party presence.
      After the election, they wanted to convert the League into a forum
      where radicalized and politically active intellectuals could discuss
      ideas and act in concert, independent of Party strictures. They were
      "uncomfortable at being trotted out as celebrities at mass meetings."
      They likewise found the lurking specter of Party functionaries coun-
      terproductive. "These idiots," Felix Morrow complained, "will drive
      useful people away." The atmosphere at the League's post-election
      meetings grew increasingly tense as factions plotted in the corners and
      shouted at one another.[17] The 1932 election, while a failure from the
      Communist point of view, marked the League of Professionals' acme as
      a front group. Thereafter, its disintegration began.

      Dissidents appeared from all sides. Some the Party labeled "Trots-
      kyites," others "Lovestoneites." In a series of meetings, the young
      turks challenged the Party's Third Period line and questioned the wis-
      dom of its "social fascist" ideology. Dissident Marxists, including
      Sidney Hook, Lewis Corey, and Herbert Solow, pushed for a "united
      front" and factional independence for the League. Malcolm Cowley
      thought their intention was to "deliberately hinder . . . the league from
      getting anything done." Progressives stood "vehement[ly]" by the or-
      ganization, but the young turks triumphed, at least to the degree that
      their determined opposition to "the Party rabbis" made it impossible
      to function any longer. League secretary James Rorty grew so tired of
      refereeing their fights that he stopped calling meetings.[18] Not long after
      the election, the group quietly expired.

      The ringleaders of the internal attack on the League of Professionals
      were very much like their Party peers in background but miles away
      from them when it came to defining the role of a radical intellectual.
      Both came from the working class and were often Jewish and urban;
      but dissident Marxists were, on the whole, better educated and more
      grandiose in their expectations than committed Party workers. Youn-
      ger Party intellectuals preferred the Reed Clubs to fronts and identified
      with the prolet cult; they saw both as means of mobility that would

propel them farther into Party circles. Young Marxist dissidents gravitated to the fronts looking for a more stimulating atmosphere, greater independence, and broader recognition. Theirs was a very idealized conceptualization of fronts as radical salons where intellectuals would come together, discuss, reach a moral consensus, then act. But they also clung to this image well past the point of innocence, so that their continued participation in fronts became a way of forcing confrontation over issues Party functionaries preferred to avoid. Their self-conceptions and the determination with which they held those self-conceptions despite their age and objective status made their survival in front politics almost impossible.

As dissident Marxists quarreled with other intellectuals over the policy of the League of Professionals, they inevitably carried those quarrels into the National Committee for the Defense of Political Prisoners. The NCDPP was the more intellectual and looser version of another front, the International Labor Defense. The NCDPP's purpose was to showcase progressives, "whose reputation or connections might best be used to bring ILD cases to a public before which the ILD itself might not be able to bring them," as one Party member explained.[19] But some young Marxists had other ideas. They joined the NCDPP rather than the ILD just as they did the League of Professionals rather than the Reed Clubs, because they were searching for the chance to discuss ideas, mingle with other intellectuals, and remain out of reach of Party discipline.[20] Once dissidents questioned the running of the League, their disagreements logically spilled over into the NCDPP.

Eight NCDPP members resigned in the spring of 1933 over the question of forming a united front with other left-wing organizations. Herbert Solow proposed and James Rorty seconded a motion that called for a united front against Hitler. Their motion was defeated and ridiculed, yet shortly thereafter "the Communist International directed the Communist Party to establish such a united front" and the NCDPP and ILD endorsed the spirit of the motion without crediting Solow at all. Solow presumably knew that the NCDPP's leadership committee, overstocked with Party members, would never accept his proposal. He offered it because he felt morally obliged to and because it would force the Party faction to reveal itself to others. After being turned down, he and the rest of the opposition could then legitimately voice their complaints. The encounter served as a pretext for a public statement they could have written before the motion was defeated. "An organization

62 claiming to struggle on behalf of democratic rights," their letter of resignation read, "which crushes all semblance of democracy within itself, is an absurd anomaly."[21]

Compounding the dissidents' grievances was the way in which the NCDPP handled their protest. Diana Trilling recalled that "for the meeting itself [where Solow's motion was discussed] the ILD lined up its regulars to bolster the vote for the Party and to swell the chorus of abuse with which we were met. Many of the 'members' who were gathered for the occasion had never before been present at a meeting."[22] Later, after the NCDPP voted in its own motion for a united front, executive secretary (and Party member) Joshua Kunitz offered a revisionist interpretation of the dispute, impugning Solow's motives and depreciating his radical commitments. Kunitz called him "childish" for trying to grab credit for an idea that actually belonged to the ILD: "No one asked the disgruntled members to run away. In a *United Front* toes are bound to be stepped upon. The more sensitive, that is the less hardened in battle, naturally shriek. The less disciplined run away."[23]

Solow's problem, then, was that he was insufficiently revolutionary and unable to subordinate his own need for glory to the good of the cause. Kunitz's interpretation was not necessarily personally contemptuous of Solow; rather, it reflected precisely the Party's expectations of intellectuals. But Solow was not trying to claim credit. He merely wanted recognition of the truth and confirmation that the Communists had been wrong and he right. He produced a copy of his resolution to demonstrate that his had been the first. He should have known better than to challenge the NCDPP leadership. The woman who took the minutes at the meeting in question insisted that his copy "does not at all agree with the notes I have." Solow persisted, but she would not back down. Instead, she contacted others who attended the meeting "and the consensus of opinion is that it [his later copy] is not what you read at the meeting."[24] History had been rewritten to satisfy the Party's needs. That Solow got in the way was relatively unimportant to much of the organization's executive committee, but supremely important to Solow. The personal dimension, his mistreatment by people he took to be Party lackeys, reinforced his interpretation of the political events. Solow now had firsthand evidence to support his complaint that the fronts served the Party and not the left. Like so many other dissident Marxists, when he lost sympathy for the CPUSA he became irreconcilably opposed to it.

Dissidents like Solow and Rorty reinforced the CPUSA's suspicion of nonaffiliated intellectuals by being belligerent, disruptive, and deliberately provocative. Certainly they did not behave in a manner consistent with Party discipline. They were not intimidated by Communist functionaries and joined fronts without any intention of playing by their unspoken rules. The younger rebel Marxists recognized that in their world success came to those who asserted themselves and the farther one was from power, the more assertive one had to be. Their "angry militancy" was a function of the Depression, their self-confidence, and their backgrounds. They learned that those who took control of their lives got what they wanted. Hitler's rise to power proved that, as did Roosevelt's triumph over polio. American workers finally gained some measure of organization via the strike. In the popular culture, heroes came in all shapes and sizes, ranging from Shirley Temple to Mae West, but shared an unwavering determination. Like Edward G. Robinson's gangster antihero Rico, dissident Marxists wanted "to be someone" in a world with little place for them. The 1930s "encouraged a righteous social anger" and "also licensed unseemly personal ambition," Diana Trilling recalled. Young rebel Marxists' poverty, ethnicity, and Jewishness, as Daniel Aaron noted, "literally and figuratively ghettoized, segregated, denied [them] 'community' with old-stock America."[25] By questioning the status quo as they did, they were able to narrow the distance between themselves and the sources of intellectual power. Theirs was the style of the underdog who had nothing to lose from the demise of the old.

No established intellectual space would accommodate them. Their ideal was a safe haven, but a safe haven full of dispute and controversy, one shaped by "freedom of discussion, proposal and criticism." Inside the NCDPP, Eliot Cohen and Solow were aggressive opponents whose arguments were "full of theory and factional vigor."[26] Yet they also were friends who ultimately shared a distaste for fronts and the NCDPP most particularly. Heated debate, for them, was not evidence of animosity, but a vehicle for developing their ideas. Progressives were neither comfortable with this model nor willing to give younger dissidents access to their own traditional safe havens to pursue it. Alfred Kazin recalled how "fundamental" the influence of a few renowned people was when it came to gaining either literary success or at least the possibility of earning a living: "Each Wednesday afternoon . . . I waited with other hopeful reviewers for [Malcolm] Cowley to sail

64   in after lunch." Mary McCarthy's fictional alter ego remembered the
same wait all too well: "Each time . . . she felt her whole career hanging
by a thread." But Cowley, book review editor at *The New Republic,*
never had enough books to go around and saved the best for established reviewers and, McCarthy thought, people who better agreed
with his politics. The arrangement hardly seemed democratic.[27] If *The
New Republic, The Nation,* and most college classrooms were closed
off to young rebels, the Party provided no adequate alternative for their
ambitions. It expected them to follow orders and do lots of Party work,
join what seemed like narrow Communist cultural organizations (like
the JRCs) and keep their mouths shut in the broader fronts. It offered
nothing more than a "sectarian attitude and bullying factional tactics."[28] There were no places where dissident Marxists could perform
the intellectual's solemn tasks.

There were occasional role models for rebels and safe havens where
they might light. One "central figure for dissidents" was V. F. Calverton, editor of the *Modern Monthly.* Calverton had a bitter public break
with the Party in 1932/33, which made his magazine a logical home
for rebels. Calverton also provided theoretical justification for dissident crusades against the Communists. He put the matter in precisely the kind of terms young dissidents might like to hear. "American Marxists in general tend to use Marxism as a substitute instead of
an inspiration for thought," he explained. "Subjective" Marxists misunderstood the doctrine but gained credibility because they endorsed
rather than challenged functionaries' power. Real Marxists knew that
Marxism could not be quoted as scripture suitable for any situation. It
was "a scientific method" that had to be constantly refined. It interacted with the present. The beauty of Calverton's explanation was that
it made nonconformity heroic. Here was someone saying young dissident Marxists were courageous and moral to buck the Party tide, that
they were "genuine, honest Communist[s]."[29]

Calverton's thesis was part of a growing interpretive framework that
helped dissidents make sense of their own clashes with the CPUSA.
Older dissidents like Calverton, Jay Lovestone, and Lewis Corey argued that the people who ran the CPUSA slavishly followed the Bolshevik model because they lacked the ability to find their way alone.
Persons of integrity and intelligence recognized that the circumstances facing Russia in 1918 were vastly different from those facing
America in 1933, but saying so meant confronting a Party hierarchy

totally dependent on the Comintern for legitimacy. As Edmund Wilson noted after returning from an NCDPP-sponsored trip to Harlan County: "The fact that the Communists in the United States are guided by the Third International and that the Communist International is dominated by Russia has tended to make them at their worst mere parrots of the Russian Party and yes-men for Stalin." It was the "yes-men for Stalin" who stood between dissidents and honest Marxism. "What we need," Ernest Sutherland Bates suggested, "is a twentieth century American Karl Marx" who could see beyond the Russian Revolution and the CPUSA.[30] Dissident Marxists imagined themselves precisely that, twentieth-century American Marxes who would use the theory, not as benefited Earl Browder and company, but as Marx intended.

Dissidents were American exceptionalists whether or not they affiliated themselves with the faction most associated with those ideas, the Lovestoneites. They believed that America had its own revolutionary patterns and potential; the CPUSA could not tap that potential, however, because its roots were so foreign. Dissidents noted several essential differences between the United States and other countries, differences that impeded the revolutionary process here. One was its proletariat, which was divided and disinclined to see its problems as problems of capitalism. Another was the traditional strength of the middle class, which such analysts as Corey argued was weakening economically but still the ideal to which Americans aspired. A third was the collision of American practicality and what Calverton called the "metaphysical trappings" of Marxism, meaning, primarily, the dialectic. Most dissident Marxists dismissed the dialectic as part of "Marx's half-baked materialist-hegelian hash." As scientists and rationalists, they could not accept "the weird heresies of the 19th century," so they simply consigned them to the attic like "superfluous baggage." Marx used the Hegelian construct "out of piety to Hegel's memory," Sidney Hook explained. But in the twentieth century, Marxists had no business believing in an inevitable revolutionary process. It was precisely this kind of blind commitment to what Marx had written, as interpreted through the Russian Revolution and Stalin, that made the CPUSA irrelevant.[31]

While the dissidents' ideas about the unique shape of an American revolution were not unlike the so-called "Right Opposition's," their critique of the CPUSA came from a seemingly contradictory source, the "Left Opposition"[32] of Trotsky. Trotsky provided both the vocabulary

66   and the mode of analysis that enabled young Marxist opponents of the Party to distinguish between legitimate Marxist theory and false interpretations of the doctrine. Trotsky argued that what dissidents confronted in 1933 or 1934 was not the failure of Marxism per se, but a failure of Stalinism. Stalin presided over an incomplete revolution, incomplete because no other nation had the simultaneous socialist revolution Marx deemed necessary for communist success. Trotsky contended that the Soviet Union could not sustain socialism and progress to communism without other revolutions to reinforce the Russian one. Stalin's attempts to build socialism in one country were, therefore, flawed and Stalin knew it. He could only temporarily maintain the illusion of true socialism by building a massive bureaucracy personally loyal to himself. This bureaucracy had to suppress dissent in order to cover over the blemishes of Soviet society. In time, Trotsky believed, the demands of the bureaucracy and the needs of the masses would contradict one another sharply and Stalinism would come undone: "The more complex the economic tasks become, the greater the demands and the interests of the population become, all the more sharp becomes the contradiction between the bureaucratic regime [of Stalin] and the demands of socialist development; all the more coarsely does the bureaucracy struggle to preserve its positions; all the more cynically does it resort to violence, fraud and bribery."[33] Younger dissident Marxists seized the idea of an illegitimate Stalinist bureaucracy because it seemed to explain why an American movement modeled on the Stalinist one might expel creative thinkers.

Yet dissidents did not see the situation quite as Trotsky did. He emphasized the necessity of "a permanent revolution," supporting work in other countries to make worldwide socialism possible. Few American dissidents—Trotskyists excepted—had much interest in other revolutions. They were most concerned about revolution, or its failure, in their own country. Even though they traced the weaknesses of the American Party to its being a "football . . . of Russian factional politics," they really had little to say about Stalinism elsewhere. In fact, they remained certain Stalin was "building the civilization of the future" in the Soviet Union.[34] The highly personal nature of their quarrels with the CPUSA made it hard for dissidents to look beyond the immediate Party situation. They took Trotsky's analysis and fused it with American exceptionalism to explain why Stalinism would not work in the United States. Although their enemies would often brand them "Trotskyites," they certainly were not, for they used Trotsky's

ideas in a manner perfectly in keeping with their sense of what constituted true intellectual discourse. They drew from and built on his
analysis without fully embracing it.

Dissidents put far less emphasis than Trotsky did, for example, on
the consequences of Stalinist rule in the USSR. Trotsky called the
Soviet Union a "degenerated workers state" whose socialist economy
was distorted by the Stalinist overlay of political and bureaucratic
structures. He critiqued Stalinism, but not the USSR because of its
socialist economy. American rebel Marxists instinctively used similar
categories, but grounded their analyses more on what they saw and felt
than theory. They were surprisingly tolerant of Stalinism abroad considering how critical they were of the impact of Stalinism at home.
Sidney Hook was apparently unfazed by collectivization or the Ukrainian famine, for he thought that "Russia today [1934] possesses more
working class democracy than any other country." Stalin, Edmund
Wilson conceded, encouraged the people to worship him too much;
but that was not enough of a problem to "throw the baby out with the
bath."[35] Rebel Marxists were neither especially interested nor especially critical of what happened in the Soviet Union. As Americans,
they saw Americanizing Marx as their first priority.

The process of Americanizing Marx implicitly impugned Stalin
and the Comintern, but more explicitly attacked the American Communist Party's Third Period line. Dissidents argued that Third Period
policies discouraged positive change. Dual unionism split the working
class and "social fascist" labels antagonized the few potential left-
wing allies available. Dissident Marxists were also quicker than Communists to recognize the threat of fascism, which, they argued, Third
Period policies exacerbated. Calverton warned that by antagonizing
"little" capitalists (the petty bourgeois), the Party pushed them toward the right. Lewis Corey agreed that the "crisis" of the middle class
made those in declining occupations vulnerable to the fascist message.[36] The solution, they thought, was to concentrate on building
links between radical factions. Dissident Marxists were "premature
united fronters"[37] advocating cooperation among Socialists, Communists, and unaffiliated radicals several years before the Comintern
adopted a similar policy. Thus they viewed their actions in the League
of Professionals and the National Committee for the Defense of Political Prisoners as attempts to force the CPUSA to embrace a more realistic
program.

Dissident Marxists, however, were themselves vague about how to make united fronts work, especially given their sometimes aggressive personal styles. Calverton in 1934 called for "a truce in the self-devouring internecine warfare which now prevails among the parties of the left" so that they might build "an authentic and not a sham *united front.*" Yet, given his other standards, which included the right to continue criticizing other factions within the front, and his special warning to the CPUSA that it must change, such a union seemed unlikely. Thus, alternatively, he advocated the formation of "a new radical party, a new revolutionary party, a new communist party which will orient itself to the American workers and farmers."[38] This latter solution was the one more often chosen by dissidents, who were too suspicious of the Party to work with it. Building counter-institutions or parallel institutions was the rebels' way of building united fronts of dissidents. As such, there were many problems they never resolved. Their ideas were unfocused and their task often got the better of them, especially since the Trotskyists were so successful at building the Communist League of America. The dissidents' strength was their critique of the CPUSA; their attempts to build radical alternatives were more hesitant, ill-conceived, and unreal.

The Non-Partisan Labor Defense, founded in 1934, showed that the dissidents either lacked imagination when it came to designing counter-institutions or were so angry with the NCDPP that they were determined to poach in its waters. It was almost identical to the NCDPP in scope and mission, except that it had no Party connections. While its organizers hoped to avoid the pitfalls of Party fronts, under the leadership of Herbert Solow the NPLD became a front of another sort, for American Trotskyists. Its most famous defendant, Norman Mini, was a Trotskyist. Mini belonged to the CPUSA when he and other organizers were arrested for violating a criminal syndicalism law in Sacramento. But as soon as he changed his party allegiance, the ILD dropped his case and denounced him as a turncoat. Mini's experience reinforced dissidents' contention that fronts were partisan organizations. Yet, American Trotskyists, as James P. Cannon recalled, "exploited to the full all the political aspects of this situation," so that the decision to defend Mini became itself a partisan one. Diana Trilling, who left the NCDPP for the NPLD along with Solow, realized in hindsight what she did not see at the time: "They [the Trotskyists] used us as the Communist Party used its fellow travelers."[39] Trilling was not dense; but she saw in the Trotskyists' opposition to the CPUSA an implied commitment to the rest of her program that did not always exist. NPLD members might have freed themselves of *Party* front groups, but they would never free themselves of the experience of being *in* front groups.

The dissidents' rival political organization, the American Workers Party, proved the point more forcefully. The AWP was precisely the kind of American Marxist party Calverton proposed. It was "revolutionary," "rooted in American soil, its eyes fixed primarily upon American conditions and problems." Best of all, it was free of all other political connections. Its head, A. J. Muste, was a Christian, a pacifist, a socialist, and a labor organizer with impressive credentials. Dissidents thought the AWP would solve all their problems with its union base, its home-grown philosophy, and its freedom from the Party taint. "The future belongs to the [A]WP—don't you think?" Sidney Hook asked Calverton in an unusually enthusiastic note. Calverton was equally excited and "willing to work (and I mean work)" to make the party a reality.[40]

Yet, once again dissidents were caught unaware because of their single-minded absorption with anti-Party politics. The Trotskyists also viewed the American Workers Party as a way of reviving their movement. Their CLA had grown increasingly dysfunctional because of Party harassment and internal divisions. The organization was badly split. One faction coalesced around Cannon, who believed in "the discipline of the party [and] the subordination of the individual to the decisions of the party" and saw those characteristics as "good sides" of the CPUSA worth replicating. Poised against him was a disproportionately younger and intellectual group of Party refugees who demanded more democracy and less interference by Cannon. Several times Cannon fought off attempts by "the parvenu-student elements, relying on the backing and encouragement of Shachtman" to seize control of the organization. In a parody of the Party behavior he shunned, he turned to Trotsky for power to preserve his position. With the CLA's small membership so divided, Cannon viewed the American Workers Party as a salvation. It would provide the opportunity to put aside petty theoretical quarrels, counterbalance the intellectuals with more workers, and "get some flesh on our bones."[41]

No sooner did rebel Marxists join the AWP than the Trotskyists made overtures to fuse it with their CLA. The working-class contingent in Muste's organization was wary. One labor organizer warned that "these . . . veterans of the Communist movement . . . will take over." But

70　intellectuals favored the fusion, expressing few doubts about potential problems in merging a party "rooted in American soil" with a movement committed to Marxism-Leninism and the permanent revolution. They could only picture interlopers in Communist Party disguises; the Trotskyists posed no real threat to them. The rebels acted in the spirit of a united front. Those who conducted the delicate negotiations to bring together the two groups, especially Hook and James Burnham, thought they took care to protect the AWP's unique character against the CLA's "theoretical dogmatism," its "lack of flexibility," and its sloganeering. Yet Burnham and Hook, for different reasons, were too trusting of the Trotskyists. Cannon's faction had no intention of abiding by the joint program "under the guise of American terminology" unless it was consistent with their Trotskyism. As CLA member Arne Swabeck reported to Trotsky, the grounds upon which the two organizations agreed to merge were "sufficiently ambiguous" to satisfy everyone without giving away too much. Dissident Marxists forgot that Cannon's organizational skills were honed in the CPUSA and that his sensibilities about party democracy came from the same organization.[42]

The CLA and the AWP officially united to become the American Workers Party in December 1934. The name of the new organization was nearly all the Musteites contributed to the merger. Despite the careful negotiations, CLA leaders walked away with every critical leadership post. Muste was the figurehead, but Cannon inherited the bureaucratic duties and Max Shachtman became editor of its *New International*. Muste was soon disillusioned. There was so much conflict between CLA theorists and AWP unionists that "the internal situation in the party has been a tremendous obstacle in our work," one report concluded. Cannon, ironically, was no more pleased than Muste. He wanted an influx of workers to offset the presence of students and intellectuals in the Trotskyist movement. What he got was "an overdose of frustrated Ph.Ds."[43] The only recruits the Trotskyists gained were intellectuals attracted by the CLA's rhetoric. The AWP made Trotsky's ideas available to dissident Marxists. Most quickly lost interest in the new political grouping; but, in the meantime, many gained an education in theory.

More than any other figure, Trotsky suggested that it was possible for rebel Marxists to realize their personal, intellectual, and political ambitions. If Stalin stood for power, Trotsky symbolized literary, cultural, and philosophical attainment. He was a thinker, well-educated, well-read, committed to the primacy of ideas. "He wrote too well," Diana Trilling once commented, "to be a tyrant." Many years after breaking with Trotsky, Irving Howe still credited him with a powerful respect of the intellectual because he or she "engage[d] in a serious political act, [and made] a gesture toward the redemption or re-creation of man." Trotsky's *Literature and Revolution* addressed cultural issues from a Marxist perspective. He was, moreover, a Jew, and many younger Marxists identified with him for that reason as well.[44] Solow was a good example of the dissident Marxist intellectual who found Trotsky a congenial role model. His roots were Jewish (the *Menorah Journal*), radical, and dissident. Like many intellectuals, his stay in the actual Trotskyist movement was very short; he could not reconcile the discipline necessary to be a Trotskyist with his doubts about theory. But his affection for Trotsky as an intellectual was much longer lived.[45] And like so many other Trotsky-influenced individuals, his enthusiasm was contagious. Such was the power Trotsky exerted over intellectuals that when James Burnham set out to influence Trotskyist Felix Morrow, whom he perceived as "sympathetic to us [Muste faction]," Morrow helped persuade him to become a Trotsky partisan.[46] Cannon's American Trotskyist group gained few working-class adherents thanks to the American Workers Party, but it was better able to spread the word among dissident Marxists.

Cannon was hardly thrilled by intellectuals' awakening interest in Trotskyism. If they did not join the movement, they often distorted Trotsky's theories. If they did join, they were notoriously fickle and resistant to discipline. Cannon thought too many such people already hurt the organization. Many joined under false pretenses, assuming that since the Trotskyists opposed Stalinism, they likewise opposed its hierarchical structure. Writer Bernard Wolfe fled the Young Communist League for the Trotskyists' Spartacist Youth looking for a more congenial atmosphere and was sadly disappointed:

> They [writers] were looked down upon as cafeteria intellectuals, parlor activists, undisciplined and irresponsible bohemians. They were defined as incorrigibly petty-bourgeois, constantly slapped in the face with their non-proletarianism. In all respects that counted they were held to be inferior people who if they had any loyalty to the cause of social overhauling at all would allow their names and public weight to be used without ever presuming to question the hallowed politicos who used them.

72 Intellectuals were, George Novack concluded, "unstable and unreliable allies of the working class" only grudgingly tolerated by Trotskyist functionaries.[47] Despite the more intellectual veneer, they were expected to play the same role in the Trotskyist parties as the Communist one: to be submissive, loyal, and allow their names to be used for the good of the cause.

It would be unfair, however, to equate the experience of intellectuals in the two movements. Because the Trotskyist organizations were so much smaller than the CPUSA, intellectuals had to play a more direct role. They sometimes felt abused by functionaries; but the movement could not afford the kinds of internal struggles that plagued the Reed Clubs or *The New Masses*. Additionally, the Trotskyists had nothing akin to the prolet cult, no cultural line, and that suggested a greater respect for intellectual independence. The CPUSA had an anti-intellectual reputation, particularly among dissidents. The Trotskyists' reputation was quite the reverse, making "their influence in the intellectual world," Cowley recalled, ". . . out of proportion with their numbers." So, Herbert Solow interested George Novack in Trotskyism. Novack interested James T. Farrell. Soon Farrell entertained the dissident community at open houses. *The New International* took its place alongside the *Modern Monthly* as a place where rebels might debate issues with vigor and honesty. Whether or not individuals actually joined the CLA or the AWP, Trotskyism had an intellectual patina the American Communist Party sorely lacked. Even a Party intellectual privately conceded that the difference between "the real communists" and "the phonies . . . is that the latter sort can write."[48]

Literary Trotskyists were especially useful in helping dissidents rationalize their opposition to the prolet cult. The Trotskyists provided an alternative radical cultural space for debate, one reasonably free of any organizational strictures. They and other dissidents shared a set of assumptions about culture and its relation to Marxism. Dissidents believed there was no justification in any Marxist movement for an artistic or literary line. Marx, Hook explained, believed in "the relative autonomy of the esthetic experience." Not surprisingly, rebels understood the prolet cult as a distortion that "flowed not out of Marxism, or Leninism," Calverton argued, "but Stalinism, which is Marxism corrupted and vitiated."[49] Yet, again, they did not hold Stalin responsible, but vilified American Communist intellectuals for their slavish commitment to Stalin. Just as dissidents extrapolated their political objections to Stalinism off their experiences with fronts, so too did some of their distaste for the proletarian culture seem to have its roots in their dislike of certain CP intellectuals. "It would be hell if the only person's works left whose style he [the writer] could imitate would be Granville Hicks or Horace Gregory or Mike Gold or Eda Lou Walton," Louise Bogan complained. Hicks, Gold, and Joseph Freeman, who Kenneth Rexroth called the "majordomo of Proletcult Rampant," all came in for their share of abuse. Letters to the editors columns were filled with prolonged debates back and forth between defenders of the prolet cult and its detractors, but shouting matches and fisticuffs were not unheard-of results of disputes. Several dissidents insisted that the whole argument had gone far enough; still the fighting continued. For the rebels, any distinctive identity they claimed for themselves would have a literary or cultural component forged in opposition to the Party line.[50]

Dissidents, though, were also philosophically opposed to the prolet cult. They were particularly troubled by what they perceived as the absence of any admiration for the creations of nonproletarians through most of history. Their definition of the prolet cult precluded subtlety; they saw "artists in uniform," in Max Eastman's phrase, marching in lockstep over the richness and diversity of modern literature. In *A Note on Literary Criticism,* the most sustained Marxist criticism of the prolet cult, James T. Farrell was troubled by the implications of this image: "To say that proletarian values will take their place uninfluenced by bourgeois values, is to contend that the cultural values and achievements that have grown out of the past are useless to the proletariat, and must therefore be destroyed." "Great proletarian art," Calverton wrote, even before his break with the CPUSA, "will not come by denying those elements [bourgeois ones] but by building upon them." Dissidents were adamant that "the post- must feed the pre-[revolutionary]."[51]

A number of elements fed the rebels' conception of a Marxian culture. One was their notions of what intellectuals did. Just as they regarded Marxism as an evolving set of ideas upon which individuals might draw, so too did they see the creative process as an interactive one that required them to reach out into the past and try out different forms, styles, and voices. If as political intellectuals they were to tailor Marxism to American circumstances, drawing on its heritage and peculiar circumstances, as creative individuals they expected to forge an

74   American culture out of the same raw materials. The independence
they revered in politics was at least as important culturally. Younger
rebels especially were more impressed by the currents of modernism
and the works of James Joyce, Ezra Pound, and T. S. Eliot than Party
writers, who often saw their works as effete and irrelevant. Some
scholars have suggested that the appeal of modernism for the New
York intellectuals was the very cosmopolitanism Communists decried. Prolet culters capitalized on their backgrounds and longed to
remake culture in a manner more consistent with both their values and
the daily life they saw around them. Other young writers, though,
wanted to escape that consciousness and move into the more rarified
world of high culture. The prolet cult denied dissidents the freedom to
be who they wanted to be.[52]

The Party's seeming unwillingness to allow them full scope as intellectuals reinforced the dissidents' ever-present sense of personal
grievance, buttressing their literary critique of the prolet cult with lay-
ers of resentments. The Party's response to Farrell's *A Note on Literary
Criticism,* for instance, further demonstrated to them that it was culturally bankrupt yet perfectly willing to enforce its appalling standards
whatever the costs. *The New Masses'* reviewer, Isidor Schneider, hated
the book. Granville Hicks, whom Farrell categorized as a mechanistic
critic, also did not like it. Dissidents expected bad reviews in *The New
Masses;* even they, however, did not expect that Farrell would be so
personally assaulted. Gold told Freeman that *A Note on Literary Criticism* "is one [of] the scurviest things I've ever read—worse than I
imagined." Freeman replied with his own denunciation of "Judas T.
Farrell," suggesting that notions of betrayal were very much a part of
the battle. Cowley tried to reunite "people of all opinions" at a party,
but the "Communists" ganged up on Farrell and he and Freeman actually came to blows. *A Note on Literary Criticism* further fractured the
Marxist intelligentsia and taught each side a different lesson. To Party
people, it suggested that those without discipline could not sustain a
true revolutionary faith. But to rebel Marxists it showed that the CPUSA
would stop at nothing to discredit thoughtful individuals.[53]

The 1934 clash at Madison Square Garden between Socialists and
Communists had a similar impact on the dissidents' strongly negative view of the Communist Party. After Chancellor Engelbert Dollfuss
moved against Austrian socialists, the SPUSA organized a protest rally.
Since it was an "open" rally, *The Daily Worker* urged Communists to

attend to "express the united front" and prevent two of the scheduled speakers from being heard. Anticipating trouble, Young People's Socialist League ushers searched the audience for disruptive banners and tried to direct the Communists into the more distant sections of the auditorium. Neither controversial speaker appeared; but the Communists kept up a disruptive roar throughout anyway. When *The Daily Worker*'s Clarence Hathaway stood up—without invitation—to address the crowd, a fight broke out. An American Civil Liberties Union commission looked into the incident and concluded that the Party was "immediately responsible" for what happened at Madison Square Garden and the Socialists secondarily so for generating "hostile feeling."[54] Dissident Marxist intellectuals, however, were far less judicious than the ACLU. The incident rallied them against the CPUSA.

The Madison Square Garden dispute brought dissident Marxists out of the shadows. Eliot Cohen and Trotskyist John MacDonald wrote an open letter of protest that Rorty, Hook, and Solow circulated. The statement expressed open hostility at the "organizationally and intellectually bankrupt" CPUSA: "No self-respecting intellectual can support a policy of disruption, infantile adventurism, breaking up workers' meetings, hooliganism, a policy of aping Fascist tactics. The Communist Party no longer has any other policy." The Party, they concluded, "has become a major barrier to the revolution," one that could not inspire the workers to action and would, thus, allow fascism to come to America. The eighteen signatories urged intellectuals to "repudiate also any of the Communist auxiliary organizations, well described as 'innocents clubs.'" In a separate letter, journalist Anita Brenner suggested that the Party refused to allow intellectuals to perform their traditional duties. "If we are asked to support certain Party activities and if our assistance as sympathetic intellectuals is accepted," she wrote, "we should . . . also be entitled to ask questions and make criticisms."[55] With these actions, dissident Marxists not only demonstrated that they were willing to stand up publicly against the CPUSA, risking the inevitable public humiliation in *The New Masses* and *The Daily Worker,* but that they were starting to unite.

It took courage for dissidents to step forward because the personal costs of opposition were often high. The Communists saw the letter as an attack on their legitimacy and so tried to turn the situation back upon itself by questioning the motives and radical credentials of those who signed it. John Howard Lawson told John Dos Passos, who signed, that fighting over who actually started the riot, the SP or the CP, was petty (although he was certain the Party was not to blame). He found the open letter quite without merit except "as a dirty attack on the Communists." Dos Passos, like Farrell, had been close to the CPUSA, so his public opposition to the Party role at Madison Square Garden provoked much hostile commentary, including an editorial in *The New Masses.* "The Communists," Lawson warned Dos Passos, " . . . feel bitterly that you're turning against them." By characterizing ideological disputes as personal betrayals, Party intellectuals like Lawson, Gold, and Freeman evaded the necessity of defending policy. In so doing, however, they made many enemies who took their response very personally as well. "Communist holyier than thouishness," as Dos Passos called it, generated an especially angry, internalized reaction to front politics that had many repercussions over the years.[56]

In the short term, though, Dos Passos's experience left him feeling more sad and impotent than angry and vengeful. "All people like us, who have no taste for political leadership or chewing the rag, can do," he told Edmund Wilson after Wilson sent him a batch of condemnatory *New Masses* clippings, "is sit on the sidelines." The situation, as far as he was concerned, was "hopeless." That Dos Passos was angry enough with the Communists to sign the open letter but not optimistic enough to think it would make a difference suggested that not all dissidents had confidence in their ability to triumph over the forces of evil. Instead, some would quickly give up on the prospects of Marxism altogether. In 1935, Dos Passos began a long disillusionment that eventually led him to the far right. His experience with Communist Party politics ultimately convinced him of the bankruptcy of all radical politics.[57]

While Dos Passos learned cynicism from the Madison Square Garden incident, others simply concluded that it was easier to work around the CPUSA than with it. Liberals, Socialists, and, occasionally, progressives ceded at least one organization to the Party and its supporters in response to what happened at the Garden. The American League against War and Fascism had been one of the few fronts that was truly diverse. Founded in the summer of 1932 as an antiwar group, it included a Party fraction as well as Socialists, representatives from the League for Industrial Democracy, liberals, and one or two Lovestoneites. Those latter forces refused to capitulate to the Communists as willingly as progressives did in other fronts. At the First United

States Congress against War, for example, they nominated Jay Lovestone to the presiding committee. Although the CPUSA twice succeeded in defeating the motion with "a thunderous roar," Lovestone's nomination was evidence of a feisty nonParty attitude. But the 1934 Madison Square Garden fracas demoralized many American League members, who felt the Party presence in their organization contaminated its work. The SPUSA, the NAACP, the Musteites, the League for Industrial Democracy, and "most of the other non-Communist organizations" disengaged from the group because the Party's behavior at the Garden, Roger Baldwin noted, "destroyed for [the] present [the] possibility of [a] united front against war."[58]

Certainly trying to reach a consensus over the Party accomplished little. The American Civil Liberties Union also split after the Madison Square Garden fight, but no one resigned and the conflict simmered for the rest of the decade. When the ACLU committee charged with investigating the incident presented its findings, two different factions filed minority reports. A few Party sympathizers objected to the Party's receiving so much blame for the fight when the SP "bait[ed] the Communists." Socialists, however, refused to accept even the lesser blame assigned them and SPUSA head Norman Thomas accused the ACLU "of supporting civil liberties only in so far as they . . . benefit . . . the Communist movement." John Haynes Holmes briefly proposed banning Communists from leadership positions in the Union, but was talked out of it by Baldwin. The report raised such strong feelings all around that Thomas continued to cite it as proof of a Communist conspiracy in the Union until 1940, prompting his opponents to beg that he give it "a decent burial after a lapse of nearly six years."[59] By 1934 there was a growing sense on the oppositional left that one could not work with the Communists, but had to either accept their domination, fight them, or concede defeat and withdraw. Long before the 1935 People's Front, the CPUSA had effectively alienated a substantial percentage of its most logical allies.

Thomas's complaints against the ACLU, Holmes's resolution, and the many resignations in the American League against War and Fascism marked the first stirrings of anticommunism as a current on the left. While dissident Marxists condemned "Stalinism" or the CPUSA, other intellectuals seemed uncomfortable with communism more generally, especially the Communist presence in organizations. John

Dewey cautioned Malcolm Cowley against joining the precursor of the American League against War and Fascism, for example, because "the Communists are going to capture [it] . . . There are good names on the Committee [founding the organization] but I don't think they are in control."[60] Dewey's concerns were commonly shared by liberals, who assumed that a Party presence almost inevitably meant Party control. Rather than joining fronts like the National Committee for the Defense of Political Prisoners, liberals trusted older and more traditional organizations like the International Committee for Political Prisoners, the League for Industrial Democracy, and the League for Independent Political Action. Their protest votes went to Thomas—or even Roosevelt—in 1932. They practiced, but did not yet preach, their own brand of practical anticommunism by avoiding any group or cause they thought tainted by the American Communist Party.

There were times, however, when liberals felt they could not be silent about the dangers of communism. In the United States, communism posed relatively little threat and most liberals were tolerant of its eccentricities. In the USSR, however, its costs were more apparent and more significant. As some intellectuals reckoned those costs, their anticommunism solidified and began to extend to the CPUSA. Eugene Lyons and William Henry Chamberlin were American journalists living in the USSR and early Soviet sympathizers. Observing the process of Stalinization firsthand disillusioned both. As Chamberlin noted in his 1934 monograph of disillusionment, *Russia's Iron Age,* Stalin undertook economic change with "uncompromising and ruthless disregard of the human cost involved." The forced labor he used to speed industrialization seemed as morally reprehensible as American slavery. The trials of engineers and other specialists who became the "scapegoats" of industrialization bothered Lyons. Most disturbing of all was the Ukrainian famine of 1932/33, a famine created by the government's determination to acquire a grain surplus to build up capital. Induced famines, purges, staged trials, and the like occurred in the USSR, Lyons and Chamberlin contended, because of the Stalin dictatorship and "the right of the rulers to decide how long it may be necessary to go on killing people." Neither reporter, though, blamed Stalin for what seemed more a function of the dictatorship of the proletariat than Stalinism per se. "Defending one dictatorship," Lyons concluded, "is in fact defending the principle of tyranny."[61] Other leftists looked at the USSR and saw the economic liberation of socialism. Lyons and Chamberlin looked at the USSR and saw only the oppressiveness of dictatorship.

Lyons's and Chamberlin's negative feelings about dictatorship grew more pronounced as they tried to report them. The Soviets denied them access to the Ukraine and American journalists helped undermine their credibility. Other reporters deliberately downplayed what they euphemistically called a "grain shortage." Chamberlin viewed the troubles he had with Soviet authorities and the friction from the left press in the United States as "the final climactic chapter in my Russian education." Lyons, evicted from the USSR because of his famine stories, was similarly stunned by the behavior of his journalist friends, particularly after rumors explained his change of heart as financially motivated.[62] The experience profoundly altered the way each man looked at communism.

Lyons and Chamberlin were outraged that other journalists deliberately lied about the famine and flourished, because it seemed such a gross violation of their role. Walter Duranty won a Pulitzer Prize for his reports out of the Soviet Union during the famine year, the very same time when the two "honest" journalists were barred by Russian authorities and denounced at home. Duranty conceded in private that up to ten million people died during the famine; but when challenged in public, he denied every word and did not admit publicly that a famine occurred until 1944. Anna Louise Strong, also on the spot in 1933, sat in Lyons's office and cried about "the horrors she had seen," but wrote only about "the glories of collectivization." Louis Fischer, reporting during the worst period of the famine, blamed peasants for refusing to harvest crops, alluding to the government's forced grain requisitions only in passing. "The peasants brought the calamity upon themselves," he concluded. Chamberlin doubted that American journalists in Russia wrote the truth; Fischer, like all the others, "was scarcely ignorant of something that was common knowledge."[63] Chamberlin and Lyons interpreted what they saw in Moscow as proof that journalists could not be objective and still admire communism. Defending a corrupt doctrine corrupted any intellectual.

The behavior Chamberlin and Lyons observed was, indeed, motivated by a very different understanding of the foreign intellectual's role in Russia. Hedging the truth was a strategy necessary to remain in Russia and continue to obtain access to information. It was a compromise that Chamberlin and Lyons found ultimately immoral. But progressive journalists had little to gain from glossing over the famine unless they believed what they did also served some larger purpose. Lyons himself recognized part of what influenced them to keep silent: "I have lied and exaggerated on things Soviet. . . . The fear of giving aid and comforts to reactionaries at home has, I confess, led me to tone down distressing facts and pull my punches." He was no longer able to sugarcoat the Soviet reality because he lost faith in it. So long as Strong and Fischer and Duranty believed that the socialist economy guaranteed things would improve, they found excuses for its bad features: tsarist holdovers, a hostile world, lack of democratic traditions, recalcitrant peasants too stubborn and old-fashioned to recognize their own best interests. Political neophytes also tended to assume that a dose of hard-bitten realism was necessary in a world filled with imperfect people and nation-states. "You can't make an omelet without breaking eggs," as Duranty once said.[64] Honest and objective journalism was bourgeois when it potentially aided reactionaries, progressives concluded. They could explain Lyons and Chamberlin as muddle-headed or sell-outs, but they could not see them as dedicated and sincere.

Liberals, however, could. Lyons's and Chamberlin's analysis of the USSR and their experiences with the American newspaper community there helped shape their feelings about communism. Always ambivalent about the new Soviet society, liberals concluded by mid-decade that the Bolsheviks had triumphed over the more democratic wishes of the people. Many agreed with Lyons's contention that there could be only one measure by which to judge dictatorships, so the dictatorship of the proletariat was no more acceptable than any other. By mid-decade, liberals replaced the phrase "Soviet socialism" with "Soviet dictatorship" or, occasionally, "totalitarianism." In so doing, they reasserted the importance of the political over economic concerns, valuing "the American ideal of democracy" more than collectivism.[65] This shift greatly affected the way they ordered their world.

Soon liberals equated Stalin's Russia with Hitler's Germany since both were "dictatorships," no matter how their leaders chose to define them. In both countries, the tight political control asserted by a relatively few people determined the structure of the other aspects of the regime. The Soviets mustered a more attractive rhetoric than the fascists, but it was rhetoric nonetheless. Thus Horace Kallen was not impressed that the Soviets called their economy socialist; as with the

German economy, the government ran it. He added that whatever the Soviets said about individual freedoms, the dictatorship of the proletariat suppressed individuals and enforced conformity in much the same way as Hitler's government. Liberals certainly acknowledged that there were differences between fascism and communism, and, if forced to make a choice, most preferred communism to fascism; but neither society seemed worth the contortions necessary to defend it. Rather, the lesson taught by the existence of so many different types of dictatorships was that democracy and "the classic liberties" were in peril.[66]

When liberals tried to convey their concerns about Russia to their colleagues, they were dismissed as defenders of the status quo and worse. Cowley called Joseph Wood Krutch's critical analysis of "class justice" in Russia "a defense of inequality and injustice." Communists found liberal comparisons between communism and fascism blasphemous. Even dissident Marxists were unwilling to entertain their point of view, although they might concede that Stalinism as a bureaucratic overlay had some features in common with Nazism. Progressives could not imagine that a society that planned and redistributed wealth might be undemocratic, even though there was little direct evidence to support their faith in political justice. Lyons discovered that trying to persuade others they were wrong about the USSR was frustrating and, ultimately, pointless. At a lunch with *The New Republic*'s staff, he recounted his Soviet experiences and was treated as though he had committed a terrible radical faux pas.[67] From these seeds, liberal suspicions of progressivism would grow.

The assassination of Leningrad Party head Sergei Kirov in late 1934 and the string of trials it prompted brought home even more clearly the incompatibility of their and other left moralities. The issue detached the last remaining liberal members from the fronts. The NCDPP confronted the matter head-on with a debate entitled "Are the Soviet Executions Justified?" If organizers expected to score points with their directness, they must have been disappointed. "To call a mass-meeting which will be attended only by partisans of the government of Russia for the purpose of debating," Horace Kallen protested, " . . . is an evasion of the issue." A debate was not good enough for him; he assumed the NCDPP would protest the Russian trials. To do otherwise was "hypocrisy." Reasoning that "no true friend of the Soviet experiment can without protest pass over conduct by the Russian government

82 which he condemns when it is German, Italian, Polish or Spanish," he
resigned. Playwright Sidney Howard quit along with Kallen, appalled
that the NCDPP "neither condones nor condemns the executions." So
too did Suzanne LaFollette, Mark Van Doren, Clifton Fadiman, and
Franz Boas.[68] Their departure marked the end of any liberal presence
in the NCDPP and effectively completed liberal isolation from the rest of
the intellectual left.

The few remaining non-Party Marxists in the NCDPP also quit the
organization because of its response to the Kirov assassination. Like
liberals, they complained about the double standard of justice the organization employed. Had American workers been tried and punished
so quickly and secretly, the NCDPP would have raised a hue and cry,
they argued. But because the trials took place in the USSR, its executive committee successfully defeated a resolution to "deplore the summary executions of those already put to death." Dissidents found the
manner in which the resolution was defeated more alarming than the
defeat itself. Many members did not even bother to vote, but care-
lessly turned over their proxies to the executive committee, who used
them to reinforce the Party position. Those who dared to support the
resolution suffered "a barrage of abuse, with name-calling and mud-
slinging." When the debate got too sticky, Party member Orrick Johns
moved "to vote unanimous confidence in the Executive Committee in
its treatment of the entire incident." Despite its alleged roots as "a
democratically-conceived, non-partisan Committee," the NCDPP did
not function democratically.[69]

Thus it was front politics at home rather than any changed evalua-
tion of the nature of Stalinism in Russia that still shaped the dissident
Marxist perspective. Whatever few good feelings liberals had about the
USSR were totally dashed by the Kirov matter. "It has completely destroyed my benefit-of-the-doubt attitude," John Dos Passos told Edmund Wilson. But dissident Marxists, like progressives, were much
more tolerant. They saw no evidence that communism and fascism
were alike. The purge following the Kirov assassination was traditionally Russian, not communist or Stalinist. Wilson resigned from the
NCDPP over the Kirov response, yet he cautioned Dos Passos not "to
give aid and comfort to people who have hopped on the shootings in
Russia as a means of discrediting socialism."[70] Still, by departing from
the fronts, dissident Marxists slowly cut themselves off from progressives as well. And, over time, the kinds of tactics used by the NCDPP and

other fronts in order to protect their pro-Soviet lines raised questions about what really went on in Russia. Party intellectuals triumphed in the NCDPP, but their sanitized front garnered little respect in the larger community.

Liberals did not allow the Kirov matter to rest there, despite little support from their peers. If the NCDPP failed to protest, there were other institutional forums. Members of the International Committee for Political Prisoners, a liberal version of the NCDPP, went straight to the Soviet ambassador. In an open letter, Robert Morss Lovett, Roger Baldwin, John Dewey, John Haynes Holmes, Lewis Gannett, Arthur Garfield Hays, Sinclair Lewis, and George Counts took a public stand against the Soviet Union for the first time. Explaining that they had kept silent so as not "to give aid and comfort to the reactionary opponents of the Soviet Union," they now felt the civil liberties issue superseded that concern. The Soviets treated them respectfully; the Soviet ambassador invited five delegates to meet and discuss the Kirov case. While the Soviets seemed, ironically, less intransigent than the NCDPP, liberals were not soothed in the least. "Will you tell him [the ambassador] for me," Holmes asked Baldwin when declining a position on the delegation, "that the fact that 117 men could be shot to death without the actual facts being given to the world in a public trial is one of the reasons why we wrote our letter?" Baldwin, America's guardian of civil liberties, came away from the meeting unconvinced that the "facts" justified the executions.[71] There was little the Soviets could do to persuade liberals to change their minds about the matter. That the rights of so many Soviets could be violated without a second thought said more to liberals about the nature of the new Russia than any ambassador or sheaf of statistics. Already suspicious of the Soviet "dictatorship," the first evidence of the purges confirmed rather than allayed their fears.

So too did it make them feel like anachronisms. No one else seemed as troubled as they did about the parallels between fascism and communism, the excesses of Soviet collectivization, or the execution of Kirov's alleged assassins. Had other intellectuals been seduced by alien values or were their own values simply passé? Historian Carl Becker complained that "the liberty that we prize—liberty of thought—means little to the mass of the people and they seem duped to support any leader or dogma which promises them bread or circuses."[72] Liberals had never really minded being out of step before. In 1935, how-

84   ever, they were disconcerted by so many seemingly thoughtful people holding such different ideas. Perhaps the emergence of extremist governments, left and right, created a new imperative traditional ideologies could not resolve. Maybe Reinhold Niebuhr was right when he suggested that "the liberal culture of modernity is quite unable to give guidance and direction to a confused generation which faces the disintegration of a social system and the task of building a new one." Maybe John Dewey's brand of liberalism was too optimistic and too idealistic; maybe there was a "pathos" about the manner in which liberals addressed social concerns.[73] Liberals were not about to throw over their philosophy in 1935, but they felt exposed and vulnerable.

Dissident Marxists also reached a crossroads in 1935, although theirs was not a crisis of faith so much as an organizational exigency. The Trotskyist and Muste factions in the American Workers Party quickly hit an impasse. The group was fractured, financially overextended, and bereft of its union base. Muste's backers refused to underwrite the Trotskyists, and Cannon returned from one speaking tour to find the party evicted from its headquarters. Workers resisted the new AWP.[74] The intellectual contingent splintered and some joined the Trotskyist faction while others quietly left the organization and gave up on politics. For many dissident Marxists, the AWP was their first and last venture into practical political organizing. By nature they were uncomfortable joining political parties and their front experiences made them even more skeptical of institutional bodies of any kind. Radical politics offered hard work with few rewards. Younger dissidents, especially, saw recruiting workers as a step backward to their pasts. The AWP experience reinforced what rebels first learned from Party fronts, that the intellectuals' tasks could not be commingled with the organizers' without compromising personal integrity. Dissidents' commitment to theory and their sense that intellectuals served the masses somewhere other than in the trenches cut them loose from organizations and left them drifting on their own.

Progressives felt their own inchoate sense of confusion in 1935. The unlimited vistas of 1930 narrowed as the New Deal stabilized the economy without substantially altering its structure. Their vague schemes for society, their notions of "planning for the masses," their "coming American revolution," had come to naught.[75] Most Americans seemed satisfied with Roosevelt and those who were not were more interested in right-wing ideas than left-wing ones. Hitler's rise sensitized them to reactionary countercurrents abroad and at home. Progressives considered Huey Long, Father Coughlin, and other demagogic leaders such serious threats to American values that they reoriented their priorities and lowered their expectations. "Did you read about the new American Liberty League?" James Neugass asked Genevieve Taggard in 1934. "Doesn't it look like a central office for all of the thousands of little fascist organizations that have lately been cropping up? I keep getting this growing feeling of emergency."[76] Communists, moreover, had not provided the guidance for which they longed. Fronts had only limited audiences and limited power. Many progressives continued to shop around for more satisfying political commitments.

American Communist intellectuals likewise felt adrift by mid-decade. The Third Period wound down. There were signs of a weakening of the policy in Moscow. In American intellectual circles, the prolet cult was no longer a sacred cow. At the John Reed Clubs' 1934 national convention, Orrick Johns denounced "sectarianism" and other speakers timidly suggested a more expansive policy. To Richard Wright, who attended the congress as a delegate, the meetings confirmed "a sense of looseness, bewilderment, and dissatisfaction among the writers." Later, in a smaller caucus, Wright learned that the CPUSA had a direction in mind; but to the larger JRCs, the prevailing feeling was one of malaise.[77]

Across the left, as the first bright promise of revolution faded, intellectuals began to reassess and concluded little, except that the future looked gloomy. There were no quick-fix solutions to the Depression, yet Americans seemed disinclined to follow radical politics. Liberals, progressives, Communists, Trotskyists, and dissident Marxists were equally frustrated by the strength of American capitalism. So too were they confused about the emergence of new international forces. There was no revolution from the left. There was, instead, the threat of counterrevolution from the right. Intellectuals were not sure what to make of fascism. Nothing in their political vocabularies prepared them for Hitler. The year 1935 was a dismal one for the intellectual left, one where reality finally caught up with their earlier radical dreams.

If their early enthusiasms quickly fizzled out, the costs of pursuing those enthusiasms had been expensive. Scattered like so much debris were many once-excited intellectuals, the "disinherited"[78] who had broken away from the CPUSA, been excommunicated, or who did not trust front politics. There had never been unity on the left; but in the

86   early 1930s there was a shared sense of optimism and hope. By 1935, intellectuals were world-weary. Change offered more to be feared than to be desired. The enthusiasm and confidence unleashed by the Depression were unsustainable under any circumstances. The intrusion of Party politics, however, made disillusionment more costly than it had to be. Fighting with the CPUSA was an experience few of the "disinherited" would ever forget.

THREE

Becoming "More Liberal":

Constructing the People's Front,

1935–1937

The Comintern's solution to the many new problems radicals faced in 1935 was to disengage from the Third Period and form broader coalitions. The Soviets nervously eyed the international situation. Stalin knew that the governments of Britain, France, and the United States were only slightly more willing to deal with him than with Hitler. Afraid that, should Hitler move eastward, the West would allow the two disagreeable governments to bleed each other dry, the Soviets changed course, making themselves appear less extreme and therefore more acceptable to the West. With this intention in mind, the People's Front against fascism was born in 1935. The Comintern encouraged member parties to build bridges with noncommunist organizations sharing certain communist goals. The Front ostensibly stood for democracy and individual liberty, although its main purpose was to support Stalin's foreign policies. Front rhetoric and intentions did not always mesh, but there were common issues that enabled Communists and progressives to come together for limited purposes.

The transition from the Third Period to the People's Front was slow, especially in the United States. The American Communist Party had already alienated many potential left-wing allies, especially the Socialists. The Madison Square Garden fight left deep scars. Upton Sinclair's 1934 gubernatorial campaign on a platform to End Poverty in

88 California (EPIC), marked another instance when the Party passed up rapprochement in favor of partisan politics. The social fascist label, pasted on Sinclair, remained the CPUSA's standard criticism of Roosevelt as well. Line changes were always difficult, for it took time to reconcile Comintern ideas with American realities.[1]

As policy, however, the People's Front had much to recommend it. Fascism was an easy enemy; it was not difficult to muster anti-Hitler sentiment on the left. Earl Browder's contention that "Communism is Twentieth Century Americanism" had its advantages. The CPUSA relocated itself within a less threatening tradition, evoking American symbols like Lincoln and the Revolutionary War. Granville Hicks finally joined the Party after much soul-searching somewhere around mid-decade. In part he did so because, as his *I Like America* demonstrated, he was able to see the compatibility of the Communists' philosophy and American values. Even though he was the exception rather than the rule, his reaction was indicative of the rising comfort level on the left with the CPUSA.[2]

The Party also won friends with constructive solutions to domestic problems. Confronting reactionary and demagogic movements at home and a new, more liberal Dr. New Deal in the White House, progressives were far more enthusiastic about the Second Hundred Days than the First. Like Roger Baldwin, many resisted Roosevelt until the Wagner Act and Social Security passed. The Party line on the New Deal was difficult to discern, but once the policy of social fascism ended, American Communists were better able to make distinctions between FDR and his opponents. While they ran Earl Browder for president in 1936, it was obvious that in a real world, where Communists never won elections, they preferred Roosevelt to Landon. Rather than attacking the Wagner Act or forming their own unions, Communist organizers lent their expertise to the new CIO. And how could they possibly attack Social Security when they had proposed a similar plan long before the Democrats did? Progressives took all of this as an indication that the Party had become more realistic and more moderate, more the all-American entity Browder and Hicks suggested it was.[3]

But the same program that charmed progressives also had to appeal to the more radical Party audience. Reconciling a program Browder himself described as "not socialism" with Marxist theory was not easy. Communist intellectuals ended up producing dual commentaries, fitting the new line into one tradition for a Party audience and another for progressives. The theoretical bends and twists were occasionally glaring. *The New Masses* presented the Front as a continuation of longtime Party aims—building working-class unity to avoid war and defeat fascism—a statement so unlikely three years before that it undercut its own message. Michael Gold quietly reversed himself on social fascism, describing an enormous gap between fascism and bourgeois democracy that he had earlier denied. A. B. Magil found the appropriate historical analogies, citing both *The Communist Manifesto* and the postrevolutionary period in Russia (1922) as examples of fronts. Joseph Freeman tried to make Communist intellectuals comfortable with the People's Front by showing that they had new worlds to conquer. "The Communist must be in the vanguard," he told a Young Communist League Writers' Congress, ". . . the direction must come from those writers who are most clear." Poet Rolfe Humphries suggested that the CPUSA "must work with what we have," adding that there were certain advantages to be had in the bargain. "Letting your light shine before men that they can see your good works," he assured E. Merrill Root, "does have some effect in the long run." Whether or not Party intellectuals liked the People's Front, and there is some evidence to suggest such arch-proletarians as Gold did not, they played their part in popularizing the new line.[4]

Dissident Marxists, however, felt no such discipline or loyalty, even though most had earlier complained of the Party's narrowness and unwillingness to work with other left-wing groups. If they saw the Party as too uncompromising in 1934, it seemed too accommodationist in 1936. Historian Louis Hacker thought Browder sold out the Party's revolutionary credentials in order to appeal to the petty bourgeois. Young socialist Hal Draper believed the new policy "kowtow[ed]" to liberals. Bertram Wolfe, reviewing a Soviet film called "Lenin in 1918," poked fun at the Front's folksiness: "Lenin was pictured as a sort of lovable old foxy grandpa who had to be told by the Central Committee and its 'leader' Stalin (even then!) when to put on an overcoat." Clearly what angered Wolfe was not the film's story line itself so much as the recipient of all its glory, Stalin. Dissident Marxists had long called for a "united front"; but when confronted with the prospect of one organized by the CPUSA, they refused to entertain the possibility that it was sincerely offered. They automatically assumed that any front advocated by the Party reflected "the interests of the reactionary bureaucracy now in control of the Soviet Union" rather

90   than Marxist theory.[5] Dissidents were not willing to concede an inch to their opponents.

The clearest articulation of what rebels thought was wrong with the People's Front came from American Trotskyists. "From its original concept," Arne Swabeck explained, "the united front, as a means of proletarian unity at any given moment in its struggle against capitalism, has been perverted by the degenerate policy of Stalinism into a coalition with the bourgeoisie." It was reformist; it encouraged "class collaboration"; it was dishonest, James Burnham argued. It disguised its pro-capitalist sentiments with hackneyed rhetoric. Its real point, Trotskyists contended, was to manipulate the American left into supporting goals it would not endorse under other circumstances.[6]

Dissident Marxists were not alone in their disdain for the People's Front. Party intellectuals understood the necessity of coalition building as a political strategy but had many questions about the cultural implications of the policy and their status once the movement widened. Even before the change of line was official, front politics overwhelmed—and overtook—the Reed Clubs. Immediately after the 1934 national JRC convention, functionaries anticipated the new direction and decided that the clubs need "'no longer exist.'" In their place, they would build a more inclusive cultural organization with a more respectable membership. The decision was perfectly consistent with the contours of the People's Front, but for Reed Club members it was a shocking violation of their trust. Young intellectuals, in particular, were stunned by the dissolution and the "high-handed way" it was done. Some would never recover from the indignity of losing their clubs so that the CPUSA could court middle-class intellectuals.[7]

The American Writers Congress initially replaced the JRCs and then spawned the new-style League of American Writers. While class background and politics earned one admission to the Reed Clubs, LAW members needed literary credentials and "some standing in their respective fields" to pass muster. This standard automatically excluded a great many, especially the poor, the young, and the radical. The inadvertent impact, as Malcolm Cowley later recalled, was generational, "leaving out the kids." Richard Wright's earnest question, "what was to become of the young writers whom the Communist Party had implored to join the clubs and who were ineligible for the new group," fell on deaf ears. The JRC's death by functionary fiat did not go unchallenged. In several cities the clubs continued unofficially for months.

The *Partisan Review* survived on its own thanks to the revenue it
generated at dances. Young writers had reason to cling to such forums;
only about half of the Reed Club membership was invited to attend the
American Writers Congress in 1935. For those who saw themselves
rendered irrelevant by the Party hierarchy in one swift blow, the People's Front seemed a foolish policy. "Already," Cowley concluded
later, "one might have foreseen a new conflict of generations."[8]

Ironically, evicting the youngsters and the proletarians had no cultural rationalization whatsoever. The American Writers Congress
floundered, trapped as it was between the older Third Period and the
newer Front. Its public "Call" was a "syntactical jumble" of slogans
from both lines. Alexander Trachtenberg coordinated the event, but
even he was not always sure how to proceed. It was easy enough to
convince the old Party hands and its rising new stars to participate.
How, though, could he induce the noncommunists? Often, he seemed
to assume that the Congress offered greater prestige than many writers
themselves believed. He was willing to include Edmund Wilson, provided he "drops from MM [*Modern Monthly*]," but Wilson "didn't go."
He successfully obtained John Dos Passos's halfhearted participation,
despite their differences, but Dos Passos was determined to "write
them a little preachment about liberty of conscience or freedom" that
would cause a stir. Moreover, he sent his paper, never gracing the congress stage at all. "I knew the comrades would have the floor most of
the time," he told Cowley later. With so few noncommunists willing to
commit, Trachtenberg fell back on trusty old Party writers like Freeman. Those progressives who were willing to participate but could not
be trusted—like Calverton's one-time protégé Michael Blankfort—
had Party cowriters assigned to monitor their progress. When the Congress finally met, the hall was full, but, Granville Hicks thought, only
because "the party simply loaded the meeting." James T. Farrell proposed ending the Congress by singing "The International," probably,
Hicks guessed, with "his tongue in his cheek," but many joined in
with gusto and "Trachtenberg's face turned red" because such revolutionary displays were not in keeping with the People's Front. Yet
"Trachty" himself included Browder on the program.[9] The success of
the 1935 American Writers Congress was limited by its organizers'
inability to pick a single line and stick with it.

Indeed, no single incident better revealed the contradictory cultural
philosophy that underlay the 1935 Congress than Kenneth Burke's

92   famous speech. Burke was neither a Communist nor a very enthusiastic
      front worker. His appearance on the Congress program was testimony
      to the new and more inclusive Party line. His paper, "Revolutionary
      Symbolism in America," might have been tailor-made for the People's
      Front. He argued that the Party's revolutionary cosmology ought to
      broaden, replacing "the symbol of the worker" with one "more ba-
      sic[,] . . . of 'the people.' " Rather than being greeted as a prophet of the
      new, he was roundly booed by the assembled crowd as "a premature
      adherent of the People's Front."[10] Burke was sincerely stunned by the
      response. If he was enlisted to bring breadth to the Congress, the par-
      tisan crowd was clearly not ready for such change. The small group
      who constituted the early League of American Writers obviously had
      much work ahead.

      The early LAW did not draw the kind of broad support its founders
      envisioned at least in part because Party functionaries had trouble
      adjusting to the freer style of front politics. The LAW was too hierarchi-
      cal. Its executive council not only controlled membership but nomi-
      nated all members, adjusting the standards it used to evaluate its po-
      tential flock while retaining the centralized power structure that had
      caused problems in so many earlier groups. One young author, whose
      résumé included "only book-reviews and a couple of short stories,"
      expressed a concern no politically correct writer ever worried about in
      the JRCS, that she lacked the literary credentials necessary to join. She
      was admitted, but the League was more interested in recruiting pres-
      tigious writers. Prestigious writers, though, were less inclined to tol-
      erate such membership scrutiny or the organization itself. "I can't
      join," Ernest Hemingway told Genevieve Taggard. His reasons were
      fairly typical; he thought the League too narrow and too Communist-
      controlled. Hemingway had a point; functionaries did have the power
      in the early LAW and they were reluctant to relinquish it for fear of
      "weaken[ing] the League's work." Looking to explain why the organi-
      zation failed to prosper, LAW leaders suggested that the dues might be
      too high; but dues were not the problem. What was wrong with the
      League of American Writers in 1935 was its image. Communist func-
      tionaries had good reasons for courting, however diffidently, famous
      middle-class writers. But famous middle-class writers could think of
      little reason to be associated with "all those reds."[11]

      The League's early activities helped perpetuate its "red" image. Its
      first two public functions were political in nature, served the Party's

interests, and were co-sponsored with other fronts. One was a protest meeting staged by the LAW, the NCDPP, and *The New Masses* after Granville Hicks lost his teaching job for political reasons. The other was a John Reed commemorative presentation coordinated with the Friends of the Soviet Union. At least one potential speaker backed out rather than appear on a platform he thought would be filled with Communists. Both events drained the League's coffers without enhancing its reputation. As a remedy, some members proposed that the organization avoid such overtly political activities and sponsor a series of public lectures called "The Mind of America" instead. Although they too lost money, at least they were popular. More importantly, the lectures brought together a more diverse group of intellectuals to talk about cultural and political issues. Relative to the JRCS, these forums were "awfully Rotarian folksy and pranksy," Rolfe Humphries commented, but they also served to "introduc[e] all the celebrities to the boys [Party intellectuals]." Still, while the lectures were memorable to those who attended, they barely kept the League alive.[12]

Compounding the League's problems was the slow disintegration of the prolet cult. As the People's Front became more focused, the notion that art was a class weapon lost its official endorsement. Walter Rideout called the Front a "killing frost" that decimated the prolet cult. More recent scholars have softened this view, arguing that the prolet cult grew more complex as it developed and became less easily identifiable as proletarianism. Certainly works with radical and proletarian themes continued to appear after 1935. But the energy that initially surrounded the prolet cult dissipated until, by the end of the decade, the only real discussions of it any longer were politically motivated repudiations. One Italian scholar, Gabriella Ferruggia, sees the decline of the prolet cult as a significant turning point in Communist literary history, one where the CPUSA not only failed to provide guidance but also lacked the ability "to respond to their [intellectuals'] demands for clear guidelines."[13] But there is little to suggest that writers clamored for more literary direction from the Party. The prolet cult was an anomaly; at no other point in CP history have the literary and political aims of the organization been in such absolute harmony. Politically attuned writers had been perfectly capable of finding themes, styles, and audiences on their own before the prolet cult and would continue to do so during and after. The cultural disequilibrium felt after 1935 was much more complex and sweeping; it was not the result of Party intel-

94 lectuals moving from a period of clear objectives to a cultural void. Rather, it was that by contrast to the apparent singular popularity of the prolet cult, culture in the later 1930s seemed much more diverse and multidimensioned.

The late 1930s were a time of cultural renewal as well as political crisis. Richard Pells suggested that, among other things, there was a "rediscovery of America" by writers, artists, and thinkers. At the Western Writers Congress of 1936—which had not yet affiliated with the LAW—speakers celebrated the literary traditions of such native sons as Jack London along with a political heritage of democracy, freedom, and homegrown radicalism. In the Southwest, folklorists and anthropologists traced the interaction of three cultures, European, Native American, and Mexican. The WPA arts projects redefined culture to include everyday objects like quilts. Such themes enhanced the People's Front, but in other ways challenged the Sovio-centrism of the Comintern. Joseph Freeman believed that Earl Browder and the rest of the CPUSA's hierarchy found *An American Testament* troubling because it "showed that my roots and loyalties, radical as they were, nevertheless were American and not Russian."[14] The celebration of an American culture was not automatically conservative, but neither did it automatically reinforce the Party line.

At the same time, aspects of the emerging culture raised new questions for intellectuals about ownership, audience, message, and value. Folklorists, for example, collected material rather than creating it and screenwriters wrote collaboratively and had little control over the final product. Were their products art? Distinctions between highbrow and lowbrow (or middlebrow) culture always existed, but during the Depression there was much crossover. Many writers relied on steady jobs writing radio scripts or children's fiction. Culture reached more people than ever before through radio, movies, and the Federal Theater, in the process creating a new status hierarchy. Russell Jacoby has argued that the generation of the 1930s was the last group of public intellectuals and generalists who could survive independently.[15] That interpretation ignores the dozens of people who supported themselves in the 1930s by turning out travel books, cook books, or mystery novels. For every Van Wyck Brooks or Edmund Wilson who dissected Emerson or wrote poetry, there were two or three Franklin Folsoms or Jerre Mangiones who patched together a living through the Writers Project, ghost-writing, and occasional commissions. The prolet cult aided such fledgling writers, providing them with their own space and an interested audience. Would the emerging intellectual community be as inclusive? The decline of the prolet cult broadened the Communist writer's potential range of subjects and themes, but lessened his or her impact.

And, finally, during the last half of the 1930s, the rise of fascism upped the political ante for intellectuals. Proletarian novels made political statements, but often implicit and ambiguous ones.[16] While the prolet cult was criticized for being bald propaganda, writers were much more likely to write propaganda after 1936 in the form of reports, speeches, and open letters opposing Hitler and fascism. International politics took center stage for the literary left, leaving the "art-for-art's-sake" intellectuals searching for alternatives. The documentary form attained great status in the late 1930s, partially funded by the New Deal. Real life seemed more dramatic than fiction. This too would have an impact on the cultural direction of the American left, as not all intellectuals were happy living under the cultural siege of antifascism. To say that the left literati moved from a culture of clearly defined expectations and terms to one that was cluttered, confused, and ambiguous oversimplifies the transition away from the prolet cult without entirely distorting the situation. There was no single style, manner, or genre that encapsulated culture after 1935, but to some degree the same could be said of the first half of the decade.

Still, whether perceived or real, there was a felt absence of consensus that made the LAW's woes all the worse. Remedying them was no easy task. In December 1935 the executive council met to discuss "League activity or lack of it." One solution was to democratize its structure so as to broaden its appeal, a choice that did not sit well with the Communists. In subsequent meetings, they considered all manner of tactics to stimulate interest: membership drives, another lecture series, and a clubhouse. The LAW threw a dinner party for Sinclair Lewis, hoping to persuade the author of *It Can't Happen Here* to become a member. It was a festive occasion, but, as a guest recalled, "clearly he did not propose to be inveigled into joining the League." Another image-enhancing idea that did not work out was a literary magazine. Communists on the council wanted to merge with the *Partisan Review*. The magazine's editors, however, declined, which was fine with progressives, who were afraid that what the functionaries wanted was "too left." To gain a wider audience, "we must be more liberal," Genevieve Taggard suggested. At the very next council meeting Trachtenberg suggested "tabling the discussion . . . until he had outlined a proposed course of action." No one, least of all Party functionaries, seemed very certain of what would make the League more popular, or even if popularity was desirable.[17]

The early LAW's failures suggested that the People's Front, coming on the heels of the Third Period, did not have that much immediate allure. Certainly the League could not be faulted for its efforts; it had gone all out to dazzle the intellectual community. Trachtenberg conceded the need "to broaden out and develop the functions of the League by calling in new blood." Where functionaries miscalculated was in trying to get middle-class intellectuals to support Party causes rather than enticing them with something more mutually advantageous. What could the Front possibly offer a middle-class writer who was left of center but not radical and not especially political? Progressives took pride in knowing "the truth," as Mary McCarthy called it, about Party front groups. That "truth" kept them out. "The revolutionary lions and the liberal lambs," one 1935 *Nation* editorial accurately predicted, "will approach one another with gingerly steps and suspicious eyes and avoid the same bed as long as possible."[18]

And it was precisely with "gingerly steps and suspicious eyes" that progressives approached the People's Front. As strategy, they appreciated it. Editorials in *The Nation, The New Republic,* and *Social Frontier* all thought uniting factions on the left a "brilliant" plan, "an olive branch" offered to those formerly alienated by the CPUSA. As policy, however, they were more uneasy. One reason was that, as the LAW experience suggested, the Front was slow getting off the ground in the United States. In *The New Masses,* for example, the process of effecting "basic changes . . . to meet the Peoples Front period" took time, well over a year. The result, "a weekly like *Time*" seemed hardly different from the old *New Masses,* a reflection of the functionaries' caution. In general, fronts followed Trachtenberg's advice about the League: "Let us admit individuals who in our judgment are helpful to us."[19] Being "helpful" to the CPUSA, however, was not high on most noncommunists' lists of political priorities.

In the League, the executive council hesitated to use the one theme that might have had some wider currency, antifascism. As late as May 1936 LAW members debated whether it was appropriate to raise the issue in a cultural organization. Some worried that it would give them too political a reputation that would chase away prominent writers. Certainly political issues had been unpopular in the past. "It is doubtful," one report noted, "whether the National League can be kept alive as a political organization if it is not kept alive as a cultural organization." But Trachtenberg was ready to test the waters with a small antifascist conference of "Leading Writers." It was never held; it did not need to be. Functionaries finally realized that "the more this United Front line is stressed, the greater the appeal to the average writer." Once the LAW began to define its "underlying purpose" as an intellectual front against fascism, its popularity increased.[20]

That popularity, however, was not universal. Some of the most prominent intellectuals the LAW sought were dubious of the Front's line and antifascism more generally. Liberals, especially, remained aloof. Reinhold Niebuhr, for example, agreed in principle that "the rising tides of fascism in every western nation are so strong as to doom anything but united opposition to them to futility"; but he could not reconcile himself to a coalition that included Communists. Was their change of line "thoroughgoing and sincere enough to insure genuine cooperation?" he asked. While he wondered if the Party had genuinely committed itself to more moderate politics, the editors of *Common Sense,* Alfred Bingham and Selden Rodman, argued Communists were settling for too little change in order to garner noncommunist support. "We are trying to build a new world," the editors lamented, "not save the old one." Liberals feared Hitler, but they feared American participation in an unnecessary antifascist war more.[21] The World War I example weighed heavily on Dewey, Dos Passos, and others. They also rejected what they perceived as the Front's basic equation: that to be antifascist and intellectual was also to be pro-Communist.

The liberals' point—that one could be antifascist without being pro-Party—limited the Front's successes until the Spanish Civil War changed everything. After Franco's Falange challenged the democratically elected Loyalist government in the summer of 1936, Germany and Italy quickly sent support. Soviet relief to the Loyalists began almost immediately after that.[22] Both acts profoundly affected American intellectuals. The former confirmed their worst suspicions about fascism. The latter, by contrast, reassured them that Stalin intended to stand by his People's Front rhetoric and assist a democratic regime. Suddenly there was more reason to be pro-Soviet and pro-Party. For many intellectuals, Spain became a holy war that symbolized the

98 struggle between fascism and democracy, civilization and barbarism. It focused energies and united—as well as divided—Americans.

The war in Spain exacerbated the split that already existed between liberals and those to the left of them. Liberals refused to see the Spanish Civil War as the last glorious stand of democracy. Rather, they were afraid that war in Spain indirectly threatened American democracy. Should the United States join the war, New Deal reforms, dissent, and civil liberties might be curtailed. Progressives' maudlin and inflamed rhetoric scared them. They tried their best to bring the discussion back to a more reasonable, and reasoned, level. John Chamberlain, for example, denied "that the cause of American political and industrial democracy was bound up with the success or defeat of the Loyalists." *Common Sense* eschewed the sensationalized headlines featured in other left-wing publications, running only one story about Spain, "Spain's Threat to America's Peace." Liberals supported the distribution of humanitarian aid in Spain but opposed lifting the arms embargo. Such attitudes further isolated them. John Haynes Holmes thought the Socialist Party's war efforts such an "unhappy business" that he resigned. Poet e. e. cummings grew so tired of his progressive friends' constant pro-Loyalist agitation that he put Malcolm Cowley firmly in his place: "If you're not uninterested in spain or something, that's your affair. And you're not. if I am uninterested, that's mine. And I am."[23] The liberal position vis-à-vis Spain was awkward because it was simultaneously antiwar, antifascist, and pro-democratic.

The dissident Marxist position on the war was different from the liberal one, but equally awkward. Marxist rebels were both antifascist and revolutionary, which created no end of complications. The elected Spanish government was a coalition and not very radical. Conducting the war was its first priority, which meant any socialist goals were secondary. Aid from Stalin improved the Loyalists' chances; however, dissidents were inherently suspicious of his meddling. There were other forces in Spain, forces with more revolutionary promise like the anarchist and separatist groups (the POUM [Partido Obrero de Unificación Marxista] and the CNT [Confederación Nacional del Trabajo], for example), that were more radical than the Loyalists, not affiliated with the Spanish united front, and therefore beyond Stalin's potential interference. But others defined the war in such a way that the POUM and the CNT threatened the antifascist fight with their revolutionary aims. Moreover, even those groups disappointed dissidents, especially the

POUM, which did join the coalition government.[24] Dissident Marxists, like liberals, were antifascist but not pro-Loyalist. They saw a far more complex war than the CPUSA acknowledged.

The Communists argued that the situation in Spain was nothing more than a simple struggle between democracy and fascism. In its version of events, the POUM and like groups threatened democracy by "complet[ing] the social revolution and possibly los[ing] the war." The Loyalists were nonrevolutionary, protected private property, opposed collectivization, and nationalized industry only for the duration of the war emergency. Joseph Lash, touring Spain as a representative of the American Student Union, was impressed. "The C.P. here has pursued a consistently fine policy," he wrote home, ". . . [and] was the first party to realize that everything must be subordinated to winning the war." "We might as well face the issue frankly," Joseph Freeman told the 1937 Writers Congress; "the majority of the Spanish people do not at present want socialism." Recognizing that progressives wanted Spain to be "the good fight," the CPUSA engaged in a fairly sophisticated and sometimes duplicitous public relations campaign to keep the cause looking pure.[25] The Lincoln Battalion was a good case in point. Party members comprised somewhere around half of this three-thousand-man American branch of the International Brigades. The Lincoln Battalion had political commissars, classes in Marxist theory, and political training; but none of these elements reached the public's ears, although, amongst themselves, Party people spoke of the great political training that recruits received.[26] Communists really wanted a Loyalist victory in Spain, but tended to misrepresent their interests.

Progressives did not question what the Communists said about Spain because they were even more sincerely and extravagantly devoted to the Loyalists. From the start, they believed the war had global implications too significant to ignore. It was, Matthew Josephson declared a mere six weeks into the battle, "our last chance to cry out" against fascism. Waldo Frank thought that "Spain . . . is the Symbol of humanity's struggle—and I love Spain as I love Hope and Beauty." Progressives almost never saw ambiguities in the fight. Louis Fischer called the war "a revolution against wide-spread poverty, for human rights, for progress." "Revolution," however, was perhaps an unwise word on Fischer's part, for progressives heartily endorsed the Communists' portrait of the Loyalists as democrats rather than radicals. The Spanish government, Maxwell Stewart reported, "frankly admits that there is no immediate possibility of a proletariat revolution." And that was as it should be; after all, one *Nation* editorial asked, "what good are farm collectives if Franco wins?"[27] The war in Spain revived progressive energies and gave larger meaning to their lives.

Progressives threw themselves behind the Loyalist cause as advocates and publicists for the Spanish popular front. They joined the Friends of the Lincoln Battalion and the American Friends of Spanish Democracy, wrote the president, and lobbied Congress to lift the arms embargo. Contemporary Historians, a group including Dorothy Parker, Ernest Hemingway, and Lillian Hellman, raised $13,000 to finance a documentary film about the war, "The Spanish Earth." Written by Hellman, Hemingway, and Dos Passos, with Hemingway as its narrator, it raised over $20,000 for Loyalist supplies at its Hollywood premiere. While Russia had once been *the* trip to make, Spain became the place everyone wanted to see. Although the journey was difficult and conditions were primitive by American standards, dozens flocked there. "It was," Hellman later explained, "rather one's duty to go." Fischer even briefly enlisted in the International Brigade because "it was not enough to write," but quickly resigned because he could not tolerate the Communist input, a complaint he did not make public. Later he served as an unofficial courier for the Spanish government and advised premier Juan Negrín. According to the House UnAmerican Activities Committee, there were eight separate pro-Loyalist front groups in Hollywood alone that managed to raise almost a million dollars. The war moved progressives like no other cause could. "Nothing so vital, either in my personal life or in the life of the world," Josephine Herbst wrote thirty years later, "has ever come again."[28]

Progressives romanticized and sentimentalized the Loyalist cause, so desperate were they for a morally unambiguous issue. They liked to imagine that freedom transcended the poverty and backwardness of Spanish life. "The Spaniard, to me at least," Theodore Dreiser said, "now seems to have a kind of proud dignity and reserve, something which humiliation and poverty cannot erase. It is handsome. It is respectable. In their rags they are proud and maybe cold. And they fight. And they do not quit." Much of their rhetoric celebrated the childlike innocence of the peasants. Occasionally, it verged on the effusive. Anna Louise Strong, for instance, enthused about "soldier boys who never had a chance to go to school" gleefully teaching one another to read and write while sitting in foxholes. Her "chief memory" of Spain,

she told Eleanor Roosevelt, "is not the horror, but the amazing confident joy." If the Loyalists were intuitive freedom fighters to progressives, the fascists represented unadulterated, almost mechanical horror. Theirs was "a new kind of warfare, without reason, without honor,
a blind malice." This "real battle of humanity" was all-consuming.[29]

The Loyalists made all the difference to the People's Front. The LAW
doubled in size by early 1937 and finally began to attract some of those
prestigious members. League activity focused around Spain; no other
single issue, including writing, consumed as much energy, publicity,
or attention. Through individual contributions, funds from an auction
of manuscripts, lectures, and a dinner honoring Theodore Dreiser, the
League raised enough money to buy four ambulances for the Loyalists.
League members circulated a petition urging Roosevelt to lift the arms
embargo. *Writers Take Sides,* published by the LAW, featured pro-
Loyalist statements by virtually every noted American author, even
those who did not belong to the organization. "Never have American
writers contributed more than we have in the present struggle," one
League *Bulletin* boasted.[30] Helping Spain brought progressives into the
League of American Writers and gave them something tangible and
satisfying to do once they got there.

The League's 1937 American Writers Congress was a monument to
the new attitude, involving progressives in every phase of an activity
that was, above all else, pro-Loyalist. From the moment the planning
began, progressives played a leading role in the Congress, and Communists, recognizing that their more extremist reputation might hamper
its success, bowed out. Trachtenberg, Gold, Hicks, Walter Lowenfels,
and Edwin Seaver absented themselves from executive council meetings altogether. Progressives wanted the 1937 Congress to be large,
nonpartisan, and moderate. "This organization has suffered tremen-
dously because of its original point of view," Helen Woodward complained at one Congress-planning session, "because it has been unable
to convince most writers that it now has a broader stand." Just how
broad the League wanted to become was reflected in the list of proposed keynote speakers the conference planners submitted: Carl Sand-
burg, Harold Ickes, John L. Lewis, Robert LaFollette, Charles Beard,
and Albert Einstein. Their list of potential resolutions was equally
mainstream: continued support for the WPA arts projects, opposition to
censorship and civil liberties infringements, and freedom for such political prisoners as Tom Mooney and the Scottsboro defendants. While

Joseph Freeman traced the history of the revolutionary tradition in American literature at the 1935 Congress, Newton Arvin looked at America's "democratic tradition." It was, as Seaver reported in *The Daily Worker,* "a People's Front Congress from beginning to end."[31]

Spain was at the center of the League's 1937 Congress and was the reason the Congress was so well attended and so popular. Writers heard more talks and saw more presentations about Spain than any other topic. Contemporary Historians showed a rough cut of "The Spanish Earth." Hemingway and other speakers related their experiences and impressions of the war. Progressives regarded the conference as an expression of their own values which happened to coincide with the Communists'. Novelist Dawn Powell, reporting back to John Dos Passos, found the meetings "impressive," especially Hemingway's speech and "The Spanish Earth."[32] Hemingway never would have headlined the 1935 Congress; nor would functionaries have been happy if he had. The Loyalist cause allowed progressives to feel in control of the League of American Writers.

Evidence to the contrary disturbed progressives. The more overt signs of a Communist Party presence frightened them. Powell enjoyed Hemingway's speech and "The Spanish Earth," but she did not like Earl Browder's appearance at the Congress's opening session. Neither did Margaret De Silver, who thought him a "vicious and a goddamned jesuitical liar and beast" who "looks like Hitler," perhaps the ultimate insult among militant antifascists. Archibald MacLeish shared the platform with Browder, but was "so disturbed" by his presence that he could not concentrate.[33] Browder symbolized the old League, MacLeish and Hemingway, the new one. The 1937-style LAW had no more room for Browder than the 1935 one had for Kenneth Burke.

The new League threatened to leave behind the Communists so important to its initial operation. The progressives who joined in 1937 were less accepting of the Party presence than the more stalwart progressives of yore. The People's Front often functioned better without "disciplined Communist" intellectuals. So, the hierarchy asked them to quietly fade from the scene. Hicks complained that there were no Party people at the 1937 Congress. He was assured, "I don't think we meant to exclude Communists as such; our main emphasis was on getting new people to read papers," which accomplished in fact what the LAW's secretary denied was a strategy. Yet Freeman suggested that the action was deliberate. "We kept our own people out as much as possible," he told another Party member. "Neither Mike Gold nor Robert Forsythe nor myself are reading papers." Freeman understood the rationale for such a decision: "This is intended to be the broadest kind of people's front Congress." But, as one of those directly affected by the decision, he felt excluded and unhappy:

> Two years ago, when they were organizing the artists congress, I heard a tovarich order the name of one of our most loyal artists stricken off the speakers list. "Who is X?" he exclaimed indignantly. "What in hell did he ever do? He served the Party for fifteen years? A fine achievement!" The artists whose achievements lay in the bourgeois world and who had only just come over to us, as honored guests of course, appreciated the point. Well maybe it's all necessary and maybe I am just not good enough for times like these.

"I have learned," he reported to Gold, "to expect nothing but heart-aches."[34]

And, many times, heartaches were what he got. Perhaps no incident so infuriated the Party's LAW fraction more than the group's prolonged and ultimately unsuccessful recruitment of Theodore Dreiser. Dreiser and the CPUSA were old enemies, having clashed over his apparent anti-Semitism in the early 1930s. But Dreiser was one of America's best-known writers, the NCDPP's founder, and strongly pro-Loyalist. League progressives badly wanted him to join. They courted him intensely, throwing a benefit dinner (for Spain, of course) in his honor, giving him the plum job of representing the League at an international conference in Paris, and inviting him to speak about his visit to Spain. They hoped he would improve the League's reputation, plus extend their pro-Loyalist fund-raising capacity. Communists, however, found "the old dope," as one Party member called him, "altogether difficult" and his opinions "peculiar."[35] Despite considerable bowing and scraping by LAW members, Dreiser did not join. No matter how abjectly Party writers behaved, sometimes their presence alone was enough to inhibit the League's new, broader function.

Dreiser was not the only one to shy away from the League. Even the more gentle Party presence deterred others as well. Reinhold Niebuhr turned down a special invitation to join, afraid that he would not have "anything to say that a group of predominantly communistic authors would be willing to listen to." Stephen Vincent Benét, William Saroyan, Felix Frankfurter, Fannie Hurst, Henry S. Canby, Struthers

Burt, and Floyd Dell also declined League memberships because, like Niebuhr, they were uncomfortable with the prospect of dealing with the Communists. Although he accepted an honorary membership in 1938, Franklin Roosevelt knew the League's reputation was questionable enough to ask that it be kept quiet, in the process undercutting the whole point of offering the membership in the first place.[36] The People's Front vastly improved the reputation of front groups, but could not extend their horizons endlessly.

The Party presence was equally troublesome to noncommunists in the American League against War and Fascism. After the Madison Square Garden fight, the CPUSA was the only political party affiliated with the group. This "gave a certain color to the false statement that the League was controlled by Communists and directed from Moscow," Robert Morss Lovett reported. Bowing to public pressure, Browder dissolved the institutional bond between his party and the ALWF in 1937. The organization also voted to rename itself the American League for Peace and Democracy in order to be "*for* something instead of *against*." The cosmetic changes did little to reassure people, especially since the League grew no more independent as a result. Its leaders canceled a 1938 antiwar speech by Harry Elmer Barnes at the last minute because, despite the name change, pacifism was "not in agreement with the principles" of the organization. So long as the Communists stood for collective security, so too would the American League. "Prospective members frequently complain that your organization is Communist-controlled," the ACLU advised the League more than a year after the Party removed itself institutionally from the organization. Looking back on the Front period, Roger Baldwin remembered that the ALPD could do nothing "sharply . . . opposed to the Communist line" without upsetting its internal dynamic. Although its official membership was eight million and it claimed to have "widened the base of the anti-fascist movement by stressing the common objective of the majority of the people," the ALPD lacked clout.[37]

The most effective front groups were those with the most limited ends, particularly pro-Loyalist ones. The Friends of the Lincoln Battalion, American Friends of Spanish Democracy, and the Committee to Lift the Spanish Embargo blended Communists and progressives with little friction. The Hollywood Anti-Nazi League, founded in 1936, was somewhat broader, but equally successful. At its peak, it boasted seven active committees, a newspaper, and two weekly radio shows.

Its president, screenwriter Donald Ogden Stewart, headed the League of American Writers from 1937 to 1939 and belonged to a number of other fronts. He also was a secret Party member. He was a good representative of the Front-era intellectual Communist recruit, middle-class, middle-aged, and respectable. He did not threaten progressives the way Gold or Trachtenberg might. Just as he was a faithful servant to the fronts, so too were many progressives. They understood that their role was to be, as Sherwood Anderson once said, "stuffed shirt[s]."[38] When fronts ran smoothly, it was because both parties could meet their parts in an implied bargain. So long as the fronts concentrated on antifascism and, particularly, the Loyalist fight, progressives did not feel the tensions they felt elsewhere.

Front politics were never mass politics, but 1937 marked their apex. The People's Front against fascism finally reached critical mass thanks to the Spanish Civil War. The Loyalist cause honestly mobilized both partners. As large numbers of progressives entered the fronts, they lost their original character, becoming less extreme and more liberal. Even Theodore Draper has conceded that "there were Communist fronts and Communist fronts." While he referred specifically to the American Student Union, most fronts in 1937 were different from what they were earlier and what they would later become.[39] Party intellectuals occasionally complained about the results, but they had more influence and authority than they ever had before. Communists always had the power to set limits in the fronts. In 1936 and 1937, however, the limits that they set did not seem all that onerous to most progressives. The People's Front briefly symbolized front politics at its finest.

FOUR

Challenging

"The Writers Congress Creed":

Left-wing Opposition to the

People's Front, 1937–1938

At the same time the People's Front seemed able to tap vast reservoirs of noncommunist support because of the war in Spain, other forces conspired to weaken it. The Moscow trials raised doubts about the Party's sincerity and front unity. The show trials enabled Stalin to reshape the Bolshevik Party into a pliant personal organization free of any rivals. He had lesser victims dispatched to the gulags in the dead of night; but he tried the revolutionary leaders, the Old Bolsheviks, in open court. In detailed confessions, they described an immense international plot to reestablish capitalism in Russia, led by Trotsky but with Hitler's connivance.[1] The Moscow trials had a large impact on the careful balance of forces keeping the People's Front afloat.

Officially, the American Communist Party stood by the Comintern's interpretation of the trials. The CPUSA suggested they eliminated a serious threat, defeated incipient fascism, and were "met [by the Soviet people] with gratitude and an increased sense of security," as Isidor Schneider reported from the USSR. The editors of *Soviet Russia Today* saw the trials as a blessing which would produce greater efficiency, raise production, and deliver "a blow in defense of peace and democracy everywhere, a blow for progress and civilization against the blackest powers of reaction and barbarism." The trials, in short, were nothing for Communists to be ashamed of, but a minor internal matter that improved Soviet socialism.[2]

This chipper official tone masked considerably more uncertainty beneath. Party intellectuals, especially, identified with the great heroes of the Bolshevik Revolution. Could they really be traitors, or had the Soviet government prosecuted them for other reasons? "One alternative," Granville Hicks recalled, "was as bad as the other." The situation got worse rather than better. The official explanation seemed weaker with each trial. "There were gaping inconsistencies and contradictions in the tales told in Moscow," James Wechsler observed. Some knew that the official line was a lie. Joseph Freeman learned from "very highly placed Soviet officials . . . that there never was a conspiracy, and that the 'evidence' at the Moscow trials, as well as the 'confessions' were pure fabrications." Making sense of the trials, even for those who had a very deep faith in the Soviet system, was a difficult and, in some cases, heartbreaking process.[3]

Most Party intellectuals eventually came to terms with their doubts about the Moscow trials but were ill-equipped to deal with the larger public outburst they engendered. No one wanted the thankless task of explaining the Party line in print. The first *New Masses* reporter to try, Joshua Kunitz, did such a bad job that he was reassigned. *New Masses* next assigned Freeman the job, but he was so distressed by what he heard from Kunitz and Soviet officials that he evaded their requests. For a time Canadian Trotskyists had a standing bet about the trials: who would be the first to break with the CPUSA, Freeman or Gold? The odds favored Freeman; but Gold did not immediately leap to the USSR's defense either. Characteristically, although traumatized by the news, Freeman was such a well-trained Communist that he tried to help another *New Masses* staff writer, Robert Bendiner, work through his doubts. His efforts were to no avail; Bendiner "had certain disagreements with the Party line" and left. Two younger Communists, Wechsler and Joseph Starobin, agreed to write a pamphlet explaining the trials; but their efforts failed as well. "The deeper we got into the maze," Wechsler recalled, ". . . the greater our own confusion became." A functionary finally advised them to avoid "an analysis of the facts" and write an exposé of Trotsky instead.[4] An exposé of Trotsky was the safer task, for the trial data itself left even the strongest Communist overwhelmed and confused.

With no hard data to prove the Old Bolsheviks guilty, the Party had to find other ways of legitimizing the Moscow trials. Gold might reason that "if Soviet nurseries, libraries, and schools are a sound development, Soviet justice must be sound," but most wanted more proof.

Legal experts helped to authenticate trial procedures, but they could not explain why so many revolutionaries betrayed their revolution. Too often, Party spokespersons fell back on the same old arguments:

> It is in the Soviet Union that the greatest victory [against fascism] has been won. The ring of Trotskyist wreckers and assassins, playing the game with the Nazi espionage system, has been dealt a mortal blow by the vigilance of the Stalinist administration. The published record of the trials can leave no impartial reader in doubt as to the guilt of the defendants.

Communist intellectuals recognized that this type of story was ineffective. As Bendiner complained when he received yet another such article, "everyone knows The NM [*New Masses*] is pro-Stalin. It is not enough for us to say that." But no one was prepared to write "a more closely-reasoned analysis of the whole subject,"[5] leaving the CPUSA's intellectual cadre few other options to carry it over the rough spot of the Moscow trials.

Unable to answer others' doubts about the trials, Party intellectuals simply told them to stop raising questions. Dedicated antifascists owed it to the cause to keep quiet and stand behind the Soviet Union, the most staunchly antifascist nation in the world. The "Writers Congress creed," Dawn Powell sarcastically reported to John Dos Passos, was to "defend the Soviet of Russia with our bare bodies." What Powell found amusing, Party intellectuals took very seriously. "Agnosticism," *Soviet Russia Today*'s editors cautioned, had no place in the People's Front; it was an ivory tower attitude no true antifascist could afford to hold. Perhaps nowhere was the whole equation of front commitments better articulated than in A. B. Magil's speech before the 1937 American Writers Congress: "When I hear sniping that is not directed against Franco, but against the People's Front government and see these people looking, with microscopes, for pimples on the shining face of the Soviet Union, I wonder, am I crazy or what? Is Spain in flames or is it not? Is the fate of humanity, of world peace, and of you and you and you, in the balance or is it not?" The solution to all the wavering, the editors of *The New Masses* suggested, was "faith in the Soviet Union and in the people's front movement in all countries." Without that faith, Earl Browder told that same Writers Congress audience, "the victory of fascism is inevitable."[6]

The CPUSA made it clear that intellectuals had only so much latitude in their public positions on the trials. Browder's comments, as virtually everyone knew, were aimed at the one prominent League member who had gone too far, Waldo Frank. The LAW's first president, he was an otherwise dedicated Fronter filled with doubts about the Moscow trials. When he first voiced those doubts, in 1935, the CPUSA arranged for him to meet privately with the Soviet ambassador. When he raised them again, in 1937, functionaries were not so sympathetic, because he visited Trotsky in Mexico and called for a public investigation of the charges against him. Once-close friends turned against the "rotter," who no longer wrote appropriate Front rhetoric but "idiotic idealistic twaddle." Clearly he was an unsuitable Front representative. So, when the Second Writers Congress convened in the early summer of 1937, President Frank absented himself from the proceedings and became, instead, the subject of Party vituperation from the stage.[7]

The response to Frank's absence was mixed. Some felt he had been driven from the Writers Congress because of his deviation from the Party line. Others considered his response amusingly naive. "Who but Frank," Lewis Mumford later wondered, "could for a moment have supposed that by aligning himself with the party Communists in the thirties he could convert them?" Few, however, missed the Party's message: intellectuals might quibble with the Party line on the trials in smaller ways, but they could not question its overall correctness without risking denunciation. Hamilton Basso summed up the prevailing Front opinion of Frank's situation when he told Malcolm Cowley: "Poor Waldo Frank! He had it coming to him, there was something shameless and inflated about his open-letter writing, but, at the same time, Browder's reply is a pretty good example of what to expect."[8] Progressives knew "what to expect" if they took a more independent line on the Moscow trials. They could be active Front members who fought fascism or they could question the official version of the purges, but they could not do both.

Neither alternative entirely suited them. They charted a middle course, carefully heeding the Party's warnings about destroying antifascist unity while carving out their own less optimistic positions on the trials. The Spanish Civil War also affected their decisions. "We must not, Hamlet-like, contemplate this tragedy so exclusively that we misjudge the USSR," one *New Republic* editorial noted.[9] Yet the very choice of the word "tragedy" suggested that progressives rejected the Party's optimistic assessment of the purges. They could see nothing good coming of the Moscow trials, no liberation from Trotskyist con-

110 spiracies, no sense in which Soviet socialism had been "saved" from fascism.

In the end, most settled for a kind of managed confusion, "keep[ing] clear of these issues." They could neither explain the trials nor reconcile them with their image of the new Soviet society. How could so many deaths be an inevitable cost of building socialism? They listened respectfully to experts, yet experts failed them in the end by reaching no more consensus than anyone else. There was enough damning evidence to make progressives uneasy, but not enough to throw over their other, more positive, images of Stalin's Russia. So, faced with a story that could be told two very different ways, many concluded that the best they could do was to just bide their time and wait for the denouement. "In the case of Russia," Josephine Herbst told Granville Hicks, "many developments leave me confused but I am willing to be patient." Editorial after editorial in *The New Republic* and *The Nation* emphasized that "we do not know enough to be sure of our ground."[10] While waiting was not a very satisfying solution, it was far less terrifying than confronting the alternatives.

Progressives also hesitated to condemn Stalin because of their long-standing belief that Russia deserved special accommodation. Its past was violent; its rulers traditionally brutal. "We do not kill our political opponents—at least not often," Upton Sinclair explained, "but in Russia it has been a custom of long standing." Such distinctions allowed them to continue admiring revolution from afar without condoning its more undemocratic features. Yet they also believed that the Moscow trials were an inevitable result of the Bolshevik Revolution. "Professional revolutionaries," they reasoned, found it difficult to make the transition from secret plotting to state building. The Old Bolsheviks lost sight of their goals and became obsessed, instead, with "the naked quest of personal power" until caught by Stalin. The result, *The Nation* explained, was nothing unique to Russia. " 'Old Bolsheviks' have in every revolution had to give way when revolutionary gains had to be consolidated."[11] Still, it was difficult to throw over nearly two decades worth of admiration for the revolutionaries who brought Russia into the twentieth century and socialized its economy. Reading over the transcripts of the 1938 trials, Cowley noted that the defendants "gave a curious impression of integrity" which did not square with his expectations. He assumed the accused were guilty, but began to imagine himself in their position. He too might break the law if there were no other way to protest. If Old Bolsheviks had to "give way" in every revolution, Cowley came to understand how it felt to be one of those disposable human beings. The experience, he remembered, was an unpleasant one.[12]

Progressives were convinced that what happened in Moscow was part truth and part fiction, part necessary and part cruel. The purges seemed both inevitable and horrible, particularly in their timing. As one typical *New Republic* editorial explained:

> Most of them [the Old Bolsheviks] are probably guilty of something, though not of the extremes of treachery that the indictment charges. Undoubtedly there was a widespread opposition in high places to Stalin . . . but it can scarcely be true that so many prominent and trusted persons were out-and-out conspirators for fascism or the return of capitalism . . . It is a strain on credulity to assert that they planned so many murders, poisonings or massacres.

Believing that the accused were guilty "of something" was hardly on a par with the official Party line. Progressives thought the idea of a conspiracy with fascists, especially, was "unthinkable."[13] Critics of the trials saw little difference between the progressive and CPUSA position—both, after all, thought the Old Bolsheviks guilty—but there were differences. The progressive interpretation was pessimistic and hinted at even deeper malaise.

The Front's dynamic hinged on progressive acceptance of the gist of the Party line on the trials. Progressives understood this, but it raised troubling questions about their integrity. Waldo Frank not only wanted to find out the truth; he also "needed to learn how free [he] was to express [his] mind." Many performed reassuring rituals of their own, although most stayed just inside the Front's boundaries. Cowley's musings "infuriated everyone" because he admired the Old Bolsheviks' nobility but expressed "so many doubts and then consciously suppressed them." Yet, Cowley saw his essays as an expression of his independence. "I was determined," he recalled, "not to be a propagandist." Bruce Bliven also sought to prove himself an independent actor vis-à-vis the trials. He wrote Stalin an open letter suggesting ways the Russian leader might regain progressive confidence: retire for a year or so to let things cool down, make all the evidence against the Old Bolsheviks public, conduct any future trials on Western lines, and abolish the death sentence. His statement was an expression of his personal discomfort with the absence of Western standards of justice in Moscow, despite what Party experts said about the fairness of the trial proceedings.[14] Progressives felt trapped between crosscurrents, their need to know what really happened and their belief that the antifascist unity forged between themselves and the Communists was more important than something that occurred in the Soviet Union.

Liberals approached the trials without progressive constraints. As civil libertarians, they found the criminal proceedings against the Old Bolsheviks wholly unacceptable and complained especially about the lack of physical evidence, the "frequent gross discrepancies" in testimony, and the haste with which they were conducted. "We would find the confessions more convincing," Reinhold Niebuhr explained, "if some other evidence beside self-accusations had been introduced to substantiate them, and if the charges of connivance with Germany and Japan on the part of the plotters had not been quite so inconceivably irresponsible." Everything happened too neatly for Eugene Lyons. "In their treason," he commented, "the Old Bolsheviks apparently have been considerably farsighted to misbehave exactly as would be most useful to Stalin, ten, fifteen and even twenty years later."[15] Liberals rejected both the Party line and the progressives' more apologetic sense that justice functioned differently in the USSR.

Liberals were quite clear about the mechanisms that produced the Moscow trials. They were neither the product of Russia's violent heritage nor some inevitable revolutionary stage to be rued but tolerated. The trials were "inevitable," Niebuhr concluded; but the force that produced them was "the Marxist-Leninist philosophy in which the end is made to justify the means," Selden Rodman explained. They were "exactly the sort of thing it *must* produce," John Chamberlain suggested. No ethical or moral considerations confined Stalin because he was building communism. "If human progress marches inexorably only through the extermination of class by class," *Common Sense* noted, "then 'anything goes.'" Lyons dismissed Party assurances that a better society would be the end result of the trials as a pipe dream: "All history proves that ends do not justify means. On the contrary, terror calls for more terror. It hardens into a system of power in which the ends are quickly forgotten." The Moscow trials violated "moral laws," Oswald Garrison Villard explained.[16] Liberals judged the purge with a very different set of values than any other left-wing faction.

They expressed those values, moreover, in terms Front supporters could not abide. The trials reinforced their distinctions between "dictatorships" and "democracies," providing additional proof that the governments of Stalin and Hitler were alike. They reminded Dos Passos that "civil liberties must be protected at every stage of every political movement that is going to have good results—at whatever costs." So too did the trials reaffirm the importance of the American democratic tradition. John Dewey figured that American radicals would finally stop worshiping Russia and realize "that we have our own job to do and have to do it in our own way." "Democracy *is* radical . . . as an end," he insisted, "and the means cannot be divorced from the end." "Democracy works," promised Arthur Garfield Hays. The immorality of the trials seemed so blatant to liberals that they blithely assumed their peers would also recognize that what dictatorships offered them was "so much crap."[17]

What liberals saw so clearly, however, others did not see at all. As John Haynes Holmes reported to Roger Baldwin: "The old issues of liberty are having a hard time these days. Liberals everywhere are forgetting their own ideals and deserting their own principles. Everywhere we are being told and taught that the end justifies the means, if the end is surely on the side of the worker in America, the Loyalist in Spain, and the Communist in Russia."[18] Progressives' inability to see the world in liberal terms disturbed them. They were shocked when the People's Front branded them accidental fascists. Villard reported to Holmes that *The Nation* received letters denouncing him as a "reactionary." Maybe, he suggested, it was time to retire. He turned over command of the magazine to progressive Freda Kirchwey, with whom he violently disagreed, sadly observing that "new times [produced] new morals." Joseph Wood Krutch, another of *The Nation*'s editors, was "less comfortable" at work. "Never before," he recalled, "had I found myself so nearly surrounded by colleagues whom I knew to be enemies or, at least, certainly not to be trusted." Granville Hicks's vocal criticism of the political line of his books department added to his anxieties. He cut back his duties. Dewey resigned from *The New Republic* in 1937, telling Dos Passos he was disappointed with its failure to encourage "independent critical thought." Villard described the whole process as a painful one: "I *do* feel a profound sense of depression," he told Holmes. "To put it more accurately, I feel that I have been left high and dry by a backwash, and I wonder if you and I, and other steadfast liberals are not merely back numbers left stranded because of the alarming clash between radical and fascist forces."[19] These experiences demoralized liberals, but also made them question the motives of the people who called them reactionaries and old-fashioned. Were they honest? What purpose did such attacks serve? Many grew resentful and suspicious of progressives.

While liberals were the Front's first casualties, dissident Marxists also questioned the Party line on the Moscow trials, although not at first. The early news of purges did not trouble them. After receiving an impassioned denunciation from Dos Passos, Edmund Wilson cautioned his friend against making any too-hasty decisions "because we really know nothing about it [the Kirov matter]." "I don't see any reason to disbelieve that they had a counterrevolutionary conspiracy," he added. Wilson was inclined to attribute the purges to a uniquely Russian mentality and set of traditions rather than anything more sinister. Moreover, he confessed, liberal carping on the subject so irritated him that he found "that I was almost driven into talking like a loyal Stalinist."[20] In 1935 and 1936, dissident Marxists, other than American Trotskyists, seemed relatively unaffected by the Russian purge.

Two years later, however, Wilson felt very differently. Writing to Cowley, he declared that the trials had "all . . . been fakes" to "provide scapegoats and divert attention from more fundamental problems." He thought "not a word" of the confessions "was true," although he allowed that the Old Bolsheviks had probably "been guilty of some kind of opposition to the regime."[21] What changed Wilson's mind? For one thing, the trials continued and that, by itself, was alarming. He also started to question the accuracy of the information coming from the Soviet Union, reminding Cowley that it was "pure propaganda" designed with the "simple" people of Russia in mind. The court procedures, he concluded, were "totally undemocratic." Nursing doubts, Wilson looked to the CPUSA's traditional enemies for answers and read "the Trotskyist and socialist stuff." Such writings, he reported, were "most illuminating."[22]

That Wilson would hear a more satisfying interpretation of the Moscow trials from Leon Trotsky and American Trotskyists—and that he would hear it through an informal intellectual grapevine—was hardly surprising. If the purges indirectly threatened the People's Front, they directly threatened Trotsky's life and reputation. He was unable to refute the charges leveled against him by the Old Bolsheviks because he was politically restrained under the terms of his Norwegian residency. The government put him under house arrest, censoring his mail and withholding his political writings. Trotsky's American followers mobilized to speak for him by putting themselves in the strongest institutional position possible outside the Communist Party and its fronts.

American Trotskyists were able to have an impact on people like Wilson partly because of their own united front tactic, executed in 1936. After surveying their bleak prospects in the American Workers Party and considering their enemy's Front strength, Cannon concluded that his group also needed to augment its ranks. His target was the American Socialist Party, then in the midst of a major factional dispute. Once the more moderate wing of the SP (the so-called Old Guard) left the organization, he began to court the Militants who remained.[23]

The tactic was not universally well received. The Musteites thought it "immoral" and opportunistic to fuse the AWP and the SP. Many Trotskyists feared that any blending of the Second and Fourth Internationals would compromise their program. Pragmatists pointed out that the size of the SPUSA relative to the AWP practically guaranteed a Trotskyist rout: "like a fly joining a brigade of elephants" was how Sidney Lens characterized the proposed merger. But Cannon was determined to capture the Socialist prize and expelled those Trotskyists who opposed him. Muste disapproved of the maneuvering and, borrowing a phrase from those conspiring against him, claimed that Cannon's action "smacks of Stalinist bureaucratic methods." He appealed unsuccessfully to Trotsky, finally resigning from the organization he founded. "Trotsky controlled his followers," he concluded, "about as autocratically as Stalin controlled his."[24]

American Socialists watched with alarm as Cannon manipulated the AWP for his own purposes. Talks between the Militants and the Trotskyists stalled, requiring a special meeting between Cannon and Norman Thomas. Cannon later recalled that the negotiations were "a difficult and sticky job, very disagreeable," and he had good reason to harbor unpleasant memories. The Militants virtually dictated the terms under which they would accept the Trotskyists, reasoning that only tight control and their seven-to-one numerical superiority would keep the new recruits at bay. A merger was entirely out of the question. Each Trotskyist had to apply individually for Socialist Party membership, pledging as he or she did to relinquish all factional journals and newspapers, even though, as Cannon pointed out, the SP was other-

116   wise tolerant of internal factions. "They made us pay," he recalled. Still, in order to get the "protective coloration of a half-way respectable party," he was willing to pay handsomely.[25]

Cannon groveled before the SP to gain the organizational strength that would make it possible to defend Trotsky. One of the first actions the enlarged SPUSA undertook was to create the American Committee for the Defense of Leon Trotsky in the late fall of 1936. The force behind the ACDLT was, of course, Cannon himself. He and his comrades persuaded six sponsors, none of whom were Trotskyists, to endorse the idea of providing Trotsky with both political asylum and a forum for responding to Stalinist charges. Although all of the sponsors were politically active, some, like the most prominent ACDLT sponsor, John Dewey, were "hardly aware of the existence of the Trotskyists as a group." They would be the ACDLT's "stuffed shirts," lending credibility to the organization. Cannon tried to structure the ACDLT like a front group, with Trotskyists in key, but invisible, positions within the bureaucracy. Although some members found the word "defense" in the organization's title "innocently but unfortunately" chosen, it accurately described the actual intention of the founders.[26]

If the ACDLT was supposed to function as a Trotskyist front, it hardly functioned very smoothly. One of its sponsors, Freda Kirchwey, resigned after Trotsky gained asylum in Mexico, figuring that its only future was as a "partisan group." Another member, journalist Mauritz Hallgren, also quit "because it seems to be all too plain that the movement to win 'justice' for Trotsky has simply become another Trotskyist maneuver." The ACDLT had several highly publicized membership controversies. Some people listed as members had no recollection of joining at all, probably because they had agreed only in the most vague of ways that Trotsky was entitled to a fair hearing. Certainly this was Mary McCarthy's experience. Four days after chatting with James T. Farrell at a cocktail party she learned that her name was on the ACDLT's roll. "I didn't think I was being asked for a signature," she later told him, but decided to attend a meeting to see what the group was like. She was not especially impressed by what she saw, but allowed her name to be used anyway. Louis Adamic's name also appeared on the ACDLT's letterhead without his direct consent. He too investigated it and concluded it was so badly disorganized that the Trotskyists had wide scope.[27] Like any other front group, the ACDLT wanted nonpartisan names behind which to hide. Like any other front group, it was not shy about getting them.

Yet there was another side to the ACDLT. Trotsky himself distinguished between the Trotskyists who *"know the truth"* and those like Dewey who "want to establish" it. Dissident Marxists fell into the latter category. They too assumed Trotsky was innocent, but they wanted evidence that would give their opposition to Stalinism moral authority. Proving that Stalin had deliberately set up the Old Bolsheviks to protect himself was tantamount to proving he had subverted the revolutionary process for selfish reasons. Liberals defended not Trotsky but his right to a fair and free trial. Dewey saw the ACDLT fighting for justice since, "as far as I am personally concerned," Trotsky's situation was unimportant. Martha Gruening, longtime NAACP activist, defended her spot on the Trotsky defense committee by arguing that "the matter is one of the importance of Civil Rights." All of these people were moved by something larger than Trotsky's "defense."[28]

There was a third ACDLT faction that received far less attention than either the intellectual Trotskyists or those who worked for abstract justice. Most of its foot soldiers came from the SPUSA. "The Party," one ACDLT report read, "is, in the most literal sense, the very backbone of the American Committee." Socialists typed and performed office work, distributed pamphlets, and arranged meetings. Their status created a rift between Socialists and Trotskyists and worked to the ACDLT's detriment. Although Trotskyists tried to convince their allies that "the cause of Socialism is at stake here," Socialists could not help but notice that the Trotskyists got to hobnob with celebrities at cocktail parties while they were beaten "by known members of the Communist Party" when they handed out literature on the street. Socialists grew quickly restive. "No sane *working class* party could possibly make the trials its most important activity," one complained. The New York City Socialist local and the Wisconsin SP branch withdrew their support of the ACDLT after Trotsky gained asylum, for fear of looking partisan. To stem the tide, ACDLT secretary George Novack met with the Socialist Executive Committee and offered kind words and promises. The Executive Committee, in turn, agreed to continue endorsing the group, but not necessarily its findings.[29] This struggle exacerbated a larger struggle between Socialists and Trotskyists for domination in the SPUSA.

By the time the American Committee for the Defense of Leon Trotsky was ready to investigate the charges against Trotsky, its reputation was already on the skids. Few illustrious personages agreed to serve on its Commission of Inquiry, so controversial were its responsibilities. Such noted civil libertarians as Arthur Garfield Hays and

118   Roger Baldwin turned it down. So too did Albert Einstein, Bertrand
Russell, Horace Kallen, Arthur O. Lovejoy, Morris Cohen, Van Wyck
Brooks, Waldo Frank, George Bernard Shaw, André Malraux, Bertold
Brecht, André Gide, H. G. Wells, and George Santayana, who was
"stirred to wrath" by the very invitation. Charles Beard refused to be "a
party to an enterprise that can have only one outcome." Carl Becker
demanded to know "what, after all, is it that Trotzky needs to be 'defended' against?" Although the ACDLT hoped to fill its Commission
with members so impressive that their findings would be widely accepted, "the *most* eligible," as Herbert Solow noted, became those
willing to serve.[30]

Even persuading John Dewey to chair the Commission was uphill
work. He had hardly been willing to sponsor the ACDLT in the first
place, as Sidney Hook, who talked him into it, recalled:

> He replied that he was tired and wanted to be left alone. Since he had
> no feeling one way or another about Trotsky and the Moscow Trials, since
> he was already seventy-eight years old, and since he was the target of every
> group soliciting political support, his weariness was understandable. Had
> anyone else requested him to sign the originating appeal, I suspect he
> would have declined.

Several months later, the ACDLT needed Dewey again and, once again,
pressed Hook into service. Reluctantly, he spoke with Dewey, but with
little conviction. Cannon decided to try himself, convinced that without Dewey "the press and public would have ignored the sessions."
Dewey was appalled by his "ward healer's charm" and nearly joined
Beard and Becker and all the others who declined. When he finally
agreed, it was neither Hook's weak appeal nor Cannon's high-pressure
one that influenced him. The Communists seemed so determined to
keep him from heading the Commission that he accepted the job.[31]

Dewey's presence might have provided the Commission of Inquiry
with the respectability it sought, but Trotskyist meddling constantly
undermined its reputation. Trotsky, his ACDLT "comrades," and ACDLT
secretary George Novack wrote to one another, plotting strategy in
a manner inconsistent with the group's supposed nonpartisanship.
Trotskyists were everywhere, meeting Trotsky's boat when he arrived
in Mexico, riding on the train carrying the Commission to Mexico
for its hearings. Novack was so obsequious that two commissioners
"threatened to resign" if he continued to interfere. He later insisted

that there had been "complete separation" between the Commission and the Trotskyists; but a letter from Herbert Solow to one of the ACDLT's financial backers, Margaret De Silver, suggested otherwise. By the end of the Mexican hearings, the integrity of the Commission was thrown into serious question by the resignation of Carleton Beals, who alleged that the investigation was biased. "There is," he declared, "on the part of the rest of the Commission, an air of hushed adoration for the master." Even the Commission's ace-in-the-hole did not escape Beals's criticism: "Doctor Dewey stares abstractedly, quizzically, once or twice asks a very, very respectful question." None of this reassured intellectuals that the Commission of Inquiry would deliver any "truths" about the Moscow trials.[32]

But there was worse to come. Several months after the delegation returned, Trotskyists drove Beals from the editorial board of Calverton's the *Modern Monthly*. Calverton had already asked for and received Beals's resignation before the threatening letters started to arrive, so he wondered if the real point of the campaign was to "stress by implication what . . . [Trotskyists are] wary about stating directly, that Carleton Beals acted in Mexico City as an agent of the GPU." This struck Calverton as being as absurd an accusation as some of the prosecutors' in the Moscow trials. He asked Beals to resign for his own reasons, because he was afraid his name on *Modern Monthly*'s masthead misrepresented the magazine's political perspective; but he was no more willing to bow to Trotskyist pressure than Stalinist. The Trotskyists lost a useful ally and a valuable forum. Calverton decided Trotsky was just as "pathological" as Stalin.[33] The Beals resignation was a public relations disaster from start to finish.

The ACDLT was a decidedly imperfect vehicle for an impartial investigation. Liberals supported it, primarily because they were too distantly involved in its proceedings to be aware of the behind-the-scenes maneuvering. Dissidents, while growing in number, were not effectively engaged by the ACDLT because they were more alert for partisan politicking and found it "unsatisfactory." Like Calverton, they saw similarities between the two Russian rivals. The ACDLT seemed too much like a front to make them comfortable. It handled "a Trotskyist matter," Alfred Kazin recalled. Trotskyists annoyed dissident Committee members like Edmund Wilson, with their constant badgering "in every mail and by telephone." Their reverence for Trotsky irritated them. It was hard to take them seriously. Louise Bogan poked fun at a newspaper account of "a whole lot of lost but enthusiastic Trotskyite souls" at an ACDLT meeting "waiting for the voice of god [Trotsky] to come in on the telephone from Mexico." When the communications riggings failed, the result, she thought, was both sad and funny. "I think Moses managed those things better," she concluded. Bertram Wolfe felt that the whole Commission of Inquiry was a sham: "The Commission was ineptly chosen, and used procedures which hurt rather than helped. I do not see how that can be denied nor how anyone can read the stenogram [of the 'trial'] without a mixture of amusement and regret that such silly questions could have been asked and such procedure used." Dissidents were not predisposed to be unconditionally supportive of the ACDLT.[34]

Still, as Meyer Schapiro argued, the ACDLT was better than "no committee at all," for Marxist dissidents were acutely interested in the Moscow trials. They suffered profoundly from the crisis of faith that Party intellectuals briefly experienced. As Liston Oak noted: "If *all* of Lenin's comrades, all the former members of the Politburo and Central Committee except Stalin and Molotov and Kalinin, were guilty of the charges made against them, then the whole history of the Russian Revolution becomes incomprehensible and incredible. Then the revolution was made by gangsters, cutthroats, renegades, spies, and traitors." Between 1935 and 1937 many Marxists passed through the same stages as Wilson: initial patience, gradual doubts, eventual outrage at the Party's response. They turned elsewhere for "*the truth.*"[35]

Learning that truth meant, in part, publicly confronting the CPUSA and its fronts. As an incident at the 1937 Writers Congress suggested, public confrontation served two purposes. Five rebels disrupted a session on criticism to ask questions about the trials and the LAW's relation to the CPUSA. William Phillips called their interruption a moral act; but Mary McCarthy told Malcolm Cowley "we're just wreckers."[36] Dissident Marxists were both wreckers and moral protesters. Both kinds of acts required public action to expose the truth and destroy what dissidents considered the Front's facade.

By publicly proclaiming their opposition to the Party line, rebels believed they acted as intellectuals should. Their honesty, however, changed their status: "I got the name of being a Trotskyite," McCarthy recalled, "which meant, in the end, that I saw less of the conventional Stalinists I had been mingling with. . . . This, then, was a break or a rupture, not very noticeable at first, that gradually widened and wid-

ened, without any conscious effort on my part, sometimes to my regret." Much as she resented being ostracized, McCarthy also enjoyed
the notoriety. Later, she said leaving her name on the ACDLT's membership list was "perhaps *the* pivotal decision of my life." History might
prove her right for doubting Stalin; but part of what made the decision
so attractive to her was the perceived cost of the gesture. The martyrdom of opposition appealed to her. So, too, apparently, did it appeal to
many ACDLT members:

> Every committee member wore an expression of injury, of self-justification,
> a funny, feminine "put-upon" look, just as if they were all, individually, on
> trial. They nodded with emphasis at every telling point, with an air of being
> able to corroborate it from their own experience. . . . And after the meeting
> had broken up, over coffee or highballs, the committee members would
> exchange anecdotes of persecution, of broken contracts, broken love affairs,
> isolation, slander, betrayal.

Saul Bellow remembered that "we [ACDLT supporters] were, of course,
the 'Outs'; the Stalinists were the 'Ins.' We alone in the U.S.A. knew
what a bad lot they were." Standing against the Front's version of the
trials became "a kind of test."[37] To willingly suffer on account of an
unpopular position was romantic verification of one's worth as an
intellectual. Once the trials became a measure of intellectual integrity,
rebel Marxists felt compelled to speak out against them.

The result was anti-Stalinism. It had its roots in the first ruptures
between dissident Marxists and the fronts, but emerged as a coherent
political doctrine only during the late 1930s. The Moscow trials forced
dissidents to look beyond their obsession with the CPUSA and confront
the Russian origins of the Stalinism they decried at home. As before,
they first listened to Trotsky and his intellectual followers. Eventually,
however, they rejected his explanation as too simplistic. Trotsky considered Stalinism an aberration created by one man. Stalin purged his
many enemies because he had no other way of imprinting his false
doctrines on the USSR. But anti-Stalinists saw the threads of Stalinism
woven into the Russian Revolution. There was a "Bolshevik amor-
ality" present from the beginning that, Liston Oak argued, grew worse
in the early postrevolutionary days. Lenin instituted one-party rule
and brutally dispatched dissenters because of the exigencies of the
civil war. Stalin and Trotsky shared the same revolutionary experience, Calverton argued; if Trotsky had power, he would likely purge

122   his enemies too. "The one-party system, *under any and all circum-stances,* is a danger in itself," concluded Oak.[38] Such an explanation came perilously close to an indictment of Marxism more generally.

Anti-Stalinism also explained other events and actions. It clarified the Spanish Civil War, for instance, and helped focus rebel Marxists' uncertainty about the nature of the forces there. Viewed through the lens of anti-Stalinism, the Russian contribution to the Loyalist cause appeared sinister. Stalin used his minimal support as an access point to gain influence over the government. He gave the once-small communist faction in the united front more power while neutralizing the anarchists and separatists who were not easily controlled. Stalin purged the POUM just as he purged the Old Bolsheviks and for precisely the same reason, self-protection. "The campaign is being carried on exactly like the Moscow trials," Anita Brenner suggested, ". . . and is in fact part of the same drive." Calverton called the Soviet role in Spain "imperialistic . . . [and] concerned with the destruction of a socialist Spain." "If socialism does not triumph in Spain," Herbert Solow warned, "the USSR—despite its butter and its posters and despite even a few tanks and men sent to Spain—will have to answer for it, and the answer will be 'Stalin.' "[39]

Spain, the progressive symbol of purity, had become another acid test for anti-Stalinists. One who passed that test was Liston Oak. A long-time Party member, he stopped in Spain after an unhappy visit in the USSR, hoping to find the clarity of purpose that eluded him in Moscow. He took a job with "the Spanish Loyalist Government against Franco" and made contacts with the communists there. They told him Comintern agents encouraged the POUM to revolt so that the Loyalists could then legitimately repress it. The father of one of his coworkers was shot for political reasons. Oak wanted out of Spain, but since he knew about an illegal Party passport ring, he was afraid he would be silenced if he tried to leave. He turned to another intellectual having doubts about the war in Spain, John Dos Passos, to get him out quickly.[40]

Dos Passos's change of heart also occurred after seeing the Spanish war up close. Like Oak, he had been strongly pro-Loyalist when he left for Spain to do preliminary research on "The Spanish Earth" with Ernest Hemingway. Before he left, anarchist Carlo Tresca warned him that the Comintern killed its enemies there. At the time, Dos Passos shrugged off the warning. Once there, he took it seriously. He tried to

look up an old friend, José Robles Pazos. Robles, doing political work
for the Loyalists, had disappeared. Dos Passos plied official channels to learn his whereabouts to no avail. Hemingway finally told him
Robles was dead, but could not tell him why. American Communists
assured him that Robles was a fascist spy; but the "higherups in Valen-
cia" gave him the impression that "he had been kidnapped and shot by
anarchist 'uncontrollables.'" Puzzled, dissatisfied, and more than a
little dubious of the explanations he received, Dos Passos was happy to
quit the film and journey home with Oak. It took two more years before
he uncovered the real story: "that Robles had been executed by a 'special section' (which I gathered was under control of the Communist
Party)" as "an example."⁴¹ What Oak and Dos Passos experienced in
Spain contradicted their image of the Loyalist cause as a pure and
honest one. Anti-Stalinism helped Dos Passos and Oak understand
why a fight once so noble had been sullied.

So too did anti-Stalinism help rebels understand the heavy-handed
propaganda campaign for Spain. Spain was a popular cause and those
with alternative perspectives were not very popular. To anti-Stalinists,
that popularity was no accident. Nobody listened to Dos Passos or Oak
because the CPUSA had effectively brainwashed intellectuals into believing a false version of the war. Lionel Trilling resented the overtones
of a situation where dissidents "live surrounded by the clouds of complex and subtle misrepresentations, . . . but one has only to open one's
mouth to have all the liberals, good, nice people, feel that one is now a
kind of reactionary." Anti-Stalinists suggested that there was a deliberate conspiracy to hide the less pleasant realities of the war "behind an
opaque screen of ignorance, misunderstanding, and downright lying."
Louise Bogan saw "The Spanish Earth" twice and noticed that "not a
word was said about Soviet Russia's part in the struggle." Worse yet,
the film ignored the more subtle dimension of the story in order to tell
one that was "sentimental and fixed." "The whole tone of it bothered
me," she told Morton Zabel, ". . . Hemingway [the film's narrator] was
having such a hell of a good time, looking at a *War*, and being disgust-
ingly noble about it." William Phillips and Philip Rahv complained
that many American intellectuals preferred this "ecstatic and foolish
faith in a classless, mystical 'Spanish People'" to the real truth about
Spain. Communists, anti-Stalinists alleged, were delighted to supply
them with lies.⁴²

The Loyalist propaganda blitz, the Moscow trials, and Stalinist in-

124   terference in the Loyalist government all appeared to be parts of a larger Stalinist power surge. The CPUSA "purged" its enemies too, anti-Stalinists declared with a certainty borne of firsthand experience, although its power was such that it could do no more than silence its critics. Several notorious cases reinforced this suspicion. Herbert Solow noted a "substitution at left tackle" after Dos Passos returned from Spain disillusioned. Suddenly *The New Masses* thought Hemingway a great writer and Dos Passos a mediocre one. Liston Oak complained of being jobless after his break with the CPUSA. He tried "the Federal Writers' Project, the Theater Project, the Art Project, [and] . . . the Information Department of the WPA" with no success. Everywhere he went, he said, the Communists sabotaged his applications, destroying his file and then spreading rumors about his character and ability to get along with others. Oak was convinced that "I am being kept off [the WPA] for one reason only—that I broke with the Communist Party and denounced Stalinism as a reactionary force splitting the labor and revolutionary movement and betraying the Russian Revolution." His experience was "only one of many" and extreme, but not atypical. As Diana Trilling later recalled: "The extent to which Stalinism dominated American culture in the years before the Second World War . . . was all but absolute. The submission to Stalinism by our opinion-forming population was not always politically conscious. It represented the fashionable trend in what was presumed to be enlightened thought." Anti-Stalinism fused the personal experiences of dissident Marxists with a larger political interpretation of events such as the Moscow trials. Purges came in all shapes and sizes, and while some were bloodier than others, all required moral action. Oak refused to "submit gracefully to Stalinist blackmail and slander," instituting a letter-writing campaign to inform as many "friends" as possible of his situation. Dos Passos chose fiction to publicize Stalinism's many evils. Both felt angry, betrayed, and vengeful.[43]

Anti-Stalinists believed that "Stalinism" threatened their survival as intellectuals. They spoke the truth, were objective and pure; that made them deserving of intellectual status. But they were persecuted by Stalinists and denied the power they earned. A free marketplace of ideas did not exist because Stalinists controlled access to key publications and editorial offices. The Party's gatekeepers, they argued, were not even motivated by any true—if misguided—Marxist commitments. They were after "new markets . . . and new conquests." The "regulars," Calverton alleged, did not believe the official line on the Moscow trials; they just mouthed it in order to keep their jobs on the Writers' Project or the League of American Writers or "remain[ed] silent and obey[ed] directives." Their primary task was "to persuade *innocents* that the 'socialist fatherland' and its foreign policy—whatever it happens to be at the moment—deserve their support."[44] While their number was small, they mobilized an immense army of progressives, although anti-Stalinists were never quite able to agree on how they accomplished it. Some thought progressives "intellectually lazy"; others said they were "spiritually terrorized"; still others argued they felt that support for the USSR was "more important than the truth." "You can get names, big names," Kenneth Rexroth complained, "on any sort of document."[45] This hegemonic theory of cultural Stalinism credited the CPUSA with immense power. Because their self-images rested on this view, anti-Stalinists always overestimated the size and strength of Communism in America.

Communists were easy targets and easily dismissed; but progressives, who had far more actual influence on the left, were not. Progressives were, Philip Rahv told Leon Trotsky, "the real mainstay of Stalinism." As such, anti-Stalinists resented them much more than Party intellectuals, especially because their response to the Moscow trials demonstrated their "moral collapse." But, in their scramble to achieve status, they could not always challenge the big-name progressive editors like Freda Kirchwey, Malcolm Cowley, or Bruce Bliven without suffering consequences. So, Alfred Kazin, anti-Stalinist yet in need of the money and credentials he could get at *The New Republic,* swallowed his pride and endured Cowley's tenure there, building up anger that would surface only years later. And Liston Oak, truly desperate for a job, groveled before Roger Baldwin and assured him he understood why Baldwin did not "break with the Stalinists."[46] Progressives were the left-liberal establishment, making them at once easy to condemn and hard to challenge.

Anti-Stalinists, consequently, chose their battles carefully. Oak, for instance, did not want his enemies to "get away with it [persecuting him],"[47] but treated Baldwin deferentially. Baldwin had respectability and clout. Oak was not as gracious with Corliss Lamont, who had money but was widely regarded as an eccentric Soviophile. Against Lamont he could allow his moral outrage full scope without threatening his livelihood. Front groups, anonymous and large, were likewise comfortable targets. By attacking them, anti-Stalinists could perform their ablutions publicly and in relative safety, contriving situations with maximum publicity and minimum personal risk. Through their flamboyant and defiant public actions, anti-Stalinists escalated the tensions between themselves and the People's Front.

Given the anti-Stalinist understanding of the forces that prevailed on the intellectual left, it is hardly surprising that one of their first goals was to create a free space where they could be anti-Stalinist without having to pacify progressives. But such a free space also threatened the Front. Thus, when William Phillips and Philip Rahv decided to reconstitute the *Partisan Review* as an anti-Stalinist journal, they instigated a major power struggle on the intellectual left. Although there were other oppositional forums, most were political and none were explicitly anti-Stalinist. Phillips and Rahv wanted a cultural magazine as well as a political one, something like the old *Partisan Review* they helped edit when it was affiliated with the New York City JRC. They were the last remaining editors before *Partisan* closed up shop, so when they created "the first anti-Stalinist left literary journal in the world," they superimposed it on the old *Partisan.* By announcing that they would turn an unofficial Party organ into an anti-Stalinist magazine, they symbolically laid claim to Marxist orthodoxy. They also declared war on the CPUSA. Party intellectuals protested; "Rahv and Phillips had TAKEN the magazine." Suddenly, long-simmering tensions between dissidents and the Front boiled over.[48]

The Party could do nothing to stop Phillips and Rahv from publishing, so had to fight them with words. Advised by attorneys that any suit to reclaim the *Partisan* might result in unwanted questions about other CP activities ("such as," Joseph Freeman told Josephine Herbst, "where and how was the Abraham Lincoln Battalion organised"), Party intellectuals decided to let them "keep the magazine they had literally stolen from our group and our movement." Thereafter, the publicity assault against them began. Michael Gold denounced Rahv as "a literary snake," "a sneak," and an "opportunist." Both *The New Masses* and *The Daily Worker* linked the not-yet-published magazine with "Leon Trotsky, the POUM, and the Trotsky Defense Committee." Some progressives also picked up the cry. The campaign was ugly, mean-spirited, and deceptive. Herbst, who herself made rude anti-*Partisan* comments, was appalled. "I wish that we could keep from yelling 'thug' and 'crook' at everyone who does not agree with us," she told

Granville Hicks. "Better," she thought, "to let them hang themselves   127
with a first number than to jump on them now."[49] When the first issue
finally appeared, the intellectual community was considerably more
divided than before.

Phillips and Rahv positively flaunted their anti-Stalinism as the
badge of honor of a new generation of intellectuals. Their first editorial
statement explicitly condemned the older "Stalinist" generation:

> The old movement will continue and, to judge by present indications, it
> will be reënforced more and more by academicians from the universities,
> by yesterday's celebrities and today's philistines. . . . Weak in genuine liter-
> ary authority but equipped with all the economic and publicity powers of
> an authentic cultural bureaucracy, the old regime will seek to isolate the
> new by performing upon it the easy surgery of political falsification. . . .
> Every effort, in short, will be made to *excommunicate* the new generation,
> so that their writing and their politics may be regarded as making up a kind
> of diabolic totality; which would render unnecessary any sort of rational
> discussion of the merits of either.
>
> . . . But *Partisan Review* aspires to represent a new and dissident genera-
> tion . . . it will not be dislodged from its independent position by any
> political campaign against it.

While Phillips and Rahv created a new *Partisan,* they also sought historical continuity between it and the old *Partisan* to establish the logic
of their evolution. They numbered their first issue "volume four."
More importantly, they rewrote the earlier history of the magazine,
alleging that while the *Partisan Review* might have been attached to
the New York City JRC, it was no organ of the prolet cult. "Formerly
associated with the Communist Party," they explained, "*Partisan Review* strove from the first against its drive to equate the interests of
literature with those of factional politics."[50] Phillips and Rahv claimed
for their magazine ideological and cultural purity.

The *Partisan Review*'s editors also saw themselves providing a free
space where the fusion of "the modernism, the estheticism, and the
avant garde impulses of the earliest years of the century with the new
historical sense that the best part of the radical movement had introduced" might occur. In asserting their earlier independence from the
prolet cult, Rahv and Phillips were, in effect, establishing their credentials as independent Marxist cultural critics. To them, any magazine
"that aspires to a place in the vanguard of literature today . . . will be

unequivocally independent." The *Partisan Review*'s cultural role paralleled its political one; both were defined by their differences with the People's Front. Organizations like LAW practiced "a kind of unofficial censorship" and an exploitation of "any successful money writer" "for its [the CPUSA's] own peculiar ends." Those ends, Rahv insisted, were "of considerably less importance culturally than politically." To Rahv, there was no better proof of intellectual degradation than the complete capitulation of art to politics. LAW's standard for good literature was the same as the JRCS': whatever mimicked the Comintern line. Both were anti-intellectual. The CPUSA, he complained, "suppress[ed] . . . intellectual freedom in the name of the defence of culture."[51]

The *Partisan*'s editors were neither as innocent nor as idealistic as their manifesto claimed to be. Phillips later invested the reorganization of the magazine with the sanctity of a moral calling: "We just felt it was important to do what you believed." Romantic though that sounds, a number of people suggest that their motives were not so much idealistic as pathological. Their "moral superiority" was too "extreme and uncompromising" for Malcolm Cowley and he disliked their "cold supercilious sneer." He saw both as the hallmarks of disillusionment. An active commitment to the revolution required flexibility, compromise, and action. "I haven't much faith," he told Edmund Wilson, "in revolutionists who run no risks." R. P. Blackmur spent an evening with *Partisan*'s editors and found them obsessed by a "conspiracy . . . against them by all good Communists—liberals—NR [*New Republic*]—*Nation*—practically everybody." Kenneth Rexroth thought them "mildly psychopathic personalities." *Partisan*'s editors, Cowley concluded, had "embarked on an anti-Communist crusade that has become a fixation."[52] To the Front's supporters, that was clear proof of intellectual weakness.

While exaggerated, there was some truth to the accusations that these anti-Stalinists were obsessed with the Front and occasionally paranoid about its power. *Partisan* theater editor Mary McCarthy offered a glimpse of that paranoia many years later, when she recalled that " 'they' [Communists] were everywhere—in the streets, in the cafeterias; nearly every derelict building contained at least one of their front-groups or schools or publications." One reason there seemed to be so many Communists under the *Partisan*'s beds was Rahv and Phillips's choice of location, deep in "Communist territory," in the same building and on the same floor as *The New Masses*' editorial offices.

Since they picked that particular location themselves, it is difficult to avoid the conclusion that they enjoyed "running a gamut" of Party intellectuals each time they rode the elevators to their offices. The daily contact with "'them,'" McCarthy recalled, served as "a concrete illustration of their power in New York at that time, a power that spread uptown to publishers' offices and to the Broadway theatre and to various cultural agencies of the Government, like the WPA Writers Project and the Federal Theatre." "They were strong," she concluded, "and we were weak." "The Partisans" very much enjoyed playing the underdog.[53]

Certainly the underdog role won them supporters, many of whom regarded the CPUSA as a terrible bully. "I don't like thuggish tactics no matter how noble the aims," Katherine Anne Porter complained. Many well-known intellectuals, including Lionel Trilling, James T. Farrell, Babette Deutsch, Bertram D. Wolfe, and Edmund Wilson all lent their public support to the magazine. Wilson even dressed down Cowley for his attacks, suggesting that his anti-*Partisan* writings were a "more serious distortion of the truth in the interests of factionalism than anything I have ever seen in *Partisan Review.*" Others were more critical. Rexroth believed that a magazine "such as they pretended to be starting" was "sorely needed," but he did not think the *Partisan Review* fit the bill. Josephine Herbst commented that Phillips and Rahv were opportunists without "the guts" to admit that they were "Trotskyites."[54] Virtually every left intellectual in the country had an opinion of the *Partisan.* It further polarized the intellectual left.

The battle over the *Partisan Review* was only the most prolonged and public of a series of fights between anti-Stalinists and the intellectual branches of the People's Front over power issues and orthodoxy. Although boundaries between Communists and their critics had never been especially fluid, divisions hardened as dissident Marxists defined themselves more explicitly as *anti*-Stalinists. The *Marxist Quarterly,* founded about a year before the *Partisan Review* reappeared, was a quick casualty of the changing climate. Its original editorial board was remarkably diverse, containing Trotskyists and dissidents along with Corliss Lamont, who provided financial support. For a few months, the group stayed together, publishing an alternative to the Party's theoretical organ, *Science and Society.* Editor Lewis Corey received comments, ideas, and the promise of articles from the whole gamut of left-wing intellectuals, from Lovestoneite Bertram Wolfe to

Party member Granville Hicks. The Moscow trials and growing tensions caused the Trotskyists to leave and then Lamont withdrew his backing as the remaining editors adopted an "attitude of complete enmity" against the USSR. Like the *Partisan Review,* the *Marxist Quarterly* was an attempt to carve out a niche for Marxist scholarship independent of the CPUSA and the People's Front.[55] It was an unlikely survivor, but one that might have lasted longer had the battle between anti-Stalinists and the intellectual People's Front not heated up.

Another battleground was the New York City chapter of the Federal Writers Project. It was, as Liston Oak learned, a hotbed of political activity. Many of the New York City writers were members or supporters of the Communist Party; but a minority were strongly anti-Stalinist. Harold Rosenberg, editor of the Writers Project magazine, became the pawn in their fights. He appointed as his assistants Lionel Abel and Harry Roskolenko, both flirting with Trotskyism. Rosenberg's writers promptly staged a work slowdown and picketed his office; the WPA fired Abel and Roskolenko, but the writers demanded more. The WPA demoted Rosenberg to managing editor and brought in Kenneth Burke from outside to serve as editor. Anti-Stalinists complained and Edward Dahlberg resigned because of the presence of "Marxist mutes." All the noise attracted the attention of congressional Communist hunters, who in 1938 investigated the Federal Writers and Theater Projects for Communist influence. Anti-Stalinists did not approve of the investigation, but they were convinced that "the cast of characters" in fronts never really changed and that a "drearily and professionally Left" cadre ran the Federal Writers Project and, increasingly, controlled left intellectual thought.[55]

Yet, the Communists were not the only ones to enforce a political standard. Although they were in a better position than the anti-Stalinists in some places, in others the anti-Stalinists triumphed. Dwight Macdonald endured a "Bloody Sunday" of acrimonious questioning by Phillips and Rahv before they allowed him to join their board of editors. His "fellow-traveling" past and his Trotskyist present both came under attack. Sidney Hook challenged the inclusion of an essay by V. J. McGill in a book on John Dewey's philosophy. McGill was a Party member who had elsewhere "deliver[ed] himself of an underhanded abusive tirade against John Dewey, passages of which are downright insulting." Hook was so relentless that the volume's editor, Paul Schilpp, declared he "wish[ed] to God . . . [he] had never seen" the McGill piece in the first place. He omitted the essay, but accused Hook of practicing a double standard, defending free speech, but "not for those who hold opinions different from their own."[57]

Barely a year after the Moscow trials began, the left intelligentsia was in the state of flux. Both inside and outside the People's Front, intellectuals had to come to grips with the meaning of the trials. Communists justified, progressives rationalized, and liberals only modified their previous position on Marxism. But for the ever-expanded group of Marxist dissidents, the Moscow trials were a milestone, a series of events so significant as to push them into active opposition against "Stalinism" at home and abroad. The emergence of anti-Stalinism as a left-wing critique of the People's Front solidified and concretized the battle between those wedded to front politics as a modus vivendi and those who favored ideological purity over compromise. In 1937, the People's Front still held the upper hand. But the anti-Stalinists were gaining momentum in 1937 and 1938. The year 1939 promised to be one of turmoil.

FIVE

"The More Developed Writers":

Managing the People's Front,

1937–1938

Anti-Stalinism reshaped the People's Front. While it was once possible for Communist intellectuals to sit back and let organizations run themselves secure in the knowledge that antifascism would rise to the surface and cover over other differences, by the end of 1937 that was no longer possible. The anti-Stalinist mission was clear and powerful. It caught the CPUSA off guard. More than ever, Communists needed progressive respectability. But progressives were also affected by the same forces as anti-Stalinists. The Moscow trials and the American Party's determination to undermine critics of the trials made them more suspicious of their allies. A quiet little mutiny began within the ranks of the fronts.

Because of the anti-Stalinist assault, the Party tightened its control over the fronts. New recruits and old hands alike understood that centralization was "inherent in the character of the party," Granville Hicks told Richard Rovere.[1] The fronts were never as centralized or hierarchical as the CPUSA, but they did become more bureaucratic. Communists were among the most organizationally skilled front members, able to make their presence felt even when their numbers were small. They carried out tactics they felt were in the best interest of the Party.

One of those tactics was a massive campaign to embarrass and undermine Party enemies. As the visible public center of opposition to the Communists' line on the Moscow trials, the American Committee for the Defense of Leon Trotsky became the focus of Party ire. Party intellectuals "hounded, threatened, and cajoled [members] to resign." They phoned them at midnight, issued warnings about their future livelihoods, and made "threats of personal violence." Kenneth Durant of Tass called Louis Adamic, implying vaguely that his future in Russia was limited should he not resign. Genevieve Taggard wrote two old friends, Sara Bard Field and Charles Erskine Scott Wood, that seeing their names on the ACDLT letterhead was "one of the saddest things in my life." It was not always easy to confront familiar people. Some of the fainter-hearted or more insecure Party members could not withstand the stress. *New Masses'* staffer Fred Dupee, for example, made only one telephone call urging resignation from the ACDLT. Mary McCarthy, on the receiving end, laughed at him and he gave up, demoralized. A few months later he joined the *Partisan Review.*[2] Most Party intellectuals, though, accepted such activities as an integral part of the Communist intellectual's political duties.

Progressives, however, had different priorities. Few were happy playing a part in the Party's campaign against dissidents or its defense of the Moscow trials. But neither did they want to threaten antifascist unity nor be attacked like dissidents were. In order to be true to their consciences and the People's Front, many devised a simple strategy: they stopped writing or talking about the Soviet Union altogether. The trend was abundantly clear in the progressive press. While *The Nation* and *The New Republic* featured dozens of happy stories about the Soviet Union before 1937, most post-1937 articles dealt with Stalin's antifascist foreign policy. The 1936 Soviet constitution, with its broad guarantees of civil liberties, merited little attention. Roger Baldwin outright refused to write about it for *Soviet Russia Today* because "it was only too apparent that the proclaimed democracy was only window dressing for dictatorship." The war in Spain offered a convenient excuse to switch topics without comment. Louis Fischer, known to millions as a specialist in Soviet affairs, for example, visited Spain and stayed for years, leaving his Soviet-born wife and children in the USSR. "I did not write a word about the Moscow trials of leading Bolsheviks," he recalled; and while his memory was faulty, the sentiment was significant. Anna Louise Strong told William Henry Chamberlin that she had learned to avoid the subject herself, for her own sanity as well as her audience's: "I haven't been writing or speaking much about Russia during the last two years. Spain and now China are much more in demand. And I could explain five Communists, ten Communists executed; but when there are so many and such unexpected people it becomes a little embarrassing." Many progressives recalled feeling guilt pangs about the Soviet Union in the late 1930s.[3] While few acted upon them, they were not just paying lip service to feelings they might have later wished they had. Their silence was the best way they could find to balance their allegiance to the People's Front with their instinctive revulsion over Russia's internal affairs.

Progressives understood their silence on the Moscow trials as a pragmatic political choice. Lewis Mumford told Herbert Solow that the matter boiled down "to one expedient or another." Solow chose to defend Trotsky, but Mumford felt "it is more expedient that the Soviet state . . . should be kept strong enough to withstand Hitler."[4] Hitler was the ghost in every progressive's attic. What happened in the Soviet Union was unfortunate, but certainly less important than defeating Hitler. If keeping silent on the trials was necessary to hold together the People's Front, then keep silent they would. They would strike a bargain with anyone, "including Beelzebub,"[5] to stop fascism. With this choice, progressives violated the traditional front bargain. They did not share their partners' pro-Sovietism, yet their partners defined that pro-Sovietism as integral to the Front. Once "cracks,"[6] as Dawn Powell called them, appeared in the foundation upon which the People's Front was constructed, progressives and Communists had increasing trouble keeping the edifice standing.

Party intellectuals were acutely aware of the defection of progressives from the active ranks of pro-Soviet propagandists. Isidor Schneider, collecting tributes on the twentieth anniversary of the Russian Revolution for *Soviet Russia Today,* complained to Joseph Freeman that few were willing to make public statements lauding the USSR. Indeed, the most visible noncommunists at the twentieth anniversary celebration staged at Carnegie Hall were Jerome Davis and Corliss Lamont, both unusually pro-Soviet. A dinner honoring the Soviet ambassador drew better attendance, but one of the two sponsors failed to show and many in the "very liberal crowd" spent the evening discussing the Moscow trials, privately and off-the-record. Freda Kirchwey summed up progressive opinion on the wisdom of the Party's Front strategy when she told Maxwell Stewart, "To my mind the effort to promote unity on the left will fail if it is predicated on a categorical declaration of faith in the virtues of the Soviet Union."[7] Progressives stubbornly stuck to their guns, unwilling to do anything more for the Communists than what was minimally necessary to keep the Front viable.

When Party intellectuals tried to elicit more, progressives balked, particularly because the anti-Stalinist critique made them more sensitive about control issues, censorship, and intellectual independence. Maurice Hindus censored his own famine stories; but when asked to alter a piece for *Soviet Russia Today,* he refused. "My answer of course is No!," he told Joseph Freeman. He was very angry that "SRT is attempting to make a prevaricator out of me." "Please don't take us bourgeois writers for children or dupes," he warned; "we are really grown up." Such constant monitoring, he guaranteed, would turn sympathizers "into implacable enemies." Albert Halper told a friend he got letters from the Communists every day asking him for favors or endorsements, but he did not cooperate. Both *The Nation* and *The New Republic* ignored Party admonitions to the contrary and printed ads for books by Trotsky and Trotskyists and for the American Committee for the Defense of Leon Trotsky.[8] The more the Party pushed, the less progressives responded favorably. Irritation grew on both sides.

Progressives began to shy away from fronts, leaving their names on the rolls but not participating in any activity that disturbed them. By 1938 their absence was noticeable. In the League of American Writers, they simply faded away. Malcolm Cowley, a League activist from the very beginning, stopped attending board meetings. So did so many others that several times the LAW could barely scrape together a quorum. Yet their nonparticipation was highly selective. They helped raise two thousand dollars for Spain in 1938, but a majority neglected to pay their five-dollar membership dues. They wrote long antifascist testimonies for *Writers Take Sides,* but were unwilling to promote the other aims of the organization.[9] Their retreat was palpable.

Communist intellectuals picked up the slack, assuming all the while that they were thereby entitled to run the League in a manner more to their liking. The LAW employed two Party members, Franklin Folsom and Harry Carlisle, as executive secretary and organizer. Folsom moved the League to the same building as Party headquarters and hired two writers close to the Party to be editors of the LAW *Bulletin.* Carlisle restructured the organization, ostensibly to make it more democratic. His program yielded a very large paper membership, but no great flood of dues or activists. In the Southwest and California, the League swallowed up extant writers' organizations, transferring their prestigious membership lists to its own. Carlisle's decentralization gave the regional organizations greater autonomy. Intended or not, though, the result gave the Party more power. A few months after the reorganization, there was "diminishing attendance" in the branches and "the liberal members sink into apathy." Disciplined Party writers and their close allies ran most regional affiliates by the end of 1938. This was especially true in Hollywood, where militant screenwriters fighting for union recognition made the local LAW branch more radical and more ambitious than any other. Soon Hollywood was so important to the national League that Carlisle and another Party member, Ella Winter, were appointed to the executive council as West Coast representatives. Even in New York City, Communist League members did their best to regain control. "We have an organized fraction now operating in New York," Folsom boasted to Granville Hicks, "and as a result, a number of important improvements in our work will manifest themselves."[10]

In the smaller circles of what Folsom politely called "the more developed writers," Communists and their closest friends worked to reshape the organization. One of their highest priorities was keeping their troops in line. Folsom distributed "reference" lists of the *Partisan Review*'s contributors and ACDLT members that helped them plot strategy. They could then puzzle out a response to Louis Adamic's simultaneous membership in the League and the ACDLT or decide when to give John Dos Passos "the works" for his heresy. Folsom even circulated guidelines to keep "the fraction" working "in the right fashion," but was careful to limit its availability; "we are not publicizing this plan," he penciled across the copy he sent Granville Hicks. The Party fraction was very flexible in its interactions with the League. Folsom fussed like a nursemaid, for example, when he finally got Cowley to attend a board meeting. But when League Communists got wind of possible trouble, they quickly instituted protective measures. "Some of our Friends might try to be a little frisky," Les Rivers warned Joseph Freeman in a letter urging him to attend a meeting where Van Wyck Brooks intended to speak his mind about the Communists.[11] "The more developed writers" in the League banded together out of self-protection because their friends were frisky all too often.

Party intellectuals battled progressive dissent, some of it unwitting, elsewhere too. The magazine *Ken,* both "anti-Fascist and anti-Communist," created unending problems for the CPUSA's cultural contingent. *Ken*'s antifascism attracted progressives, who were either ignorant of or unconcerned by the other half of chief editor Arnold Gingrich's philosophy. It proved difficult to disengage eager antifascists from the magazine. Repeated warnings to Ernest Hemingway about Gingrich convinced him to remove his name from *Ken*'s board of editors but did not stop him from writing for the publication. George Seldes also ignored what the Communists had to say about Gingrich's anticommunist reputation, and when he left the magazine it was because of a clash over his editorial work.[12] No matter how much bad press the Party circulated about *Ken,* progressives seemed to keep frustratingly open minds about it.

When the first issue finally hit the newsstands with "red-baiting captions" written by Gingrich, Party intellectuals could stand it no more. Folsom sent Gingrich a letter—on LAW letterhead and phrased to sound official—condemning the cartoons. At the next LAW executive council meeting, he asked for retroactive approval of his action and got, instead, a reprimand. He was admonished in future not to take any action "without the approval of the National Council." Even a more overt Party presence in the LAW did not seem to help Folsom fight *Ken.* Gingrich continued publication, unmoved by the Party's actions. He was, however, influenced by another institution. The Catholic Church threatened a national boycott of the magazine because of its allegedly pornographic contents. Gingrich tried to pacify the Catholics, Meyer Levin recalled, by dismissing all the "Jewish reds" who worked for him. His job on the line, Levin turned to the nearest thing he could think of to a union, the League of American Writers. Having just been stung for taking independent action, however, Folsom "bucked it [Levin's letter] right over to *The New Masses*" and then *The Daily Worker.* Rather than being appreciative of those efforts, Levin was furious. Bringing the CPUSA to his defense made him look like a Party member and that was the last thing he wanted. When *Ken* finally collapsed, it was because of the Catholic Church's boycott.[13] Folsom and the rest of "the more developed writers" could neither stop *Ken* nor make progressives see what was wrong with it.

The LAW's rehabilitation of Waldo Frank was another instance when progressives' antifascism triumphed over the Party's more per-

138 sonal wishes. Frank had many close friends in the League, friends who wanted to bring him back into the fold. A year and a half after he was effectively banned from the 1937 Writers Congress, Cowley moved that the LAW executive council invite him to "report on his recent trip to Spain," a safe subject since he was passionately pro-Loyalist, and offer him the chance to "reestablish his status as a League member by paying his back dues." Knowing such a proposal was in the works, Folsom urged his writers to attend. Some did, but not enough to shape the outcome. Frank spoke to the organization, duly chastised by his exile. He alluded to his absence at the Congress as nothing more than a misunderstanding.[14] That the League of American Writers could embrace him even after he directly challenged the Party line with his public questions about the Moscow trials demonstrated that the CPUSA never fully controlled the group. Yet his humble behavior also revealed that progressives would rather get along with the Communists than clash with them. The former fact limited the scope of the Party cadre within the organization; the latter, however, could work to their advantage.

Progressive flexibility cut both ways, though. Willing to pacify the CPUSA when necessary, progressives did not automatically see the world as Communists did. When Party intellectuals tried to force matters, they usually fell in line, but the cost was more grist for the anti-Stalinist publicity mills. William Carlos Williams's run-in with two rival publications, the *Partisan Review* and *The New Masses,* suggested that, more and more, progressives were perceived as pawns in a war between the two rival Marxist factions. Williams was no political innocent, but he defined himself first as a poet. An occasional *New Masses'* contributor, he sent a poem to the *Partisan Review.* Precisely why he did, given the enormous controversy surrounding it, is unclear; perhaps its politics meant less to him than its proclamation of cultural freedom. The *Partisan's* editors regarded Williams's submission as something of a coup and listed him as a "contributor." When *The New Masses's* editors saw that listing, "they refused to print me." "You know, of course, that I have no reason for liking *The Partisan Review,*" he told Phillips and Rahv. "I have, at the same time," he added, "no partisan interest in *The New Masses.*" It was precisely this attitude that confounded Party intellectuals and anti-Stalinists alike. Williams accepted *The New Masses'* terms, withdrawing his association with the *Partisan* because his connections with *The New Masses* were "of longer standing." The incident reflected badly on the Communist intellectual cadre; the *Partisan Review* publicized it to the hilt; and yet Williams's recantation was both incomplete and temporary. He published in the *Partisan Review* a year or so later.[15] Both sides tried to use Williams. Neither fully succeeded.

Williams pursued his own interests, but found it increasingly difficult to negotiate between the anti-Stalinists and the CPUSA. Progressives had little sympathy for anti-Stalinists, who seemed obsessive and dogmatic; but many were only slightly more comfortable with the Communists. Most of all, they feared public association with either faction. One solution was disengagement, easier to do from anti-Stalinist strongholds, like the ACDLT, than Party ones. Front connections became more problematic. The ACLU even sued the *American Mercury* for suggesting that it was a Communist front. Famous intellectuals once again grew leery of standing on the stage with Party members for Party causes. Invited to chair one LAW function, Sherwood Anderson "started to say yes, but was afraid to."[16] In so doing, he reneged on another part of the front bargain.

The Party built bigger and better paper fronts to compensate. The LAW altered its membership requirements, simplifying a process that was originally by invitation only. By the end of 1937, it circulated application blanks. For the cost of a year's dues and a commitment to the League's aims, anyone could join with little fuss. The League also broadened its definition of "writing." The first members produced "highbrow" culture; even "political writers" were suspect. As the People's Front widened into the still more inclusive Democratic Front of 1938, the LAW likewise democratized, welcoming screenwriters, radiowriters, how-to writers, and "pulp" writers. Its elder statesmen were sometimes appalled, but Party intellectuals, many of whom themselves produced scripts and screenplays and cookbooks, liked the changes because they made the organization less elitist. The League tripled in size between 1937 and 1939, increasing its total membership to about 750. Participation, however, declined; only 35 percent of the organization paid its dues.[17] This was fine with Party intellectuals, who found names easier to manage than souls.

One advantage of the bigger but less active fronts was that the Party cadre could take a more direct role without challenge. As others disengaged from the LAW, Communists worked their way back into the bureaucracy and, since "the liberals [progressives] were lazy, while the

140 Communists did all the work," they could hardly complain. The active progressive membership faded after the 1937 congress and was replaced with a new crop of Party people and their friends: Joshua Kunitz, William Z. Foster, Ruth McKinney, *Soviet Russia Today* editor Hope Hale, and Dashiell Hammett. Altogether identifiable Party members were about 10 percent of the membership by 1939; another 10 percent were extremely close to the CPUSA. On the executive councils, however, Communists and their close supporters were somewhere between a fourth and a third of those elected and an even higher percentage of those who actually participated. This did not guarantee that the organization could be easily influenced, as Franklin Folsom well knew; but by manipulating quorums, the Communists could at least potentially shape policy. "The more developed writers" had an ally in League president Donald Ogden Stewart, who secretly belonged to the CPUSA. Most of the rest of the officers were progressives who supplied status but little else to the organization. So untaxing were his duties as a vice-president, for example, that Upton Sinclair did not even know he was an officer for more than a year of his two-year term.[18] The LAW still relied on big names at the top, but progressives had less influence in its expanded ranks.

Party intellectuals also pursued the strategy of amassing names rather than committed supporters when it came to the one area where they were most desperate and progressives least willing to comply, the Soviet Union. In 1939 they solicited four hundred signatures on an open letter listing ten differences between the Soviet Union and Nazi Germany. The number of endorsers seemed large at first glance (although perhaps not as large as promised, since only 165 of the alleged 400 names were made public), but many were public Communists or their private allies. Some of the others might have signed under false pretenses, the victims of a more determined Party presence in the fronts. An "initiating committee" approached the LAW for access to its mailing list and gained it, thanks to increased Communist participation on the executive committee. When the letter was sent out, it looked like an official League message, prompting at least one member to assume the organization officially endorsed the statement.[19] Easier access to the fronts and the ability to mobilize names gave the CPUSA power in the People's Front up until the very end.

At the same time, the campaign to obtain signatures in support of the USSR showed that progressives were not as cooperative as a few years before. Less than 15 percent of the LAW's membership responded favorably, a return rate actually lower than the percentage of Party members and close friends within the organization. Few seemed willing to go very far out on a limb for the USSR. At *The Nation,* the editorial response to the "400 Letter" was almost perfunctory, except for a complaint that the statement failed to present an accurate picture of life in the USSR. Chief editor Freda Kirchwey refused to endorse it altogether. *The New Republic*'s chief editor, Bruce Bliven, not only refused to sign but urged his fellow editors to keep their names off as well. Several endorsers of earlier statements did not appear on the "400 Letter": Malcolm Cowley, Theodore Dreiser, Louis Fischer, Robert Lynd, and Dorothy Parker.[20] Progressives no longer accepted on faith the notion that active pro-Sovietism contributed to antifascism. Rather, most saw expressing public support for the USSR as a task performed solely to placate the CPUSA.

Progressives communicated their displeasure by refusing to be as tolerant as they once were of the Communists' needs. Many lost their awe of Party discipline and refused to be intimidated. Communists could once elicit progressive cooperation largely through guilt, chiding their partners for failing to measure up to their values. By 1938 and 1939, progressives were more assertive about *their* values and let the Party know when *it* failed to measure up. "*New Masses* had certainly become a place where slogans are thrown around promiscuously without any attempt to answer anything," Josephine Herbst complained to Granville Hicks. *New Masses*' attempts to "expose" General Krivitsky, a former member of the Soviet secret police whose story of Stalinist repression in Spain appeared in the *Saturday Evening Post,* raised progressive hackles, even though many agreed that he probably was a fraud. *The Nation*'s editors reproached the magazine for "sniping" without the facts. Cowley privately thought Krivitsky a "bastard," but asked Louis Fischer to write something other than a factless CPUSA denunciation of him for *The New Republic.* Progressives came to see the Communists' "doctrinaire vendettas" as good reason to stand up for their principles.[21]

The emergence of the Special Committee on UnAmerican Activities under Representative Martin Dies made it more critical for progressives to disassociate themselves from the CPUSA. Even though they strongly opposed its methods and goals, its power scared them. Haughty opposition was only possible so long as it ignored them.

142   Those who felt misrepresented had to decide which was worse, remaining publicly identified with the CPUSA or cooperating with investigations most thought illegal. Even the American Civil Liberties Union was not immune. Its initial policy of scornful noncooperation ("no representative of the Union should appear before the Dies Committee except under subpoena") gave way after several witnesses called it a Party front. ACLU leaders frantically pursued Dies for "an opportunity to appear before your committee." The Union's legal counsel even considered filing a writ of mandamus to force the situation. Ultimately several leaders sent voluntary statements to the Committee and invited its investigators to examine the ACLU's records, accommodating the congressional body despite the directive to the contrary.[22] Upton Sinclair, whom witnesses identified as a Party member, sent an affidavit denying any such membership and assuring the Committee that he had devoted his entire political career to showing "I am not a Communist and why."[23] Sinclair was, in fact, not a Communist, but as a strong supporter of the People's Front he did associate with plenty of Communists. That he and others like him were willing—even eager—to draw distinctions between themselves and the CPUSA suggested that the original bargain upon which the People's Front was based no longer functioned.

Meanwhile, the rhetoric of the Front itself undermined progressive support for Party aims. Earl Browder told them communism was "twentieth century Americanism," but he was primarily concerned with protecting the Russian Revolution. Communists continuously pitched the Front as a coalition of democrats fighting fascism; yet noncommunists more commonly associated democracy with America than the USSR. The Moscow trials disabused most of their earlier belief that socialism guaranteed political freedom or individual justice. In 1936, they still believed that "the Soviet system has always contained far more genuine democracy than outsiders have realized." By 1938, many blamed the Bolsheviks for "repudiat[ing] political democracy completely." In a world filled with repressive societies, the United States looked suddenly good by comparison. Although class inequalities still existed, many argued, the principles of democracy and equality were codified. Three books that came out in 1938 and 1939, George Counts's *The Prospects of American Democracy*, Lewis Mumford's *Men Must Act,* and Max Lerner's *It Is Later Than You Think,* reaffirmed the importance of freedom and urged Americans to see that their own democratic heritage provided the best protection against fascism. "We have looked back to history, and we have found a usable past," Lerner wrote, "and one that we can call ours."[24] Noticeably absent from this equation was the USSR or the CPUSA. If progressives' best defense against fascism was democracy and their usable past was their own, the very notion of allying with the Communists to protect values the Communists did not share became problematic at best.

By the end of 1938, progressives were more likely to draw distinctions between what the Front stood for (antifascism and democracy) and what the Party represented (communism), asserting their support for the former and their independence from the latter. Van Wyck Brooks detailed the differences for the Connecticut branch of the League of American Writers. The LAW, he asserted, was not "as a body, communistic." Thus "its common denominator is *liberalism . . .* Its object is to enlist American writers in the cause of democratic thought and action." Communists played little role in shaping either the League or the People's Front more generally, which was important to Brooks, since he did not think very highly of them. The speech was not just heretical from a Party perspective, but deliberately confrontational as well. He "hope[d] very much *The New Masses* will rake me over the coals" in order to generate "other personal statements" that would begin a dialogue about CPUSA input in the Front. He could then sit back, his duty done, and avoid the LAW, "except for voting." But too many other progressives also wanted little to do with the LAW besides voting. They did not pursue the matter. Neither did the CPUSA. The Party faction packed the Connecticut meeting but contributed only to the general "confusion" which marked the end of his talk. When the League reprinted his speech, Franklin Folsom asked Granville Hicks to write a sidebar defending the CPUSA. Hicks's piece was exceedingly even-handed. Genevieve Taggard, very much the Party partisan, demonstrated that *tact* was the word of the hour when she told Brooks she did not always share his opinions, but "valued the honesty and sincerity of your statement."[25] What distinguished this episode from earlier clashes between progressives and Communists was that it was a comparative nonclash. It was only by allowing progressives the room to disagree within ever-widening parameters that the Communists were able to remain within the Front.

Only a few months after the Brooks incident, both groups had to again confront the widening gap between League progressives and communists. For purposes of incorporation, the LAW needed a statement of aims. Several progressives regarded this as an opportunity to "set the record straight . . . that . . . the League is controlled by *no* political party." The subcommittee assigned the task of drafting the statement split and turned over two statements to the executive committee, one composed by Party member Isidor Schneider and a second written by progressive Oliver LaFarge. Schneider's version emphasized typical Party rallying cries; it was a brief and glorious document about unity on the left and antifascism. But the executive council adopted LaFarge's instead, which, as progressives hoped, declared the organization composed of writers "of every shade of political conviction, from Republican to Communist." What held this diverse group together was "a true, deep, aggressive belief *in freedom and democracy*" and not any particular opinion on the USSR. Schneider never mentioned the Soviet Union at all. LaFarge did, claiming for League members the explicit right to "our individual opinions of the Soviet Union's internal political system."[26] The statement, in short, replaced the "Writers Congress creed" with the freedom to dissent from the Party line on the Moscow trials. Despite the growing preponderance of Party friends within the LAW hierarchy, progressives again demonstrated that they could prevail in the fronts when the issue mattered to them.

By early 1939, the strain of getting along had begun to take its toll on the League. The theme of the Third American Writers Congress, scheduled for the summer of 1939 was therefore noncontroversial, the writer's craft. Even that failed to rally progressives. Many followed Brooks's lead and disengaged except for voting. With a membership base three times as large as during the glittering 1937 congress, willing organizers were still in such short supply that the Communists took over and planned much of the event themselves. Progressive celebrities were also unavailable to grace the stage, leaving the planners no choice but to tap the more traditional CPUSA entertainment stable: folk singer "Aunt" Molly Jackson, folk musicologist Alan Lomax, Dashiell Hammett, Hope Hale, Joseph Freeman, Albert Maltz, and A. B. Magil. The result was disappointing. Not only did the meetings seem filled with Communists, to intellectuals accustomed to thinking in high cultural terms, the participants themselves seemed below standard. Many, Malcolm Cowley recalled with a clear sniff of disapproval, "earned their standing through publishing in the cheapest sort of popular magazines." Yet it was not pulp magazine writers who most stood out at the 1939 congress; it was representatives from the movies. Screenwriters were roughly a third of the congress sponsors and so visible a presence that the next conference was scheduled for Hollywood.[27] But screenwriters, like pulp fiction writers, were still marginal in many progressives' eyes. Their primary virtue, as far as Party functionaries were concerned, was their radical fervor. The 1939 LAW congress offered the interested public proof that many progressives had lost interest or faith in the organization. Without them, the kind of show the Communists could stage-manage seemed an inferior product.

In other fronts, the tensions between Communists and progressives manifested themselves in more overt ways. The merger of two pro-Loyalist front groups, one with substantially more Party control than the other, produced the North American Committee for Spanish Democracy, which had a "stormy, sectarian career." The Medical Bureau to Aid Spanish Democracy was almost entirely Party affiliated; the American Committee for Spanish Democracy had far more progressive input. Progressives were initially wary about fusing the two, so extracted "an agreement by the communists to play down their role." Yet, as Roger Baldwin noted, "the Communists were in on the ground floor of the organization and managed to get their personnel pretty much in charge." Superior organizing paid off. Progressives tried to replace the Party member in charge of the treasury but were "overruled." When the group turned its attention to postwar refugee problems, the Communists insisted upon helping only communist refugees. Progressives complained, then the Party fraction loaded meetings with its supporters or deliberately stayed away to keep the other side from gaining a quorum.[28] What happened in the North American Committee to Aid Spanish Democracy was the triumph of an energetic minority aided by the hesitation of the majority. Unable to prevail democratically because they could not trust progressives, the Communists used underhanded tactics to achieve their goals.

Even in Hollywood, the supposed bastion of Communist power, front groups could not stay happily wed. The Motion Picture Democratic Committee, founded in 1938 to help elect Democrat Cuthbert Olson governor of California, suffered a classic clash between dubious progressives and its Party contingent. After the 1938 election, the group nearly faded. Both progressives and Communists wanted to

146 revive it, but some progressives also wanted the MPDC to go "on record . . . as a democratic organization." In February of 1939, Philip
Dunn drafted a statement of purpose for the Committee which included the following plank: "We hereby reaffirm our categorical opposition *to any and all forms of dictatorship,* whatever the economic
philosophy behind them." He had "one hell of a time" getting the
MPDC's board of directors to accept even an amended statement, one
that modified "dictatorship" with the word "minority," so as to distinguish the Nazis from the Soviet dictatorship of the proletariat.[29]
Dunn, like many progressives, believed that fronts were democratic
and could, at any time, be used to express the popular will. That assumption was often naive; yet when they pushed, the Party was forced
to stand behind its democratic rhetoric. The relationship between the
two partners often seemed more adversarial than cordial.

It was left to Archibald MacLeish, his politics tempered by his ap-
pointment as Librarian of Congress, to raise a question even he was
afraid to answer. If the Front was democratic and the Communists
were not, why bother with them at all? Why not cut them out of the
coalition and reconceptualize antifascism as a "*pro*-democratic policy" rooted in American values that put "the dignity of man" first?[30] A
year or two earlier, the very suggestion would have provoked angry
Party denunciations and heated progressive debate. In 1939 it engendered neither. Rather, there was only a deadly, ominous silence. For
their own reasons, progressives and Communists both felt a growing
urgency in their Front tasks. At the same time, however, their coalition
had grown too fragile to risk debate. By containing their disputes and
focusing, instead, on antifascism as a positive, attainable goal, they
could hold together their coalition a little longer.

Yet, the end of the Spanish Civil War rendered their goal immediately unattainable, raising more questions about the nature of front
politics. The Loyalists provided the one bright spot in an increasingly
dark world, "an antidote to the poison . . . in Germany," Josephine
Herbst remembered. The last shreds of progressive idealism were sustained by the Spanish peasants' fight to prove "you cannot hold any
people in slavery." So too was the war the "decisive" issue holding
progressives in check. Once the government fell to Franco, many lost
hope. Some even gave up altogether. Unwilling to concede that the
right side could be defeated, they were anxious to find someone to
blame. Anti-Stalinist tales of a war within a war gained more cur-

rency. Most had very "mixed political feelings" about Spain, the Soviet Union, and their own commitments.[31] When the war in Spain ended, the People's Front against fascism lost its center.

The spring and summer of 1939 were times of "general disheartenment" for progressives. War loomed; Spain was lost; Stalin seemed determined to track down and punish every enemy. Many felt they were simply going through the motions while repressing alarming thoughts. Anna Louise Strong, for example, wrote down all her doubts about the Soviet Union "in words that Krivitsky and Hearst would approve" and then burned the paper. The League of American Writers fell into debt and it, like other fronts, languished for lack of an active membership.[32] A few months before, progressives still had a positive agenda. After Spain, however, it was impossible to feel optimistic about anything, including the continuation of the Front. Progressive apathy hung in the air, largely because the question "what next?" was too horrible to contemplate.

SIX

"Bystanders" and the

"Tit for Tat Front": The Emergence

of Extremism on Either Side of

the Front Barrier, 1939

Both within and outside the People's Front, the more moderate forces went into retreat after 1938. Progressives disengaged and left the fronts more and more to Party intellectuals. Liberals lost their momentum and faltered, fearful of collective security, uncomfortable with anti-Stalinism, and confused by the Front. Anti-Stalinists and intellectual Communists continued to wage war in what William Carlos Williams called the "tit for tat front"[1] without them. Polarization resulted since the willing fighters on either side were angry, determined, and extreme. The first casualty of their fight was the one value liberals and progressives came to cherish more than any other, democracy. By the time of the Nazi-Soviet Pact, there was such intense conflict on the left that force, deception, and outright lies became standard practices. "Intellectual freedom," the rallying cry on either side of the Front barrier, was more an empty promise than anything else.

Progressives and liberals shared a deep commitment to democracy, but it was not enough to unite them in the fractious atmosphere of 1939. One stumbling block to cooperation was their different notions of what democracy was. So long as progressives defined it as the antithesis of fascism and liberals as the antithesis of dictatorship, they did not have very much common ground, because Stalin's Russia figured into their equations differently. Progressives hardly ever called the USSR a democracy, but they accorded it a kind of unofficial democratic status because of its antifascist foreign policy. Liberals considered it a dictatorship, a threat to American democracy rather than a partner. Defending democracy meant collective security to many progressives, whereas most liberals felt avoiding a European war was the only way to preserve American freedoms. Still, the Moscow trials, the spread of fascism, and the fall of Loyalist Spain heightened concern all round that democracy was more fragile than they ever suspected. Liberals and progressives remained far apart in other ways, but they grew closer as their concerns about political freedoms intensified.[2]

Anti-Stalinists and Communists, however, grew further apart. The CPUSA opposed fascism and paid lip service to the ideals of American democracy, but its first allegiance was to the one true socialist country, the USSR, and its leaders. Anti-Stalinists had little to say about fascism,[3] were ambivalent about the outcome of the socialist revolution in Russia, and vociferously critical of its present leadership. Party intellectuals fervently believed in Marxism. Anti-Stalinists were not even sure of their Marxist faith. To American Communists, Stalinism *was* socialism. American Trotskyists were equally comfortable with their position that the USSR could be both Stalinist and socialist, even though one was a natural stage and the other a bureaucracy unnaturally imposed upon it. In either case, their Marxism was reified by the Russian Revolution. Anti-Stalinists did not have such a strong stake in the Revolution; they claimed to be interested in Americanizing Marx, after all. Yet, Marxism really stood or fell for most of them on the Soviet example. With time, most would become disillusioned of both. Their anti-Stalinism slowly gave way to a more general anticommunism.

As so often happened on the dissident left, the reconsideration of the Soviet Union that turned so many anti-Stalinists into anticommunists started with the Trotskyists. The year 1937 was an important one for them. Their schemes to use the SPUSA to counteract the People's Front were a limited success. They could not match the Front in numbers, but they were able to make themselves heard. They had an impact on dissident Marxists. The American Committee for the Defense of Leon Trotsky kept public an issue the CPUSA preferred to bury. The very vehemence with which the party denounced the ACDLT and the fear the Trotsky issue struck in progressives suggested that intellectual Trotskyists had done well for themselves. But all was not well in the Socialist Party, where nonTrotskyists, particularly working-class nonTrots-

150   kyists, resented the direction their organization seemed to take. They disapproved of all the energy poured into the ACDLT, found the Trotskyist position on the Spanish Civil War impossible, and assumed that James P. Cannon and company plotted to take over their party. Everyone saw the split coming, including Trotsky, who directed his followers to leave the organization; but the Socialists acted first and expelled them. Throughout the fall of 1937, American Trotskyists, their numbers swollen by Socialist converts, laid the groundwork for a new political organization, the Socialist Workers Party.[4] In the process, they raised a question about the nature of the Soviet Union that would have a profound effect on anti-Stalinist thought.

As American Trotskyists began to draft their own party platforms, several intellectuals had a crisis of conscience reconciling Trotsky's claim that the Soviet Union was a "workers' state" worthy of defense with the Moscow trials and what they knew of the purges. Joseph Carter and James Burnham argued that the only institution in socialist Russia with any power whatsoever was the Stalinist bureaucracy, "*now functioning solely as a reactionary force*," and on the brink of overtaking the socialist economy. Trotsky's response was dismissive; the Soviet workers' state was like a diseased liver, he explained, unrecognizable because it was bloated by the infection of Stalinism. The remedy for what ailed these intellectuals was not more discussion, but less. They suffered from what Cannon called the "intellectual soul sickness." Trotsky urged Burnham to get away from the claustrophobic circles of New York academe and travel to Mexico to sit at the feet of the master. Burnham preferred to stay in New York, but got the message. He recanted. Still, the new party codified his doubts, accepting his draft of a statement on the USSR which suggested that the Stalinist bureaucracy contained the "elements of a new, i.e. capitalist class." More importantly, despite their best efforts, Trotsky and Cannon could not contain the debate he started. Another group of rebels introduced a resolution at the SWP's founding convention declaring that since "there is no workers' democratic control of the means of production in Russia, . . . there is no workers' state." They were expelled; others were not so easily defeated. A growing network of American Trotskyists quietly discussed the troubling question until there was "a small minority," as Emanuel Geltman recalled, that was "opposed [to the SWP's position on the Soviet Union] but loyal." This small "but influential" group slowly spread ideas that emerged simultaneously elsewhere.[5]

In only a few months the impact was visible. Heretofore, most dissidents assumed that Soviet socialism would eventually overtake Stalinism. The precise opposite, however, appeared to have occurred. One *Modern Monthly* editorial noted that "with startling suddenness the realization has dawned on large sections of the radical and labor movement . . . that the Soviet economy so long regarded as essentially socialist has actually nothing in common with socialism." Trotsky was wrong when he called the Soviet Union merely a degenerated workers' state, V. F. Calverton concluded, "since the [Soviet] workers have no more share in determining the direction of the state than the German workers do in influencing the policies of Hitler's Reich." His comments cut straight to the point: stripped of that one crucial difference, Stalinism and Nazism seemed very much alike. "Authority is monolithic," Philip Rahv noted; "property and politics are one." Consequently, maybe "all these years radicals the world over have been imposed upon, ensnared by an elementary plot of mistaken identity." Calverton too asked, "Can it be that the radical movement has been victimized by a political cant?" If, he reasoned, the USSR had become a "servile state" where everyone worked for Stalin and a dictatorship controlled all power, then what existed was not socialism but "state capitalism."[6]

The implications of this line of argument were significant. Not only was the Stalinist dictatorship destroying the last vestiges of socialism in Russia; it was also deliberately misleading the interested international community on that point. If all this were true, Scott Nearing commented to Calverton, "it needs a lot of rethinking." How could it happen? Many anti-Stalinists conceded that it would have been impossible to destroy the Bolshevik Revolution so quickly had there not been mechanisms and institutions easily abused by Stalin. But to follow out that line of thinking too far was to condemn Lenin and write off the Russian Revolution as a failure. The ground upon which anti-Stalinists were willing to defend the Revolution continually shrank. Once they could no longer assuage their tremendous misgivings about Stalinism by seeing it as a transitory phenomenon, the "shadow" to socialism's "substance" or "a hybrid society, neither capitalist nor socialist," many began to have doubts about Marxism as a doctrine. Logically, we might expect them to declare the Russian Revolution a false revolution and turn their attention elsewhere. They were, after all, interested in Americanizing Marx and strongly opposed to what Calverton called the subjective use of Marx by the two Russian rivals. But they were wholly unable to separate their feelings about the Russian Revolution from their belief in Marxism. So they isolated flaws: Liston Oak blamed the "absolutism" of Marx, Sidney Hook "the underestimation of *democratic processes*," and Calverton the "authoritarianism" of Marxism for allowing Stalin to deflect the Revolution. Despite the different names each gave these weaknesses, what they all found so appalling about Russia was the way in which the dictatorship of the proletariat became, in Ernest Sutherland Bates's phrase, a "'dictatorship over the proletariat.'" While they sat on the other side of the People's Front barrier from progressives, anti-Stalinists were themselves growing more appreciative of democracy and more critical of its absence internationally.[7]

Yet it was not the absence of democracy they saw in Stalinism that rankled anti-Stalinists as much as the intentional falsification of Stalin's aims and his misuse of Marx. And if they could do little to halt Stalinization in Russia, they hoped to do much to stop the process within the American intellectual community. Although they numbered Stalin's crimes in the hundreds, none of them generated as much outrage as the CPUSA's "efforts to stifle independent left-wing expression." The process of Stalinization seemed quickly identifiable and potentially stoppable at home. Weaken the power of the intellectual People's Front, they figured, and you would have weakened the power of American Stalinism. As anti-Stalinists saw it, the Front defined standards and coerced intellectuals to abide by them or suffer the embarrassment of dissent. Using "the tactics of the underworld," it "menac[ed] the intellectual freedom of those left-wing writers who are known to be opposed to the bureaucratic dictatorship in Moscow." More than fifty years after the Front collapsed, Diana Trilling remained convinced that it "was formidable" and that the Stalinist "propaganda network penetrated deep into our society."[8] Anti-Stalinists might not be able to stop the purges, but they might weaken, or even collapse, the intellectual People's Front.

In their eyes, the crusade against the Front was a moral one, but intertwined with their moral outrage were personal and professional issues. This was a fight against the left establishment. Anti-Stalinists fused their philosophical opposition to Stalinism with feelings of betrayal and resentment, literary competitiveness, and personal ambition. They measured morality in personal terms: if the Front failed to value them as creative or critical human beings, it had to be flawed. "No intellectuals of any consequence" actually supported the Party, Calverton claimed, but the intellectual Front's many agencies seemed omnipotent. Terry Cooney has shown that one difference between anti-Stalinists and those who were active in front groups was that the latter signed on at the WPA while anti-Stalinists "resisted . . . the obvious attractions of expanding bureaucracies and secure public jobs" they deemed second-rate and immoral. Perceptions of status, sacrifice, and integrity thus made some feel self-righteous and unjustifiably marginalized as they compared their situations to those of their peers in the Front. Many equated irresponsible or unprincipled politics with unprincipled thought or writing. Good people with honest ideas ought to gain ascendancy in a free intellectual marketplace. But, in reality, gatekeepers like Malcolm Cowley stood guard over the most powerful journals and the most respected organizations, enforcing a political standard that demeaned the critical content of fiction and nonfiction alike. William Phillips later argued that what happened in the 1930s was a lowering of literary standards that enabled the CPUSA to expand its appeal. Political hacks and sentimental journalists gained credence thanks to the Party at the expense of those who better deserved success. Anti-Stalinists often believed they were personally persecuted by the Communists' tactic, both as political actors and intellectuals, and this assumption drove them to expose the evil that was the People's Front.[9]

"I'm gathering some material on the CP attempts to dominate the intellectual world," Suzanne LaFollette told Bertram D. Wolfe in 1939. Wolfe had nothing to provide her, but plenty of other anti-Stalinists had tales, personal examples, and horror stories that circulated through the community and, less frequently, gained an outside audience. Herbert Solow ran through a laundry list of examples in a piece called "Stalin's Spy Scare," which talked about John Dos Passos and the Spanish Civil War, William Carlos Williams and *The New Masses,* Liston Oak and the *Partisan Review.* Solow concluded with a personal experience: "The present writer has repeatedly been warned of dire consequences should he continue telling unpleasant facts about Stalinism." Solow had much worse examples, but he kept those to himself. His deposition on Whittaker Chambers sat in a safe deposit box in New York City. Should anything happen to Chambers, the one-time Party intellectual who claimed to have been a spy for the CPUSA, the deposition was to be given over to Sidney Hook, who could then instigate charges against the Party.[10] Most anti-Stalinists did not venture into the subterranean labyrinth of alleged Party spies, but confined themselves to questions of freedom of expression and access to the media. The difference, however, was more a matter of degree than substance; anti-Stalinists believed that the methods the CPUSA used to control information and access to information were authoritarian, dictatorial, and totalitarian.

As the most prominent symbol of what anti-Stalinists came to regard as cultural Stalinism, the League of American Writers became a popular target. Frances Winwar and Babette Deutsch both submitted their resignations to LAW in 1939, complaining about the one-sidedness of its line. Deutsch criticized its officers' failures to answer her questions about the Moscow trials. Winwar disliked the group's seeming pro-Sovietism. "I do not feel that the Soviet Union has been the most consistent defender of peace," political dissent, or democracy, she noted in her resignation letter, made public to the *Times*.[11] There was worse to come. Standing before the entrance to the third writers' congress, novelist Florence Becker distributed a private manifesto called "Culture Is in Exile." Becker alleged that she was forced to adopt such a tactic because the League leadership would not allow her to raise issues internally. The LAW, already under assault elsewhere, was not inclined to be lenient. She was "called before the credentials committee and told that giving out of these leaflets was a violation of discipline." After she was "terminated" by the larger national board, she tried to enlist the support of others, including Van Wyck Brooks, Edmund Wilson, and Lewis Mumford. Becker's intention was to make as much noise as possible, forcing the kind of confrontation that occurred in order to demonstrate that "your [LAW's] claims to democracy are pretty tenuous."[12] Deutsch, Winwar, and especially Becker acted in typical anti-Stalinist fashion, publicly pushing an agency of the intellectual People's Front until its friendly demeanor gave way to its more aggressively pro-Party core. They wanted to show that the League of American Writers was not the culturally independent group it purported to be, but one that was "Stalinist-controlled."[13]

Sidney Hook was more outraged than Becker by what he perceived as the Front's attempt to claim the rhetoric of intellectual freedom for its own, but he was not content to merely fight the LAW. In December 1937, anthropologist Franz Boas organized a faculty group at Colum-

bia University protesting the manipulation of science for Hitler's ends
in Nazi Germany. The organization called itself the University Federation for Democracy and Intellectual Freedom. In the spring of 1938,
Boas collected signatures on a manifesto attacking a German physi-
cist's denunciation of "Jewish science" that included broader statements about intellectual freedom. By December, he had over a thousand names on the statement. From these beginnings, the American
Committee for Democracy and Intellectual Freedom was founded. It
proclaimed Lincoln's birthday an appropriate moment to celebrate the
free exchange of ideas at home as well as to speak out against the
absence of such freedom in the fascist states. The ACDIF did supremely
well among scientists and social scientists, boasting a membership of
over two thousand. With its resources, it was able to put on an impressive public show. It is hard to assess the ACDIF's place on the left.
In some ways, it operated like a front; but Boas had taken his stand
against the Moscow trials and refused to sign the "400 letter." But to
Hook, one feature of the ACDIF stood out above all others: it "condemn[ed] . . . the German and Italian ideologies but . . . kept silent
about the Communist type." The ACDIF seemed a "Communist Party
front that was . . . successful in concealing its true character,"[14] and
a particularly insidious front since it denied in reality what it proclaimed in its title, intellectual freedom.

In response, Hook "decided to launch a new movement." He
brought together a small group of anti-Stalinists just on the verge of
giving up on Marxism and a few liberals to discuss ways of seizing the
initiative away from the intellectual People's Front. Socialist Frank
Trager, Ferdinand Lundberg, Eugene Lyons, and John Dewey joined
him for meetings during the fall of 1938. Each had been badly burned
by the Front's agencies. Each, therefore, had good reason to scorn "this
massive phenomenon that was corrupting the springs of liberal opinion and indeed making a mockery of common sense." By December,
they had a manifesto, drafted by Lyons, that defined "the least common denominator of principle on which the intellectually honest
could join together." They called themselves the League against Totalitarianism.[15]

Their manifesto challenged the left's traditional political categories
by altering its definition of "totalitarianism." Earlier, all left intellectuals shared a linear political spectrum that identified "socialism"
and "fascism" as polar opposites and "capitalism" somewhere in be-

156   tween. "Totalitarianism" had been their synonym for fascism. As Mary Van Kleeck explained, "historically, the word 'totalitarianism' has been used by the Fascist states to describe their concept, but does not apply to the concept of government in the theory of Communism." In the mass circulation press, however, "totalitarianism" described both fascism and communism, much as "dictatorship" described both forms of social organization to liberals. What the two forms of government shared was total state control. By the late 1930s, the term "totalitarian" was used to describe governments without democracy, with infallible leaders (what liberals called dictators), single-party political monopolies, terrorism, and complete governmental control over all forms of communication and expression. Anti-Stalinists tiptoed carefully around the word, using phrases like "totalitarian trend" rather than directly labeling the USSR totalitarian.[16] But the League against Totalitarianism did just that:

> Under varying labels and colors, but with an unwavering hatred for the free mind, the totalitarian idea is already enthroned in Germany, Italy, *Russia*, Japan and Rebel Spain. There, intellectual and creative independence is suppressed and punished as a form of treason. Art, science and education—all have been forcibly turned into lackeys for a supreme state, a deified leader and an official pseudo-philosophy.[17]

The manifesto took the left's linear conception of politics and bent it into a circle, identifying the point where fascism and communism met as "totalitarianism" and describing its opposite as "democracy." In other words, it directly challenged the Front's raison d'être.

The League further alienated leftist sensibilities by linking front politics to the spread of cultural totalitarianism. Its manifesto spoke of a "panic among intellectuals" which made them

> exalt one brand of intellectual servitude over another, to make fine distinctions between various methods of humiliating the human spirit and outlawing intellectual integrity. Many have already declared a moratorium on reason and creative freedom. Instead of resisting and denouncing all attempts to straitjacket the human mind, they glorify, under deceptive slogans and names, the color or the cut of one straitjacket rather than another.

The "totalitarian idea" that was already "enthroned" in other countries was "all too evident" in the United States. American intellectuals, "infect[ed]" by "energetic agents" and "subsidized propaganda," edged toward authoritarianism and cultural repression, tendencies the League against Totalitarianism intended to resist.[18] The manifesto was a declaration of war against the intellectual People's Front. When the group finally went public in the spring of 1939, though, it was clear that its organizers borrowed ideas from the very fronts they reviled, for its manifesto appeared not as the work of the League against Totalitarianism, but as the Committee for Cultural Freedom's. The name change suggested that Hook and company had quietly absorbed a key lesson of front politics: that words like "freedom" attracted a broader audience than the more politically problematic "totalitarianism."

The CCF was, in fact, the first successful anti-Front front. It marked the convergence of anti-Stalinism and liberalism and the beginning of their joint evolution into liberal anticommunism. It succeeded where the American Committee for the Defense of Leon Trotsky failed, by defining a common ground acceptable to liberals and anti-Stalinists, albeit not all of either group, undisturbed by Trotskyists. Its program was an amalgam of liberal and anti-Stalinist ideas. "Totalitarianism" as the CCF used it was far closer to the liberals' understanding of political categories than the anti-Stalinists'. And its public rhetoric was both affirmative and liberal. Its "positive end[s]" included defending civil liberties and cultural freedom.[19] Dewey envisioned the CCF as an ACLU without front connections. Yet this side of the CCF did not often prevail. The more assertive members were the anti-Stalinists with personal grudges against the Front and a rapidly shifting Marxist perspective. They conceived of the CCF as an aggressive anti-Front agency. As Hook told the New York *Times,* it would challenge such organizations as Boas's, the League of American Writers, and the American League for Peace and Democracy. It became a tool of a few individuals determined to make Front intellectuals pay for their sins.

They took control of the CCF by being more tenacious, more determined, and more extreme than its liberal majority. They constantly undercut liberal attempts to bridge the Front and draw progressives into the kind of pro-democratic agency Archibald MacLeish envisioned. While Hook assured the *Times,* anonymously, that the CCF intended to fight groups like the ACDIF, Dewey simultaneously negotiated with Boas to fuse the two organizations. Presumably suspecting who spoke to the *Times,* Dewey assured Boas that he was "surprised and chagrined" when he saw the story, attempting to smooth over differences. His best efforts at compromise failed. He could neither persuade Hook to back down nor persuade Boas to be forgiving. Boas declared he could not work with Hook. Rather than question Hook's efforts to further rile Boas, Dewey came to doubt that Boas really wanted compromise. In the end, the experience strengthened Hook's position.[20] This pattern repeated itself throughout the spring and summer of 1939. Dewey pursued a program of accommodation designed to detach progressives from the Front. Hook and the other anti-Stalinists made outrageous demands on progressives, alienating them and provoking responses by the CPUSA. Those responses made CCF liberals more anticommunist. By the Nazi-Soviet Pact, they had moved closer to the anti-Stalinists tactically, while the anti-Stalinists, deradicalizing at a rapid rate, were more accepting of some liberal ideas.

Anticommunism also prevailed in the CCF because Hook and the other anti-Stalinists successfully tapped liberals' feelings of helplessness. Fighting the Front became noble; those who fought it were persecuted because of their high moral values and not because they were old-fashioned or their views unpopular. Hook encouraged members to take pride in their supposed torment. He argued that a good reason to sign the CCF manifesto was that "every official group is suspicious about it." While the organization took a beating in the Party press, it was not as besieged as he imagined. According to one scholar of the ACDIF, the CCF's founding had a "rapid and perceptible" negative impact on the former group. The American Jewish Committee slashed its operating grant from $12,250 to $1,400 and could promise no more after that. Certainly the fact that a strongly anti-Stalinist CCF official, Frank Trager, was also an AJC official, probably affected its declining financial prospects. Boas wrote another AJC official that he was concerned about the CCF because "up to this time nobody has accused us of 'red' inclinations."[21] Hook encouraged CCF members to see themselves as the persecuted rather than the persecutors Boas believed them to be. It was a compelling picture.

Yet Hook's views were not indicative of the anti-Stalinist position more generally so much as a portend of things to come. Many anti-Stalinists disliked the CCF. Dwight Macdonald thought it was too much like the organizations it opposed, "one more emotional, witchburning, classless-middle-class outfit like the League for P[eace] & D[emocracy]—but with totalitarianism substituted for fascism as the bogeyman." Many anti-Stalinists complained that it lacked a class analysis and failed to identify socialism as a precondition for real cultural free-

dom. Afraid that others might presume the CCF spoke for them, they
created "still another committee," the League for Cultural Freedom
and Socialism. It shared the CCF's indictment of the People's Front
for "outlaw[ing] all dissenting opinion" in the United States and also
condemned the German, Japanese, Italian, Spanish, and Stalinist re-
gimes for suppressing freedom abroad. But its membership, which
included Calverton, Macdonald, the *Partisan Review*'s editors, and
several intellectual Trotskyists, opposed "that currently fashionable
catchword: 'Neither communism nor fascism.' "[22] In another fifteen
years much of the organization's surviving membership belonged to
the CCF's successor organization, the American Committee for Cultural
Freedom, suggesting that the general direction in which most anti-
Stalinists traveled was toward the anticommunist center and away
from Marxism.

But if many anti-Stalinists were unwilling to embrace the CCF,
some progressives were more receptive, at least to its pro-democratic
agenda. That they were at all willing to consider the organization with
open minds showed how far they diverged from their Party allies.
What their Front partners considered an insidious threat to left harmony, they sometimes accepted at face value. A few could not honestly discern any difference between the CCF's aims and the Front's.
After reading a copy of its manifesto, Sherwood Anderson saw nothing
more than "a simple declaration in favor of cultural freedom." "My intention was solely to aid freedom of speech and a general defense of
civil liberties," William Carlos Williams explained after signing the
statement. When a Party member suggested that the group had other
motives, he was sincerely puzzled: "There surely was nothing in the
letter I saw to suggest an attack [on the Front]."[23] Communists and
their closer progressive friends read something in the document that
those who leaned more toward the center did not. Neither was wrong;
the document expressed both points of view. The Party interpretation
prevailed within the Front, but that should not obscure the willingness expressed within more moderate Front circles to consider an alliance with liberals in the name of democracy, individual freedom,
and cultural autonomy. The CCF represented the last slim chance for
compromise.

The moment passed, unrealized, because, inside and outside the
CCF, forces struggled to assert and respond to the manifesto's other
message. Party intellectuals played up Hook's comments about the

160   organization's anti-Front perspective so that it might be dismissed as a "Trotskyist trap." Hook blasted the *Times* reporter for including in an article his (Hook's) opinion that the CCF would go after fronts, insisting that he made clear those were his "personal views," which should have been "kept off the record." His commentary was just as much a propaganda effort as the CP's description of the CCF as "Trotskyist." Although he believed in "cultural freedom" and defeating "totalitarianism in all its forms," as he suggested to prospective members, Hook really only wanted to attack the Front. Progressives might have been confused by the specifics, but they got the gist of this battle of words. Despite Dewey's best efforts, most quickly recognized that the CCF intended "to separate the sheep from the goats," which, in progressive terms, meant threatening antifascism's already shaky alliance. The more the Party and its friends played up this theme, the more progressives leaning toward the CCF saw something new and sinister there. Williams, for example, suddenly noticed "that the League [CCF] was being seized by a group for purposes rather subversive to its published intentions." Whether or not he actually believed that, like other progressives he lived in "a world of realities and not absolutes," where fascism threatened democracy.[24] If fascism could only be defeated by uniting various left-wing forces, then the CCF, whatever its rhetoric, threatened that unity and, therefore, democracy.

Even though progressives nominally accepted the Party's verdict on the CCF, their response to it was feeble and ineffective. Most had little to say about the group; many, like Williams, could neither remember its name nor the content of its missives. When they did comment publicly on it, they often used the opportunity to further distance themselves from the CPUSA and its "Writers Congress creed." Freda Kirchwey's *Nation* editorial, for example, devoted nearly as much space to the CPUSA as the CCF, and most of what she said was unflattering:

> The Communist Party is a nuisance or a menace to all its opponents. Whatever its line may be, its tactics are invariably provocative and often destructive. Not only do Communists try to inject partisan ideas into the program of most organizations in which they are active; not only do they fight ruthlessly and tenaciously to make those ideas prevail; they also have been guilty, in many known instances, of using against their enemies methods of attack that were both unscrupulous and callous.

"Stand for freedom throughout the world, by all means," *The New Republic* urged the CCF, and "speak out strongly against violations of civil liberties in Soviet Russia as well as every other country." Progressives were not anxious to support the CCF because they thought it "honest but not innocent,"[25] but neither were most overtly hostile toward it.

Since progressives were not willing to take the lead in a campaign against the CCF, Communists were forced to launch their own attack. In many ways their initial assaults were more pitched at progressive sensibilities than anything else. They even conceded that their allies were welcome to have "reservations . . . about Communism or the Soviet Union" so long as they ultimately recognized that the CCF hurt antifascist unity. Correctly reading their partners' willingness to accord the organization sincere, if misguided, motives, they briefly assumed that they might be able to detach—or at least appear willing to detach—its well-meaning majority from its fanatical minority. Only a handful of members, they asserted, some fifteen with disruptive histories, supported the goal Hook too candidly admitted to the *Times*. The rest "must certainly be unaware of the real purpose of the committee" and were likely more shocked than Dewey when they opened their morning papers. "A good many of the 96 signers of Dr. Hook's manifesto have publicly expressed their indignation at his tricky maneuvers," the Hollywood monthly *Direction* asserted, "and some of them have already resigned from his committee." But no one did resign and Party intellectuals became less polite, remembering that membership disputes within the ACDLT had gone a long way toward undermining its credibility. Unable to produce resignations, they engineered one. Someone, later no one was sure who, told Columbia University professor David Muzzey that the CCF and the ACDIF had merged and he gave them a letter of resignation to help transfer his membership "from one to the other." Party members at Columbia University and League of American Writers secretary Franklin Folsom then used his letter to try to induce others to resign, omitting the part about a merger. As a tactic, it was supremely unsuccessful; only two more people resigned. When Muzzey returned and discovered how he had been used, he quickly contacted the CCF and its next *Bulletin* carried his story under the headline "A Plain Fraud." Hook could then fairly claim that the CPUSA played a "disruptive role . . . behind the scenes."[26] Communists within the Front and anti-Stalinists within the CCF thus both gained the upper hand, playing off one another's actions in an ever-escalating campaign that left those in the middle puzzled, confused, and uncertain.

A similar polarization of forces manifested itself in the ACLU with

162   disastrous results. There too the term *totalitarianism* became the springboard for a larger fight over the legitimacy of certain tactics and behaviors. Early in 1939, liberal lawyer Morris Ernst proposed that the Union's board of directors approve a statement condemning "all totalitarian governments—Fascist, Nazi, or Communist—as the antithesis of civil liberties." John Finerty, a veteran of the ACDLT's Commission of Inquiry, and Elmer Rice, whose opposition to communism dated to the early 1930s, mustered the votes necessary to adopt the proposal, which then moved to the national committee. There, after four hours of heated discussion, it was defeated. Ernst, Rice, and Finerty, meanwhile, used the new statement of principles, which at that stage had been endorsed by the board of directors but not yet defeated by the national committee, as reason to revise a 1937 pamphlet, "Should We Defend Free Speech for Nazis in America?" Although there was little actual difference between the old and new pamphlets, the title, "Why We Defend Free Speech for Nazis, Fascists, and Communists," implied that all were "totalitarian." Immediately after the board of directors changed the pamphlet title, the national committee voted "not to adopt any formal statement in opposition to any particular theory or form of government." Progressives Mary Van Kleeck, Robert Dunn, and Corliss Lamont then argued that the pamphlet should be changed as well, but it never was. Various anti-totalitarian statements circulated among ACLU liberals for months thereafter, and Lamont, Van Kleeck, and Dunn fought with Rice, Ernst, and Finerty. Only three months after the debate began, the organization was so badly divided that Roger Baldwin suspected the only solution was "the resignation of the entire Board and its reconstitution as a harmonious working unit."[27] As one of the few organizations informally straddling the Front divide, the ACLU approached a virtual impasse based on its board members' increasingly divergent attitudes about communism.

The incident confirmed suspicions both ACLU factions harbored about the other and, like the CCF controversy, strengthened the more extremist forces. Anticommunists plotted to advance their concerns. Well aware that the whole matter was likely to be controversial, they introduced the statement at an unusually small board meeting and struck with the pamphlet change before the resolution had worked its way through appropriate channels. When the antitotalitarianism statement came before the national committee, moreover, they hushed up debate, anticipating trouble. "These minutes are not to be given out," read the copies of the statement sent to board members. They also benefited from Baldwin's unwitting connivance. He recalled that for harmony's sake, he picked agenda items according to who would attend each meeting, making it possible for anticommunists to manage a majority. On the other side of the barricades, the pro-Front ACLU faction resorted to familiar belittling rhetoric to advance its position. Van Kleeck accused Rice of employing "fascist-like" tactics to get the resolution passed and then unfairly resuscitating it through the pamphlet title. "You know all too well how Nazism came in Germany," she slyly commented. Rice responded with fury, insisting that "intelligent adults" ought to be able to discuss differences of opinion "without recourse to personal abuse." Compromise, in the form of a milder statement by Arthur Garfield Hays, did not satisfy either side, and Rice told him that if he could not be "clear-cut . . . it would be better not to make any [statement]." By the time the CCF made public its manifesto, the ACLU was already polarized and had "no real possibility of constructive progress" for the foreseeable future.[28]

Extremists like Hook and Folsom or Rice and Van Kleeck gained the upper hand in these controversies because they had clearly formulated agendas and felt strongly about the issues involved. Many liberals and progressives hesitated, unsure of where they stood on such matters or unconvinced of their ultimate importance. They were, in Van Kleeck's word, "bystanders"[29] who watched helplessly as the fighting escalated around them. Yet many such bystanders eventually became engaged because of the more extremist positions advanced by champions of the People's Front and their anti-Stalinist opponents. Hook, for example, simplified the Communists' tasks by making ill-timed and unfortunate remarks about the League of American Writers just as Van Kleeck's personal remarks suggested to Rice that she used character assassination because her arguments had no validity. Representatives of both sides could legitimately call the other undemocratic at some points. This left wavering liberals and progressives uncomfortable but unwilling to renounce their long-standing positions. Once extremists were able to establish even minimal credibility for their actions, liberals would never again be quite so forceful in their defense of free speech for Communists and progressives would never again be quite so comfortable about public denunciations of the Soviet Union. The changing nature of the People's Front facilitated the construction of a more extreme anti-Front ideology just as the increasing intensity of anti-Stalinist rhetoric forced the Communists to take the fronts more in hand.

SEVEN

"A Pretty Pickle":

The Nazi-Soviet Pact and the Breakup

of the Intellectual People's Front,

1939–1940

By the summer of 1939, the coalition between progressives and the CPUSA hung by a single antifascist thread. Progressives did not want to be associated with the Communists in any significant way. Communist intellectuals were no happier than their allies. They feared that the situation was about to slip from their control, if it had not already. Could they continue to hold progressives in check, simultaneously fight anti-Stalinists, and survive against a public wary of "totalitarianism"? Much to the anti-Stalinists' extreme frustration, the answer was yes. If the Front wavered, it did not completely fall apart. So long as antifascism united progressives and their Party allies, some semblance, however imperfect either partner considered it, of front politics existed. But in August of 1939 an outside force, the Nazi-Soviet Pact, undermined the People's Front, leaving both progressives and Party intellectuals to redefine their tactics, strategies, and goals.

Progressives clearly never suspected that Stalin and Hitler would sign a mutual nonaggression pact. Although they believed war was imminent, they assumed it would pit Stalin and Hitler against one another. When the first news of the Pact came, they were utterly and absolutely shaken. Many recalled exactly where they were when they heard the news, just as they would a few years later when the Japanese attacked Pearl Harbor. Matthew Josephson and Roger Baldwin were both at Martha's Vineyard that August and heard someone suggest that a pact was in the works. Both dismissed the idea as impossible. Whatever their flaws, Baldwin believed, the Communists "could at least be relied upon to be anti-fascist." When word came that the treaty had indeed been signed, it was "the biggest shock of my life. I was never so shaken up by anything," he recalled. Josephson was "stunn[ed]." Many took the news very personally. Josephson, for example, complained that "Stalin never considered how people like me would feel," while Malcolm Cowley feared he had been "thrown overboard" by the Communists.[1] The Pact stopped the Front's coalition in its tracks.

American Communists were just as stupefied as progressives, which hardly reassured their partners. Despite their supposed inside connections with the Kremlin, Party leaders knew nothing of an impending pact. For twenty-four hours *The Daily Worker* had no comment as those who might have offered wisdom struggled to assimilate the news. Afterwards, it was obvious that the Party improvised its responses, initially trying to do the impossible and explain the Pact in antifascist terms. Party intellectuals denied that it signaled any cooperation between the Soviet Union and Hitler's Germany. Rather, they promised, it was a ruse or some brilliant antifascist stratagem about to unfold. Long trained to have faith in their leaders, American Communists waited, at least publicly confident that all would be revealed, for, as A. B. Magil said, it was "just as impossible for the USSR to pursue a reactionary policy in any field as it is for a fascist government to pursue a progressive policy."[2]

Failing to find an antifascist vocabulary to explain the Pact, Communist interpreters described it as "a *pact* for peace," an ironic conclusion considering the scorn Communists had for "Umbrella Face" and the whole Munich episode. Yet they were not willing to concede what others suggested, that the Nazi-Soviet Pact was "Stalin's Munich," as *The New Republic* called it, since it "was offered with an utterly different motive." It would provide real peace, not appeasement. Communists had "no evidence that could satisfy a six-year-old," but believed this nonetheless. "Hitler won't attack," Anna Louise Strong assured Eleanor Roosevelt a few days after it was signed. Such a view left her hopelessly unprepared for what was about to happen. "It continues to look more and more like peace, doesn't it?" she asked her correspondent a few days later.[3] Roosevelt did not think so, but certainly Communists did. Their public line was as relentlessly optimistic about the meaning of the Pact as it had been about the meaning of the Moscow trials.

The progressive press was no more inclined to buy this cheery version of the Pact than the trials. *The New Republic* allowed that Stalin "had good superficial reasons" for signing the treaty, but refused to believe it would work out any better than the Munich accord had. The editors scoffed at the CPUSA's attempts to glorify what was essentially a matter of Realpolitik; "we take a little unholy delight," they confessed, "in their [the Party's] present discomfort." *The Nation* was somewhat more sympathetic, but not much. Its editors decided to wait and see what happened rather than second-guess Stalin. All progressives, however, immediately recognized that the Pact seriously undermined the antifascist status quo. "Her [Russia's] proudest boast was the clear and simple line of her foreign policy," *The New Republic* explained; ". . . it has now been lost." "It is hard to say which was worse," Lewis Mumford wrote in his diary, "the agreement itself or the apologies that were made for it by the Communist[s]."[4]

Many people, including some Communists, shared his opinion that the CPUSA behaved shamelessly. As always, Party rhetoric covered up very human doubts by members about the unfolding policy emanating from Moscow. "Anything may happen now," Joseph Freeman warned Robert Gessner. The problem was, everything and nothing did. Events moved forward, but the organization stalled. "Leadership," Richard Rovere noted, "is not coming from the party." Even at the highest levels, he complained, there were "decisions and indecisions," and those "serve only to undermine the confidence of party members themselves." Granville Hicks agreed:

> The leaders of the Communist Party have tried to appear omniscient, and they have succeeded in being ridiculous. They have clutched at straws, juggled sophistries, shut their eyes to facts. Their predictions have almost uniformly been proved wrong within twenty-four hours. They have shown that they are strong in faith—which the future may or may not justify—and weak in intelligence.

It was hardly surprising that Rovere and Hicks and others like them could not find a reasonable explanation for the Pact or a leader willing to give them one. Browder himself was confused by the treaty. But he did not say so in public and he and his lieutenants spoke confidently only to backtrack later. Their stalwart positions merely compounded the negative impact of the Nazi-Soviet Pact by revealing that at the highest levels Party policy depended on external factors, factors over which neither Browder nor any other American had much control.[5]

The CPUSA finally sorted out its response to the Nazi-Soviet Pact more than a month after the accord was signed. In late September and early October, Browder received two messages from Moscow on his shortwave radio set. The Comintern designated antifascism outmoded as a strategy. The war in Europe pushed the Western capitalist democracies "into a phase of most acute and profound crisis." Communists' duties were to defeat capitalism and to stay out of war. Under such circumstances, the "United Front and the People's Front lose significance." "The time to stop Hitler, to fight Fascism and Nazism by gathering democratic nations into a popular front against totalitarian aggressors," *Black and White,* a Hollywood monthly closely associated with the Party, declared, "was *before Munich.*" The Party's new policy was anti-Front, anti-capitalist, and anti-war.[6]

The so-called "Yanks Aren't Coming" period of American Communism marked the return of some older Party positions, like opposition to war, and the rejection of its more recent antifascist and, to an extent, pro-New Deal policies. While Party intellectuals sounded like America Firsters with their isolationist rhetoric, the new line was consistent with their desire to protect the achievements of the Bolshevik Revolution. Still, they were mindful of the relationship between their new line and their old one. Browder explained that "what we have to deal with is an imperialist war in which the rulers of both sides are equally guilty; it is not a war waged for the destruction of fascism, but is carried on to extend and perpetuate imperialist control over the world. The character of this war in no principal respect can be said to differ from that of the late world war." As for American involvement in such a war, Michael Gold was adamant that the only beneficiaries would be bankers and industrialists. Civil liberties would suffer and the advances gained by organized labor during the 1930s would be lost.[7] Over time, the Party's position would become more extreme and would give way to a more pervasive antiliberalism that made Franklin Roosevelt once again an enemy. The new CPUSA line was not popular with very many Americans.

The Party's version of the Red Army's invasion of Poland was especially strained, providing the intellectuals who were to publicize it with little raw material upon which to build a sustained defense. *Black and White* conceded that Russia was "seemingly violating a state with which she was not at war," but then insisted that matters were not as they appeared. The Poles had taken land from the Soviets at the end of World War I; the Polish government was reactionary, not democratic. What the Russians did might be justified solely by the past, such editorials implied, but the Soviets had nothing but good intentions when they marched westward. Certainly Anna Louise Strong believed that "the reception given the Red Army by the East Poland population . . . differs from Hitler's brutal invasion and from Chamberlain's cynical abandonment of the Poles." With the Nazis invading Poland from the west, the Russians did the Poles a favor. "Millions of people are sleeping better nights and having fewer cold sweats about their future now that the mighty Red Army is guarding a third of Poland's people against destruction by fascism," poet Bob Brown reported. Indeed, "she [Russia] saved millions of Poles from being bombed, shelled, bayoneted and machine-gunned by Nazi generals." The Poles, *New Masses* confirmed, were "not confused" by what happened because they did not read "American commercial papers." They "seem to know when they are well off."[8] The notion that Stalin helped Poland by invading and occupying it was so patently outrageous that it inflamed rather than placated intellectuals.

Soviet actions in Poland accelerated the Soviets' downward public relations trend. In July, progressives could imagine no scenario that would put Stalin and Hitler on the same side of an issue. In September, they cast aside their initial hesitations and concluded that the Pact represented a deliberate and long-term policy change. By November, they considered Soviet foreign policy "communist imperialism," or even, Vincent Sheean suggested, "fascist." What Stalin had done, *The New Republic* concluded, was demonstrate that its role in an international antifascist coalition was "insincere propaganda." Once they cracked "the mystery of Moscow," progressives found little reason to celebrate.[9]

Even within the Party, the Polish news took its toll. Several Party intellectuals resigned. Most were the neophytes, Front-period recruits whose sense of what the organization was like was based on the antifascist coalition. When the policy changed so quickly and so cynically, they felt betrayed. This was not how they pictured radical politics. Unable to reconcile what happened with what they expected, several left. The organization's most publicized post-1935 intellectual recruit,

Granville Hicks, was also its most publicized post-Pact dropout. Although Kyle Crichton, Robert Minor, Joseph Lash, Samuel Sillen, and Earl Browder talked to him about the Pact, he resigned anyway. His choice made Richard Rovere reevaluate, because he was "the most loyal communist I know." "I cannot follow the Communist Party toward what I think is suicide," he told a comrade at *The New Masses*. Robert Gorham Davis, another of Hicks's close friends, almost left the Party, changed his mind, and then changed it again and quit. Only a few left the Party after Poland, but the Hicks defection alone, explained to the press, added to the CPUSA's woes.[10]

As the Party changed its line, justifying the Pact and the Red Army's march into Poland, fronts forged on the commonality of antifascism suddenly became potentially superfluous. In the League of American Writers, the organization did not know what to do, but the Communists stood firm while progressives were more likely to see indecision as a repudiation of antifascism and bolt. So many of the figurehead officers resigned that the League had to print new letterhead without any names on it. Honorary president Thomas Mann departed, as did vice-presidents Van Wyck Brooks and Archibald MacLeish. Those who quit made clear that the Communist presence shaped their decisions. Mann condemned the League for too closely following Soviet policy without regard for its members' feelings. Oliver LaFarge did not resign but complained of "the violent series of reversals and somersaults recently performed by the American Communist Party." Where, he demanded of Franklin Folsom, did the LAW stand on this matter?[11]

LaFarge was not alone in wanting to know. Progressives hoped for reassurance that they could still trust the LAW, but most suspected they would not receive it. Vincent Sheean warned Folsom that "intellectuals will not feel in a mood of approval toward the present foreign policy of the Soviet Union or toward the developments that may be expected in the immediate future." The League had to work around that attitude, but also the Communist minority's increasingly intransigent antiwar stance. When the executive council finally drafted a policy statement concerning the Second World War, "unity among writers" rather than reacting to "rapid moves and countermoves in the international arena" was its main concern. So the organization's policy remained no policy at all, although the statement assured members that the League was both antiwar and antifascist.[12] In the autumn of 1939, neither partner was yet willing to abandon the fronts. But holding together a coalition half committed to antifascism and half to Soviet foreign policy was not easy.

The Soviet invasion of Finland altered both the progressive and Party strategies. Poland was hard enough for progressives to accept; Finland was beyond the pale. Progressive reaction to Finland was sharp, sure, and negative. This was a clear example "of calculated and unprovoked aggression by a large power against a small neighbor," *The New Republic* declared. Frederick Schuman thought there was no "shadow of justification, legal, ethical or political" for Stalin's action. "No conqueror ever had a worse press than Stalin has today," Freda Kirchwey noted. Even Anna Louise Strong had to agree that Finland offered "the worst case against the Soviets."[13] Progressives were primed to find the Soviet invasion of Finland an outrage. If the CPUSA wanted to win back their sympathies or even just maintain unity within the fronts, it would have to produce a morally sound interpretation of Stalin's actions.

Yet, with even less basis for an antifascist interpretation and less inclination to provide one, the Party was completely unyielding over "brave little Finland." *Soviet Russia Today* and *The New Masses* implied the Finns were both fascist and aggressive with little success. It was almost impossible to make people cheer for a Goliath who attacked David, even though both journals carefully omitted mention of the Soviets crossing the border unprovoked. Party apologists expended less ink explaining the invasion than mounting a campaign against the press. They insisted reports coming out of the country were biased so as to create sympathy for what Lillian Hellman called "that fine, lovable little Republic of Finland that everyone gets so weepy about."[14] This Party diversion practically guaranteed that one side or the other within the fronts would have to give.

The Party's Finnish story did not even satisfy all of the remaining comrades. Ralph Bates, Spanish Civil War hero and an effective Party speaker, announced in December 1939 that he was "getting off the train" on account of the "disaster in Finland." He also argued that it was high time progressives reevaluated their front activities. "All sympathizers with the Soviet Union, from the Left to the Center, have until recently thought that the defense of the Soviet Union was a defense of their own political principles." But their aims were no longer consistent with the Soviets' and the CPUSA should not be trusted any longer. "The Communist Parties all too frequently sought to use Popular Front

organizations for party aggrandizement," he warned. Intellectuals
ought to beware.[15]

Many LAW progressives heeded his warning. "The [only] question in my mind," LaFarge commented, "is whether or not the League is strongly influenced either directly by the Communist Party, or indirectly by a reluctance to offend the Communist Party." Either circumstance made him unhappy. Kenneth Fearing told the organization to stop playing "fast-and-loose" with its principles. Horace Gregory thanked the League for "the opportunity to keep my name off [its statement regarding the war] and my conscience clear." Albert Halper suggested that the League "should fold up and call it a day" rather than continue to sling "all this cultural bolony [sic]." There were so many protests that the organization devised a form letter of acknowledgment. Three League branches, in Washington, Connecticut, and Chicago, closed. Although the executive council twice extended the deadline for endorsement, nearly two months after the noncommittal policy statement first circulated slightly more than half of the membership still had not responded. It was adopted only on a bureaucratic technicality; the majority of those who expressed an opinion favored it.[16] Passivity was one way progressives could register their displeasure with an organization many had already written off as Communist-controlled.

Indeed, after the invasion of Finland, Party intellectuals were less inclined to humor progressives than to pursue their own antiwar policy. Unconstrained by front etiquette, they used their bureaucratic superiority to promote the Party line. Even as the LAW applied for a bank loan to compensate for missing progressive dues, Folsom wanted to publish an antiwar round robin, and "the more developed writers" on the executive board created the Keep America Out of War Committee. Although it had no official status, its partisans acted as though it did, appearing before the executive board to ask for a clearer policy on the war and for a greater commitment to its programs. They demanded and got League backing for public antiwar meetings in several cities. Philip Dunn defended the possibility of U.S. support for the Allies at one meeting, "to a running commentary of jeers, boos and hisses." He debated Carey McWilliams, Dalton Trumbo, and Theodore Dreiser, all antiwar, which hardly made the forum balanced. Such actions deeply troubled progressives. Newton Arvin thought that the League had become "cynically indifferent to the rudimentary principles of democracy within its own ranks." In response to his complaint, he doubtless got one of the LAW's form letters assuring him that "it is the essence of a democratic organization that people speak their minds, [but] that they accept the majority opinion on the basis of free discussion" afterwards. Yet there was little evidence that the League operated on a majority basis; rather, its Communists pursued their own aims and were, as Malcolm Cowley complained, "willing to destroy the united front organizations they founded rather than lose control of them."[17]

The earliest fights for post-Pact control over the League occurred in the local organizations. The Northern California branch never had the quorum necessary to discuss the new statement of aims, so it did not bother to go through the official process of endorsement. Two members (Elsa Gitlow and Hans Otto Storm) protested and threatened to withhold their dues until the matter was duly discussed and officially voted in. Their comrades finally gave them two alternatives, "stand by it [the new statement] or resign." The minutes do not record which they chose, but they got a courtesy discussion well after the statement was national policy.[18] In Hollywood, another two members waged their own war against the antiwar trend. Novelist Irving Stone proposed amending the local bylaws to counteract the Party's bureaucratic control by forcing a full membership vote on all international policy issues. When that was "voted down by [a] large majority," he and other board members argued until 1:30 A.M., at which time he resigned his position as "a one-man guard against communistic influence." A few weeks later, screenwriter Sheridan Gibney proposed a resolution "condemning Russian aggression against Finland." He was immediately replaced by Donald Ogden Stewart as chair of the Hollywood chapter.[19] Party strength in the local LAW affiliates enabled a minority within the organization to squash dissent, but progressives did not go down without a fight.

At the national level, the fight between Communists and progressives over changing League policy was much closer. Progressives warned that making the League antiwar "might antagonize some of the more liberal elements." A few years before, the Party fraction would have taken that concern seriously; in 1940, however, the People's Front was only a memory. They pushed on, relentlessly. The Keep America Out of War Committee demanded a more "explicit" antiwar statement. In the spring of 1940, a subcommittee produced a draft, which divided the executive committee with its "complete denuncia-

tion of help for the allies." The committee, "most of them Communists," appointed another subcommittee, which produced another
antiwar statement. By this time, the Nazis marched on France, giving
progressives a new ideological weapon. Samuel Grafton introduced an
amendment tempering the antiwar line with a declaration of support
for American defense "against foreign invaders." The amendment
passed by one vote; the Party contingent then slightly altered the language to weaken it. Three weeks later, though, the full force of collective security hit the executive committee in the form of another
amendment, by Oliver LaFarge, that "reaffirm[ed] *established* policy . . . to urge aid to those who are battling against the Fascist powers."
Folsom and company staved off an immediate vote in order to gather
their forces and collect absentee ballots, an unusual procedure. In the
end, progressives lost; but it was the absentee votes that turned the
tide. Suspecting, like Irving Stone, that the larger membership was
more antifascist than antiwar, Marjorie Fischer moved that the statement and the LaFarge amendment be put to a full LAW vote. That was
defeated as well. Thoroughly disgusted, the remaining progressive officers finally admitted defeat, resigned, and turned over the League to
the Communists and their friends.[20]

Those who left in the spring and summer of 1940 insisted they were
driven from the organization by an undemocratic Communist minority. The Communists twice violated their trust; once by reneging on
the anti-fascist front and a second time by manipulating the League
bureaucracy. Nora Benjamin "felt badly" about resigning, but had to
because "my heart does not belong to Daddy Stalin." LaFarge complained he was "forced" out by policy "not freely and democratically
determined" but "subservient to . . . a single political party." Malcolm
Cowley noticed that almost half the executive committee quit between
the time of the Pact and the antiwar statement. "No policy," he concluded, "should have been adopted that would lead so many active
members to resign."[21] The Communists and their allies, however, no
longer cared what Cowley, or any other progressive, thought. They
wanted to convert the League of American Writers from an antifascist
agency to an antiwar one, and were prepared to do whatever it took to
make it consistent with the new Party line.

At the same time, they also wanted to maintain the illusion that the
League was something different. Strapped for cash, they went ahead
with their plans for *Bulletins* and forums nonetheless, pretending to be

174   the shining League of 1937. Most intellectuals knew otherwise. The
Fourth Congress of American Writers, held in 1941, was "a rather sad
affair." Looking over the list of its sponsors, Kenneth Rexroth was
struck by "how many signers of former similar manifestos were missing, and why they were missing." Agnes Smedley heard that Edgar
Snow was to be the main speaker until the LAW hierarchy examined his
speech "in support of Roosevelt" and took him off the program. John
Dos Passos listened to parts of the Congress on the radio, laughing at
the juxtaposition of Rockwell Kent's antiwar speech and news of the
Nazi invasion of Russia. "Well, he'll get different orders tomorrow
from his bosses," he predicted.[22] Even Folsom had to concede that life
in the League was much easier before the Pact, but he was full of
excuses for the decline. "Over three-quarters of the membership has
steadfastly maintained its anti-war position," he insisted, and many of
those resigned because they could no longer continue to call themselves writers. Folsom blamed WPA cuts and the political climate for
decreasing the League's effectiveness. What he failed to note was that
members remained on the rolls for years, whether or not they paid
dues or participated at all. Even his figures suggest that there was a 25
percent membership turnover after the Pact; the turnover of active
members was undoubtedly higher. The carryover of sponsors from the
third to the fourth congress was only 24 percent and twelve of sixteen
officers elected in 1939 had resigned by mid-1940.[23] Intellectual Communists hoped the LAW would retain enough of its past aura to be as
prestigious as the front it once was, but it was more important to them
that it be a pliant pro-Party, antiwar organization.

What happened to the League of American Writers happened to
other fronts as well. In organization after organization, the minority
Communist fraction prevailed over the progressive majority through a
combination of bureaucratic cunning and progressive disengagement.
In the Motion Picture Democratic Committee, Communists and their
allies passed a quick statement of neutrality much like the LAW's first
wait-and-see statement about the war. Progressives condemned the
close vote and countered with a resolution supporting Franklin Roosevelt, "to define our split of purpose and opinion with the Communist
Party—since we can get no place until we do state this split." The
resolution was defeated; still, the board agreed to take the matter to the
membership directly. But Hollywood was filled with Communists and
their comrades and the motion was soundly defeated. Thereafter, pro-

gressives withdrew from the MPDC, leaving it to those forces more closely allied with the CPUSA.[24]

The American Committee for Democracy and Intellectual Freedom was more independent of Party connections than most other front-type organizations, but equally susceptible to struggles of an antiwar nature. Its small pro-Soviet fraction presented it with an antiwar petition in November 1939. Both its governing councils divided over whether or not to endorse the statement. Finally, because of the closeness of the votes, its officers decided to circulate their own open letter promoting both "freedom of discussion" and the kinds of measures antiwar activists regarded as necessary protections of minority opinion. This was, in short, an antiwar statement without direct mention of the fact. The measure weakened the ACDIF's prestige among the larger scientific and social scientific academic community. It retained a core of dedicated members, but was never again able to produce a national event like its 1939 celebration of Lincoln's Birthday.[25]

In the American Student Union, the changing Party line also spelled disaster. Initially Communist and progressive factions agreed to take no position on the Pact. Soon, however, Communists disregarded that policy and promoted U.S. isolationism. On Armistice Day, ASU head Joseph Lash sent Roosevelt a letter urging Hitler's defeat, since this was established Union policy. Communist members organized antiwar protests and denounced Lash. After the Soviet invasion of Finland, tensions increased as the organization prepared for its annual convention. Two sets of position papers circulated before the meeting, one Communist and the other not. The authors of the progressive statement, Lash, Molly Yard, and Agnes Reynolds, expressed their concern that a majority decision would not prevail at the convention since "increasingly good ASU'ers have dropped into inactivity because of actions and policies" taken by the Communists. The Communists did lots of organizing; progressives disengaged; and when the convention met in late December 1939, the Communists were easily able to defeat a resolution condemning the Soviet action. Thereafter, chapters disaffiliated or ceased to exist and two-thirds of the ASU membership dropped by the wayside. In his study of the organization, Robert Cohen contended that the Party faction "brazenly violated democratic process within the ASU" to achieve its goals. The process, he suggested, had a dramatic impact on the way nonCommunists perceived Communism.[26]

In the American League for Peace and Democracy progressives

176   tried, but quickly failed, to halt assimilation of the Communist change
of line. Like other fronts, the group's first response was to "neither
condemn nor approve the actions of the Soviet Union." Roger Baldwin, at least, thought this resolution "by implication gives it [the Pact]
approval" so as "to not offend our Communist constituency." Feeling
they had lost the first round, progressives reasserted themselves in
September with a resolution condemning the Pact and the Russian
invasion of Poland. This motion was defeated fourteen to one by the
board. ALPD head Harry F. Ward later explained to the Dies committee
that the Communists were able to triumph despite their minority status (he estimated that Communists were only 12 percent of the organization's membership) "through sheer ability and willingness to do the
'Jimmy Higgins' work." Whether or not Party members earned the
right to dominate the American League, Baldwin thought the invasion
of Poland constituted "an act of aggression" to which the group ought
to react. When it did not, he resigned, suggesting that "the cleavage
[between progressives and Communists] is so profound . . . that no
reconciliation is possible." It was only after the Soviet invasion of
Finland that the ALPD passed any kind of response to the war, a resolution favoring an arms embargo against the USSR with the proviso that
Stalin's actions were not as aggressive as Hitler's. This "satisfied nobody"; remaining progressives resigned, and before long the American
League for Peace and Democracy ceased to exist. A new, smaller, less
prestigious, but more easily shaped front, the American Peace Mobilization, took its place.[27]

In both the ASU and the ALPD, the situation was complicated by
investigations conducted by the Dies committee. Lash suspected that
the Communists schemed to dominate the ASU, but was afraid that
making public accusations would alienate the remaining noncommunists in the organization. So too did he fear that any "open break with
[the] ycl [Young Communist League] . . . plays into [the] hands of [the]
dies committee." Having so long denied Communist control, Lash recognized that to reverse himself at this late date would make his life
more miserable than the Communists'.[28] Ward was more candid before
Dies; his testimony did not help the ALPD any and certainly made his
life more miserable than it otherwise would have been. He admitted
that the ALPD was partially funded by the CPUSA. He also conceded that
the Party influenced the group to the extent that "we were . . . prevented from taking any position in opposition to Communist policy,

for they would have withdrawn and thus wrecked the united front," a statement consistent with front politics that sounded unusually sinister in the fall of 1939. As a result of this public drama, liberals and socialists on the ACLU's board of directors pressed for his resignation as their chair, arguing he "completely discredited" the ALPD.[29] For Ward and Lash, front leadership carried penalties that only became obvious after the Pact. Yet neither felt very comfortable contributing to the post-Pact red scare. Ward stood by the fronts as they became more overtly Party entities. Lash, on the other hand, joined those who hoped to find another way of political engagement, separate from both Dies and the Communists.

Many progressives did not give up on front politics so much as on their Communist partners, at least temporarily. They hoped to re-create the Front's forward momentum without relying on the CPUSA. They wanted "a new organization, mainly educational in character, of progressive elements on the left." Refugees from the fronts, including some recently resigned Communists, met on Sundays at Max Lerner's house, but they "could find no agreement on a minimum program," Granville Hicks recalled. There were those who wanted the Independent Left group, as it was tentatively called, to build a large movement while others were content with small discussion groups. There were antifascist interventionists and antifascists who endorsed only support for Britain and France. More debilitating were the divisions created by the front experience. Several group members, particularly Hicks and Lerner, were intolerant of anything that sounded remotely pro-Party. Others tempered their disapproval of current Party policy with concerns about the growth of anticommunism. Members of both factions already felt they had compromised all they could, so each "stood out for his full program." Lacking a consensus, the group fell apart early in 1940.[30] Its failure reinforced progressive fears about their inability to act on their own.

As the experience of the independent left group suggested, progressives were not quite sure what to think about the American Communist Party and had trouble identifying their role apart from it. Cowley noted that he was "standing pretty much alone, in the air, unsupported" without it; but he also felt corrupted and "unclean" because of it. For a long time he had been "not a man but an institution, a name to be signed to petitions, a possible speaker at meetings."[31] Suddenly, he was on his own. Much of what progressives gained from the People's

178   Front—the sense that they were on the cutting edge of change and part
of a larger cause that had real possibilities—disappeared with the con-
version of the fronts into a more tightly knit pro-Party apparatus. And
those features disappeared in a particularly ugly way, for the very
people who had once courted them turned against them, out-foxing
them in the fronts and slamming them in the Party press. "When the
locomotive of history takes a sharp turn," *The New Masses* noted in
a cartoon, faithful progressives like *The New Republic, The Nation,*
Heywood Broun, and Louis Fischer joined the usual lineup of the
Party's enemies, Eugene Lyons, James T. Farrell, Sidney Hook, and
Max Eastman. Joseph Lash was surprised at how vicious the Party
attack against him was after he broke with the ASU. "It was absolutely ferocious," he told the House UnAmerican Activities Committee. Could these be the same do-gooders with whom progressives had
worked for so many years? Maybe, but maybe not. "Suddenly," Roger
Baldwin recalled, "the Communists were different people."[32]

Progressives had some difficulty reconciling their earlier image of
the CPUSA with the Communists' post-Pact behavior. It was hard to
see them as sympathetic figures any longer; but accepting the anti-
Stalinists' more negative view meant admitting their own guilt. If the
Communists were totalitarian, then progressives had "compromised
with despotism," Lewis Mumford explained. While some conceded
such a compromise necessary, others preferred to think they were in
control of the Front—or should have been. "I wanted what the Communists wanted," Baldwin later said, "and I traveled the United Front
road—not the party road—to try and get it." In hindsight, though, traveling the united front road required more care, perhaps, than progressives recognized at the onset. One *New Republic* editorial excused the
Communists by blaming progressives for being unrealistic: "It should
have been remembered all the time that if communists joined democratic and popular fronts, it was because it served their strategic purpose to do so, not because they cherished democratic ideals." Freda
Kirchwey reconciled two very different images of the CPUSA by defining it as "a split personality." One half promoted "a wide variety of
democratic ends," while the other pursued "old-line conspiratorial
contrivings." Since progressives allied only with its good half, most
saw no reason to be ashamed or embarrassed by their radical forays. As
Cowley said, "I can't forget that all this business started with high
purposes and dreams of a better society." That he ended up "in a

pretty pickle" was unfortunate, but no reason to repudiate his earlier
actions.[33]

However unfairly the Party cadre behaved in the LAW or the ALPD,
progressives did not contribute to the general post-Pact red scare. Van
Wyck Brooks told V. F. Calverton: "I shall never join in the witch-
hunt against Communists, but I cannot wish them well." Progressives
watched, stunned, as the Dies committee summoned such Party leaders as Earl Browder, Alexander Trachtenberg, and William Z. Foster
along with expert ex-Communist witnesses like Jay Lovestone to learn
about front groups, which became known by the more sinister Party
designation of "transmission belts." When the Committee published
in its records the ALPD's Chicago and Washington, D.C., chapter mailing lists or membership lists, there was strong progressive outrage and
the ACLU protested the action as "guilt by association." Kirchwey compared Martin Dies to Hitler.[34] Those who had not sworn off politics
were vociferous in their denunciations of the civil liberties violations
involved. No doubt, those who protested were mindful that an expanded hunt for Communists and "fellow-travelers" might include
them. Still, progressives simply refused to believe that the Communists threatened democracy or were dangerous.

Thus they continued to have little in common with anti-Stalinists.
Even though both were refugees of the fronts and, in a sense, victims of
the Party's wish to manage those agencies, progressives regarded anti-
Stalinists as the enemies of freedom. Never would they credit them
with a constructive political analysis. Most dismissed anti-Stalinism
as a set of quirky "personal quarrels," an explanation borrowed from
Party propaganda and never given up because it was too compelling. "I
had some damned persistent enemies, notably Sidney Hook and Jim
Farrell," Cowley told Lewis Mumford. He blamed them for his demo-
tion at *The New Republic,* a much easier explanation than acknowledging that "I wasn't getting any too damned popular" after the Front
fell apart. Cowley's "explanation in terms of personalities" made sense
to progressives who saw anti-Stalinists as quibblers and nay-sayers
without the stomach for the compromises necessary for collective action. Cowley's picture of the anti-Stalinists at *The New Leader* was not
completely inaccurate; but he failed to realize that he too had reduced
conflict to personalities: "Its contributors minify [*sic*] almost all political issues into conflicts of personalities, with bright boys bedeviled
by stupid but somehow sly and potent Stalinists—stage devils pulling

wires behind the scenes . . . I suppose they calculate that they can weaken the opposition by discrediting those whom they regard as its leaders." That kind of explanation made Cowley's attempts to get on with the difficult business of politics seem noble while denigrating the anti-Stalinists' intellectual style. Many progressives believed that this style not only hurt the antifascist cause but also contributed to "the tide of intolerance that has been rising on the right." Whether or not Communists seemed like "different people," anti-Stalinists seemed just the same as always, "perfect pest[s]" with no real program of their own.[35]

Progressives also had little respect for the few of their colleagues who defended the Pact, whatever their motives. It was easy to snipe at someone like Anna Louise Strong, who claimed to enjoy the "mental agility" necessary to keep up with changes in Soviet foreign policy. It might have been harder to deal with the likes of Carey McWilliams, who "could understand why the Soviet Union had done what it did from the point of view of national self interest"; but most progressives did not bother. Rather, they just wrote them off as antifascist dropouts. Some of those who broke ranks did so because they were opposed to American involvement in the war. Most progressives did not acknowledge that or credit pacifists with any principles. And since, as anti-Stalinists were fond of noting, progressives occupied the intellectual power-structure, they could use their power to silence their enemies. They were much more likely to exclude Pact defenders and peace advocates from their magazines than they ever were anti-Stalinists. *The New Republic* told one poet outright that his works were unpublishable "for political reasons—in this case the political reason being that we can't share your feeling about the new Russian policy." So too did they shun people who seemed to betray them. The Pact "ruptured friendships," McWilliams recalled. "A great many people have stopped speaking to us," Dorothy Parker's husband, screenwriter Alan Campbell, confessed to Alexander Woolcott. Donald Ogden Stewart fought with his long-time pal Robert Benchley. Lillian Hellman quarreled with the whole cast of her play "The Little Foxes" after refusing to allow them to do a benefit for Finland.[36] In many different ways, progressives punished their colleagues for unpopular views.

The new progressive position was, thus, impossible: simultaneously antifascist, anti-antiwar, anti-anticommunist, and anti-Party. Progressives' inconsistent responses to the newly altered League of

American Writers demonstrated just how confused they were. It was hardly popular. Ernest Hemingway, for example, pitied the poor souls helped by the LAW's Exiled Writers Committee, not because they were imprisoned but because they were "used as an object for collections ... [by] Folsom and Co." Still, not everyone automatically ruled it beyond acceptable bounds. Agnes Smedley applied for LAW membership in 1941, decided she "acted too quickly," wrote Cowley for the "inside story of the League," and got an earful in return. Marjorie Fischer proved willing to serve on the Exiled Writers Committee even after she broke with the LAW, until Folsom told her that the group "felt it would be better if you did not sit with the committee." Some progressives were angered by the FBI's investigation of the LAW. But all were acutely aware that the organization had a bad reputation. Robert Morss Lovett, appointed by the Roosevelt administration to a government position, apologized to his superior for his League membership because his signature on the call to the 1941 Writers Congress "embarrassed you and the Department [of the Interior]." By not endorsing the LAW, they angered Party intellectuals. By denying that it was a threat, they angered anti-Stalinists and left themselves vulnerable to anticommunist attack. What their casual and noncommittal attitude actually said about the League was that it had "outlived its usefulness."[37]

In many ways, progressives believed they had outlived their usefulness as well. "Here I am," Clifford Odets noted in the spring of 1940, "indecisive because I do not know truly what I feel and believe." It was a "nightmarish season," McWilliams remembered, whether progressives were antifascist or pro-Soviet. After a few brief stabs at political activism, many simply gave up. "For the moment I want to get out of every God damned thing," Cowley told Edmund Wilson early in 1940. But he did not completely disengage from politics and became a "war monger" by 1941.[38] For every Cowley who decided to remain a political intellectual, though, there were two or three others who faded back into the less political world they inhabited before the Depression. The Nazi-Soviet Pact did not necessarily sour progressives on front politics; but it often disillusioned them about politics altogether, and particularly the involvement of intellectuals in political controversy.

Life was no simpler in the American Communist Party. Its partisans lost all credibility within the larger intellectual world. It was impossible to be respected as thinkers when others saw your position as "simple and mechanical." Anti-Stalinist Charles Yale Harrison suggested that after the Nazi-Soviet Pact Michael Gold and his comrades were forced to exchange the tweed jackets of academe for their more traditional proletarian leather ones.[39] While his comment was meant to mock the CPUSA, in some ways it was apt. The Party intellectual's world constricted after the Pact, no matter how much functionaries pretended otherwise. The qualities, particularly commitment and discipline, that progressives once admired in their allies became symbols of the CPUSA's intellectual sterility. Most outsiders concluded that radical politics and judicious intellectual pursuit were inconsistent occupations. Dedication to the Party became reason to question an intellectual's objectivity. Never again would Party intellectuals be accorded much outside respect.

Most Party intellectuals accepted the turn of events with some grace; one, however, could not. The Nazi-Soviet Pact was the final indignity in a series of episodes that reinforced Joseph Freeman's doubts about the compatibility of Communist activists and cultural independence. For years there were "rumors that he was intermittently accused of nonconformity." Each clash left him uneasy about his loyalties. As Waldo Frank noted, "he felt the hurdles in the Communist command." Finally, the Nazi-Soviet Pact and the ensuing line change precipitated his break, although the Pact itself mattered less to Freeman than the question of "whether a writer, even a writer committed to the communist brand of socialism, had the right to maintain his moral and intellectual integrity."[40] But was this simply a case of a good writer ruined by too much political duplicity? Freeman was hardly the ordinary Party intellectual. No one else was as subject to oversight by functionaries as he was; few took such "guidance" so seriously. He was eager to please and easily offended by criticism. Freed of the constraints of Party discipline and the demands of the movement, he produced no magnum opus on a par with *An American Testament*. Whether or not his troubles really were the result of a clash between intellectual integrity and Party discipline, he framed them as such, and many others, both inside and outside the Party, felt as he did, that Communism and cultural autonomy were incompatible.[41]

Freeman and others quickly discovered that leaving the Party did not solve all their woes. While the experience might have been initially "liberating," as Richard Rovere said, ex-Communists faced many practical problems. "One does not easily retreat from a position one has taken after great turmoil and held at some cost," Granville Hicks recalled. Rovere and Hicks adjusted more easily to life on the outside. Since they were Front-period recruits, they were not as tightly bound to the Party apparatus as others.[42] Freeman, like Liston Oak a few years before, had few outside resources. "I was completely broke and isolated," he told Floyd Dell more than a decade later; "it was difficult for me to get work because the Communists . . . fought me as a 'renegade' and the anti-Communists . . . held my 'background' against me."[43] He was, in some ways, a Communist for life. One of the problems with being an "ex" was that many remained small-c communists for life. They did not stop holding political opinions when they left the CPUSA. Their opinions just no longer corresponded with the Party line. Defining oneself politically was very difficult, especially since the public continued to define many ex'es only by their pasts. Few of the post-Pact renegades followed the path taken by earlier dissidents, anti-Stalinism, although many were mildly anticommunist. Hicks tried to be both progressive and anticommunist. His friend Rovere joined the Socialist Party. Freeman rejected anti-Stalinism, anticommunism, and progressivism. Instead, he reveled in private life and literary concerns, confident that by rejecting politics altogether he was finally his own person.

Part of the difficulty ex'es had adjusting to life outside the CPUSA was functioning without their once-closest friends. They received little of the rancorous abuse heaped upon earlier dropouts; however, the older implication that they had failed to be strong enough or good enough people still came through. Commenting on Hicks many years later, Earl Browder thought that "he never should have joined any political party" because he "represented a type of sensitive intellectual unfitted for the harsh realities of political decisions." As it became clear his beliefs diverged from the rest of *The New Masses*'s staff, Hicks recalled that everyone was outwardly polite and that one colleague even invited him out for a drink. Yet the need to maintain discipline was intense. "The next morning," he added, "Dick [Rovere] heard A. B. Magil say to Joe North, 'You know, Sillen is really a better critic than Hicks.'" "The line," Hicks concluded, "had already changed."[44] And so it was for the few intellectuals who left the CPUSA over the Pact. The Party world just quietly closed behind them as though they had never existed.

Party intellectuals said little about such people or the general impact and consequences of the Nazi-Soviet Pact on their organization because they were "prepared for stormy weather," as a newly revised verse in a Party song advised. On the surface, the change of line would seem to be one of the most difficult the organization ever had to make, but it was executed swiftly and silently. Denied the luxury of time or the sense of expanding horizons that characterized the last line change, they had no choice but to plunge ahead. Budd Schulberg recalled that intellectual functionaries became a lot more visible after the Pact. Robert Gorham Davis thought this was because "they had to work desperately to hold the line."[45] All the functionaries in the communist world, however, were not enough to protect the CPUSA from the post-Pact red scare. The Roosevelt administration cracked down on the organization. Earl Browder was tried and convicted for falsifying information on a passport application in the 1920s. Anti-Stalinists were in a position to affect public opinion. A broader wave of anticommunism—much of it on the political right—also helped shape policy. And progressives were in no mood to actively defend those who had betrayed them. Many Communists and former Communists appeared before the Dies committee, the latter sometimes happily denouncing the CPUSA. In 1940, Congress passed the Smith Act, and while it would not be used against the CPUSA until after World War II, its existence suggested that Americans were not in a tolerant mood.[46] All in all, 1940 was a dismal year for American Communists, and intellectuals were no exception. The year 1941 would prove to be little better.

The Nazi-Soviet Pact halted the forward momentum of progressives and intellectual Communists. Many would never again regain any political momentum at all. Even in the darkest moments of their antifascist fight, both had been supercharged by a sense of moral righteousness. Antifascism—opposing Hitler—was an unambiguous cause. It provided creative inspiration, allowed intellectuals to feel a sense of purpose, and was, at the same time, popular. Antifascism brought everything together, intellectual success, respectability, accolades, recognition, and political rectitude. The Pact forced intellectuals to make hard choices. Were they antifascist or pro-Soviet, isolationist or for collective security, writers or political animals? So too did the Pact sully the once-noble cause of antifascism. In the post-Pact atmosphere intellectuals were forced to reevaluate the meaning and value of front politics.

Curiously, it was progressives more than Communists who retained their faith in front politics. Many felt personally burned by the Pact but continued to believe that the concept was workable, even necessary in a world where political compromises had to be effected. "Though the record of the united front . . . has been one of universal failure," Roger Baldwin wrote in 1941, "the method has proved sound in principle as the only practicable means of united popular forces with any chance at all of overcoming reaction."[47] Although the base would be narrower each time, progressives and the CPUSA built similar coalitions during World War II and the Henry Wallace campaign of 1948. Such a choice did not mean, as anti-Stalinists assumed, that progressives never learned from one experience with the Communists to another. Rather, it meant that they continued to find important issues in common with the CPUSA and continued to believe they could work for those issues without unduly compromising their integrity. "I may have been mistaken in my judgment," Frederick Schuman told the House UnAmerican Activities Committee, ". . . but . . . my motive . . . had nothing to do with . . . sympathy with communism."[48]

The Communist Party, by contrast, never had quite so much faith in front politics again. Whereas it plunged into another round of mainstream activity during World War II, thereafter it preferred a more limited course. It quickly repudiated the very idea of accommodationist policies after its brief wartime experience. The Henry Wallace presidential campaign brought Communists and progressives together once again, but the result was more the illusion of a front than an actual coalition, like the clumsy fronts of the early days or the post-Pact League of American Writers rather than the slick 1937 antifascist apparatus. After Wallace failed, the Communists went underground in the hostile political climate and never really reemerged in anything more than truncated condition.[49] The People's Front against Fascism really was, as Harvey Klehr titled his book, "the heyday of American Communism."

EIGHT

Countering

"Totalitarian Liberalism": The Demise of

Anti-Stalinism and the Emergence

of Liberal Anticommunism, 1939–1940

The Nazi-Soviet Pact that so shocked People's Front intellectuals seemed consistent with Stalinism to liberals, Trotskyists, and anti-Stalinists. It confirmed, intensified, and broadened certain aspects of their critique of Stalin's Russia. Anti-Stalinists believed that the Party's shameful behavior following the line change would embarrass progressives, provoke them to recant, and shift the balance of power away from them. But progressives followed another script. Consequently, the Nazi-Soviet Pact did not end quarrels on the left; it made them worse. As anti-Stalinism lost its Marxist perspective, it transferred its concerns. Liberal anticommunism emerged in 1940 and provided intellectual legitimacy for a post-Pact red scare that directly challenged progressive integrity and the Front's legitimacy.

Liberals were remarkably prescient about the Pact. An article in the March 1939 issue of *Common Sense* described "that coming Nazi-Soviet Pact." In a side-bar, editors Alfred Bingham and Selden Rodman noted that "whatever the public may believe, readers of 'Common Sense' will not be unprepared for such an event." The popularity of "totalitarianism" to describe both communism and fascism suggested that an alliance between representatives of both doctrines was, in Benjamin Stolberg's word, "inevitable." Indeed, Bingham and Rodman predicted, "Communism and Fascism may yet find that they have more in common than the public suspects."[1] Since liberals already equated communism and fascism, the alliance between the Soviets and the Nazis had a certain logic for them that eluded others.

Prescience did not mean that they were mentally prepared for the Pact and what it signified, however. Most were shocked and disappointed. John Haynes Holmes was one of the most outspoken of the USSR's critics, but he felt "sick over this business, as though I saw my father drunk and my sister on the street." Still, he was ashamed; he wished he had done more to oppose Stalin. John Dewey searched for a silver lining and found one. Thanks to the Pact, he predicted, "the hypnotic spell [of Marxism] is now broken."[2] Intellectuals would be forced back to their American roots. But Dewey was hardly thrilled by the Pact. No one was; it meant war.

Liberals were much more worried about the prospect of an antifascist war than most other intellectuals. They were older and more satisfied than other leftists with the reforms that had occurred in their lifetimes. They remembered the last war. They remembered the 1920s. But even younger liberals could be strongly antiwar. Certainly the editors of *Common Sense* were. They watched uneasily as some intellectuals denounced the Soviet Union, afraid that these "embittered ex-Communists are poisoning the atmosphere." They dealt with the Pact much as they had the Spanish Civil War, by ignoring its consequences whenever possible in a journal devoted to current events. Regarding the stories of Soviet atrocities in Finland, for example, Bingham and Rodman believed that "we have no more reason to fly to the defense of Finnish democracy than of Spanish democracy or Czech democracy." Although there were individual liberals who felt more strongly about Finland (Holmes vowed to put the Finnish flag in his pulpit and play the Finnish national anthem to his congregation), as a group they were largely antiwar. This left them with little in common with progressives, even after progressives soured on the Soviet Union. Their antiwar attitudes, manifested in organizations like the Keep America Out of War Congress, effectively isolated them from most progressives and left them, once again, on the sidelines.[3]

The Pact brought together liberals and some anti-Stalinists by accelerating the latter's disillusionment with Marxist politics. In one sense, the Pact confirmed the central premise of anti-Stalinism, demonstrating that "the real political content of Stalinism" was cynical self-protection. But in another, it made it harder for many intellectuals

188   to distinguish Stalinism from communism. Was Stalin really the only reason why "everywhere, including the Soviet Union, it is not the social revolution but the counter-revolution which has triumphed?" Simply blaming Stalin seemed too easy. Anti-Stalinists were prepared to reassess following the Nazi-Soviet Pact, so that they might sort out "what is living and what is dead" in Marxism.[4]

During the next year, Edmund Wilson, Max Eastman, Lewis Corey, Bertram Wolfe, and Sidney Hook each found more that was "dead" than "living" in Marxism. Marx's great contribution to philosophy, they decided, was "his sense of the great part played by economic relations in determining political and cultural ways of life." But each condemned his dictatorship of the proletariat and blamed the dialectic for Marxism's undemocratic potential. The dialectic, Wilson explained, promised that, whatever happened, "the human story [will] come out right." It was relatively easy to show that Stalin used the dialectic cynically, justifying his brutalities in the name of Marx's ends and suggesting that, thanks to historical inevitability, the USSR would reach those ends no matter what the short-term costs. Yet it troubled anti-Stalinists that Marx failed to anticipate someone like Stalin misusing the dialectic. Stalin succeeded partially because the mechanisms to consolidate and maintain his power already existed. His rule originated "not only in Lenin's power-politics but in the religious belief in a benignly-evolving universe which lay behind those policies," Eastman argued. Until 1940, most assumed that the dialectic they always found so unscientific and antiquated played little role in Lenin's revolution.[5] Stalin's rapid rise and iron control over the USSR suggested otherwise. For many anti-Stalinists, the Nazi-Soviet Pact finally collapsed their Marxism.

What was left was not liberalism. Former anti-Stalinists often detested that label. They were uncomfortable with the center; it seemed too wishy-washy. They never quite lost their stereotype of liberalism as a sweet and naive doctrine promoted by dreamers and optimists. They, by contrast, felt they had seen the ugly underside of politics. Communists circumvented the law. The People's Front proved that they manipulated bureaucracies for their own purposes. They could not respond with idealism, hoping and wishing that Communism would go away like they thought the liberals did. Former anti-Stalinists were afraid that liberalism was too polite to deal with as wicked a doctrine as Communism. They had their own ideas about how to proceed in the wake of the Nazi-Soviet Pact.

In the short term, the Nazi-Soviet Pact revived precisely that gentle liberal do-goodism some former anti-Stalinists mocked. The treaty roused Committee for Cultural Freedom liberals from their apathy. John Dewey predicted that the next threats to cultural freedom would be alien registration and sedition laws. These were familiar dangers and liberals knew how to react. The CCF considered ways to protect dissent, including Communist dissent. It amended its declaration of principles to guarantee free speech and dispatched a letter to Congress demanding that Martin Dies be removed as head of the House Special Committee on UnAmerican Activities. It also passed a resolution re-defining its purposes, since "the emergency [created by the People's Front] . . . no longer applies," as Dewey noted. "In view of certain changes in the cultural climate," the Committee oriented itself more "toward domestic manifestations of totalitarianism," an overly broad sentiment, but one most liberals took to mean fighting reactionaries. CCF liberals saw the Pact as a vindication of their position. Progressives, they predicted, would soon join them in a pro-democratic campaign. Having emphasized the negative side of anti-totalitarianism for so long, they were ready to concentrate more on its positive side.[6]

Committee anti-Stalinists, however, were fixated on anticommunism. They even implied that the liberal agenda played right into Party hands: the Communists wanted others to believe it lost power because they could maneuver better if people assumed they were weak. The CPUSA's cultural and intellectual tyranny did not disappear; it went underground, making it all the more insidious. To smoke out its continued supporters became an anti-Stalinist obsession. Sidney Hook wanted to individually confront all four hundred who signed the letter challenging the Committee's definition of "totalitarianism," asking each to directly state his or her post-Pact views. His letter draft was so vitriolic that Dewey intervened, afraid that it "imitate[d] . . . their tactics." Hook found his mentor's version "mild," and when it failed to get the results he wanted, pressured the organization to take a harder line. Ferdinand Lundberg was prepared to repeat the entire process with all eight hundred members of the League of American Writers, but the board voted "to refrain from doing this at this time."[7] CCF anti-Stalinists thought it unlikely that the crisis on the left might be over.

While CCF liberals organized radio shows and panels to demonstrate the potential impact war might have on civil liberties, anti-Stalinists were hard at work refining their understanding of communist "totalitarianism." Hook articulated the rudiments of his postwar position, defining communism as something so different and dangerous that traditional liberal niceties might not apply. He denied, for example, that Earl Browder's civil liberties had been compromised when officials at Harvard University refused to allow him to speak. There was "no issue of civil freedom involved." What was involved, he suggested, was a "calculated" Party policy "to stir up confusion." Communists would con liberals into guaranteeing their civil liberties; then the CPUSA "would abrogate the Bill of Rights the day it took power." As if that were not reason enough to differentiate between the Party and other political organizations, Hook also suggested that it was unique among parties because it was "subsidized and controlled by a foreign power." Were Party members entitled to the "cultural and civil freedoms" granted to other American dissidents? That was "a matter . . . for the United States courts to decide." Hook was uncharacteristically hesitant about these opinions in 1940, but his drift was pretty clear. The dangers posed by the CPUSA were significant. Unless it were checked, American democracy would lose.[8]

Despite initial liberal action, Hook's perspective gained ascendancy in the CCF. It did so for several reasons. One was the doggedness of Committee anti-Stalinists compared to the relative passivity of the liberals. Dewey resigned as honorary chair in November 1939, because "the Stalinite action" (meaning the Pact) ended the emergency situation that brought him out of retirement in the first place. Like Dewey, after an initial round of membership drives and radio symposia, liberals hung back. Not so the former anti-Stalinists, who continued their campaign to spotlight each front. Each round of investigations made them more determined and liberals more unsure of their previous assumptions. Equally significant was the reception the Committee got from others. Progressives did not flood the organization; the group claimed 169 members in September but only 140 two months later. A second invitation to Franz Boas's group for fusion yielded another polite negative. Boas was no happier to work with Hook after the Pact than before.[9] Soon some liberals were willing to concede what Hook, Eugene Lyons, and others had argued all along, that the Nazi-Soviet Pact changed nothing, that the Communists still controlled the cultural and intellectual scene.

As liberal ground shifted and former anti-Stalinists consolidated their control over the CCF, the result was a changed policy toward communism. Whereas liberals once had a rather laissez faire attitude toward the CPUSA, assuming that its doctrines were irrelevant for most Americans, now they were suspicious, fearful, and armed with prophylactics to prevent its spread. "What Should the Attitude of a Liberal Be toward the Dies Committee?" one CCF-sponsored radio panel asked. Different panelists had different answers, but all recognized the need for such a committee. The CCF also endorsed attorney Morris Ernst's plan requiring any organization applying for postal privileges to make public its officers, donors, bylaws, and printed materials. Ernst, a veteran anticommunist in the National Lawyers Guild in the midst of an ACLU fight over the same issue, argued that registration would expose fronts to the interested public. His own ACLU, however, considered it a violation of privacy. Every other liberal organization agreed; the CCF stood alone in support of Ernst's plan.[10] The CCF was the first liberal institution to assert that it was incumbent upon scrupulous liberals to help expose totalitarianism.

"Stalinist Outposts in the United States" showed precisely what role liberals should play in the exposure of totalitarianism. It was a consumer's guide to organizations that classified fronts from most to least dangerous: those "under outright C.P. control," those "under Communist influence," and those "in close collaboration with the Communist Party." It brought the liberal approach to social problems—rational, legalistic—to the hunt for communists. It created standards and system for a process the Dies committee performed haphazardly and without concern for individual rights. Author Ferdinand Lundberg "checked and rechecked" the Dies committee's research, rejected its "extremely undiscriminating" processes, and reminded his readers to remain "coolheaded." The CCF even consulted an attorney before publishing to make sure "there is nothing libelous in the report." While his methods were liberal, however, Lundberg's assumptions owed more to former anti-Stalinists like himself. He took it for granted that the professed aims of any front organization did not represent its actual purposes. "Superficial activity" performed "for a worthy cause" could be "merely a screen for the essential totalitarian activity which, in differing degrees, is carried forward by the separate cogs in the Communist machine." Lundberg's scientific criterion proving CPUSA control was "the actual personalities in charge of organizing activity" and "concrete information as to their affiliation with the Communist Party." Lundberg believed that Party members were automatically exponents of totalitarian propaganda whose presence, no matter what the cause or how few their numbers, posed a threat to democracy. No organization could be free of the totalitarian taint unless all its members were not communists.[11] Although the CCF's information-gathering process was more thoughtful than Dies's, exposure of duplicitous communists was their shared goal.

"Stalinist Outposts" was one of the CCF's last acts. It never officially dissolved; it ceased functioning. But it was the first truly liberal anticommunist organization in America. From its definition of "totalitarianism" to its commitment to exposure, it articulated a new variety of anticommunism, one more moderate than had before existed. Traditionally anticommunism was a doctrine of the far right. In the 1930s, anti-Stalinists made a variant of it a doctrine of the far left. The Committee for Cultural Freedom created a liberal vocabulary for anticommunism by defining communism as the antithesis of democracy. It was on the cutting edge of liberal change. Perhaps nothing better illustrated its significance than the postwar emergence of the American Committee for Cultural Freedom. The ACCF shared its unofficial parent's commitment to legalistic and careful exposure of communism. Unlike its parent, however, the ACCF was large, powerful, influential, and linked into an international network of like-minded organizations.[12] The Committee for Cultural Freedom formalized the changing liberal perspective on communism.

Liberal anticommunism also influenced, and was influenced by, post-Pact debates within the American Civil Liberties Union over similar issues: exposure, the meaning of Communist Party membership, totalitarianism, and civil liberties for Communists. But while there was relative consensus within the CCF, the ACLU was the scene of a stormy and prolonged fight over the appropriate attitude liberals ought to adopt toward the CPUSA. The Union's diverse membership was already polarized. The split between liberals who inclined toward at least mild anticommunism and progressives who were squeamish about trampling the civil liberties of Communists was especially pronounced on the organization's board of directors. There, the two factions, in each case a minority of members, were evenly balanced.[13]

The Nazi-Soviet Pact tipped the balance—only slightly and only on the governing boards—in favor of the anticommunists. It also caused Roger Baldwin's defection to the anticommunist side. Until the Pact, he was a willing, even enthusiastic, participant in several fronts. Watching those fronts disintegrate made him suspicious of CPUSA motives and actions. During the earlier ACLU fights, he was neutral. As the group approached its more serious 1940 crisis, he had a new understanding of what it meant to be a Communist. "I will no longer participate in any organization with members of the Communist Party to accomplish any end," he told an acquaintance in March 1940, because "there is an obvious conflict between the attitude of the Communist Party to civil liberties and our own."[14] Baldwin joined the former anti-Stalinists and liberals who were determined to free the ACLU of its front reputation. His turnabout helped set the stage for a shift in ACLU policy.

What precipitated the crisis, though, was not Baldwin's reassessment so much as anti-Stalinist pressure. About a month after the Pact, Sidney Hook sent the board a letter resigning because ACLU board chairman Harry F. Ward signed that "slanderous attack" on the CCF, the "400 Letter." "In many circles within and without the ACLU," he explained, "people are asking whether Harry Ward, its Chairman, is not more of a liability than an asset." The Union's anticommunist board faction quickly picked up his complaint. Margaret De Silver, Oswald Garrison Villard, John Dos Passos, John Haynes Holmes, Morris Ernst, and E. A. Ross supported him. Their motives were mixed; but many had bad experiences with front groups that they transformed into larger anticommunist philosophies. "Just when is Harry Ward resigning?" Roger William Riis wanted to know. No one was more outraged than Norman Thomas. He thought Ward's signature on the open letter constituted "an attack upon all of us who joined the League [Committee] for Cultural Freedom." He was so angry that he took his complaints to the public, violating board tradition, in order to try Ward "before the bar of public opinion."[15]

However the "bar of public opinion" judged Ward, the ACLU's board ruled Thomas out of order. Progressives felt that he should never have attacked a fellow board member in print and a report commissioned by the board concurred. Thomas "used his standing as a Board member" in a manner that could "make his further presence embarrassing."[16] That response infuriated anticommunists. It did not surprise Margaret De Silver. "When I first came into the room," she told Thomas, "the fellow travelers were looking so complacent I knew we were licked." She detected a pattern. Their opponents triumphed, she added, because liberals "lost confidence": "These goodhearted people will always in all important and critical issues in the future fail to act, and will thus yield to the pressure of a minority group which never does fail to act, and acts in unison. This to my mind destroys the effectiveness of the Union increasingly." Board anticommunists had a conspiratorial interpretation of Thomas's rebuke and Ward's continued leadership. A "Communist bloc on the board," they concluded, hampered Union democracy. But they had only "evidence . . . which falls short of proof" of its existence. Two investigations revealed no such bloc.[17] Anticommunists saw those investigations as further proof of conspiracy. Communists and their friends seemed to prevail on the ACLU's board because no one challenged them. These experiences confirmed what Hook only hinted at, that liberals who failed to be part of the anticommunist solution themselves contributed to the problem.

Reinforcing the anticommunists' suspicions was their inability to shake the alleged Communist bloc's hold in order to put the ACLU on record as favoring the principle of exposure. Despite their disproportionate representation on a subcommittee assigned the task of writing a public report on the Dies committee and their desire to "turn out 'a middle-of-the-road report' which would help lead liberals into a position of 'pragmatic realism,'" they did not prevail. Theirs was hardly a laudatory report; but many board members thought it "impl[ied] a rather fundamental endorsement of the Dies Committee." It did endorse the principle of exposure, certainly: "the only defense of a democracy against movements which use the 'Bill of Rights' in order to destroy the 'Bill of Rights,' is to expose them by a thorough-going investigation." But the larger board of directors excised that statement, and many others, from the final product. This was, Holmes argued, another lesson in Realpolitik Communist-style: "The opposition began its familiar work of 'boring from within . . .' [I]n the face of this opposition, we liberals did what we usually do—instead of fighting for what we believed in we sought to make concessions and compromises."[18]

When the next round of bureaucratic fighting began, Union anticommunists were better prepared. The 1940 nominating committee submitted to the board a policy statement quietly written by Baldwin. It declared that it would be "inappropriate for any person to serve on the governing committees of the Union or its staff, who is a member of any political organization which supports totalitarian dictatorship." Harry F. Ward, who still chaired the board, ruled it "outside the Committee's authority," a decision the board upheld by a single vote. By another single-vote majority, the board instructed the larger national committee that "there is no occasion to adopt a resolution setting up standards of qualification for membership." But in a third close vote, the board defeated Mary Van Kleeck's alternative statement, which declared that board members need only have "complete and consistent support of civil liberties as guaranteed in the Bill of Rights of the Constitution."[19] Neither minority board faction was able to succeed. The more conservative national committee, however, approved the anti-totalitarianism resolution largely thanks to anticommunist efforts "to get out the vote." Progressives protested that the election was unfair because anticommunists flooded the meeting with their supporters, "not more than two or three of whom had attended a meeting of the ACLU for several years past." Those who could not attend in person sent proxies. In the end, the newly elected board of directors belatedly endorsed the measure too.[20] Flushed by their victory, the anticommunists pressed on.

That same evening, Holmes replaced Ward as board chairman and served notice to his opponents: "It may be, that our conflict is not over. The Resolutions passed . . . involve certain implications of action, which, it seems to me, must be fulfilled, if these Resolutions are to be regarded as anything more than an idle gesture."[21] He intended to purge the ACLU of communist influence. Only one public Communist served on its boards, Elizabeth Gurley Flynn. Although, as Baldwin noted, "Miss Flynn has not hampered the work of the Union at meetings,"[22] she became the anticommunists' target. Their choice meant they had to buck enormous odds. The progressive board faction was the least of their problems. The incoming mail ran two-to-one against the resolution; "local committees . . . are practically unanimous in condemning our resolution." Baldwin predicted the Flynn expulsion would cost the organization perhaps a thousand members and five thousand dollars in lost revenues. Anticommunists felt they had done their duty, nevertheless. Flynn was "not a free agent," Holmes told De Silver.[23] If they did not challenge her and the other Communists in the Union, no one else would, and the Communists would remain in control by default and duplicity.

Their attitude was uncompromising, even in the face of opposition. Baldwin disregarded the generally negative response in the affiliates. "Something further will have to be done," he suggested, "to educate them to what our policy *should be*." Holmes instructed his secretary to ignore all letters from "Communists, fellow travelers, and readers of the *Daily Worker* and the *New Masses*." Baldwin publicly maintained

196   that the anti-totalitarianism resolution did not "change the fundamental policy of the Union over the twenty years of its existence." Press
releases said almost nothing about the Flynn matter; anticommunists
tried to keep a tight lid on the information that circulated. Holmes, for
example, bureaucratically buried Alfred Bingham's proposed compromise measure, which would have expressed regret at Flynn's reelection but allowed her to serve out her term. The board did not approve
it, but Holmes did not want the national committee to learn of it for
fear it would "confuse the issue." Anything less than a total victory
seemed to him a surrender of principles—and "I cannot recommend
surrender."[24]

They did not surrender. In early March of 1940, Dorothy Dunbar
Bromley filed a motion, written by Baldwin, calling for Flynn's resignation from the ACLU's board of directors. Flynn refused in print,
prompting two more counts against her and forcing a "trial" to decide
her fate. On the evening of May 7, the board met to discuss and deliberate. For six hours members listened and, finally, deadlocked over
Bromley's initial motion "that Elizabeth Gurley Flynn is not entitled to
retain her directorship on the Board on the ground that she is a member of the Communist Party." Holmes ruled against virtually all of
Flynn's objections to both the substance and process of the "trial"
and cast the deciding vote against her. The board then sent her outside
and considered " 'punishment.' " Baldwin pressed, unsuccessfully,
"for non-ouster" to avoid subsequent factionalism. Flynn was not even
invited back in to hear the verdict—Holmes later apologized—and
Baldwin, once her lover and still a friend, never saw her again.[25]

The anticommunists removed Flynn but still had to gain endorsement from the national committee. Each committee member received a
carefully edited packet of information and a ballot. Progressives complained the official summary was "quite misleading." Since Holmes
refused to allow them to include a statement of dissent, they published
their own pamphlet, "Crisis in the Civil Liberties Union," and did a
brisk mail-order business. Holmes "was greatly disturbed by the publication of the pamphlet" and sorely aware of its potential impact. The
national committee approved Flynn's ouster by a mere two votes, a
narrow victory, but one that anticommunists felt they earned. Therefore, the continued circulation of "Crisis" seemed unfair. So, Baldwin
wrote and Ben Huebsch introduced a resolution to prohibit any expression of minority opinion that might "jeopardize the Union's integ-

rity and cripple its functioning." The board of directors tabled the
resolution, Holmes broke a tie vote to untable it, it was defeated, and
the pamphlet continued to circulate.[26] In 1976, the ACLU reversed itself and declared that Flynn's "expulsion was not consonant with the
basic principles on which the ACLU was founded."[27] In 1940, however,
Holmes and the rest of the anticommunist board faction were so afraid
that Communism threatened those same basic principles that they
were willing to bend them to protect democracy. Their decision represented "the turning point in the attitude of *liberals* toward civil liberties."[28] The result was liberal anticommunism.

Over the years, progressives developed an easy explanation for
what happened in the ACLU. Flynn alleged Holmes and others sold out
their principles to "play with Mr. Dies." They were "mercenary": they
"capitaliz[ed] . . . [on] our anti-Communist stand" to gain large contributors and a better reputation. Others suggested that the Union wanted
to " 'cleanse' itself of Communists" for political reasons. Members
heard rumors of "various conferences with Congressman Dies," although there was only a single cocktail party encounter between Dies,
Congressman Jerry Voorhis, Arthur Garfield Hays, and Morris Ernst.
We shall probably never know what went on at that meeting. Baldwin
described it as an unsuccessful attempt to persuade the two congressional representatives to let the ACLU clear itself of charges that it was a
front. Abraham Isserman noted that the conversation dealt "principally, with Communists and the work of the [Dies] Committee." Corliss Lamont believed that Hays and Ernst conceded the necessity of
purging visible Communists from the body in order to halt Dies committee attacks.[29] It really does not matter whether there was an official
deal with the Dies committee or not, since anticommunists felt compelled to remove Flynn and eliminate CPUSA influence with all due
speed for their own reasons.

Their motives were decidedly mixed. They were resentful of progressive power within the ACLU and felt helpless to stop its movement
in a leftward direction. They could not credit progressives or Communists with any principles, so they could only see them as power-
hungry and conspiratorial. Yet the anticommunists were themselves
power-hungry and conspiratorial. They wanted to put their stamp on
the organization whether or not a majority supported them. They justified their questionable maneuvering by presenting an image of the
Communists as secret plotters who used democratic procedure to de-

fend "a wholly temporary, partial and fragmentary definition of civil liberties." How else to explain why a majority failed to support them? Thus, Union anticommunists believed they acted for the good of the organization. In this, they added another element to liberal anticommunism, the notion that there were experts who could detect and combat communism better than most others. They, of course, were the experts, whose experiences with Party treachery enabled them to make informed and intelligent decisions that others, particularly those "infected with the virus of Communism," were incapable of making. At the same time, they were also concerned about the ACLU's reputation.[30] Their power in an anticommunist age was at least partially incumbent upon having a squeaky clean image. If the public associated the Union with frontism, then it could neither do its job nor enhance its individual members' abilities to do their jobs as intellectuals. Liberal anticommunism served several simultaneous agendas, a political one, an intellectual one, and many personal ones.

Other organizations quickly followed the ACLU and CCF's lead and embraced liberal anticommunism. The American Federation of Teachers, a union with Front sympathies, quickly purged itself of unsightly Party connections. Although the most determined anticommunists had long since broken with it and joined the rival Teachers' Guild, anticommunist sentiment within the union grew in response to the Pact. Liberal anticommunists opposed the reelection of Jerome Davis as union president. Davis, like Harry F. Ward, was an inveterate front supporter but not a Party member. George S. Counts ran against him on a platform that urged that the AFT "strongly condemn and oppose any attempt at manipulation of the American Federation of Teachers, or its program and policies, by a Communist." The election was close, but Counts won and the AFT passed a resolution critical of the Dies committee's methods, but not denying its right to exist. Most locals fell into line behind the national organization. Even its most allegedly Communist-controlled branch, New York City, voted to reject all undemocratic governments "whether they be Nazis, Communist, Socialist or Fascist." As a *Common Sense* reporter noted in early 1940, "right now a Communist Party-liner does not have a ghost of a chance in the A.F. of T."[31]

Several organizations informally banned all Communist membership to protect themselves from the kinds of manipulation about which "Stalinist Outposts" warned. The Keep America Out of War

Congress, for example, included liberals, ex'es, and other radicals and former radicals. Its organizers were willing to admit Trotskyists, provided they "not bore from within (and I mean bore in both senses) nor capture nor blow up" the group, newly deradicalized Bertram Wolfe told Kenneth Rexroth; but "we cannot admit loyal Stalinists at present, even though some of their programmatic statements on war sound like ours." What was the difference? Wolfe thought the Trotskyists, whose track record of swallowing up other organizations was quite lengthy, sincerely antiwar. The CPUSA, on the other hand, was "not honestly and reliably anti-war"; it only followed its current program because a foreign power told it to do so.[32] The Intercollegiate Socialist Society also opposed admitting Communists into the organization and would not allow any kind of cooperative venture with them even after the Nazis invaded Russia. General secretary Joseph Lash justified these decisions with claims of expertise acquired in the American Student Union.[33] The founders of the Union for Democratic Action, a pro-interventionist body at a time when the CPUSA was isolationist, did not have to worry about Communist membership; but they were "virtually all bitterly anti-Communist" and "not interested . . . in repeating the sad experiment of the Popular Front" after the Party changed lines.[34] Liberals were increasingly convinced that any Party presence in an organization spelled its doom as an independent force.

The Union for Democratic Action reflected that new liberal anticommunist position. Its policy statements routinely used the word "totalitarianism" as the CCF and the ACLU had, to describe communism and fascism. Soviet entrance on the Allied side of the war forced the organization to substitute "the Axis powers" for "totalitarianism" when describing the enemy, but members could hardly be described as enthusiastic supporters of the Allies' new partners. As early as 1942, there were signs that the Union envisioned no postwar harmony with the USSR. At an International Policy and Peace panel, one-time Party member Ralph Bates proposed that the UDA make a statement recognizing that the "Soviet Union will play its part" in creating and maintaining the peace, but the motion was "modified . . . [so that] no specific mention of Russia [was] made." Domestically, the Union was obsessed with "Communist attempts to penetrate the American liberal and labor movement," and, particularly, the UDA. A memo to local affiliates, for example, warned against the Communists: "Even without voting rights, Communist infiltration can do irreparable damage to the organization." When the Dies committee called the Union "a communist organization," rather than laughing off what everyone in the group believed a ludicrous charge, officers mounted a round robin campaign to make sure it was not so associated. Even though members regarded Dies and his cohorts as "bad," most were "heartily in favor of the job the Dies Committee was created to do."[35] The Union for Democratic Action, soon to become Americans for Democratic Action, fit firmly into the new liberal anticommunist tradition.

As liberal anticommunism took shape after 1940, it quickly left behind the most determined anticommunists who had been so influential in its early formulation. They were too extreme, too negative, and, often, too undemocratic for liberals and still-radical anti-Stalinists to tolerate for very long. Such anticommunists made even sympathetic persons uncomfortable with the intensity of their feelings and the elaborate nature of their conspiracy theories. Liberal anticommunists accepted institutionalized and carefully monitored means of exposure, but only rarely admired or respected those who participated in the process too enthusiastically. Anti-Stalinists saw their repudiation of Marxism as an indication of the too-obsessive nature of their anticommunist beliefs. Extreme anticommunists stood alone politically. Their isolation intensified the very qualities others disliked in them and caused them to imagine that the Communists were more powerful, more ruthless, and more dangerous than they actually were.

Extreme anticommunists were very cynical about their intellectual peers. Their attitude was both haughty and confrontational. They assumed they were the only intellectuals with any kind of personal integrity in a world where others compromised the very beliefs that defined intellectual responsibilities. Others, they figured, disliked them because they were above reproach. "Do not try to hide your face from unpleasant truths by attributing any personal 'bitter' motivations to me," Sidney Hook wrote Corliss Lamont in the fall of 1941. Hook would continue to send Lamont letters for decades, lecturing, preaching, and generally denouncing him for his positions in the 1930s. Whether Lamont ignored him or responded did not really matter; he just needed to remind Lamont at regular intervals that he was not fit to have the public's respect.[36] Hook never fully indicated precisely what he thought motivated Lamont to take the positions he did, intellectual laziness, revolutionary cunning, or the prospect of personal gain.

Charles Yale Harrison, however, seemed very clear about what drove progressives to take the stands they did: "Now that the Communists have lost thousands of members and sympathizers, this business of bleeding all over the place for the Soviet Union isn't going to be as profitable as it used to be. The lads are now quite definitely on the disband wagon. But never fear, they'll find another phoney cause to-morrow—they always do." Calculating, petty, corrupt, and mean, these "habitues of New York coffee shops" would never be anything more than caricatures of intellectuals.[37]

What extreme anticommunists wanted of progressives was some expression of contrition. "There can be no hope for American liberalism," Eugene Lyons explained, "until it renounces its recent totalitarian past." Max Eastman agreed, telling *The New Republic*'s readership that he would admire them if they admitted "you cannot serve democracy and totalitarianism." These were to be not just acts of intellectual honesty, but repayment for past injustices. Hook reminded his readers of these progressive "crimes": "They have justified purge, frame-up and political murder . . . [T]hey have lied about principled opponents of Stalinism, blackened their reputations, and whenever possible cut them off from their sources of livelihood."[38] Progressives neither desired Eastman's respect nor thought it necessary to grovel for Hook's forgiveness. Yet, as the range of Hook's complaints against progressives suggested, any penitence they offered for their actions should have included acknowledgment of the practical folly of front politics and the damage they did to people like Hook. Progressives were disinclined to comply on either score,[39] which made extreme anticommunists angry, frustrated, and even more suspicious of their motives.

Because progressives did not repudiate the Front, anticommunists assumed it lived on in a smaller, secretive, more concentrated, but still functional form. To a degree, all anticommunists believed this; but extreme anticommunists believed the most extreme version of it. The highly public collapse of the People's Front facade failed to reassure them of the CPUSA's lost potency. The Communists merely exchanged "new fronts for old," Lyons wrote in *The Red Decade,* and those new fronts, since they were less immediately identifiable, were more threatening. "Let no one assume . . . that the Communist periphery is a ghost town," he warned, so long as there were plenty of people left to support "the innumerable committees, leagues, bureaus and congresses" created by the CPUSA.[40] Extreme anticommunists had little tangible evidence but much faith in this view of an active, menacing Communist Party.

Lyons's "red decade" thesis made it difficult for extreme anticommunists to get along with the rest of the intellectual community. Their absolute need to expose others, and particularly other intellectuals, alienated many. When people recoiled at their methods or their more fanciful accusations, extreme anticommunists interpreted their actions as further proof of conspiracy. The more convinced they became of conspiracy, the more extreme their accusations became, and the more the community rejected them. This cycle pushed them farther and farther to the margins. After Benjamin Stolberg described the American Federation of Teachers as "the only AFL union controlled by the Communists," former AFT president Jerome Davis took him to court. Davis charged Stolberg and the magazine in which he published, the *Saturday Evening Post,* with libel. The outcome of the trial indicated where the nexus of power lay on the left. Davis engaged Arthur Garfield Hays of the ACLU to represent him. Stolberg had only Eugene Lyons in his corner and Lyons "proved a poor witness." The *Saturday Evening Post* settled out of court, giving Davis $11,000.[41] The case reinforced Stolberg's conspiratorial beliefs, especially since something so obvious to him remained unacknowledged by others. The more extreme anticommunists further undermined their status and narrowed their options by antics such as Stolberg's. They scorned, and were scorned by, what John Dos Passos called the "subsidized liberal"[42] magazines (*The New Republic* and *The Nation*), but converted a basic difference of opinion into a conspiracy theory.

Eugene Lyons's attacks on the liberal press, even more so than Stolberg's, demonstrated the gap between extreme anticommunists and the rest of the intellectual community. Lyons was convinced that a Communist-controlled press tailored opinion for its own benefit even after the Pact. Those few anti-Party books that saw the light of day, he said, did poorly in "the liberal and quasi-liberal press" and amongst the "many reviewers for major newspapers and magazines."[43] His *Red Decade* received respectable enough reviews in such publications by anticommunist reviewers like Max Eastman and William Henry Chamberlin; but Lyons was not satisfied that he received fair treatment. He publicly accused Corliss Lamont of interfering with the distribution of his book. Lamont, he complained, "has intimidated one of the country's largest book distributors into withdrawing 'The Red De-

cade' and has tried unsuccessfully to do it with others." Like Jerome
Davis, Lamont decided to sue. Lyons hoped to enlist ACLU support, but
John Haynes Holmes consulted with Lamont (who was a Union board
member) and then told Lyons this was "nothing more nor less than . . .
a straight and simple suit for libel" and not a civil liberties case. In the
end, Lyons felt let down by liberals and retreated even farther to the
right.[44] Lyons exaggerated the reception accorded his book and found
an easy explanation for its unpopularity. Thus his confrontational attitudes and immoderate views signaled danger to liberal anticommunists, who saw in such behaviors the possibility of undemocratic actions. Holmes liked *The Red Decade* and read it "with satisfaction and
admiration" but "wish[ed] that the book had been written in a somewhat kinder spirit.""I looked in vain," he added, "for even the briefest
confession of the fact that you yourself had known days when you
were as enthusiastic over revolutionary Russia as the rest of us."[45] It
was the extremism of the position more than its actual message that
distinguished someone like Lyons from someone like Holmes.

But Lyons's book could not be the kinder portrait liberal anticommunists wished for. He lacked their equilibrium. He was prepared for
the possibility that in the hunt for Communists "innocent bystanders
may get hurt." Liberal anticommunists balanced individual rights
with the public good, fitting anticommunism into a larger tradition of
democratic liberalism. Lyons thought such careful accounting possibly foolish, for the dangers posed by Communism were "infinitely
greater"[46] than anticommunism's threat to civil liberties. Liberal anticommunists flinched at such excesses, which, in turn, reinforced extreme anticommunist paranoia and, ultimately, isolation.

No issue more clearly separated liberal anticommunists from their
more energetic counterparts than the question of public exposure via
government hearings and investigations. Both assisted the government
in its post-Pact anticommunist crusade. Liberal anticommunists, however, were generally reluctant participants while extreme anticommunists were more enthusiastically cooperative. Jay Lovestone appeared
before Dies under duress, carefully disassociating himself from "a
great deal of the procedure of the committee." Bernard Grebanier, like
Lovestone an ex-Communist, appeared before the Rapp-Coudert committee investigating Communist infiltration in education in New York
State, with less trepidation. He willingly spoke about his past and,
when asked, confirmed the identity of nine Party members who were
fellow instructors at Brooklyn College at public hearings and named

thirty-one privately. Grebanier's testimony helped lead to the dismissal of several colleagues. He was vaguely uncomfortable with his role in the investigation, but not especially contrite. "I hadn't supplied a single name that they didn't have," he explained. His fellow instructors, most of them liberals, disapproved. His students booed him in the corridors.[47] Grebanier had been too obsequious for liberal anticommunists and had failed to demonstrate enough concern for the subtleties of liberal anticommunism.

Without the support of the liberal community, extreme anticommunists sailed right past the political center and toward the political right very quickly. Some joined forces with Martin Dies or other congressional investigators or right-wing organizations. J. B. Matthews served as an expert on Dies's staff after breaking with the American League against War and Fascism in 1934. Morris Ernst struck up a friendship with J. Edgar Hoover, and the proposal he pitched to various intellectual organizations concerning registration of organizations "subject to foreign control" found its official voice in the Voorhis Registration Act.[48] Anticommunist politicians welcomed the added weight of any intellectual endorsement, while extreme anticommunists, who felt deserted by their peers, were happy to receive acceptance anywhere. Although some would deny their conservatism until the end, most were swept in a more conservative direction by their anticommunism.

By the end of 1940 anti-Stalinism was collapsing as a separate political category. Many of its one-time advocates, like Sidney Hook, were in transit to the political right. Isolated pockets of anti-Stalinism still existed, most notably in the *Partisan Review* staff offices, but most *Partisan* staffers ultimately joined the liberal anticommunist ranks. Only anti-Stalinism broadly defined as Marxist opposition to Stalinism continued to exist in any systematic way, and that was within the American Trotskyist movement. Yet, the Pact prompted an internal crisis within the Socialist Workers Party because not all Trotskyists could sustain Trotsky's confidence that Stalinism and Marxism were incompatible entities. "On the face of things," Irving Howe recalled, "we were quarreling about language: what to *call* the Stalinist dictatorship we all abhorred."[49] But the quarrel was not about semantics, but about Marxism, Stalinism, and Trotskyism.

Trotsky never even entertained the possibility that the Nazi-Soviet Pact would alter his qualified support of the Soviet Union. War, he conceded, might give Stalin enough force to completely end socialism, but so too might it accelerate a world revolution. In the meantime, he insisted, "we do not change our course." Neither the Red Army's invasion of Poland nor its occupation of Finland swayed him in the least. Whatever Stalin did was a "'lesser evil'" than Hitler. It was imperative, he told his American supporters, to "defend the social basis of the USSR, if it is menaced by danger on the part of imperialism."[50] Trotsky's faith in the Bolshevik Revolution never wavered.

Not all SWP members were as confident as their mentor. Max Shachtman and James Burnham wanted the organization to debate the meaning of the Pact because it marked a major policy change within the USSR. Conveniently, both sat on the SWP's board, which met to discuss the matter on a day when James P. Cannon, always loyal to Trotsky, was absent. Burnham proposed and the board agreed to convene the larger national committee to discuss the matter. The board asked him to draft a preliminary statement on the Soviet Union and the Pact, a request already suggesting its bias given Burnham's past concerns about the USSR's status as a workers' state. Cannon attended the next meeting and denounced the motion, but could not reverse it. Party discipline demanded that he do as directed by the board and arrange for the larger meeting and distribute copies of the statement. He did so, but ungraciously, assuring the national committee that there was "nothing particularly new in the policy of the Stalin bureaucracy." Burnham and Shachtman protested. Cannon called them disrupters who violated the essence of a vanguard party with their constant requests for debate. Soon the organization had another factional dispute on its hands.[51]

Cannon's "Majority" faction, a label which gave them the aura of orthodoxy, approached the upcoming discussion as a tactical matter rather than a theoretical one. Cannon's first priority was making sure he prevailed. He sent an emissary to Trotsky and began to court young Trotskyists, Shachtman's traditional power base. He helped precipitate a sudden "financial crisis" at the *Socialist Appeal,* forcing staff cutbacks that conveniently purged the Minority faction. Because the Minority predominated in New York City, he brought in Majority functionaries from outlying regions.[52] Soon his supporters were in place to do battle over the nature of the Soviet Union, a debate that to Cannon's way of thinking had been already decided by Trotsky.

The Minority politicked themselves, but accused Cannon of deliberately ignoring the theoretical side to their dispute. This, they argued, was typical. Cannon ran the SWP in an autocratic manner, refusing to allow discussion, debate, or even democracy. Their tactic successfully broadened their support base. Their position paper, "War and the Bureaucratic Conservatism," indicted the SWP's leadership and especially Cannon for creating "bureaucratic conservatism"; war in Europe only served to exacerbate its tendencies. It was *"apparatus politics"*:

> Its chief base, in any organization or movement, larger or small, is the "apparatus." Objectively considered, the goal and purpose and aim of the bureaucratic conservative tendency is *to preserve itself*. To this aim all else is, in the last analysis, subordinated.
>
> It is for this reason that the politics adopted by the bureaucratic conservative tendency tend always toward being *conservative*. It is the defender of the *status quo*.

Cannon used Trotsky to imbue his apparatus with legitimacy, the statement explained. When the Minority questioned Trotsky's pronouncements, they likewise threatened Cannon's authority, so he quickly closed off discussion. "More and more we find that the Cannon faction *resists* every new idea, every new experiment."[53] The implications were impossible to miss; "bureaucratic conservatism" was just another name for Stalinism. The Shachtman-Burnham group cleverly identified themselves as innovators stifled by Stalin-like bureaucrats.

The Majority did not answer the accusations, but offered up its own interpretation of Minority motives. Cannon branded them habitual malcontents, unable to commit to revolutionary politics because they were "petty bourgeois" intellectuals. They joined the organization but remained reserved, avoiding all the difficult tasks of party building, and then left when "someone steps[ped] on . . . [their] toes." They "should quit politics and read poetry for a while,"[54] he told a friend. Burnham and Shachtman were hardly surprised by Cannon's comments; he had never been very amenable to theoretical discussion within the organization nor very open to democracy. What did surprise them was that Trotsky, the "intellectual and . . . big city man," as Burnham called him, picked up the theme. Thinkers, Trotsky noted, "are more or less outsiders from the general current of the workers' movement." The Socialist Workers Party had only enough room for one theoretician, apparently, and that one was Trotsky. This "anti-intellectual 'tough-guyness' " seemed especially "ludicrous," a Minority member recalled, because "it had been one of our [swp's] boasts that intellectuals were coming over to us."[55] The only way some Trotskyist intellectuals felt they could maintain their integrity was to regroup on their own.

As Trotsky suggested, "from a scratch" the swp developed gangrene only treatable by amputation. The climax came in April 1940, at the national plenum. Cannon's Majority prevailed and expelled the Minority "until such time as they signify their readiness to abide by convention decisions." Cannon took little joy in his victory, however, for roughly half the swp followed the Minority out the door. So too did it take *The New International,* most intellectuals, and much of the youth movement.[56] When all was said and done, the American Trotskyist movement proved to be no more supportive of intellectual freedom than the cpusa seemed to be.

The Minority immediately created its own Workers Party, as a more democratic alternative to the swp. More than anything, however, the Workers Party came to symbolize the continuing contradictions of anti-Stalinism. As one commentator noted, it was "founded on doubt." Burnham quickly gave into that doubt, resigning less than a month after it was founded because "by no stretching of terminology can I any longer regard myself, or permit others to regard me, as a Marxist." His *The Managerial Revolution,* published in 1941, suggested that he edged toward the same type of analysis as other deradicalizing anti-Stalinists, except that what others called a totalitarian state he called a managerial one. Its essence was bureaucratic. Its leaders were bureaucrats, experts who sought to rationalize the economy for their own benefit, excluding both the bourgeoisie and Marx's working class from power. It was, in effect, a dictatorship, except that Burnham was more interested in economics than politics.[57] Such a view made him an outcast, even among anticommunists. Yet, as Dwight Macdonald noted, his defection from the Workers Party "was a special blow" to those who "stood for a more democratic and less orthodox party."[58] Burnham's resignation, the European war, and Trotsky's death at the hands of an assassin quickly reduced the Workers Party's ranks to 323. Although it grew during the war, afterward it scaled down until it re-created itself as the Independent Socialist League in 1949. Under Shachtman's leadership the Independent Socialist League went back into the Socialist Party in the 1950s. Shachtman, however, followed the more common anti-Stalinist trajectory, moving to the right. Like Burnham, who also shifted rightward, he was never quite able to distinguish socialism from Stalinism.[59]

The Socialist Workers Party fared little better than the Workers Party in the short term. Trotsky's death was a shock, leaving the American movement, already weakened by the split, rudderless. External persecution made the SWP's situation even worse. In a curious irony, Trotskyists were the first official victims of the post-Pact red scare. Twenty-eight SWP leaders were indicted under the provisions of the Smith Act. The Communists, setting an odd precedent, supported the government's indictment of their traditional enemies, little realizing that the law would soon be used against them too. James T. Farrell formed a Civil Rights Defense Committee for the twenty-eight, an organization with a familiar cast of characters, including John Dewey, Mary McCarthy, and Edmund Wilson. Although the Committee endured the usual Party attacks, without the People's Front to buck, it gained far more intellectual credence than the earlier American Committee for the Defense of Leon Trotsky. The Socialist Workers Party survived the crippling blows and continues to exist today. Although many of its intellectuals fell away over the years, the continuing commitments of a radical party, as Alan Wald has persuasively argued, helped intellectuals keep the Marxist faith in a way those like Burnham, who distanced themselves from the movement, could not.[60]

The Marxist faith was not easy to keep in the aftermath of the Nazi-Soviet Pact. Party intellectuals, like their Trotskyist counterparts, often held onto it through their disciplined involvement in practical radical activities. Anti-Stalinists rarely could. Their doubts were too numerous and their actual commitments too few. But they had trouble really letting Communism go. It colored their ideology, in many cases, for the rest of their lives. Anti-Stalinism was a short-lived phenomenon. But the anticommunisms it helped spawn—both liberal and extreme—were much longer lasting.

NINE

The "Official Creed":

The Legacy of the 1930s

Intellectual Left

The People's Front did not, with time, fade into hazy memory. It remained a potent and powerful symbol for the intellectuals who actively remembered it. Its meanings were many, as were the lessons it supposedly taught. Its capacity to divide the left intellectual community continued unabated through the 1940s and 1950s. Yet, its reputation grew more tarnished over time. If it represented the left-wing intellectual establishment in the 1930s, its remaining defenders represented precisely the opposite in postwar America. The new intellectual establishment was liberal and anticommunist. A new generation and a new set of values gained ascendancy.

After 1940, front politics lost what little respectability they had in the 1930s. World War II might have revived them, but did not. Progressives were warier than in 1937 and 1938. They supported the war, admired the Soviet contribution, but were less willing to put themselves back into front organizations. Two swift policy reversals did little to help the CPUSA. As Granville Hicks observed, "the party made the new shift [away from isolationism after Hitler invaded the USSR] with more grace than the preceding one, but I don't believe their gracefulness is going to get them much." Stalin's dissolution of the Comintern likewise failed to impress. Even the announcement of a new, broader "political association" to replace the Party seemed cynical and self-serving. "Under any name," Freda Kirchwey explained, "communism smells about the same to the people who don't like it."[1] Party membership rose during the war, but intellectuals only tolerated the organization.

Nothing better demonstrated progressive wariness than the fortunes of that one-time centerpiece of the intellectual People's Front, the League of American Writers. Its reputation improved little after the invasion of the USSR. By the end of 1942, it was $3500 in debt and completely dependent on personal loans from its leading members. Its leaders gambled heavily on a Writers-Win-the-War Congress. But even its list of sponsors was anemic.[2] The conference, moreover, never materialized, for the League's efforts were eclipsed by a more popular wartime organization, the Writers Mobilization. It succeeded where the League failed, bringing together many writers in support of American war aims.

One of the reasons why the Writers Mobilization was more attractive than the battle-scarred LAW was that its reputation was pure. Progressives never endorsed the full League program, for that meant supporting the "Writers Congress Creed." But they needed the LAW to fight fascism, so accepted the Communist input. During the war, however, they could fight fascism without making such compromises by joining the service, working for the government, or allying with patriotic groups. They could circumvent the CPUSA entirely. They were liberated from the "Writers Congress Creed."

Still, antifascism, converted to all-out support for the Allies, tenuously linked them with the CPUSA and distinguished them from anticommunists. While liberated from the "Writers Congress Creed," progressives could actually muster a much more enthusiastic admiration for Stalin's waging of the war than they ever could for his purges.[3] That prolonged the 1930s quarrels. They read into anticommunists' discomfort with the wartime alliance with Russia a lack of sufficient enthusiasm for the war. The "hang-back boys," as Bruce Bliven called them, were "liberals . . . Socialists, ex-Socialists, Trotskyists or ex-Communists" so obsessed with communism that they "refus[ed] to take any real part in the struggle between fascism and democracy." Theirs was a "phenomenon by itself" prompted by disillusionment, a sense of persecution, and "neurotic and unstable personalities." Yet, as Bliven noted:

> Some of the I-hate-Russia group have found this attitude extremely profitable, financially and otherwise. These gentlemen make a fat living out of

retelling endlessly the story of how dreadful the USSR is. They can now get
big fees from mass-circulation magazines whose pages would certainly be
closed to them on any other subject. Socially, too, doors are now open that
would otherwise be barred. Perhaps they enjoy, unconsciously, being taken
seriously, for the first time in their lives by the "solid, respectable elements" in the community.[4]

Bliven was right. Anticommunism remained strong in the popular
imagination and was reinforced by anticommunist intellectuals. There
were not very many "hang-back boys." There were, though, a great
many intellectuals who endorsed the war but were lukewarm about
the USSR. As John Dewey told the *New York Times,* "It is possible
to rejoice in Russian victories over the common enemy without ide-
alizing Stalin's regime of terror." Anticommunists believed that progressives never learned, apologizing for Stalin all over again, although
Liston Oak thought Bliven and his counterpart at *The Nation* were
"true innocents, displaying the persistent naiveté of liberals" rather
than "not-so-innocent agent[s] of a foreign power." The picture was
both powerful and inaccurate: progressives just kept joining front
groups to be used by a Comintern that "despised them as cowards."[5]

Between the time of the Nazi-Soviet Pact and Pearl Harbor, anticommunism gathered momentum. By 1943, anticommunists had enough
strength to publicize an open letter protesting the film version of *Mission to Moscow,* Ambassador Joseph Davies's sympathetic memoir of
his years in the USSR. Sixty-six signed the statement, which called the
film's release "a political event to which no thoughtful American can
remain indifferent." The letter accused the "Mission to Moscow" pro-
ducers of presenting "the kind of historical falsifications which have
hitherto been characteristic of totalitarian propaganda." Many of the
signatories, including Sidney Hook, Bertram Wolfe, James T. Farrell,
Norman Thomas, and Ferdinand Lundberg, were ACDLT veterans still
determined to force a public acknowledgment of Trotsky's innocence.
But they were not just concerned that the film misrepresented the
Moscow trials. "'Mission to Moscow,'" the letter warned, "has the
most serious implications for American democracy." Progressives
complained that the letter credited an essentially trivial film with too
much power. Several refused to sign it because it was so obsessed with
the trials and rehashed old ACDLT battles. Hook believed that the open
letter was completely eclipsed by a far more effective studio campaign
"with the active help of every Stalinist organization in the country."

212   But it was not really fair to judge its success against a studio promotion undertaken to sell a film. All things considered, anticommunists did quite well with their "Mission to Moscow" campaign, quickly gathering an impressive and large list of sponsors.[6] They proved they were both ready and able to flex their muscles. They had progressives on the run.

"Things are really pretty bad in Washington as regards the people who belonged to united-front organizations," Malcolm Cowley reported to Kenneth Burke in 1942. He was in a position to know, having been exposed to the full force of the anticommunists' wrath. Tapped by Archibald MacLeish to serve in the Office of Facts and Figures, his Front-period record held up his confirmation. Martin Dies told the House of Representatives he was "one of the chief Communist intellectuals of this country" with seventy-two questionable associations. The FBI kept a thick dossier on him, questioning his friends and tracking his activities. "Ex-communists (J. B. Matthews, Whittaker Chambers of *Time,* Eugene Lyons and somebody close to Sidney Hook, if it wasn't Sidney himself)" supplied the government with information. MacLeish gave Cowley a quick look at the FBI file, which, indeed, included an interview with Hook along with two other ex'es. After briefly trying to correct the record, Cowley abandoned the task and the job. His progressive friends were shocked by his experience. Van Wyck Brooks felt it "was a scary trick they played on you." Felix Frankfurter called him a "victim" of "blind irrationality." Freda Kirchwey thought his investigation "part of a much larger affair which begins to look extremely menacing." Menacing, indeed, and, to Joseph Gollumb, particularly so since "guys like you and me with the records of antifascist activities dating far back" were threatened by relative slackers in the war against Hitler. "Yet," Gollumb commented, "they seem to be in a position to throw stones at us and get away with it."[7]

Cowley was not the only target of a wartime anticommunist campaign. Frederick Schuman and Jerre Mangione both endured investigations after they sought temporary employment with the government. Muriel Rukeyser became the target of a full FBI investigation when she accepted a job at the Bureau for Publications and Graphics. Josephine Herbst returned from lunch one day to her job at the Office of the Coordinator of Information to find her desk padlocked and two government investigators waiting to question her. Schuman and Mangione were ultimately cleared; but Rukeyser resigned and Herbst was

fired because of information collected by the FBI from anticommunist informants, including her friend, novelist Katherine Anne Porter.
Robert Morss Lovett, government secretary to the Virgin Islands, was
asked to resign after the House Appropriations Committee held up
funding for the territory until he was dismissed. The assault against
"ordinary, decent people" seemed clear to The New Republic. It
started with disgruntled ex- and anti-communists, who passed "not
very accurate" information on to the FBI and the Dies committee, who
then used that material "to strain anti-fascists and liberals out of the
government." Progressives feared the consequences of this crusade. "If
Dies and his friends can get away with their persecution of Lovett,
Schuman and the others," The New Republic warned, "no American is
safe."[8]

Anticommunists were not immune to investigation of their radical
pasts, but they were able to gather strength and build for themselves a
support network during the war years. The Partisan Review continued
to preach the anti-Stalinist line; Dwight Macdonald's short-lived Politics created a second bastion for left-wing anti-Stalinists. And extreme anticommunists gained an organ of their own, The New Leader.
Though the publication had been a social democratic forum, a 1944
change of editorship put such strong anticommunists as Leon Dennen,
Max Eastman, Hook, and Eugene Lyons in charge. It became, in Alan
Wald's apt phrase, "a halfway house for right-wing social-democratic
anti-communists from which virtually no one returned." Although
each of these journals had a different editorial line, all shared a distaste for front politics and a moral righteousness about the necessity of
speaking out against them. "There are plenty of subversive activities in
America which constitute a threat to democratic institutions," the new
New Leader editorial board declared; "having them officially exposed
to public inspection would serve a good purpose."[9]

Progressive hesitation and anticommunist sentiment helped reinforce the larger public conclusion that while Stalin might be a wartime friend, Communists were not to be trusted on a continuing basis.
Stalin bolstered his sagging public relations image by waging all-out
war against Hitler. American Communists, however, could not prove
themselves like the Russians did. They garnered little wartime sympathy. No one beyond a very small circle of Party sympathizers and old
civil libertarians really paid much attention to the persecution of Communists. A Committee to Free Earl Browder made no headway until

Roosevelt had him released from prison on the eve of the Soviet foreign minister's visit. The government repressed and spied on Communists, despite their eagerness to fight the war. Donald Ogden Stewart and Ella Winters had their mail intercepted by the FBI. Draftees and recruits with Communist pasts often got assigned to obscure places, removed from the fighting and outside of sensitive projects. Enlistee Dashiell Hammett spent the war in Alaska on a base so remote that even the FBI had trouble locating him.[10] No matter how hard the CPUSA tried to mainstream itself, it could not.

The Party's attempted wartime transformation made matters no better. Inspired by the dissolution of the Comintern and the spirit of the Teheran Conference, Browder disbanded the Party and replaced it with the Communist Political Association. The CPA was supposed to work within the two-party system in alliance with existing parties. It was American and not revolutionary. But "Browderism," as it was called, quickly lost out. The CPA had many problems, not the least of which was Moscow's disapproval. Browder misunderstood Stalin's motives for dissolving the Comintern. He was not signaling national movements to become more independent; he just wanted to maintain harmony with the West for the duration of the war. The Communists purged Browder and reinstated the organization's former name and status. His downfall reinforced the CPUSA's public relations problems. Having repudiated the politics of moderation, it adopted its logical alternative.[11]

The controversy had implications for intellectuals as well as workers. The spirit of Browderism spilled over into the cultural arena. *New Masses'* editor Isidor Schneider opened the discussion with a 1945 analysis of "writers' problems." He described a series of felt obligations and restrictions that affected the work of the writer who, as he coyly put it, "took his stand with the labor movement." In the end, though, he suggested that the stereotype of the Party intellectual forced to conform to literary dicta or spend time writing "for the needy 'Left' publications . . . without payment" was self-induced and self-inflicted. "No writer," he concluded, "need worry about being politically correct if his work is faithful to reality," implying that no writer was ever asked by the CPUSA to compromise his work. Several months later, Albert Maltz challenged this optimistic vision. He believed that what Schneider saw as a self-inflicted role was in fact "*induced in the writer by the intellectual atmosphere of the left wing.*" Maltz was not wholly opposed to using art to express politics, but he thought that the Party literati had "converted" the phrase "art is a class weapon" from "a profound analytic insight" into "a vulgar slogan." "Writers must be judged by their work," he wrote, "and not by the committees they join." Yet Maltz did not really ask for the Party to change so much as for individuals to be less "narrow" and "shallow" in their judgments of others and more a part of "the great humanistic tradition of culture" themselves. But, as one film historian noted, Maltz's article was perceived as "the literary equivalent of the Browder line." Hollywood writers initially stood behind him as a protest against what they saw as the New York-centeredness of Communist culture. Once the big guns of the Communist literary movement (Schneider, Michael Gold, Samuel Sillen, and Joseph North) pronounced that he "preach[ed] . . . a terrible confusion," however, Maltz realized that he stood alone and faced "the choice of being expelled from the party or of . . . repudiating . . . [my] positions." He recanted.[12]

The episode barely made a wave outside of Party circles, yet touched several of Maltz's intellectual comrades. The CPUSA did not ask writers to put on "straitjacket[s]"[13] after the Browder episode, but the Maltz episode entered the noncommunist left's "cultural memory"[14] as yet another example of precisely the kind of narrow cultural vision and confining intellectual role Schneider denied. Of course, Schneider undercut his own position by resigning from *The New Masses* and leaving the CPUSA because he could not complete his novel "in the hullabaloo about the Maltz article." He explained why to Malcolm Cowley:

> After all these years in organization work I've lost what capacity I've had, which was never very much, to take the political mind. . . . I thought I could work effectively in left cultural organs and organizations, and maintain literary values at the same time. . . . As I now see it I would have been more effectual even in the political aims I set myself had I continued writing.

Guy Endore complained in the aftermath of the Browder purge "of years, years of being treated like a little boy, years of being called to hell, years of being told again and again how I erred." Schneider's inability to complete his novel while at *New Masses* and Endore's weariness at being directed by Party functionaries spoke to a much larger issue than a literary line. Both felt that it was impossible to function as an intellectual should while performing their duties as Party members. "Political necessities," as Schneider called them, made good writing impossible.[15]

The emerging cold war delivered more blows to an American Communist movement already reeling from the Browderism debacle and the Maltz controversy. Party leaders were tried and jailed for violating the Smith Act. The FBI launched an all-out investigation of thousands of American Communists, questioning their coworkers, opening their mail, tapping their phones. The "separate world," as Ellen Schrecker called it, of Party fronts, summer camps, and labor unions that insulated the CPUSA could not survive the siege. Members left, as they always had, but new ones did not join.[16] The Wallace campaign of 1948 showed the impact of all the propaganda, investigations, and innuendo. Wallace was seen as an extremist and, worse, "a prisoner of the Commies."[17] The CPUSA was in an impossible position after the war.

Anticommunists, especially liberal ones, by contrast, were in a good position to influence how both policymakers and the public saw Communism. Their opinions appeared in newspapers and magazines. Their arguments circulated through the Truman administration. Many held academic positions. Hannah Arendt's 1951 book *The Origins of Totalitarianism* articulated in greater depth ideas anticommunists first raised in the late 1930s.[18] The very same people who lamented the power progressives seemed to have over educated public opinion in the 1930s themselves had tremendous resonance after World War II.

At its best, liberal anticommunism also had a social agenda that appealed to a generation raised on the New Deal. While some intellectuals "vulgarize[d] . . . [their anticommunism] into a politics barely distinguishable from reaction," as Irving Howe wrote, others wanted to protect and extend Roosevelt's domestic programs, fight for civil rights, and defeat poverty.[19] Liberals were not automatically supportive of American society. They were often critical of its conservatism, its middlebrow culture, and its continued inequities. Americans for Democratic Action, a postwar version of the Union for Democratic Action, represented the most left-wing version of liberal anticommunism, one so liberal right-wingers considered it subversive.[20] Some liberals felt this positive agenda enhanced the other half of their philosophy. "You don't fight Communism by being AGAINST IT," Archibald MacLeish explained, "but by being FOR something immeasurably better."[21] Like John Dewey, who saw anticommunism as only the first step toward a larger liberal agenda, some postwar liberal anticommunists wanted to build something immeasurably better.

All too often, however, anticommunists were *against* more than they were *for*. Liberal and more extreme anticommunists went to great lengths to distinguish themselves from one another, but the features they had in common often made them tacit partners against progressives. In his autobiography, Sidney Hook denounced William Phillips, Philip Rahv, Mary McCarthy, and Alfred Kazin on political grounds, generally for their failure to condemn Soviet crimes loudly enough or often enough for his tastes. McCarthy and Kazin, on the other hand, were highly suspicious of Hook's politics, seeing him as a Johnny-one-note when it came to communism. Yet, all worked with one another to defeat "totalitarianism." Nathan Glazer later remembered that "we did try—or most of us did—to distance ourselves from the most intense anti-communists: yet we also ended up pretty much in the same camp as they." The reason why, he suggested, was that "American anticommunist intellectuals did not spend much time on proportionality."[22] Anticommunism became their single-minded focus.

The Europe-America Group demonstrated some of the complexity of the situation. Founded in 1947 by McCarthy, Kazin, Macdonald, and others, it was part of a broader movement to help "independent democrats and socialists" redefine "internationalism [and] . . . distributive economic justice" in a postwar world. McCarthy remembered recruiting another group of members to broaden its base. They were more anticommunist. Soon, this "Sidney Hook gang," "tried to steal our treasury" and wrote a strongly anticommunist plank into its manifesto: "We regard Stalinism as the main enemy in Europe today." The "Hook gang" converted the Europe-America Group into a kind of Marshall Plan for intellectuals in other countries, "a relief group" that rewarded anticommunists with money. McCarthy liked to tell the story this way, but the differences between Hook and his friends and the presumably more principled McCarthy group were not always so clear. There is some evidence to suggest that the Europe-America Group's initial tone did not express its founders' internationalist vision so much as their need to cater to European intellectuals who were more socialist and less anticommunist than they were. The Europe-America Group, like so many other ex-anti-Stalinist organizations, was filled with people who liked to debate, fight, and intrigue and expected organizations to accommodate that style. As one of McCarthy's biographers has pointed out, 1947 was not the 1980s; Hook's "gang" was not yet conservative. McCarthy had far less reason to harbor suspicions of his motives. Differences within the group were more rhetorical than substantive.[23]

Liberal and extreme anticommunists also seemingly worked at cross purposes to protest the largest postwar front gathering, the Waldorf Cultural and Scientific Conference of 1949, but the matter was, again, more complex. Liberals wanted access to the meetings to voice their opposition to the explicit pro-Sovietism of the conference. Extreme anticommunists predicted they would not get it and formulated more aggressive plans. McCarthy, Macdonald, and a few others easily obtained tickets to the Waldorf and two minutes of stage time each. Their goal was "to ask embarrassing questions" of the Communists and their now smaller circle of supporters. Hook was not granted an opportunity to speak, although it is not clear if he was excluded for political reasons or because his request came too late. He brought together more extreme anticommunists, called them American Intellectuals for Freedom, and proceeded "to make trouble." Armed with $5,000, they took a hotel room at the Waldorf and disrupted meetings, issued false press statements, and intercepted mail. As McCarthy's biographer noted, in her later accounts of the Waldorf Conference, "it isn't the Stalinists who gave the rebels [McCarthy group] a run for their money, but the Hook crowd." Neither Macdonald nor McCarthy liked to be linked with Hook. But they too belonged to American Intellectuals for Freedom, which met, on occasion, at Macdonald's house. Hook coached McCarthy on how to hold the floor at the conference. Hook's later politics were much more embarrassing to them than his earlier anticommunism. But even at the time, liberal anticommunism gained stature through juxtaposition with more extreme varieties. And extreme anticommunists forged ahead where liberals sometimes feared to tread. Both could, at times, see the other as "principled."[24]

The collaboration of the two factions was most evident in the American Committee for Cultural Freedom, built out of the remnants of the CCF and the AIF. Although the ACCF was part of an international network of anticommunist organizations, it was more conservative and more anticommunist than most other affiliates, reflecting, as it did, the contribution of such people as Hook, Eastman, and James Burnham. Representing no political program and opposing only "totalitarianism," it was genuinely diverse.[25] But it was not the liberal anticommu-

nism of the McCarthys, Macdonalds, or Kazins that drove the ACCF.
Rather, it was the more extreme anticommunism of the Hooks and the
Diana Trillings.

The reason was that the early ACCF operated from a siege mentality.
"Whatever the Communist Party is for," a member of a much smaller
rival organization, the Emergency Civil Liberties Committee, complained, "they are against." The ACCF's strenuous campaign to undermine the ECLC and secure its own ascendancy as the protector of
cultural freedom strengthened its more extreme side. The battle for
cultural freedom, which the CCF hoped to win in 1939/40, was refought
in the early 1950s. The ACCF pursued the ECLC as diligently as anticommunists ever went after any front, although the attorney general's office
did not consider it subversive. When the ECLC convened a 1953 conference on the Bill of Rights, the ACCF reacted by sending all participants telegrams asking if they were "aware that this organization is a
Communist front with no sincere interest in liberty in the United States
or elsewhere." ACCF head Irving Kristol publicly identified ECLC director Clark Foreman as "a gentleman with an inordinately long record of
association with Communist front organizations." Challenged to prove
his allegations, he retreated to the phrase "popular front." A year later,
the ECLC honored Albert Einstein and the ACCF called the tribute "exploitation."[26] Like its parent organization, the ACCF was run by extreme
anticommunists who triumphed over the more hesitant liberals.

When called upon to defend their ideals more assertively, liberal
anticommunists in the ACCF panicked at the prospect of being linked
with front politics. Joseph McCarthy surely represented illiberal values, but he was also anticommunist. Progressives, including the ECLC,
strongly opposed him. Many ACCF members did not want to endorse
him, but neither were they happy standing with progressives. For two
long years, the ACCF did its best to ignore McCarthy. Extremists finally
forced the issue. At an ACCF-sponsored forum, "In Defense of Free
Culture," Max Eastman denied the existence of a red scare, blamed the
excesses of anticommunism on liberals who were not anticommunist
enough, and called McCarthy "a clear-headed patriot of freedom."
Some liberals were concerned. The very next day, James Wechsler
introduced a resolution expressing ACCF disapproval of McCarthy. It
was debated, ruled out of order, and never passed. Most members
neither liked McCarthy nor wanted to support what William Phillips
called the "CP view of America." "To oppose both Stalin and McCar-

thy," Eliot Cohen reasoned, "is to equate them,"[27] and it was this odd logic that shaped the ACCF's desire to avoid saying anything at all. McCarthy presented the ACCF with an impossible situation, for he was totalitarian in method but anti-totalitarian in goals. Liberal anticommunism had no vocabulary to understand McCarthy and no ways of restraining him.

The ACCF waited until McCarthy was weak enough to be safely and expediently denounced without "playing the game of the Stalinists." Even then, some members only agreed to take a stand because, as Sol Stein told Hook, it was "unpleasant but necessary if we are to get a more sympathetic following in the academic community." *McCarthy and the Communists,* commissioned by the organization, articulated the liberal anticommunist view that it was important to "combat communism responsibly." Extreme anticommunists resigned in protest.[28] Still, many believed that, even without the most extreme anticommunists, no qualifying adjective affected the ACCF's anticommunism.

Stalin died, McCarthy was censured, and the witch-hunt slowly subsided; but the ACCF remained staunchly anticommunist. In 1955, an internal memo complained that the organization lost sight of its original anticommunist goals. Members were urged to refocus "on [the] primary threat to cultural freedom: Communist totalitarianism." A year later, James T. Farrell resigned as chairman of the board, signaling the departure of the more liberal elements within the organization. A world tour made him critical of American foreign policy. "We have a rigid, hysterical, one-track fear of Communism" that was easily manipulated by other countries, he explained. Domestically, Farrell thought the ACCF had veered off track: "The Communist problem in the United States has now become minor rather than major. We no longer need to emphasize over and over again that we are the only intellectual anti-Communist committee, nor to think that we are the best experts in fighting Communism." Speaking on behalf of the board of directors, Diana Trilling suggested that "Farrell's resignation was thoroughly welcome."[29] Indeed, liberated of such critical input, the ACCF would continue on its anticommunist way into the 1960s.

The ACCF had "too much of reactionary anti-Communism" in it because liberals allowed themselves to be swept along in the anticommunist crusade without questioning the "excessive response that could be demanded from American institutions."[30] The case that pitted the symbol of unreconstructed progressivism, Alger Hiss, against the sadder-but-wiser ex-communist, Whittaker Chambers, showed both liberal faith and their hesitant doubts. All agreed Hiss was guilty, but liberal anticommunists were troubled by aspects of the trial, nonetheless. Richard Rovere considered the case "a red herring." Mary McCarthy thought it showed that a police mentality was ineffective against Communism: "Hiss is in the penitentiary, but he continues to tantalize us. We wanted the truth and all we got was his body." Despite these doubts about the political use of the trial or the government's equation of jail time with containing Communism, liberals were willing to accept Chambers' word over Hiss's because he was both knowledgeable and contrite. "Most anti-Communists have been through the Communist mill," explained Diana Trilling, "which has given them a first-hand knowledge of the Communist technique, personnel and idiom."[31] Chambers, with his pumpkin patch microfilm, was a more believable witness than Hiss because Hiss had not made a public confession. The curious conundrum of liberal anticommunism was the confession, which provided proof of a wicked past and a contrite present. The expectation that there would be confessions forthcoming, though, left no room for the innocent.

The conviction and execution of Ethel and Julius Rosenberg was another example of a case where liberal anticommunists felt both confident of two Communists' guilt and hesitant about their conviction. Their "uneasiness" concerned their sentence, although liberal anticommunists were, again, convinced they were spies. But death was an extreme punishment. Moreover, "if we execute the Rosenbergs," McCarthy noted, "we still will not have their confessions." And that suggested the drawbacks of a witch-hunt. You could convict people of espionage without changing their views. Liberal anticommunists did not want Communists' "bod[ies]"; they wanted their hearts and minds. If the Rosenbergs recanted, that would have reassured liberal anticommunists that liberal techniques worked against Communism, that when confronted with the truth, rational people would acknowledge it. The ACCF actually made their confessions a precondition "before any appeal for clemency can be regarded as having been made in good faith."[32] Liberal anticommunists were not as easily satisfied as their more extreme counterparts.

Liberal anticommunists were especially troubled by the witch-hunt when they were the ones performing the rituals of exposure. It was much harder to sit on the other side of the desk, answering questions and identifying friends and coworkers. The contradictory obligations of privacy, friendship, freedom, and fear haunted them. Bertram Wolfe, for example, agreed to sketch out the general impact of communism, but worried that if asked by HUAC about former friends he would violate his "old-fashioned notions about not readily revealing information which I learned purely because I was in a relation of confidence with other individuals." He might talk specifically about former friends, "if I felt that such individuals threatened our safety"; however, talking about old friends was clearly a gray area for him. The ritualistic nature of informing bothered McCarthy. Watching Arthur Miller before HUAC, she was struck by its expectation that he "*act*" like an informer, "defin[ing] himself as the kind of person who would interpose no obstacle between them and their right to know."[33] The emerging phenomenon of the professional witness also heightened liberal anticommunist anxieties about exposure. As Chambers joined ex'es like Elizabeth Bentley and Martin Berkeley as a professional witness, they had to confront the possibility that exposure was a business with rewards both personal and monetary. Rovere noted in 1942 that informers were "moved either by spite against their former friends or by a simple desire to save their own hides."[34] All exposure was not alike, apparently. Honest, unselfish, valuable testimony given freely would reveal the flaws of the Communist system. But being a witness under duress or for money or to extract revenge sullied the process. Unfortunately, liberal anticommunists never quite knew how to encourage the one without also taking information from the other.

Rovere might well maintain a cynical approach to informers in 1942, since Dies had not called him to testify. Once the House Un-American Activities Committee began its postwar hearings, people with Communist pasts and anticommunist presents were likely witnesses before the group, forcing them to come to terms with exposure and informing in a very personal way. As Victor Navasky has noted, "playing the informer runs against the American grain," even when one believes in the cause. A number of liberal anticommunists never quite reconciled their behavior before HUAC with their abstract distaste for revealing secrets about others. James Wechsler protested Lillian Hellman's description of him as a "friendly" HUAC witness in *Scoundrel Time,* demanding that the "defamatory" label be replaced. Subsequent editions described him as a "cooperative" witness, which he liked no better. Clearly Wechsler did not want to be perceived as someone who willingly answered the committee's questions. Michael Blankfort characterized his naming of names before HUAC as an accident tricked out of him. Like Wechsler, he did not want to be identified with the institution or the process despite his appearance.[35] Granville Hicks recorded the agonies he experienced when HUAC summoned him. He privately gave the committee names, but was "reluctant" to appear at a public session. "I could not logically plead the Fifth," he recalled, nor was he "opposed on principle to the investigation of Communism." He "had doubts about the way in which Congressional investigations were conducted and about the results they were able to achieve." He finally appeared before HUAC as requested and provided it with the names it wanted and felt "no damage was done." "I had no choice," he later claimed. His soul-searching was typical. And he "had my neighbors to think about."[36] Liberal anticommunists felt that refusing to cooperate would leave others rightly questioning their motives.

By the middle of the 1950s, most liberal anticommunists justified their encounters with investigatory bodies as unpleasant duties intellectuals had to perform for the greater social good. Few were pleased with everything HUAC did; but most were "impressed by the fairness and decency of the process" and all believed in the need for such committees to exist.[37] The larger cold war culture helped reassure them that exposing communism was the moral thing to do. Liberal anticommunists both contributed to that culture and received support from it. Elia Kazan's *On the Waterfront,* for example, substituted mobsters for Communists to make informing more acceptable. Two years before, Kazan testified before HUAC. James Rorty and Moshe Decter expressed the liberal anticommunist view of exposure in their ACCF-sponsored book on McCarthy. "Speaking out fully and frankly," they wrote, "serves to establish the credibility of the witness. It is probably also the best method of vindicating one's own values." Informers were thus "extolled as . . . model[s] whom others should emulate," Lewis Coser noted. They had, moreover, "an active support system within the liberal community," Victor Navasky argued. There were smaller problems, but exposure generally served the community and publicly demonstrated one's commitment to the right values. It was not just a duty, but a ritual or rite that proved one's willingness to be cooperative.[38]

Progressives refused to perform these rituals and were, consequently, suspect. Diana Trilling even went so far as to argue that by "neglect[ing] to do their own principled job of intellectual housecleaning," progressives provided "HUAC and McCarthy . . . [with] the field they had for their incursions upon democratic freedom." Most progressives no longer defended the USSR, so anticommunists faulted them, instead, for failing to participate in the "current sport of fighting communism" except in the most abstract and noncommittal of ways. William Henry Chamberlin called them "anti-anti-communists." The term itself suggested the deliberately adversarial relationship anticommunists perceived between themselves and active progressives. Anti-anticommunism did not denote a different intellectual position; it represented no legitimate position at all. Progressives "did not act like intellectuals" when they suspended their critical function in the 1930s in order to support the Soviet Union. While they might grow dubious of the USSR or lose interest in politics, they could not "get rid so easily of the stinking albatross [of Stalinism]," as Sidney Hook told Corliss Lamont. Progressives continued to identify "good causes" with the CPUSA. They insisted on protecting its ability to do damage in a free society. Hicks acknowledged that he, as a liberal anticommunist, valued what most people of "the *PM–Nation–New Republic*" stripe did, but was "not very well satisfied" that they selected their values for the right reasons. His description was reminiscent of an older means-versus-ends debate; good values adopted for the wrong reasons were as impossible as fighting fascism by condoning Stalinism. The more extreme anticommunists saw the situation in the most personal terms. What was wrong with anti-anticommunists, Chamberlin declared, was their "venomous hatred for the ex-Communists whose revelations made possible the smashing of at least some . . . conspiracies," in short, their failure to value what he did as an intellectual.[39] Liberal anticommunists did not believe that progressives selected their values to annoy and denigrate their colleagues, but they could never exactly decide whether they were muddled thinkers or just adopted that protective coloration.

Liberal and extreme anticommunists debated the amount of damage anti-anticommunists were capable of doing, their motives, and the range of their control. The most extreme anticommunists continued to hold a very conspiratorial view of the intellectual world, one where "submission to Moscow" was the ticket to success. They, by contrast, suffered. "I have paid a certain penalty for my change in attitude," John Dos Passos told HUAC. It was all part of a whole, his suffering, the ambitious anti-anticommunists who "learned from the subtle and diligent propaganda fostered by the Communist Party" what to think, and the self-deprecating "melodramatic myth" anti-anticommunists encouraged of a witch-hunt that cost them "career[s], reputation[s], and even . . . liberty." Others rejected the notion of an outright conspiracy, but remained convinced that progressives held an unfair—and undeserved—advantage. Anti-anticommunists "love to denigrate their power," Diana Trilling concluded. "Liberal anti-Communism was not, and still is not, the recommended path to professional success," she added after her inflammatory remarks about *Scoundrel Time* cost her a publisher. Trilling's comments better described the 1930s than the 1970s, although, even in the 1930s, she did not seem to suffer conspicuously for her views.[40] By the 1970s, liberal anticommunists denigrated *their* power but prospered because of *their* views.

Their identification with outsiders was so great that they refused to recognize that change had occurred since their 1930s salad days as anti-Stalinists. They continued to picture themselves as eager and needy and thwarted by the "great abuser[s] of power," who were older, more established, less principled, and omnipotent. They were the "have-nots" unable to compete with the undeserving "haves." Never were the many levels of anticommunist resentment for the People's Front—class, ideological, generational, and personal—better captured than in a letter from Alfred Kazin to Malcolm Cowley:

> When I was young and unknown, you were unfailingly snotty. Later, you were unfailingly surly and even worse. But what you don't understand was that, at a time when I was trying to make my way out of the tenements, to rise above the misery of my life, you were not only directly unfriendly, but presented the interesting spectacle of a literary socialist who was certainly betting on the wave of the future, while I was losing my faith in the only religion [Marxism] I had.[41]

Times changed, but many anticommunists seemed loathe to let go of this image. When they read that anti-anticommunists were persecuted by congressional committees and the State Department, they mustered little sympathy. Progressives whined, Trilling noted, "even while . . . they exercise[d] an immeasurable influence as opinion formers." McCarthy's friends viewed Hellman's suit against her as a metaphor of the unequal powers wielded by two very different women: Hellman, made wealthy by her self-serving view of the McCarthy era and misrepresentation of her past, and McCarthy, honest but poorer and, therefore,

226   vulnerable to Hellman's determined attempt "to wreck" her.[42] The underdog image was too central to anticommunists' identities to let go.

Times, of course, had changed and anticommunists often left the
periphery for the center. "Everyone on PR [*Partisan Review*] is now
teaching," Philip Rahv bragged in 1950, "which shows you how far
things have gone." The *Partisan Review* eclipsed *The Nation* and *The
New Republic*. No postwar front group approached the status of the
American Committee for Cultural Freedom or the more left-wing
Americans for Democratic Action. A 1970 poll which asked intellectuals to identify their most influential peers included McCarthy, Kazin, Harold Rosenberg, and Hook along with a whole new generation of
cultural and political analysts like Daniel Bell, Leslie Fiedler, and
Nathan Glazer who cherished their ideals and values.[43] Whether or not
they were willing to admit it, liberal anticommunists were the intellectual leaders of postwar America.

With success came accommodation to the status quo that would
have been unthinkable to these same people as young Marxists in the
1930s. Even though many never felt they got all that they deserved
(particularly because progressives never got the comeuppance *they*
deserved), the 1950s brought them unprecedented opportunities. How
could they help but admire a society that was so fluid and so open that
it enabled them, as Jews, immigrants, and the sons and daughters of
unskilled workers, to succeed? Their newfound attachment to American society was also a comparative one. The United States represented
the antithesis of totalitarianism, whatever its smaller flaws. Certainly
an intellectual needed "to criticize what needs to be criticized in
America," Hook contended, but he or she must never lose sight of the
larger context, "the total threat which Communism poses to the life of
the free mind." Intellectuals must choose "between endorsing a system of total terror and *critically* supporting our own imperfect democratic culture." Hook's assumption that there was a choice to make and
his refusal to consider the existence of other alternatives directly contradicted the message of the People's Front, the internationalism of
the Wallacites, and the laissez faire attitude anti-anticommunists had
toward Party members. "I chose the West," declared Dwight Macdonald, and while he was personally disinclined to celebrate all things
American, he nevertheless accepted Hook's assumption that he had to
take a position in this "fight to the death between radically different
cultures."[44]

Macdonald distinguished those who recognized the political realities of the postwar era, "the practicals" "not much affected by Communism," from the "idealists or doctrinaires." Reinhold Niebuhr's "children of light" were very much the same thing, political innocents too impractical to fathom the depths of evil. The "practicals" replaced the New Dealers following Roosevelt's death, marking the triumph of liberal anticommunism at the highest levels. It was harder-edged, less dreamy, and more pessimistic than the heady liberalism of John Dewey, but still committed to equality, justice, and freedom. Arthur Schlesinger called it "vital center liberalism," a force very much created by the 1930s: "The Soviet experience, on top of the rise of fascism, reminded my generation rather forcibly that man was, indeed, imperfect, and that the corruption of power could unleash great evil in the world." Vital center liberalism was not just anticommunism tempered by traditional liberal concerns. It was a doctrine of disappointment, a concession that there were no utopias, just evil and corruption that must be held in check. The good qualities of democracy were not those that liberated, but those that controlled. The result was a more conservative and cautious set of policies. One historian of the Americans for Democratic Action, for example, noted that "ADA liberals, chastened by the harsh realities of the Great Depression and fascism, disenchanted with Marxist polemics, and skeptical of ideal solutions, placed a premium on bargaining and compromise," and they were on the extreme left edge of the vital center. Yet liberal anticommunists never really confronted the extent to which they protected the status quo. Former anti-Stalinists continued to regard themselves as "genuine radicals"[45] whose ideas were automatically on the cutting edge.

But anticommunism was rather different from anti-Stalinism. Philip Rahv suggested that anti-Stalinism had "the true pathos and conviction of a minority fighting under its own banner" that gave it a grandeur or nobility. Postwar anticommunism, however, "has virtually become the official creed of our entire society."[46] Being a radical anti-Stalinist was hard, requiring sacrifice and integrity. Being a liberal anticommunist, by contrast, was easy and at least potentially profitable at the expense of others. The very process of becoming the intellectual establishment brought out the same characteristics anti-Stalinists identified with their enemies: compromise, complacency, and an inflated sense of self.

The ascendancy of liberal anticommunism after World War II confused progressives. They felt very adrift. The characteristics they valued, compromise and improvisation, meant nothing in a society where moral absolutes shaped the unwritten rules. Stalin, their erstwhile ally, had proved to be no better than any other leader. Socialism produced no better society. Politics in their own country were inexplicable. Many found it simpler to withdraw altogether than make sense of the unfamiliar terrain. They could discern no legitimate intellectual rationale for liberal anticommunism, only benefits that might accrue to those who assuaged their guilt by voicing its platitudes:

> The trouble is [Matthew Josephson suggested] that the repentant liberals overwhelmed with guilt at having sent $5 to Loyalist Spain prematurely, now try to hang on to the coat-tails of the McCarthy's [sic]. They say: we know better than anyone else how to save the country from the few wretched Communists still surviving. And each outdoes the other in repenting, recanting, or whining or offering to commit atrocities against Communists or any other shameless and unrepenting heretics.

But, Waldo Frank noted, "Communism in the United States is a problem so infinitesimally small" as to constitute no threat whatsoever.[47] Progressives could not subscribe to postwar liberal anticommunism, but neither did their front experiences suggest any useful alternatives.

Postwar politics were difficult for progressives. Very few were pro-Soviet, although many favored a more conciliatory foreign policy toward the USSR. The American politician most associated with that stance, Henry Wallace, did not greatly benefit from their support, however. Most thought him a tool of the Communists. Roger Baldwin called accepting Party support "morally indefensible."[48] Progressives were trapped between the liberal anticommunist domestic agenda (minus its anticommunist aspects) and the Communists' foreign policy. Only one issue truly moved them, and it was unpopular, the red scare. The possibility that the Party was any kind of threat to the government seemed laughable. "What," Arthur Garfield Hays asked at a hearing to consider outlawing the CPUSA, "is all the excitement . . . about, Congressman?"[49]

Protecting civil liberties, particularly the civil liberties of political minorities, became progressives' postwar cause. Anticommunists charged that, like their earlier antifascism, this too was a smokescreen that covered over their naive or deliberate support for the CPUSA. Although progressives could be faulted on their motives in other ways, their postwar defense of civil liberties actually suggested that they had learned from the 1930s. Front politics required them to support a lesser evil, Stalin, in order to combat a greater one, Hitler. But civil liberties were a purer cause. Even if they championed the rights of Communists, how could they be suspect since they promoted a long cherished liberal value? Although badly outnumbered as intellectuals in the 1950s, by fighting for civil liberties, progressives were able to re-create some of the fighting spirit that carried them through the 1930s.

But championing civil liberties also had its self-serving aspects. Progressives, after all, were called before committees, had their passports confiscated, and their ability to write screenplays or speak on campuses blocked. They knew they were vulnerable to accusations of "fellow traveling" or suspicious associations. They were more interested in the problems of people like themselves than Communists' similar or worse problems. The prosecution of Party leaders under the Smith Act elicited relatively little progressive attention. The Rosenberg case was more interesting because it was easier to identify with two otherwise ordinary people sucked into a nightmarish web of conspiracy charges, but a number of progressives tiptoed around their innocence or guilt: "If they execute the Rosenberg's [sic]," Joseph Freeman told Floyd Dell, "it will be one of the silliest, as well as one of the cruelest acts any government has ever committed. Whatever the Rosenberg's [sic] did or didn't do, there is no excuse whatsoever for making them the first spies ever to be executed in peacetime."[50] Progressives were more inflamed about loyalty oaths and congressional hearings, issues with the most potential to affect them as well as Communists. Championing these causes was easier than defending Communism.

Taking up the civil liberties banner not only protected and vindicated progressives, it also enabled them to think badly of their 1930s enemies and feel good about themselves. Called before the Rapp-Coudert committee in 1940, Freeman refused to testify, citing the "moral principle involved in all this." "For my own sake, for the health of my soul," he continued, "I refuse to be an informer." Two years later, when asked to name Communists within the ASU, Joseph Lash sounded similarly noble when he declared, "I do not want to buy immunity for myself at the cost of telling on these people."[51] Liberal anticommunists, by contrast, seemed perfectly willing to sell out their souls. Freeman was "appall[ed]" that so many intellectuals passively or actively aided Joe McCarthy:

The liberals make me sad. By approving McCarthy's alleged aim, the destruction of Communists, while deploring his methods, they played right into his hands. That great literary critic Granville Hicks has written a piece explaining why he gave McCarthy the names of fellow-members of his Party unit at Harvard. He said he knew this would bring hardship to these people, and possibly ruin, but if he did not give the names, he would go to jail. Certain people who were on the New Masses with Hicks *have* gone to jail.

Progressives considered liberal anticommunists weak-willed and self-serving, "hiding out in rabbit holes," I. F. Stone wrote. Malcolm Cowley detected "the symptoms of the medically recognized disease called paranoia": "guilt, insecurity, suspicion, fear, messianism." Several implied that anticommunism had its financial and personal attractions. Matthew Josephson concluded that Max Lerner's "future would be anticommunist, and it would be a fairly prosperous future," while Lillian Hellman believed that "the children of timid immigrants . . . make it so good they are determined to keep it at any cost." Stone thought Whittaker Chambers' self-image distorted. "To say, as he does, that in deciding to testify he was 'disregarding all risks, accepting all consequences,'" he scoffed, "is certainly laying it on thick when the consequences included $75,000 from the *Saturday Evening Post* for the serial rights to his memoirs."[52] Ironically, progressives' view of anticommunists' was precisely anticommunists' view of them: cynical, self-serving, conniving, and dishonest.

Progressives found it easy to believe such things about anticommunists because, in practice, liberal anticommunism seemed a contradiction in terms. "The liberals run without fighting," Cowley noted glumly. Carey McWilliams later argued that the ACCF helped spread anticommunism by using liberal language to promote conservative causes. He was not surprised to learn that it had CIA connections. Stone felt a similar "split personality" lurked within the ACLU in the person of Morris Ernst, who "at one and the same time . . . advises the Civil Liberties Union and J. Edgar Hoover." Roger Baldwin admitted that a "too conciliatory" attitude toward the Communist hunters probably protected the organization against attacks.[53] Progressives expected little of the ACCF, but the American Civil Liberties Union was another story. Despite the Flynn episode, many hoped it would lead the fight against McCarthyism. Its failure to do so alienated many progressives and reinforced their suspicion that any form of anticommunism must inevitably be conservative.

The ACLU so profoundly disappointed postwar progressives that some fled its ranks for the Emergency Civil Liberties Committee. The ACLU's record on communist-related civil liberties was weak. It did little to protest the blacklist, allowed four years to pass before labeling the government's case against union leader Harry Bridges a civil liberties matter, stayed out of the Smith Act trials until they reached the appeals stage, and would not take a stand on the question of the limits of congressional subcommittees. In 1953, it barred Communists from its membership, in the process subverting its own democratic procedures. The board of directors favored such a measure; but, as the board minutes noted, "a majority of popular votes has been recorded against" the proposal. The board dismissed that vote as opposed to the particular phrasing of the proposal rather than its spirit and vowed to clean up its draft. Local affiliates demanded input; Norman Thomas proposed restructuring the organization to take away affiliate power. When that failed, he threatened to resign unless the anticommunist measure was approved on an interim basis. Union progressives could not buck this kind of "blackmail." "I am tired of all this," declared Corliss Lamont after his renomination to the board was rescinded and then revived via petitions. On the evening that the "Liberties Union Vote[d] Strong Anti-Red Stand," as the New York World Telegram headline read, progressive opposition "collapsed so completely that it didn't even bother to show up." The ACLU's cautious politics resulted in the creation of the Emergency Civil Liberties Committee in 1951. It was, as the ACLU board noted in the midst of a fractious debate over Thomas's proposals, "waiting eagerly to pick up the pieces."[54]

Yet the ECLC and similar progressive attempts to regroup and fight against liberal anticommunism ran into problems of their own. In order to function at all in the postwar climate, the ECLC expended considerable energy denying that it was a front group. To do otherwise was to invite investigations and inquiries. Thus the organization issued a standard statement that "we will not judge our country by one standard, and other countries by a less rigorous democratic standard." Such denials became a way of life during the cold war and progressives were not immune to their necessity. Some, however, found the whole process tedious, and it is likely that such obeisance to anticommunism caused some attrition in organizations like the ECLC. "I don't

232   see why one should waste one's time answering charges that aren't half believed by the chargers," Cowley opined. He remained politically active but pledged "not to join anything." Matthew Josephson also felt demoralized "by all the incredible nonsense that is propagated everywhere." "The James Burnhams," he complained, "have the facilities of Life Magazine and an audience of twelve million."[55] The Emergency Civil Liberties Committee made little difference in a world progressives felt they could not control.

Progressive momentum was further slowed by the time and mental energy diverted into personal responses to anticommunist attacks. Finding and keeping jobs was hard; being politically active and still keeping jobs was harder still. Cowley learned to use the preemptive strike, providing potential employers with a list of his past associations to save himself the unpleasantness of getting and then losing teaching jobs. He also suffered the embarrassment of being monitored by the FBI. While he "didn't have anything to conceal," it was demoralizing to be followed and easy to feel threatened by the security apparatus involved. Active progressives had to be continually aware of the impact their commitments might have on others. As early as 1942, Roger Baldwin told the UDA he was "the wrong man to sign" their round robin against the Dies committee because "I was for long identified with movements in which the C.P. took part." Screenwriter Guy Endore was almost afraid to burden his friends with his problems for fear of hurting them too. "The sense of guilt by association is [so] strong," he told Carey McWilliams after he was blacklisted, "that you hesitate ten times before you call on anyone."[56] Isolated, fearful, and uncertain, progressives could not challenge the status quo.

Progressives were never able to bounce back after the People's Front collapsed. Some lost interest or belief in politics; others joined the anticommunist crusade; most simply could not regain their passion after 1939. No cause seemed as clear-cut as antifascism, no battle as stirring as the Spanish Civil War. Bucking the system was more perilous and less clear-cut than before. Progressives never had the certainty their opponents, or even their Communist partners, had. They agonized, debated, balanced, and rebalanced. Their front experiences made them even more hesitant than before, a quality again reinforced by the times. And they did not prosper. In part that was because they were older than anticommunists and perhaps legitimately past their primes. But it was also true that they could not coexist very easily with anticommunists, so once anticommunists triumphed, progressives gave way like the Old Bolsheviks they once admired. They were not entirely graceful about the process, but neither could they reverse the trends. They gambled on the People's Front and lost. Unwilling to concede their error, they had to turn over their chips to another generation of players.

"Newcomers . . . Forcing
Themselves toward the Fore":
Some Conclusions

What happened in the 1930s had profound consequences for
America's intellectuals. In few areas of society was the fight over communism as clear, as strident, or as sustained as it was in their circles. Working with the American Communist Party became a lightning
rod that attracted and focused power. Where intellectuals stood more
generally on political, social, and cultural issues and how they perceived their roles as intellectuals were all mediated through that one
issue. Most intellectuals understood the symbolism and used it to
make judgments about others. Those judgments affected friendships,
feuds, publishing opportunities, memberships, and editorial lines.
Anti-Stalinists and representatives of the People's Front debated communism a lot, but its meaning became a shorthand, expressing far
more than it would at first appear.

The long war was actually more about intellectual integrity than
communism or anticommunism. All of the individuals in this study
shared a single objective, bringing their special talents to bear on social
problems in the 1930s. But there were different ways to accomplish
that, and therein lay the rub. Neil Jumonville has argued that American
intellectuals divide into two cultural traditions, one epitomized by the
detached critic and the other by the realist. Critics were "outsider[s]"
whose cultural objectivity required separation and dispassion. Real-

ists worried about "becoming too ethereal, abstract, or disconnected from everyday real life,"[1] so relished involvement in the world. These two categories describe two political styles equally well. Detached outsiders argued that intellectuals must remain above the fray, delineating an ideal, and pointing out where efforts to achieve it fell short. Realists believed that intellectuals must lead the way, converting theory into functional social reality. Anti-Stalinists embraced both the detached cultural and political roles. Progressives were more likely to be activists directly involved in political change and lessening the gap between "highbrow" and "lowbrow" culture. These categories are oversimplifications and not all intellectuals neatly fit into one camp or the other. Still, there was no consensus on the appropriate relationship between an intellectual and his or her society. Rather, there was intense debate.

Generational differences at least partially determined these contrasting intellectual styles. Each generation rebelled against social expectations and traditions; each chose to model itself on an idealized version of what intellectuals did. Most of the older generation were white, male, middle-class, old-stock, and Protestant. They grew up in a society that was structured and hierarchical, but increasingly unable to cope with the industrial, social, economic, and ideological changes that occurred during the Progressive Era. They were trained to be well-rounded, genteel, and somewhat remote, but that role made no more sense to them than their elders' responses to change. The new world seemed to push them aside and devalue creative and critical work. So, they retreated and were "concerned about Freudian psychology and exotic literary movements which were as remote from the common man as the abstruse calculations of astronomers," George Soule recalled. However inaccurate that portrait might have been, it nevertheless primed progressives to become activists who forged links with the people. "No more ivory tower," *The New Republic* gleefully declared, and dozens of progressives climbed down. "We are many and we write for many," Vincent Sheean told the 1939 Writers' Congress.[2] For men and women who once saw themselves as socially irrelevant, the persona of the activist-intellectual was irresistible.

The next generation of intellectuals rejected this attitude and the role it represented. They had a better claim to speaking for or to the masses, but like their elders, rebelled against the stereotype into which society seemed to force them. The ivory tower was considerably more attractive to those farthest removed from it by birth. Anti-Stalinists wanted to be like the scholars they admired, thoughtful, distanced, and with a "passionate attachment to the search for truth." Their ideal led them to see "the political and intellectual struggle against Stalinism . . . [as] perhaps even the central moral obligation of intellectuals."[3] Progressives liked the activist role because it was a repudiation of their background. By the same token, anti-Stalinists also flirted with the unfamiliar, a poor but ambitious intellectual's vision of what real intellectuals did.

Neither group was actually able to live out all its fantasies. Progressives tried to be like the social activists they admired, but they could not even work up the gumption to join the CPUSA. They talked about factories, but lived in a world of relative privilege, high status, and secure pay. Anti-Stalinists modeled themselves after men they considered sophisticated and noble thinkers, Edmund Wilson, Max Shachtman, and Leon Trotsky. They frequented literary salons and met famous writers, but they could not float through life as effortlessly as their elders seemed to. They fought poverty, prejudice, academic restrictions against Jews, and an old boys network that funneled editorial positions, fellowships, and book reviews toward the more traditional elite. There always seemed to be one more hurdle to leap. Progressives' failures were personal ones they attributed to their weak wills. But the next generation's inability to get exactly where it wanted to be and accomplish what it believed needed to be done was easily blamed on an outside force, the previous generation.

The younger generation's sense of injury originated from the seeming inequity of circumstances. Anti-Stalinists and progressives built separate institutions, but the power and status possessed by those networks was uneven. Progressives not only had control of journals, publishing houses, and organizations, they also regarded the next generation as alien and threatening. They were little inclined to help young men and women they could not understand who seemed ungracious and ungrateful. Still, anti-Stalinists needed to get past them somehow to accomplish their goals. How could they gain access to progressives' status and power networks? Deference would do it, but younger intellectuals refused to kowtow to those they considered their intellectual inferiors. So, they confronted them head-on, questioning their integrity. Anti-Stalinists craved intellectual stature and despised those who already had it. They had a clear sense of injustice and outrage. "I think that you, like most middle-aged writers, resent the young newcomers who are forcing themselves toward the fore," Albert Halper told William McFee, "and, like most men in the saddle, you do not want to be unseated."[4]

Further aggravating the anti-Stalinists' sense that they were snubbed by people undeserving of power was the progressives' choice of an alliance with the CPUSA. From the progressive perspective, it was the logical choice, but one that outraged the younger generation. The Party gave progressives confidence because it seemed so actively committed to radical social change. Fronts let them think they mingled with "real" people, coal miners, union organizers, even unshaven literary functionaries who drank too much and wrote too little. The romance of the radical world seduced them so much that they accepted what the Party told them often without question. They never really wondered, for example, why it was that antifascism rose and fell with Communist cooperation when they were the vast majority of front supporters and certainly its more prestigious and powerful members. But progressives were generous and trusting of their allies. Despite their veneer of cynicism and sophistication, they had an old-fashioned faith in progress. Like Lionel Trilling's fictional hero, John Laskell, they could not believe Maxim Gifford's (really Whittaker Chambers') tales of the darker side of the CPUSA.[5]

The younger generation was not so easily impressed by the Communist Party. They were more familiar with it, less in awe. And they did not carry the same high intellectual status as progressives. The CPUSA accorded them little respect and thwarted their literary, creative, or critical dreams. Party functionaries expected them to serve in the ranks while courting and coddling more famous intellectuals to use their names. Younger intellectuals regarded the CPUSA as the institution that stood between them and their natural rise to the top. Its power was artificial. It duped and bewitched the naive and promised rewards to the ambitious. Party functionaries lied to get what they wanted and progressives accepted their lies. Although their views mutated from dissident Marxist to anti-Stalinist to anticommunist, members of the younger generation remained convinced that the CPUSA was anti-intellectual. Whether "Stalinist" or "totalitarian," it forced creative individuals to limit themselves to orthodoxies. No intellectual should be connected with the CPUSA. But many intellectuals were. This was the supreme abuse of progressives' enviable status.

Generational conflicts always occur, but some are more intense than others. This one was especially so because there were so many differences between anti-Stalinists and progressives. The Depression heightened differences, as did the backgrounds of the two generations. Circumstances made power particularly valuable and particularly likely to remain in progressives' hands. Anti-Stalinists struggled against great odds to become intellectuals. In the process, they came to deeply value the role they so idealized. Progressives, stereotyped as careless pseudoradicals, dishonored and debased their struggle. Anti-Stalinists felt both a sense of persecution and a need to avenge their beliefs.

The Moscow trials, the Spanish Civil War, and battles between American radical factions shaped what William Phillips described as a "profoundly traumatic shift of consciousness."[6] Front politics never had much meaning for the younger generation. Anti-Stalinism was hard to reconcile with what they observed of Marxism in practice. So, members of the younger generation became anti-totalitarian and anti-communist. Given their backgrounds and experiences, it was hardly surprising that their outlook was democratic, even if their methods were not always. Having matured into an intellectual community where they thought the powerful corrupt and raw power more important than any moral virtue, they were rightfully suspicious of authority.

Although anti-Stalinists saw themselves as totally without success in the hostile and alien People's Front period, they changed the nature of the Front's alliances. The 1937 Front was a model of antifascist cooperation, despite its occasional problems. Progressives participated in it comfortably and Communists trusted that there was a shared core of values that would keep the system functioning smoothly. The 1939 Front was a very different institution, one profoundly affected by the persistent anti-Stalinist voice. Progressives were not willing to discard the idea of front politics as unworkable, but they found the People's Front increasingly unworkable. They were suspicious of their partners, sensitive to accusations that they were "fellow-travelers," and anxious to disassociate themselves from the CPUSA. Communist intellectuals no longer trusted their partners either, reasserting themselves in the fronts as a more visible minority in order to protect their interests. The Moscow trials and the defeat of the Spanish Loyalists might have provoked these changes even without an oppositional voice, but certainly not to the degree that they ultimately occurred. The American Committee for the Defense of Leon Trotsky, the revived *Partisan Review,* and the Committee for Cultural Freedom made progressives more sensitive and Communists more determined. By the same token, liberal talk about civil liberties, personal freedoms, and the differences between dictatorship and democracy encouraged progressives to think seriously about the Front's prodemocratic rhetoric.

The Nazi-Soviet Pact shifted the power balance away from the older generation and slowly elevated the members of the younger, anticommunist generation into the authorities and the power-wielders. Despite their other differences, they acted like any other intellectual generation upon reaching the top. They institutionalized their own values and priorities in the doctrine of liberal anticommunism. They promoted a reasoned exposure of Communism, a more cosmopolitan culture, and a detached intellectual style. But once in power, they discovered what progressives already knew, that it was not quite so easy as they imagined to flesh out their ideals. They became the status quo themselves, with power over others that made them just as arbitrary as the progressives they despised.

Thus, when Mary McCarthy accused Lillian Hellman of being a "dishonest" writer, she meant that Hellman did not measure up to a new, postwar, intellectual canon McCarthy helped define. Hellman's prose was dishonest because it pandered to a more popular and less "highbrow" taste. Her politics were dishonest because, as an unrepentant former Communist, she was unable to think for herself. Her intellectual credentials were dishonest because she would not admit that she bore some complicity for the crimes of Stalin. Since Hellman was not willing to confess her own failings, McCarthy was. Indeed, she positively relished it as her duty. Exposure was consistent with McCarthy's commitment to liberal anticommunism. It also served a very personal end, however, by bringing Hellman down a peg or two in the public's eyes. She wanted nothing less than a full public confession from Hellman that her whole life had been a fiction and her politics a lie. This would make Hellman finally honest, as well as vindicate McCarthy's own position and her noble suffering. Hellman was no more inclined to make that confession than most other progressives because she thought McCarthy's position unconscionable and herself more a victim than her foe ever was. Their legal battle encapsulated the whole struggle between anticommunists and progressives, reflecting

240   the personal, intellectual, cultural, and political dimensions of the war.

Yet, as the McCarthy-Hellman feud suggested, once Communism ceased to have direct impact as an issue, the long war between anti-Stalinists and progressives degenerated into a series of vindictive personal quarrels between survivors. Even from the beginning, no matter how much intellectuals couched their opinions in abstract terms like *democracy, antifascism, purity,* and *honesty,* there was always an element of self-interest to their claims. To some historians, that conclusion might condemn all of its participants equally as selfish human beings who found ways to make their petty squabbles sound like grandiose intellectual battles. But to demand more objective behavior, to ask intellectuals to act solely on the basis of their ideas, expects too much of people with experiences, hopes, and dreams. All 1930s intellectuals did precisely what intellectuals are supposed to do; they tried to mediate between the abstract and the human. Somewhere between the supposedly dispassionate criticism of the anti-Stalinists and the well-intentioned activism of progressives was a more workable middle ground. If the intellectual left failed in the 1930s, it was in finding this middle ground.

NOTES

Abbreviations

ACCF   American Committee for Cultural Freedom Papers, Tamiment Library, New York University.

ACDLT   American Committee for the Defense of Leon Trotsky Papers, Tamiment Library, New York University.

ACLU   American Civil Liberties Union Papers, Seeley G. Mudd Manuscript Library, Department of Rare Books and Special Collections, Princeton University Libraries.

ADA   Americans for Democratic Action Papers, State Historical Society of Wisconsin, microfilm copy.

AGH   Arthur Garfield Hays Papers, Seeley G. Mudd Manuscript Library, Department of Rare Books and Special Collections, Princeton University Libraries.

AFSD   American Friends of Spanish Democracy Papers, Rare Books and Manuscripts Division, New York Public Library, Astor, Lenox, and Tilden Foundations.

AH   Albert Halper Papers, Rare Books and Manuscripts Division, New York Public Library, Astor, Lenox, and Tilden Foundations.

ALS   Anna Louise Strong Papers, University of Washington.

AM   Albert Maltz Papers, State Historical Society of Wisconsin.

AS   Arne Swabeck Papers, Hoover Archives, Stanford University.

AT   Alexander Trachtenberg Papers, State Historical Society of Wisconsin.

242	B&W	*Black and White.*
	BB	Bruce Bliven Papers, Special Collections, Stanford University.
	BDW	Bertram David Wolfe Papers, Hoover Archives, Stanford University.
	BH	Benjamin Huebsch Papers, Library of Congress.
	CAL	Collection of American Literature, Beinecke Library, Yale University.
	CM	Carey McWilliams Papers, Special Collections, UCLA.
	CS	*Common Sense.*
	DK	Dale Kramer Papers, Newberry Library, Chicago.
	DW	*Daily Worker.*
	EB	Earl Browder Papers, Duke University.
	EL-H	Eugene Lyons Papers, Hoover Archives, Stanford University.
	EL-O	Eugene Lyons Papers, University of Oregon.
	ER	Eleanor Roosevelt Papers, Franklin D. Roosevelt Library, Hyde Park, New York.
	EW	Edmund Wilson Papers, Beinecke Library, Yale University.
	FD	Floyd Dell Papers, Newberry Library, Chicago.
	FK	Freda Kirchwey Papers, Radcliffe College.
	FOIA	Freedom of Information Act Files.
	GE	Guy Endore Papers, Special Collections, UCLA.
	GH	Granville Hicks Papers, Syracuse University.
	GT	Genevieve Taggard Papers, Rare Books and Manuscripts Division, New York Public Library, Astor, Lenox, and Tilden Foundations.
	HLM	H. L. Mencken Papers, Rare Books and Manuscripts Division, New York Public Library, Astor, Lenox, and Tilden Foundations.
	HS	Herbert Solow Papers, Hoover Archives, Stanford University.
	HUAC	House UnAmerican Activities Committee, *Hearings* (Washington, D.C.: Government Printing Office).
	IDSP	Ithiel de Sola Poole Papers, Hoover Archives, Stanford University.
	JD	John Dewey Papers, Center for Dewey Studies, Southern Illinois University.
	JDP	John Dos Passos Papers, University of Virginia.
	JF	Joseph Freeman Papers, Hoover Archives, Stanford University.
	JFI	John Finerty Papers, University of Oregon.
	JHH	John Haynes Holmes Papers, Library of Congress.
	JR	James Rorty Papers, University of Oregon.
	JWK	Joseph Wood Krutch Papers, Library of Congress.
	KAP	Katherine Anne Porter Papers, University of Maryland.
	KR	Kenneth Rexroth Papers, Special Collections, UCLA.
	LAW	League of American Writers Papers, Bancroft Library, University of California at Berkeley.

LF	Louis Fischer Papers, Seeley G. Mudd Manuscript Library, Department of Rare Books and Special Collections, Princeton University Libraries.
LO	Liston Oak Papers, State Historical Society of Wisconsin.
MB	Marc Blitzstein Papers, State Historical Society of Wisconsin.
MC	Malcolm Cowley Papers, Newberry Library, Chicago.
MC2	Malcolm Cowley Papers, Annex, Newberry Library, Chicago.
MDZ	Morton D. Zabel Papers, Newberry Library, Chicago.
MM	*Modern Monthly.*
MQ	*Modern Quarterly.*
MVK	Mary Van Kleeck Papers, Sophia Smith Collection, Smith College.
MXQ	*Marxist Quarterly.*
N	*Nation.*
NI	*New International.*
NL	*New Leader.*
NM	*New Masses.*
NR	*New Republic.*
NT	Norman Thomas Papers, New York Public Library, microfilm copy.
NYT	*New York Times.*
OF	Osmond Fraenkel Diaries, Seeley G. Mudd Manuscript Library, Department of Rare Books and Special Collections, Princeton University Libraries.
OGV	Oswald Garrison Villard Papers, Harvard University.
PL	Peggy Lamson Collection, Seeley G. Mudd Manuscript Library, Department of Rare Books and Special Collections, Princeton University Libraries.
PR	*Partisan Review.*
R&HML	Robert and Helen M. Lynd Papers, Library of Congress.
RB	Roger Baldwin Papers, Seeley G. Mudd Manuscript Library, Department of Rare Books and Special Collections, Princeton University Libraries.
RC	Robert Cantwell Papers, University of Oregon.
RML	Robert Morss Lovett Papers, University of Chicago.
RN	Reinhold Niebuhr Papers, Library of Congress.
RR	Richard Rovere Papers, State Historical Society of Wisconsin.
RRO	Raymond Robins Papers, State Historical Society of Wisconsin.
SA	Sherwood Anderson Papers, Newberry Library, Chicago.
SC	*Socialist Call.*
SCH	Stuart Chase Papers, Library of Congress.
SH	Sidney Howard Papers, Bancroft Library, University of California at Berkeley.
SO	Samuel Ornitz Papers, State Historical Society of Wisconsin.
SP	Socialist Party Papers, Syracuse University, microfilm copy.

244   SRL   *Saturday Review of Literature.*

       SRT   *Soviet Russia Today.*

       SWP   Socialist Workers Party Papers, State Historical Society of Wisconsin.

       VFC   V. F. Calverton Papers, Rare Books and Manuscripts Division, New York Public Library, Astor, Lenox, and Tilden Foundations.

       WL   Walter Lowenfels Papers, Special Collections, UCLA.

       WWC   Western Writers Congress Papers, part of the Carey McWilliams Papers, Bancroft Library, University of California at Berkeley.

Introduction

1   Michiko Kakutani, "Hellman-McCarthy Libel Suit Stirs Old Antagonisms," NYT (3/19/80), c-21. Carol Brightman, *Writing Dangerously: Mary McCarthy and Her World* (New York: Clarkson Potter, 1992), 597–622, gives a very detailed account of the case.

2   See, for example, John Dewey, "Democracy Is Radical . . . As an End, and the Means Cannot Be Divorced from the End," CS, 6 (1/37), 10.

3   The word and concept are Lawrence Goodwyn's from *Democratic Promise: The Populist Moment in America* (New York: Oxford, 1976).

4   Wald, *The New York Intellectuals* (Chapel Hill: University of North Carolina Press, 1987), 13.

5   Lyons, *The Red Decade* (1941; New Rochelle, N.Y.: Arlington House, 1970). Quotations are from pages 15 and 16. The book became a source for the government as it investigated communism in America. The Internal Security Investigation on the League of American Writers, for example, cited it in its reports. See FOIA papers on the LAW.

6   William Wright, *Lillian Hellman* (New York: Simon and Schuster, 1986), 388.

7   A good example of this type of memoir is Sidney Hook's *Out of Step* (New York: Harper and Row, 1987) or Diana Trilling's "Liberal Anti-Communism Revisited," in *We Must March My Darlings* (New York: Harcourt, Brace, Jovanovich, 1977).

8   All have written on the period. See Hook, *Out of Step,* Trilling, *The Beginning of the Journey* (New York: Harcourt, Brace, 1993), and Phillips, "What Happened in the 30s?" *Commentary* 34 (September 1962), 204–12.

9   The phrase is Philip Abbott's, from his *Leftward Ho!: V. F. Calverton and American Radicalism* (Westport: Greenwood Press, 1993), 96.

10   William O'Neill, *A Better World* (New York: Simon and Schuster, 1984), 386. He uses the word "better" to describe the anti-Stalinists on page 376.

11   Ibid., 384.

12   Paul Hollander, *Political Pilgrims* (New York: Oxford University Press, 1981), 435.

13   I find O'Neill's characterizations unsatisfying because he consigns so many intellectuals we might expect to find in his category of "liberal and left-wing anti-communists" to his "anti-Communists as a whole" category, thereby dismissing them as extremists who "were often as bad as American Communists, even if in a better cause." See pages 376–77.

14   Cowley, "The Sense of Guilt," in *And I Worked at the Writer's Trade* (New York: Viking Press, 1978), 133–52; the three quotations in the paragraph are from pages 151, 134, and 152.

15   See, for example, Matthew Josephson, *Infidel in the Temple* (New York: Alfred Knopf, 1967) or Carey McWilliams, *The Education of Carey McWilliams* (New York: Simon and Schuster, 1978). Lillian Hellman's *Scoundrel Time* (New York: Bantam Books, 1976), 40–41, blames not only anti-Stalinists but, more specifically, "the children of timid immigrants" for refusing to stand up to McCarthyism. On page 44 she comments that "I was wrong" about personal liberties in the USSR.

16   Pells, *Radical Visions and American Dreams* (New York: Harper and Row, 1973), 311.

17   Aaron, *Writers on the Left*, 2d ed. (New York: Avon, 1965), 407.

18   Warren, *Liberals and Communism* (Bloomington: Indiana University Press, 1966). Quotations are from pages 5, 232–33, and 233. The new edition of the book, published by Columbia University Press in 1993, includes an introduction by Warren that situates the work within the burgeoning new historiography.

19   Langer, *Josephine Herbst* (Boston: Little, Brown, 1983); Leonard Wilcox, *V. F. Calverton: Radical in the American Grain* (Philadelphia: Temple University Press, 1992); Ludington, *John Dos Passos* (New York: Dutton, 1980).

20   The fact that some recent literary biographies focus on figures with unusual sexual histories or personal quirks is not meant to detract from those works, which usually treat sensitive subjects with judiciousness. Rather, my point is that these figures are often more interesting as people than as contributors to the debates of the 1930s. Perhaps the most obviously partisan biography to appear in the last decade is William Wright's of Lillian Hellman. Wright makes a persuasive case that Hellman distorted her life history for her own advantage. Scholars should be aware of his argument; but it cannot be generalized across the People's Front. His sympathies clearly lie with such anti-Stalinist Hellman critics as Diana Trilling and Mary McCarthy.

21   As quoted in Moses Rischin's review of some of the biographies of the New York intellectuals, "When the New York Savants Go Marching In," *Reviews in American History* 17 (June 1989), 290. In addition to the three works reviewed by Rischin, and discussed later here, the writings on the New York intellectuals include Gilbert's own *Writers and Partisans* (New York: Wiley and Sons, 1968), William Barrett, *The Truants* (Garden City: Anchor/Double-

246   day, 1982), and Irving Howe's portrait of them in *Decline of the New* (New York: Harcourt, Brace and World, 1963).

22   Bloom, *Prodigal Sons* (New York: Oxford, 1986).

23   Cooney, *The Rise of the New York Intellectuals* (Madison: University of Wisconsin Press, 1986).

24   Jumonville, *Critical Crossings* (Berkeley: University of California, 1991).

25   Wald, *The New York Intellectuals*. His conclusions explain what he means by "counterinstitutions."

26   Steven Biel's *Independent Intellectuals in the United States, 1910–1945* (New York: New York University Press, 1992), 4, challenges the "uniqueness" of the New York intellectuals, arguing that an older community of scholars came together in the 1910s and 1920s who were already concerned with many of the questions that later united the New York group, particularly the issue of independence. While I have some problems with the boundaries of the particular community he imagines in the 1910s and 1920s, I agree that the quest for independence was not an issue that mobilized only the New York intellectuals.

27   Wald, "Culture and Commitment: U.S. Communist Writers Reconsidered," in *New Studies in the Politics and Culture of U.S. Communism*, ed. Michael E. Brown, Randy Martin, Frank Rosengarten, and George Snedeker (New York: Monthly Review Press, 1993), 289. Wald calls for a literary reevaluation of CP writers, but I think he would also agree that a broader reevaluation of Party intellectuals would be equally valuable. Another view of the same inequality of writings on the 1930s intellectual left is in Gabriella Ferruggia, "Organizing the 'Ivory Tower': The Communist Party and the United Front of Intellectuals during the Late Thirties," *Storia Nordamericana*, 6 (1989), 142–43.

28   Murphy, *The Proletarian Moment* (Urbana: University of Illinois Press, 1991).

29   Foley, *Radical Representations: Politics and Form in U.S. Proletarian Fiction, 1929–1941* (Durham: Duke University Press, 1993), 85.

30   Wald's "Culture and Commitment." He suggests we consider the following dimensions of Communist writers' productions: the Jewish-American literary tradition, the African American literary tradition, the "premature-socialist-feminists," popular genres, and cultural differences. As of this writing, Wald is at work on such a study, one that students of the 1930s literary left eagerly await.

31   Bloom, *Left Letters* (New York: Columbia University Press, 1992).

32   Rabinowitz, *Labor and Desire* (Chapel Hill: University of North Carolina Press, 1991).

33   Myers, *The Prophet's Army* (Westport, Conn.: Greenwood Press, 1977). Wald's *New York Intellectuals* also delves into Trotskyist history in some depth. There are other works on the Trotskyists, but they have been written by participants. On the Socialist Party, the two significant works are David Shannon, *The Socialist Party of America* (New York: Macmillan, 1955) and Frank Warren, *An Alternative Vision* (Bloomington: Indiana University Press, 1974).

Robert J. Alexander, *The Right Opposition* (Westport: Greenwood Press, 1981), examines the Right Opposition internationally, including a chapter on the Lovestoneites.

34 Draper, *American Communism and Soviet Russia* (New York: Viking, 1960). Coser and Howe, *The American Communist Party* (Boston: Beacon, 1957).

35 Klehr, *The Heyday of American Communism* (New York: Basic Books, 1984), 415.

36 Draper, "The Popular Front Revisited," *New York Review of Books,* 32 (5/30/85), 46. Draper has been extremely critical of both the writers and the writing of subsequent work: "A good deal of recent work on American communism deals with the Communists by leaving out the communism or making it innocuous." This comes from his "The Life of the Party," *New York Review of Books* 41 (1/13/94): 46.

37 Ottanelli, *The Communist Party of the United States* (New Brunswick: Rutgers, 1991), 4.

38 See "Revisiting American Communism: An Exchange," *New York Review of Books,* 32 (8/15/85): 40–43. Quotations are from Jim Prickett, 42, and Gary Gerstle, 43.

39 Michael E. Brown, "The History of the History of U.S. Communism," in *New Studies in the Politics and Culture of U.S. Communism,* quotations from pages 15, 17, and 27. Draper's "Life of the Party," 49–51, dismisses Brown's work and the other efforts in *New Studies* as "politically sick" in their obsession with American Communism.

40 There have been some works over time that have attempted to look at the politics of certain groups of intellectuals. One is Art Casciato's excellent dissertation on the League of American Writers, "Citizen Writers" (Ph.D. diss., University of Virginia, 1986). Eric Homberger's "Proletarian Literature and the John Reed Clubs, 1929–1935," *Journal of American Studies,* 13 (August 1979): 221–44, looks at the John Reed Clubs. Larry Ceplair and Steven Englund, *The Inquisition in Hollywood* (Garden City: Anchor Press/Doubleday, 1980), is the best of several books on screenwriters. Ellen Schrecker's *No Ivory Tower* (New York: Oxford University Press, 1986) briefly treats the pre-1940 period with regard to colleges and universities, and Monty Penkower's *The Federal Writers' Project* (Urbana: University of Illinois Press, 1977) examines that topic.

41 From his essay in *The God That Failed,* ed. Richard Crossman (New York: Harper and Brothers, 1949; reprint, 1954), 184–85.

ONE The Lost Generation,
Social Activists, Communists, and the Depression

1 Donald Ogden Stewart, as part of a speech to the League of American Writers in 1937.

2   From Josephine Herbst, "Communism and the American Writer," *Newberry Library Bulletin,* 5 (8/59), 104. Steven Biel, *Independent Intellectuals,* suggests that one reason for this particular myth was Cowley's *Exile's Return* (rev. ed., New York: Penguin, 1956). Cowley certainly did play a role in the process, although he himself pointed out that what attracted most of the expatriates about Europe was not "values . . . [but] valuta" (page 81).

3   Cowley, *Exile's Return,* 27. On the college culture of the rebels see Helen Lefkowitz Horowitz, *Campus Life* (Chicago: University of Chicago Press, 1987), chap. 4.

4   May, *The End of American Innocence* (Chicago: Quadrangle Books, 1959, 1964), 257.

5   On Holmes, see his *I Speak for Myself* (New York: Harper and Brothers, 1959). On Baldwin and Strong, see Tracy B. Strong and Helene Keyssar, *Right in Her Soul: The Life of Anna Louise Strong* (New York: Random House, 1983), 55–60. On Kirchwey, see *These Modern Women,* ed. Elaine Showalter (rev. ed., New York: Feminist Press, 1989), 5–6.

6   There is a great deal of literature on the impact of feminism on women. Perhaps the most influential book is Nancy Cott's *The Grounding of American Feminism* (New Haven: Yale University Press, 1987).

7   On the impact of war on intellectuals, see Aaron, *Writers on the Left,* 59–67, and May, *End of American Innocence,* 355–98.

8   Quotations are from Brooks, "The Literary Life," in *Civilization in the United States,* ed. Harold E. Stearns (New York: Harcourt, 1922), 179–97, and Cowley, *Exile's Return,* 72. Aaron's *Writers on the Left* offers a good portrait of writers in the 1920s.

9   Quotations are from Robert B. Westbrook, *John Dewey and American Democracy* (Ithaca: Cornell University Press, 1991), 276; Dewey, *Liberalism and Social Action* (New York: Putnam, 1935), 56; Dorothy Thompson, *Dorothy Thompson's Political Guide* (New York: Stackpole and Sons, 1938), 64. See also Joseph Wood Krutch, *Was Europe a Success?* (New York: Farrar and Rinehart, 1932), 45.

10   Quotations are from Niebuhr, "The Liberal Illusion," *Christian Century,* 56 (4/6/39), 542–44. See also his "After Capitalism—What?" *The World Tomorrow,* 16 (3/1/33), 203–4; *Moral Man and Immoral Society* (New York: Scribner's Sons, 1936), xi–xxv; "The Pathos of Liberalism," N, 141 (9/11/35), 303–4, which specifically attacks Dewey's positivist liberalism. The best Niebuhr biography is Richard Wightman Fox's *Niebuhr* (New York: Pantheon, 1985).

11   See Aaron, *Writers on the Left,* 23–47.

12   Gold, "Why I Am a Communist," NM, 8 (9/32), 9. There are dozens of memoirs that recount experiences like Gold's.

13   On *The Masses,* see Joseph Freeman, *An American Testament* (New York: Octagon Books, 1936), 53–58, and Floyd Dell to Freeman, 1/18/52, FD, Dell-Freeman sect.

14   Theodore Draper's *The Roots of American Communism* (Chicago: Dees,   249
1957; reprint, 1985) and *American Communism and Soviet Russia* (New York:
Random House, 1960; reprint, 1986) detail these changes in far more detail.

15   Quotations are from Gold, "John Reed and the Real Thing," NM, 3 (11/27),
7; Minor, as quoted by both Bertram Wolfe, *A Life in Two Centuries* (New York:
Stein and Day, 1981), 153; Ella Winter, *And Not to Yield* (New York: Harcourt,
Brace and World, 1963), 118; Freeman, *An American Testament*, 321; John
Howard Lawson to John Dos Passos, n.d., c. 1935, JDP, ser. 2, box 2. The two
descriptions of Gold are Freeman's *American Testament*, 257, and Michael
Blankfort's conversation with the author, 1/23/82, Beverly Hills, California.

16   On Cannon and the American Trotskyist faction, see his book *The History
of American Trotskyism* (New York: Pioneer, 1944). On the Lovestoneites, see
note 26.

17   Hindus's term appeared in a letter to Freeman, 5/21/39, JF, box 153. In the
early 1930s, the two most influential functionaries overseeing artistic matters
in the CPUSA were V. J. Jerome and Alexander Trachtenberg; but Earl Browder
himself interfered to a surprising degree. On the 1920s, see Joseph Freeman,
"Ivory Towers—White and Red," NM, 12 (9/12/34), 20–24.

18   Quotations are from Claude McKay, *A Long Way from Home* (San Diego:
Harcourt, Brace, Jovanovich, 1970), 139–40, and John Howard Lawson to John
Dos Passos, n.d., c. 1934, JDP, ser. 2, box 2. On *The Liberator* and *New Masses*,
see Aaron, *Writers on the Left*, 109–20 or Walter Kalaidjian, *American Culture
Between the Wars* (New York: Columbia University Press, 1993), 35–47. Gold
was not very popular, either as a writer or a person. See James Bloom, *Left
Letters*, 14; Floyd Dell to Joseph Freeman, 7/12/51, FD, Freeman-Dell sect.;
Albert Maltz, "The Citizen Writer in Retrospect," oral history collected by Joel
Garner (Los Angeles: UCLA, 1983), 217; Josephine Herbst to Granville Hicks,
9/21/37, CAL.

19   See David Felix, *Protest* (Bloomington: Indiana University Press, 1965).

20   Quotations are from Lovett, "Liberalism and the Class War," MQ, 4
(11/27–2/28), 192, and Dos Passos to Edmund Wilson, 9/19/27, in *The Fourteenth Chronicle* (Boston: Gambit, 1973), 371. Among those who note in their
memoirs or letters the personal impact of the case were Heywood Broun, Matthew Josephson, Roger Baldwin, Marc Blitzstein, Carey McWilliams, and Herbert Solow.

21   The details of the CPUSA's 1920s policies are in Draper, *American Communism*. Readers should remember, though, that Draper's book focuses on
policy-making at the highest institutional levels. We know much less about
how individual organizers received or changed national policies.

22   Quotation is from Esther Corey's "Lewis Corey (Louis C. Fraina), 1892–
1953: A Bibliography with Autobiographical Notes," *Labor History*, 4 (spring
1963), 112. Corey briefly told his radical history to Bertram Wolfe as Wolfe
prepared to give a deposition on his behalf many years later. A copy, dated
3/5/52, is retained in BDW, boxes 4 and 78. The details of his experience with

250   the movement in the early 1920s are also in Draper, *The Roots of American Communism,* 293–302. Draper recalled that only "a small party circle at the top" knew that Fraina and Corey were one; letter to author, 8/29/77. Some writers also maintain that John Reed was disillusioned with the links between the CPUSA and Moscow when he died; see, for example, Robert A. Rosenstone, *Romantic Revolutionary: A Biography of John Reed* (New York: Knopf, 1975), 373–78, or Draper, *Roots,* 291–93. There is, however, dispute on this point.

23   The first quotation is Eastman's title, *Since Lenin Died* (London: Labour, 1925), from which the second quotation comes, p. 129. Notice that he had to use an English publisher to print his book. The description "extinct" comes from Eastman's *Love and Revolution* (New York: Random House, 1964), 491. William O'Neill offers a somewhat psychobiographical portrait of Eastman in *The Last Romantic* (New York: Oxford University Press, 1978).

24   "Dog days" comes from Cannon, *History,* 80. On the founding and early days of the Trotskyists, see Cannon's book, 40–59; Jack Alan Robbins, *The Birth of American Trotskyism* (privately published, 1973); chapter 13 of Arne Swabeck's unpublished memoir, "Early Days of American Trotskyism," AS, box 4.

25   The second quotation is Shachtman's from *Genesis of Trotskyism* (privately published, second ed. 1973), 8. The phrase "City College boys" comes from Cannon's *History,* 29. On Shachtman's impact on the next generation, see Irving Kristol, *Reflections of a Neoconservative* (New York: Basic Books, 1983), 11–12, and Irving Howe, *A Margin of Hope* (New York: Harcourt, Brace, Jovanovich, 1982), 49.

26   Robert Alexander, *The Right Opposition,* 6–28, Draper's *American Communism,* 377–441, and Bertram Wolfe's *A Life,* 464–551, discuss these developments in more depth. On American exceptionalism, see Harvey Klehr, "Leninism and Lovestoneism," *Studies in Comparative Communism,* 7 (Spring/Summer 1974), 6–12. The Lovestoneites always denied the connections between themselves and Bukharin. Fraina was, for a time, associated with the Lovestoneites.

27   Matthew Josephson's *Infidel* offers a colorful picture of the impact of the Depression on intellectuals. Steven Biel, *Independent Intellectuals,* 31–53, points out that given the model of independence, autonomy, and intellectuality to which writers aspired, freelance journalism was desirable but not very marketable. Granville Hicks's *Part of the Truth* (New York: Harcourt, Brace, and World, 1965) describes his teaching experiences. McCarthy's *The Group* (New York: Harcourt, Brace and World, 1963) presents an interesting picture of a young intellectual trying to make a career for herself in the character of Libby. Much of Diana Trilling's *The Beginning of the Journey* is about the struggle of two middle-class New York Jews to replicate a middle-class standard of living during the early 1930s. People like Edwin Seaver, Rolfe Humphries, and Isidor Schneider always seemed to be begging for jobs or hustling letters of recommendation in the hopes of winning literary fellowships. Yet even so august a presence as Edmund Wilson constantly fought with *The New Republic*'s editors about pay-per-word and the number of cuts made in his articles.

28 The quotations are from Oak in a letter headed "Dear Friend," n.d., in VFC, box 12, and Baldwin's testimony before Dies, 3/31/39, ACLU, vol. 2075. The one Party member the Union employed was Joseph Freeman, who served as publicity director for the organization during part of the 1920s. The milieu of radical young people is best captured by Wald in *New York*, 27–45, or Cooney in *Rise*, 10–37. On Jews in academe, see Diana Trilling, "Lionel Trilling: A Jew at Columbia," and Lionel Trilling, *Speaking of Literature and Society*, ed. D. Trilling (New York: Harcourt, Brace, Jovanovich, 1980), 411–12, or *Beginning*, 268–77.

29 Quotations are from Hicks, *Part*, 92–93, and Josephson, *Infidel*, 155. See also George Soule, "Hard-boiled Radicalism," NR, 65 (1/21/31), 261–62; Kenneth Burke, "Boring from Within," NR, 65 (2/4/31), 326; Malcolm Cowley, "Ivory Towers to Let," NR, 78 (4/18/34), 260–63.

30 On the League for Independent Political Action, see CS, 1 (4/13/33), 17, for its program and Alan Lawson, *The Failure of Independent Liberalism* (New York: Putnam's Sons, 1971), 39–46, or Westbrook, *Dewey*, 445–52, for a secondary analysis. On sacrificing capitalism for liberalism, see Sidney Hook, *John Dewey* (New York: John Day, 1939), 157.

31 Quotations are from Sherwood Eddy, *A Pilgrimage of Ideas* (New York: Farrar and Rinehart, 1934), 255; Lincoln Steffens, "Bankrupt Liberalism," NR, 70 (2/17/32), 15, and NR, 81 (1/16/35), 279.

32 Quotations are from Josephson to Malcolm Cowley, n.d. [1932], MC, incoming; Trilling, *Beginning*, 180; Dreiser to Fisher C. Bailey, 4/6/32, *Letters of Theodore Dreiser*, ed. Robert Elias (Philadelphia: University of Pennsylvania, 1959), 576; Dos Passos, "Writers and Society," republished in *The Strenuous Decade*, ed. Daniel Aaron and Robert Bendiner (Garden City: Anchor Books, 1970), 292; Broun, "All Quiet along the Rubicon," CS, 2 (7/33), 4.

33 George Soule in *Challenge to the New Deal*, ed. Alfred Bingham and Selden Rodman (New York: Falcon Press, 1934), 63. See also "Questionnaire on Social Objectives," NR, 82 (4/17/35), 274–75.

34 The quotations are from Mumford to Brooks, 9/14/32, in *The Van Wyck Brooks–Lewis Mumford Letters*, ed. Robert E. Spiller (New York: Dutton, 1970), 82; Roger Baldwin, in Peggy Lamson's oral history of him, *Roger Baldwin* (Boston: Houghton Mifflin, 1976), 195; Cowley, *The Dream of the Golden Mountains* (New York: Viking, 1964), 43. See also Diana Trilling, *Beginning*, 179.

35 Quotations are from Anderson to Charles Bockler, 11/22/32, SA, outgoing; Matthiessen, "The Education of a Socialist," in *F. O. Matthiessen*, ed. Paul Sweezy and Leo Huberman (New York: Shuman, 1950), 12; N, 137 (7/26/33), 86; Heywood Broun, "It Seems to Me," N, 130 (4/23/30), 483. Three memoirs that delineate some reasons why intellectuals did not join the CPUSA are Malcolm Cowley's *Dream*, 116–19, George Seldes's, *Tell the Truth and Run* (New York: Greenberg, 1953), xxiv, and Jerre Mangione's *An Ethnic at Large* (New York: Putnam's, 1978), 121–23.

36 Quotations are from Broun, "Apology for Not Being a Communist," N, 141 (9/4/35), 274; Josephson, "The Road to Indignation," NR, 66 (2/18/31), 13;

252 Arvin to Malcolm Cowley, n.d. [c. 1932], MC, incoming; Arvin to Hicks, 11/6/30 as cited in Leah Levenson and Jerry Natterstad, *Granville Hicks* (Philadelphia: Temple University Press, 1993), 47; Cantwell to Arvin, 11/15/33, RC, box 1; Williams, "Poor Doc, Nobody Wants His Life or His Verse," NM, 6 (12/30), 22. Two more cynical views are Lillian Symes, "Our Liberal Weeklies," MM, 10 (10/36), 7–10, and Diana Trilling, *Beginning,* 205–6.

37   Quotations are from "Honorable in All Things," oral interview with McWilliams conducted by Joel Gardner (Los Angeles: UCLA, 1982), 85–86; Michael Blankfort's HUAC testimony, as quoted in *Thirty Years of Treason,* ed. Eric Bentley (New York: Viking, 1971), 467; Rexroth, *Excerpts from a Life* (Santa Barbara: Conjunctions, 1981), 27; Mumford to Malcolm Cowley and Edmund Wilson, 8/17/32, MC, incoming; Eddy, *Pilgrimage of Ideas,* 326–28; and Dreiser to Evelyn Scott, 10/28/32, *Letters,* 615. T. B. Bottomore, *Critics of Society* (New York: Random House, 1966), 126, uses the phrase "[living] on borrowed Marxism" to describe intellectuals in the early 1930s.

38   Quotations are from Michael Blankfort, conversation with the author, 1/23/82; Meyer Levin, *In Search: An Autobiography* (New York: Horizon, 1950), 98; and Cowley, *The Dream,* 117. See also Lewis Mumford to Cowley and Edmund Wilson, 8/17/32, MC, incoming; Dreiser to Dallas McKown, 6/9/32, *Letters,* 586–87; and Matthiessen, "Education," 11–12.

39   Wilson's article appeared in NR, 65 (1/14/31), 235–38. The other quotation is from Sherwood Anderson to Paul Rosenfeld, 4/7/31, SA, outgoing.

40   Quotations are from Joseph Wood Krutch, *Was Europe,* 37; Davis, "The 'Logic' of History," *Harpers,* 169 (8/34), 335; Dewey, "Democracy Is Radical," 10.

41   Quotations are from Davis, "The Collapse of Politics," *Harpers,* 165 (9/32), 386, and Beard to Solow, 8/10/n.d., HS, box 1. Chamberlain, "Would Socrates Be a Marxist?" CS, 4 (12/35), 6–7.

42   Richard Wright, *American Hunger* (New York: Harper and Row, 1944; new ed., 1977), 39–40. For several different interpretations of the Third Period, see Frasier Ottanelli, *The Communist Party,* 17–48; Coser and Howe, *The American CP,* 178–235; Klehr, *Heyday,* 12–17; or Philip Jaffe, *The Rise and Fall of American Communism* (New York: Horizon, 1975), 34–37.

43   Foley, *Radical Representations,* 87. Much of the subsequent discussion of proletarianism has been informed by Foley's book. Cary Nelson's *Repression and Recovery: Modern American Poetry and the Politics of Cultural Memory, 1910–1945* (Madison: University of Wisconsin Press, 1989), 152–64, shows that the field of poetry clearly demonstrates the absence of a single cultural standard on the left. Poets used many different styles and forms during the Third Period, only some of which we might define as stereotypically proletarian. His work raises questions about "lost" works that are erased from the "cultural memory" because they contradict the way people want to remember certain eras. Walter Kalaidjian's *American Culture Between the Wars* makes a similar argument.

44   Quotations are from Klehr, *Heyday,* 75; Foley, ibid., 76; and Murphy, *Proletarian,* 75. Some of the Kharkov documents are in JF, box 177. Firsthand accounts include Ellis et al., "The Charkov Conference of Revolutionary Writers," NM, 6 (2/31), 6–8; Josephine Herbst, "Yesterday's Road," *New American Review,* 3 (4/68), 84–104; Michael Gold, "Notes from Kharkov," NM, 4 (3/31), 4. Among those who attended the sessions were Gold, A. B. Magil, Joshua Kunitz, Herbst, and John Herrmann. A traditional view of Kharkov is Max Eastman's in *Artists in Uniform* (New York: Knopf, 1934), 3–29, or Deming Brown, *Soviet Attitudes toward American Writing* (Princeton: Princeton University Press, 1962), 45–46. Aaron, *Writers on the Left,* 236–40, raises and then essentially dismisses the possibility that this version was politically motivated.

45   Quotations are from Gold's address to the 1941 LAW congress, as cited in *Mike Gold: A Literary Anthology,* ed. Michael Folsom (New York: International Publishers, 1972), 246; Ellis, "Charkov," 8; Freeman, "On the Literary Front," NM, 6 (1/31), 4; Kazin, *Starting Out in the Thirties* (Boston: Little, Brown, 1962; new ed., Ithaca: Cornell University Press, 1989), 12. On the Reed Clubs, see Homberger, "Proletarian Literature," 232–35, or Helen Harrison, "John Reed Club Artists and the New Deal: Radical Responses to Roosevelt's 'Peaceful Revolution.'" *Prospects,* 5 (1980), 241–46. On artists, also see Robert C. Vitz, "Clubs, Congresses, and Unions: American Artists Confront the Thirties," *New York History,* 54 (1973), 425–47, or Kalaidjian, *American Culture Between the Wars.* There is a little on 1920s theater in Pells, *Radical Visions and American Dreams,* 252–54. My information on dance comes from Stacey Prickett's paper, "The Workers' Dance League: Politicized Dance in the 1930s," presented at the American Culture Association conference, New Orleans, 4/93. My thanks to the author for providing a written transcript. Two examples of the unexpectedly diverse ways in which the prolet cult might differ from my traditional styles are through the use of what Cary Nelson calls "found materials" (excerpts of workers' correspondence rephrased and used as poetry) and through text interacting with drawings. See Nelson, *Repression and Recovery,* 104–6 and 218–21.

46   Quotations are from Dell, cited in Philip Abbott, *Leftward Ho!,* 28; Dell to Joseph Freeman, 7/12/51, FD, Freeman-Dell sect.; Bloom, *Left Letters,* 14; and North's introduction to *New Masses: An Anthology* (New York: International, 1969), 23. On Gold, see Bloom, ibid., 14, and Murphy, *Proletarian,* 64–68. Both, especially Murphy, challenge the traditional view of Gold as a "hack." Michael Folsom also attempted to rehabilitate Gold's reputation, but it is hard to find another intellectual so widely condemned as Gold.

47   Most of my information on the early Reed Clubs comes from Homberger, 232–35, and his piece on the JRCS for *The Encyclopedia of the American Left,* ed. Mari Jo Buhle, Paul Buhle, and Dan Georgakas (Urbana: University of Illinois, 1992), 649–50. The quotation and the story of their founding come from Harrison, "John Reed Club Artists," 242–43.

48   Quotations are from Rexroth, *Excerpts from a Life,* 29; Wright, *American Hunger,* 67; Vitz, "Clubs, Congresses, and Unions," 428.

254　　49　Rabinowitz, *Labor and Desire*, 25. I am not a specialist on the topic of the prolet cult and the reader will find a more sophisticated analysis in a number of other books: in addition to Rabinowitz's *Labor and Desire*, Foley's *Radical Representations*, Bloom's *Left Letters*, Aaron's *Writers on the Left*, Rideout's *The Radical Novel*, James Murphy's *The Proletarian Moment*, and Pells's *Radical Visions*. The traditional interpretation of the prolet lit as simplistic (and bad) revolutionary propaganda is rightly under attack from a number of scholars, especially Murphy and Foley. I hope I have conveyed their sense that, to paraphrase Foley, our evaluations of it need to be revised but we need not celebrate it (page 443).

50　Quotations are from Elmer Davis, "Red Peril," SRL, 8 (4/16/32), 662; Breuer to Sherwood Anderson, n.d., SA, incoming; Ficke to Floyd Dell, 10/9/34, and to R. C. Lorenz and Jay DuVon, 5/19/31, both in FD, incoming; and Louis Adamic, "What the Proletariat Reads," SRL, 11 (12/1/34), 321–22. Foley amends Adamic's assertion, arguing that there was "a small but growing group of working-class and middle-class readers," 106–7.

51　Quotation is from Anderson to Alan Calmer, 1/2/36, SA, outgoing. See Anderson's "Danville, Virginia," NR, 65 (1/21/31), 266–68; Cowley's "The Flight of the Bonus Army," NR, 72 (8/17/32), 13–15; Wilson, *The American Jitters* (New York: Scribner's Sons, 1932); Rorty, *Where Life Is Better* (New York: Reynal and Hitchcock, 1936). The impact of the prolet cult varied from field to field. It seemed strongest in literature, theater, and journalism, but faced countercurrents more often in poetry, art, and literary criticism.

52　Quotation is from Cowley, speech before the first American Writers Congress, *American Writers Congress* (New York: International Publishers, 1935), 60. See also "Proletarian Novels," N, 139 (12/19/34), 700; Kenneth Burke, "The Nature of Art under Capitalism," N, 137 (12/13/33), 677; and Heywood Broun, "It Seems to Heywood Broun," N, 130 (7/16/30), 59.

53　See Murphy, *Proletarian Moment*, chap. 1.

54　A short but useful definition of front groups is provided by Dan Georgakas in *The Encyclopedia of the American Left*, 248. A more critical view is in Diana Trilling's *Beginning*, 197–98.

55　On FSU see Sylvia Margulies, *The Pilgrimage to Russia* (Madison: University of Wisconsin Press, 1968), 37–44, or Joanne Melish's "American Soviet Friendship," in *The Encyclopedia of the American Left*, 29–32.

56　The quotation is from Joseph Freeman to Louis Fischer, 9/22/32, JF, box 164. Waldo Frank's *Dawn in Russia* (New York: Scribner's Sons, 1932), 3, captures the skepticism bred of too much publicity.

57　HUAC, *Investigations*, 78th Congress, 2nd Session, pt. 1, 465.

58　Quotation is from NCDPP's constitution, copy retained in HS, box 8. There is no one satisfactory source on the NCDPP. The Samuel Ornitz papers (at the State Historical Society of Wisconsin) and the Herbert Solow papers (at the Hoover Institution) both contain some material. A careful reader can also glean some information from the clearly biased material contained in Francis X.

Gannon's *Biographical Dictionary of the Left* (Boston: Western Islands, 1969), 145–47. Diana Trilling, an NCDPP volunteer, recalled that the NCDPP had offices in the same building as the ILD and just a few blocks away from CPUSA headquarters. See *Beginning,* 198–99.

59   Quotations are from Oak, "Bloody Harlan," NR, 70 (3/9/32), 102; ACLU report, "The History of the Miners' Struggle in Harlan and Bell Counties," 4/32, p. 17; ACLU papers, reel 91; and Frank, *Memoirs of Waldo Frank,* ed. Alan Trachtenberg (Amherst: University of Massachusetts Press, 1973), 182.

60   D. Trilling, *Beginning,* 194, 198, 199.

61   Quotations are from Cowley, "Kentucky Coal Town," NR, 70 (3/2/32), 67; Hicks, *Part;* Wilson to John Dos Passos, 2/29/32, in Wilson, *Letters on Literature and Politics,* ed. Elena Wilson (New York: Farrar, Straus and Giroux, 1977), 222; Anderson to Wilson, late summer 1931, SA, outgoing.

62   See Felix, *Protest,* 169, 221–22.

63   Quotations are from "The Communists and the Scottsboro Case," NR, 66 (5/13/31), 343, and Edmund Wilson to Sherwood Anderson, 6/24/31, SA, incoming. The question of Party involvement in the case is addressed by Robin D. G. Kelley, "Scottsboro Case," in *The Encyclopedia of the American Left,* 684–86. Dan Carter's book *Scottsboro: A Tragedy of the American South* (Baton Rouge: Louisiana State University Press, 1969; 2d ed., 1984) presents the case more generally.

64   Hindus, *The Great Offensive* (New York: Smith and Haas, 1933), 27.

65   Quotations are from John Dos Passos to Dudley Poore, 10/28, *14th Chronicle,* 388; Thompson to Sinclair Lewis, 11/16/27, as quoted in Marion Sanders, *Dorothy Thompson* (Boston: Houghton Mifflin, 1973), 121; Dewey, *Impressions of Soviet Russia and the Revolutionary World* (New York: New Republic, 1929), 4.

66   Quotations are from Dewey, *Impressions,* 10 and 116, and Niebuhr, "The Land of Extremes," *Christian Century,* 47 (10/15/30), 1241. Oswald Garrison Villard's "Russia from a Car Window, Part I," N, 129 (11/6/29), 515–17, and Dorothy Thompson's *The New Russia* (New York: Holt, 1928) convey the same kind of enthusiasm.

67   Quotations are from Dewey, *Impressions,* 122, and Chamberlin, "Soviet Russia's First Steps toward Democracy," *Current History,* 20 (4/24), 34. Most of the accounts already cited express similar concerns. See also Harry F. Ward, "Civil Liberties in Russia," N, 120 (3/4/25), 234–37. On liberals and the Soviet Union during the 1920s, see Sister Margaret Kinney, "The Independents: A Study of the Non-Communist Left in the United States, 1919–1929" (Ph.D. diss., Syracuse University, 1973), 134–46, or Peter G. Filene, *Americans and the Soviet Experiment, 1917–1933* (Cambridge: Harvard University Press, 1967), 131–56. Dewey's book, written at the end of the 1920s, mentions nothing about the succession crisis, so uninterested in the official government was he.

68   Quotations are from Dos Passos, *The Best Times* (New York: New Ameri-

256   can Library, 1966), 195; Krutch, *More Lives Than One* (New York: Sloan and Associates, 1962), 200; Villard, "Russia from a Car Window, Part V," N, 129 (12/4/29), 654; and Villard, "Russia, Part I," 515.

69   Quotations are from Duranty, NYT, 4/19/28, sect. III, 3, and Fischer, "Russia's New Revolution," N, 130 (3/19/30), 323. Counts, *The Soviet Challenge to America* (New York: Day, 1931), 110–20. Peter Filene (*Americans and the Soviet Experiment,* 287) shows that the number of books on the USSR doubled as the Depression worsened, but initial interest in the Five Year Plans was small.

70   Quotations are from Eddy, *Challenge,* 36, and Fischer, "Why Stalin Won," N, 130 (8/13/30), 176. On Stalin, see "Stalin as the New Lenin," NR, 63 (7/23/30), 276, and Walter Duranty, *I Write as I Please* (New York: Halcyon, 1935), 180–82. Blankfort, conversation with author, 1/23/82. Dewey's *Impressions* never even mentions Trotsky or Stalin at all. On Trotsky, see Duranty, 179–81; Nathan Asch to Malcolm Cowley 10/3/31, MC, incoming; Jerome Davis, "Trotzky's Side of It," N, 130 (5/28/30), 629–30; Louis Fischer, "Lenin, Trotzky and World Revolution," N, 139 (8/15/34), 186.

71   Quotations are from Freeman, *American Testament,* 415, and Gold, as quoted in Villard, "The Russian 'Purging,' " N, 139 (12/26/34), 729.

72   Quotations are from Eastman, "The Doctrinal Crisis in Socialism," MQ, 5 (winter 1930/31), 427, and Wilson "Stalin as Ikon," NR, 86 (4/15/36), 271–73. Eastman and another of Lenin's admirers, Sidney Hook, both studied as graduate students with John Dewey. Both turned Lenin into a kind of pragmatist and Marxism into an offshoot of Dewey's pragmatic philosophy.

73   "Leftbound Local," NR, 182 (8/17/32), 6–7.

TWO   The Emergence of a Left-wing Opposition, 1932–1935

1   Michael Gold, *The Hollow Men* (New York: International Publishers, 1941), 31.

2   Quotation is from Joseph Freeman to Floyd Dell, 6/16/53, FD, Dell-Freeman sect. On Trachtenberg, see John Gerber's entry in *The Biographical Dictionary of the American Left,* ed. Bernard K. Johnpoll and Harvey Klehr (Westport: Greenwood Press, 1986), 387–88. North has written both a biography of Minor, *Robert Minor: Artist and Crusader* (New York: International Publishers, 1956), and an autobiography, *No Men Are Strangers.* On Forsythe/ Crichton, see his *Total Recoil* (Garden City: Doubleday, 1960).

3   Bessie to Guy Endore, 1/22/34, GE, box 72.

4   Quotations are all from Freeman to Floyd Dell, 7/1/51, FD, Dell-Freeman sect. This letter recounts the story of Freeman and the literary commissars in great detail. *An American Testament* supposedly treated Leon Trotsky too kindly. Different writers reported different experiences with Party censorship. Granville Hicks claimed that he wrote his John Reed biography without interference, but Robert Gorham Davis recalled that he and Hicks were scru-

tinized by a functionary when they wrote a pamphlet on anti-Semitism. Edwin Seaver never felt controlled by Trachtenberg at *Soviet Russia Today*, but James Wechsler remembered getting into trouble for not submitting a copy of his manuscript before publication. Budd Schulberg was greatly angered by the Party's attempts to shape *What Makes Sammy Run*.

5   There is, of course, dispute on this point. Those of the Harvey Klehr–Theodore Draper school see little adjustment to the line once it reached this side of the Atlantic and, in fact, would argue that once the CPUSA became "the American appendage of a Russian revolutionary power" in the early 1920s, as Draper's concluding sentence in *The Roots of American Communism* reads, "nothing else so important ever happened to it again" (p. 395).

6   Quotations are from Abbott, *Leftward Ho!*, 28; Seaver to the First American Writers Congress, *American Writers Congress*, ed. Henry Hart (New York: International Publishers, 1935), 101; Foley, *Radical Representations*, 117; Gold's "Proletarian Realism," NM, 6 (9/30), 5; Hicks, "The Future of Proletarian Literature," NM, 11 (5/22/34), 23–24; and Gold, "John Reed," *New Masses Anthology*, 307. Murphy, *Proletarian Moment*, particularly chapters 1 and 4, talks about the evolution of the prolet lit. Foley also traces its changes, including "the welcoming hand . . . increasingly extended to radical writers of petit bourgeois origin" (p. 90).

7   Alan Calmer used a generational model to explain the JRCs in his "Portrait of the Artist as a Proletarian," SRL, 16 (7/31/37), 3–4, 14. Many accounts, both primary and secondary, stress that the Reed Clubs were principally interesting to younger writers with working-class backgrounds.

8   All quotations, except the last, are from an unsigned memo on the JRCs for which Freeman has claimed credit, JF, box 180. "Draft Plan for Reorganization of the Cultural Movement," July 1934, AT, box 1, contains Trachtenberg's ideas for the JRCs and the final quotation. Kunitz's ideas are cited in the former source.

9   All quotations are from the minutes of the First National Conference of the JRCS, 5/30/32, JF, box 153, except Carlisle's, which is in Orrick Johnson's report, "The JRC Convention," NM, 8 (7/32), 14, and those coming from the "Draft Manifesto of the JRCS," NM, 7 (6/32), 4. In a similar vein, see also the minutes for the next day of the conference, "Memo Concerning Reorganization of the Literary and Professional Sections of the Movement," n.d., JF, box 153, and Michael Gold, "Notes from Kharkov," 5. Gold apparently came away from Kharkov with the sense that "every door must be opened wide to fellow-travelers."

10   All of the quotations but two come from Freeman's "The Crisis in *The New Masses*," 1933, JF, box 161. The word "monotonous" is Newton Arvin's description in "Not So Hot, but . . ." NM, 6 (12/30), 22, and the comments about shabby treatment are from Louis Lozowick's letter of resignation from NM to Alexander Trachtenberg, 2/27/33, JF, box 177. See also Hicks to V. F. Calverton, 1/8/33, VFC, box 5.

11   All quotations are from Freeman's memo cited above. The greatest advo-

cate of a still broader magazine was William Browder, Earl Browder's brother. To follow Browder's advice, however, would have unleashed a storm of complaints and far greater interference from the Party hierarchy.

12   All quotations except the last one are from Freeman's memo. The last one comes from a letter from Freeman to Earl Browder dated 8/5/37 and marked "not sent" in JF, box 151. He does not specify who asked him to resign and it is not immediately obvious from the context whether he meant other staff members or functionaries of the Party.

13   Alan Calmer addressed the generational tensions in his "Draft Plan for the Reorganization of [the] Cultural Movement," n.d. (ca. summer 1934), AT, box 1. On Gold, see Freeman's memo. On Freeman and functionaries, see William Browder to Freeman, 8/14/33, and Freeman to Browder, 5/21/34, both in JF, box 163. The tensions producing the JRCs are discussed in the last chapter.

14   Quotations are from *Culture and the Crisis* (New York: League of Professional Groups for Foster and Ford, 1932), 3; Mumford to Van Wyck Brooks, 4/10/32, *Brooks–Mumford Letters*, 78–79; Mumford to Malcolm Cowley and Edmund Wilson, 8/17/32, MC, incoming; Dos Passos to Edmund Wilson, May 1932, *Fourteenth Chronicle*, 409; and Frank to Cowley, 8/5/[32], MC, incoming. Matthew Josephson's recollections in *Infidel*, 149–54, help capture the early headiness he felt, yet Cowley's in *Dream*, 114–15 suggests that progressives were not entirely comfortable with the rhetoric of the manifesto. Several years after the fact Newton Arvin complained to Granville Hicks that his name was simply signed to the manifesto without his permission. Arvin to Hicks, 12/26/34, GH.

15   Quotations are from Josephson, *Infidel*, 152 and 151–52.

16   Quotations are from Bill Browder to Joseph Freeman, 8/26/33, JF, box 163, and Malcolm Cowley, "A Remembrance of the Red Romance, Part I," *Esquire*, 61 (3/64), 127.

17   Quotations are from Hook, "Breaking with the Communists," *Commentary*, 77 (2/84), 51, and Morrow to "Jim" [Farrell?], 3/22/33, JF, box 154.

18   Quotations are from Cowley to Edmund Wilson, 2/2/40, EW, and Rorty to H. H. Lewis, 7/22/33, VFC, box 13. Cowley's and Rorty's recollections differ on the breakup of the League. See also Hook, *Out of Step*, 187–88, Cowley, *Dream*, 123–24, and Josephson, *Infidel*, 165–66.

19   Orrick Johns in the NCDPP executive committee minutes of 8/16/34, HS, box 8.

20   While Diana Trilling's recollection of why she and her husband Lionel joined the NCDPP should be taken with a grain of salt, the bravado she expressed with her cynicism about "'innocents' club[s]'" and her assertion that they would have never joined "were it to have been the liberal organization which it pretended to be" were common sentiments. See *Beginning*, 194–96.

21   Quotations are from the letter of resignation signed by Louis Berg, Anita Brenner, George Novack, Lionel Trilling, Elliot Cohen, Diana Rubin [Trilling], Elinor Rice, and Herbert Solow, 5/8/33, HS, box 8. Diana Trilling presents a

view from the NCDPP office, but her perspective should not be taken as representative. *Beginning*, 207.

22   Ibid., 213–14.

23   Kunitz to Albert Margolis, 5/10/33, HS, box 8.

24   The exchange between Solow and Grace Allen, who took the minutes of the meeting in question, is Allen to Solow, 5/2/33, Solow to Allen, 5/10/33, and Allen to Solow, 5/11/33, all in HS, box 8.

25   The phrase "angry militancy" comes from Alfred Kazin's *Starting Out*, 12. The other quotations are from Trilling, *Beginning*, 205, and Aaron, "Some Reflections on Communism and the Jewish Writer," in *The Ghetto and Beyond*, ed. Peter I. Rose (New York: Random House, 1969), 257. Warren Susman talks about status among intellectuals in the 1930s in his *Culture as History* (New York: Pantheon, 1973; new ed., 1984), 169. See also Allen Guttman, *The Jewish Writer in America* (New York: Oxford University Press, 1971), 134–40.

26   Quotations are from the dissidents' letter of resignation from the NCDPP and Diana Trilling, *Beginning*, 205.

27   Quotations are from Kazin, *Starting Out*, 15, and *The Group*, 198. McCarthy's actual recollection of Cowley is in her "Fellow Workers," *Granta*, 27 (summer 1989), 112.

28   Dissidents' letter of resignation to the NCDPP.

29   Quotations are from Michael Blankfort, conversation with the author, 1/23/82; Calverton, "Marxism and the American Pattern," MM, 10 (1/37), 9; and Calverton to Haakon Chevalier, 9/12/33, VFC, box 3. See also his "The Crisis in Communism," NM, 7 (4/33), 140–45, 151. On Calverton, see Leonard Wilcox's biography, *V. F. Calverton*, or Philip Abbott's *Leftward Ho!*. The latter argues that Calverton was a more influential thinker than most scholars recognize.

30   Quotations are from Edmund Wilson, *The Thirties: From Notebooks and Diaries of the Period*, ed. Leon Edel (New York: Washington Square Press, 1980), 212, and Bates in *American Philosophy Today and Tomorrow*, ed. Horace Kallen and Sidney Hook (New York: Furman, 1935), 61. On Herberg, see his "The Crisis in Communism," MM, 7 (6/33), 286–87.

31   Quotations are from Calverton, "Marxism and the American Pattern," 10; Kenneth Rexroth to Louis Zukofsky, 3/10/31, KR, box 23; Sidney Hook, "Experimental Naturalism," in *American Philosophy Today*, ed. Kallen and Hook, 208; and Hook, *Toward an Understanding of Karl Marx* (New York: Day, 1933), 73. See also Max Eastman, *Marx and Lenin* (New York: Albert and Charles Boni, 1927), 109, 113–17; Calverton, *For Revolution* (New York: Day, 1934); Lewis Corey, *The Crisis of the Middle Class* (New York: Covici, Friede, 1935); and the editors, "Challenge," MXQ, 1 (1937), 4. Hook and Eastman had a very long debate in MM over the dialectic. See Wilcox, *Calverton*, 100–102, for the details. On Calverton and American exceptionalism, see Abbott, *Leftward Ho!*, 162–77. I am clearly using the term "American exceptionalism" fairly broadly here.

32   These terms are Soviet designations, not American, and only imperfectly apply to American intellectuals like Calverton and Corey. In fact, dissident Marxists in general would have disapproved of any attempt to force their work into a Soviet mold.

33   Trotsky, "The Soviet Union Today," NI, 2 (7/35), 118. See also his *The Revolution Betrayed* (New York: Pathfinder, 1937; new ed., 1972).

34   "Editorial," MM, 7 (1/34), 707.

35   Quotations are from Hook, "On Workers' Democracy," MM, 8 (10/34), 541, and Wilson to John Dos Passos, 1/31/35, JDP, ser. 2, box 4. Even Max Eastman, perhaps more critical of Stalin's imprint on the USSR than other rebels, still found some good things to say in his "Discriminations about Russia," MM, 8 (9/34), 479–85.

36   Quotations are from "Will Fascism Come to America: A Symposium," MM, 8 (9/34), 453–78, and Corey, *Crisis*. See also Sidney Hook, "The Fallacy of Social Fascism," MM, 8 (7/34), 342–52.

37   I borrow the term from one used by the right to describe progressives in the People's Front, "premature anti-fascists."

38   The quotations are from "The Pulse of Modernity," MM, 8 (5/34), 197, and "The Pulse of Modernity," MM, 7 (10/33), 518.

39   The two quotations are from Cannon's *History*, 199, and Trilling, *Beginning*, 212. The NPLD's provisional statement is in HS, box 9. A series of letters exchanged between Solow and Norman Thomas beginning 5/5/34 in NT, reel 3, shows how instrumental Solow was in forming the NPLD. There are many documents on the Mini case in MVK, box 38.

40   Quotations are from AWP's founding statement, "Toward an American Revolutionary Party," issued in pamphlet form; Hook to Calverton, n.d., VFC, box 8; and Calverton to Muste, 10/28/33, VFC, box 11. Perhaps it says something about the limits of Calverton's conception of the AWP that his pledges of work were "among the intellectuals" rather than the workers.

41   The quotations are from Cannon, *History*, 93; Cannon to Vincent Dunne, 4/21/32, in *Communist League of America, 1932–34*, ed. Fred Stanton and Michael Taber (New York: Monad, 1985), 89; *Militant*, 9/31; and Cannon, *History*, 186. See also the Shachtman faction's statement, "The Situation in the American Opposition," 6/4/32, SWP, reel 32.

42   Quotations are from Oliver Carlson, "Recollections of American Trotskyist Leaders," *Studies in Comparative Communism*, 10 (Spring/Summer 1977), 164; "Summary of Negotiations (AWP & CLA)," 8/30/34, SWP, reel 32, 3; and Swabeck to Trotsky, 3/9/34, SWP, reel 32. On Muste, see Jo Ann Robinson, *Abraham Went Out: A Biography of A. J. Muste* (Philadelphia: Temple University Press, 1981), 54–57. Arne Swabeck also offers a version of the whole negotiations in "Baptism in Fire," a chapter of his unpublished memoirs, 9–10. Hook claimed credit for persuading Muste to agree to fusion, but Burnham and Calverton also took part in the negotiations; see Hook, *Out of Step*, 202–3. The Calverton papers, box 1, contain a statement from the Los Angeles branch of

the earlier AWP dated 8/1/34 expressing outrage at the way negotiations proceeded. Immediately after fusion Hook left the organization and Burnham went over to the Trotskyist faction.

43   Quotations are from "Report on Activity of New York District Workers Party, December 15 1935 [1934?] to May 15 1935," 9 SP, reel 127, and Lillian Symes to Calverton, 2/13/34, VFC, box 15. See also "Statement on the Internal Party Situation," June Plenum [1935], SWP, reel 32. For Muste's point of view, see *The Essays of A. J. Muste*, ed. Nat Hentoff (New York: Bobbs-Merrill, 1967), 162–67.

44   Quotations are from Trilling, *Beginning*, 212–13, and Irving Howe, "Leon Trotsky: The Costs of History," in *Steady Work* (New York: Harcourt, Brace, World, 1966), 119. On Trotsky's influence on young Jewish intellectuals, see Alan Wald, "The *Menorah* Group Moves Left," *Jewish Social Studies*, 38 (summer/fall, 1976), 319–20. I have also based my analysis on some ideas suggested to me by Daniel Aaron in a letter, 5/2/82.

45   On Solow, see Wald, ibid., or his "Herbert Solow: Portrait of a New York Intellectual," *Prospects*, 3 (12/77), 418–60.

46   Burnham to Calverton, 5/31/34, VFC, box 2.

47   Quotations are from Wolfe, *Memoirs of a Not Altogether Shy Pornographer* (Garden City: Doubleday, 1972), 37, and Novack, "Marx and Intellectuals," NI, 2 (12/35), 230. Trotsky himself warned in 1938 that "an intellectual with an education gained in the Stalinist party, that's a dangerous element for us." *Writings of Leon Trotsky, 1937–38* (New York: Pathfinder, 1970), 297.

48   Quotations are from Cowley, "The Sense of Guilt," 148, and John Bright to Joseph Freeman, 12/4/33, JF, box 163. On the spread of Trotskyism through intellectual circles, see Wald, *New York*, 46–74.

49   Quotations are from Calverton, "Criticism on the Barricades," MM, 10 (8/36), 15, and Hook, *Toward an Understanding of Karl Marx*, 88.

50   Quotations are from Louise Bogan to Rolfe Humphries, 7/6/35, in *What the Woman Lived: Selected Letters of Louise Bogan*, ed. Ruth Limmer (New York: Harcourt, Brace, Jovanovich, 1973), 93, and Rexroth to Malcolm Cowley, n.d., MC, incoming. One example of the sustained level of argument may be found in MM in the months following some of Max Eastman's articles on U.S. and Soviet culture. See MM for most of 1934. Edmund Wilson's "Art, the Proletariat and Marx," NR, 76 (8/23/33), 41–45, also registers some belligerence. To a degree, William Phillips and Philip Rahv's later presentation of themselves as anti-prolet cult even during their Party phase grows out of a similar need to distinguish between good intellectuals and bad ones.

51   Quotations are from *A Note on Literary Criticism* (New York: Vanguard, 1936), 91; "The Pulse of Modernity," MQ, 6 (summer 1932), 7; Louise Bogan to Rolfe Humphries, 7/6/35, in *What the Woman Lived*, 93. Eastman's *Artists in Uniform* is about the impact of Stalinization on Soviet culture but also contains two chapters at the beginning on the American movement.

52   This analysis was influenced most heavily by Irving Howe's *A Margin of*

Hope, 57–59, Terry Cooney's *Rise of the New York Intellectuals,* 67–94, Alexander Bloom's *Prodigal Sons,* 11–67, and Wald's *New York,* 75–97. Carey Nelson, Barbara Foley, and Walter Kalaidjian have all suggested that these people included some of the New Critics who helped create a negative stereotype of the prolet cult.

53   Quotations are from Gold to Freeman, n.d., and Freeman to Gold, 1/5/37, both in JF, box 152, and Malcolm Cowley to Dale Kramer, 11/1/50, DK, incoming. Another version of the incident is James Thurber to Kramer, 8/5/50, DK, incoming. Schneider's review appeared in NM, 17 (6/23/36), 23–25; Hicks's in NM, 17 (7/14/36), 23. Overall, the reviews of Farrell's book were not as negative as might be expected.

54   Quotations are from DW, 2/16/34, 1, and "Report on the Madison Square Garden Meeting," 1934, ACLU, reel 91. The latter also provides a reasonably clear chronology of events. Contrast that with Oakley Johnson's Party view of "Madison Square Garden and the 'United Front,'" *Monthly Review,* 1 (6/34), 12–16.

55   Quotations are from "An Open Letter to American Intellectuals," MM, 8 (3/34), 92–93, and Brenner, NM, 10 (3/20/34), 21. Hook, *Out of Step,* 189, claimed that he did not sign the open letter, but his name does appear.

56   Quotations are from Lawson to Dos Passos, n.d. (c. 1934) in JDP, ser. 2, box 2; Endore to NR, 2/27/34, GE, box 74; Dos Passos to Robert Cantwell, 1/25/35, JDP, ser. 2, box 2. "To John Dos Passos," NM, 10 (3/13/34), 8–9, was the editorial.

57   The quotation is from Dos Passos to Edmund Wilson, 3/23/34, *14th Chronicle,* 435. On Dos Passos's disillusionment, see Virginia Spencer Carr, *Dos Passos: A Life* (Garden City: Doubleday, 1984); Townsend Ludington, *John Dos Passos* (New York: Dutton, 1980); or John P. Diggins, *Up from Communism* (New York: Harper and Row, 1975).

58   Quotations are from DW, 10/2/33, 1; Hillman Bishop's *The American League Against War and Fascism* (New York: privately published, 1936), 8; Roger Baldwin to J. B. Matthews, 2/20/34, RB, box 7. On the early League against War and Fascism, see Baldwin's files on the organization; J. B. Matthews, *Odyssey of a Fellow Traveler* (New York: privately published, 1938), 135–85; Robert Morss Lovett, *All Our Years* (New York: Viking, 1948), 258–67; and Bishop's quirky analysis.

59   Quotations are from Harry F. Ward to Baldwin, 3/2/34, and Thomas to Corliss Lamont, 4/5/34, both in ACLU, vol. 712, and Osmond Fraenkel to Thomas, 12/15/39, ACLU, vol. 2064. The original report and both minority dissents are in ACLU, reel 91. On Holmes, see board minutes for 2/26/34 and 3/5/34, ACLU, reel 5.

60   Dewey to Cowley, 7/21/32, MC, incoming.

61   Quotations are from Chamberlin, *Russia's Iron Age* (Boston: Little Brown, 1934), vii; Lyons, *Assignment in Utopia* (New York: Harcourt, Brace, 1937), 571; Chamberlin, ibid., 152; Lyons, ibid., 621–22.

62   Quotation is from Chamberlin, *The Confessions of an Individualist* (New York: Macmillan, 1940), 159. See Lyons to Lewis Gannett, 3/6/35, EL-O, pt. 2. A

typical comment was Jack Conroy's about Chamberlin, whom he called "a cheap careerist" (Conroy to V. F. Calverton, 3/23/33, VFC, box 3). Party intellectuals inevitably thought that the disillusioned sold out to better their careers.

63   Quotations are from Fischer, *Soviet Journey* (New York: Smith and Haas, 1935), 171; Lyons, "Epitaph for Anna Louise," 5, EL-H, box 5; Chamberlin, "The Ukrainian Famine," N, 140 (5/29/35), 629. James Crowl, *Angels in Stalin's Paradise* (Washington, D.C.: University Press of America, 1982), and S. J. Taylor, *Stalin's Apologist: Walter Duranty, the New York Times' Man in Moscow* (New York: Oxford University Press, 1990), are good secondary sources.

64   Quotations are from Lyons to Gannett, 3/6/35, EL-O, pt. 2, and Duranty in NYT, 3/31/33, 13.

65   Quotation is from John Dewey, "A Great American Prophet," CS, 3 (4/34), 6. See Joseph Wood Krutch, "Class Justice," N, 136 (5/3/33), 490. Dos Passos to Edmund Wilson, 12/23/34, *Fourteenth Chronicle,* 458–59, applauds Chamberlin's *Russia's Iron Age.* Thomas Lifka, "The Concept 'Totalitarianism' and American Foreign Policy 1933–1949" (Ph.D. diss., Harvard University, 1973) discusses the evolution of the word *totalitarianism* in more depth than I can here.

66   Henry Hazlitt's *Instead of Dictatorship* (New York: Day, 1933) talks about the concept of dictatorship in depth. See also Horace Kallen, *A Free Society* (New York: Ballou, 1934), 39–40, and his statement in "Will Fascism Come to America—A Symposium," 467–68; Chamberlin, *Collectivism: A False Utopia* (New York: Macmillan, 1936), 37–59, and *Confessions,* 166–75. The quotation is from John Dos Passos to Malcolm Cowley, 5/28/35, *Fourteenth Chronicle,* 477.

67   Quotation is from Cowley, "Europe Was a Success," NR, 81 (1/9/35), 253. Lyons, *Assignment,* 628, talks about his experience.

68   Quotations are from Kallen's letter of resignation, 12/26/34, HS, box 8, and Alfred Hirsch to Sidney Howard, 1/9/35, SH, box 6. I have not been able to find a copy of Howard's letter of resignation, but the material in boxes 5 and 6 of his papers suggests the scenario for his resignation pretty clearly.

69   The quotations are from the minutes of the 1/17/35 NCDPP meeting and the letter of resignation submitted by Walker, Wilson, and Margolis on 1/25/35; both are in HS, box 8.

70   Quotations are Dos Passos to Wilson 12/23/34, *Fourteenth Chronicle,* 459, and Wilson to Dos Passos, 1/11/35, JDP, ser. 2, box 4. John Haynes Holmes expressed an almost word-for-word reaction to the Kirov matter in a letter to Emma Goldman, 4/17/35, JHH, cont. 183.

71   Quotations are Baldwin et al., 2/15/35, EB, reel 1; Holmes to Baldwin, 2/8/35, JHH, cont. 183; and Baldwin in NYT, 2/12/35, 17.

72   Becker to George Lincoln Burr, 9/12/33, as quoted in Burleigh Wilkins, *Carl Becker* (Cambridge: MIT/Harvard, 1961), 142.

73   See Niebuhr, *Reflections on the End of an Era* (New York: Scribner's Sons, 1936), ix, and his "The Pathos of Liberalism," 304.

74   See Cannon, *History,* 189–215.

75 Both phrases are George Soule's from his *The Coming American Revolution* (New York: Macmillan, 1934).

76 Neugass to Taggard, 8/26/34, GT, box 13. Frank Warren, in *Liberals and Communism,* does a fine job of demonstrating in more detail the breakdown of the progressive ideology by mid-decade.

77 Quotations are Johns, "The John Reed Clubs Meet," NM, 13 (10/30/34), 25, and Richard Wright in *The God That Failed,* 136. See also Max Gordon, "The Communist Party of the 1930s," *Socialist Revolution,* 6 (1–3/76), 15–21, and Foley, *Radical Representations,* 117–26.

78 The phrase comes from the title of Jack Conroy's proletarian novel *The Disinherited.*

THREE Constructing the People's Front, 1935–1937

1 Klehr, *Heyday,* 167–85, and Ottanelli, *The Communist Party,* 83–105, both show, from within their contrasting frameworks, how the process of switching lines occurred. Both agree, however, that it did not happen instantly. Both also discuss the EPIC campaign.

2 Browder, *What Is Communism* (New York: Workers Library, 1936), 188. The Lincoln analogy is in the same passage and in his *Lincoln and the Communists* (New York: Workers' Library, 1936), 5. See also Samuel Sillen, "Old Abe Lincoln in 1939," NM, 30 (2/14/39), 23–25. Nathan Glazer, *The Social Basis of American Communism* (New York: Harcourt, Brace and World, 1961), suggested that Party membership rose from 24,500 in 1934 to 42,000 by 1936 and hit a peak in 1938 at 55,000 (pp. 92–93). Hicks, *I Like America* (New York: Modern Age, 1938). On his earlier hesitations about joining the CPUSA, see his *Where We Came Out* (New York: Viking, 1954). Hicks's most recent biographers, Leah Levenson and Jerry Natterstad, contend that "Hicks would have joined even if there had been no change in Party policy." See their *Granville Hicks: The Intellectual in Mass Society,* 85.

3 See Klehr, *Heyday,* 186–206, and Ottanelli, *Communist Party,* 137–57. On Baldwin, see Peggy Lamson, *Roger Baldwin,* 193–94. Some other examples of changes of heart on the New Deal are Stuart Chase to J. Mildred Schwartz, 3/16/39, SCH, box 1, and Heywood Broun, "The 1936 Election," in *The Collected Edition of Heywood Broun* (New York: Harcourt, Brace, 1941), 376–78.

4 Quotations are from Browder, *The People's Front* (New York: International, 1938), 168; Freeman to the YCL, 4/3/37, JF, box 129; Humphries to Root, 2/4/37, as quoted in *Poets, Poetics, and Politics: America's Literary Community Viewed from the Letters of Rolfe Humphries, 1910–1969,* ed. Richard Gillman and Michael Paul Novak (Lawrence: University Press of Kansas, 1992), 137. The paraphrased comments are from " 'Misunderstanding' Moscow," NM, 16 (8/13/35), 3; Gold, "The United Front in France," NM, 16 (8/6/35), 15; and Magil, "An Answer to Ernest Boyd," NM, 18 (1/14/36), 16–19. Freeman ex-

pressed private dissatisfaction with the cultural People's Front in a letter to Gold, 1/17/38, JF, box 152.

5   Quotations are from Hal Draper, "The American Student Union Faces the Student Anti-War Strike," *American Socialist Monthly*, 5 (4/36), 7; John West [James Burnham], "The Question of Organic Unity," NI, 3 (2/36), 18; Wolfe's review of "Lenin in 1918," n.d., BDW, box 23; and Hacker, "Mr. Browder Studies History," N, 142 (4/22/36), 526–28.

6   Quotations are from Swabeck's "The Real Meaning of the United Front," NI, 2 (10/35), 182, and Burnham, *The People's Front: The New Betrayal* (New York: Pioneer Press, 1937), 11.

7   The first quotation is from a letter from Leon Dennen to Max Eastman, cited in Eastman, *Heroes I Have Known* (New York: Simon and Schuster, 1942), 203n; the second is from Matthew Josephson's *Infidel*, 364. On the breakup of the JRCS, see also Malcolm Cowley, "1935, the Year of the Congress," *Southern Review*, new ser., 15 (4/79), 275; Richard Wright in *God That Failed*, 136–37; Mangione, *An Ethnic*, 124. Barbara Foley, *Radical Representations*, 79, 119–24, presents a rather different view, seeing little connection between the sudden interest in middle-class intellectuals and what she calls a "rhetorical mellowing" of the prolet cult (p. 79). While several of the stories of the JRCS' demise come from anticommunists, there are still plenty of other versions that generally confirm their narrative. I also find it otherwise difficult to explain the fairly rapid disappearance of the JRCS.

8   The quotations are from "Call for the American Writers Congress"; Cowley in "Symposium, Thirty Years Later: Memories of the First American Writers' Congress," *American Scholar*, 35 (summer 1966), 496; Wright, in *God That Failed*, 136; Cowley "1935," 275. See also Gilbert, *Writers and Partisans*, 135n. Rolfe Humphries to Theodore Roethke, 12/24/35, in *Poets, Poetics and Politics*, 125, nicely captures some of the younger generation's resentment.

9   Quotations are from Cowley, *Dream*, 271; LAW ex. comm. minutes, 2/2/35; Wilson to Dos Passos, 5/9/35, JDP, ser. 2, box 4; Dos Passos to Cowley, n.d. (c. spring 1936), MC, incoming; Hicks, "Symposium," 496; Hicks, *Part*, 130; Cowley, *Dream*, 279. My information on Blankfort comes from an interview conducted 1/23/82. It is very difficult to know how to assess the firsthand accounts of the conference because they are so shaped by politics. Hicks's assumptions about the Party stacking the meeting, for example, may not be accurate. And Trachtenberg's reaction to "The International" is probably exaggerated.

10   Burke's speech is included in *American Writers Congress*. The description of Burke as a "premature adherent of the People's Front is Cowley's, from "1935," 279.

11   Quotations are from Eva Goldbeck to Malcolm Cowley, c. spring 1935, MC, box 3; Hemingway to Taggard, 9/17/35, GT, box 8; Katherine Buckles to Granville Hicks, 12/23/35, GH; Robert Hallowell, as quoted by Buckles in a letter to Hicks, 10/5/35, GH. On membership and dues, see ex. comm. minutes, 6/12/35 [fragment], LAW, pt. 2. Another example of a fairly well known writer resisting

266 the LAW is Newton Arvin. See his letter to Granville Hicks, 12/26/34, GH, detailing the many reasons he would not sign the Call to the 1935 Congress.

12 Quotation is from Humphries to Theodore Roethke, 2/4/36, in *Poets, Poetics and Politics,* 129. On the Hicks matter, see ex. comm. minutes 6/3/35, LAW, pt. 2, and Katherine Buckles to Hicks, 6/4/35, GH. On the Reed memorial, see ex. comm. minutes, 8/15/35, 8/29/35, 9/12/35, 9/19/35, 10/10/35 (all in LAW, pt. 2), and Buckles to Hicks, 10/5/35, GH. On the failed lecture series, see minutes 8/8/35, 8/29/35, 9/5/35, 9/26/35, 10/3/35, 10/10/35, 10/30/35, and 11/6/35, in LAW, pt. 2.

13 Quotations are from Rideout, *Radical Novel,* 243, and Ferruggia, "Organizing the 'Ivory Tower,' " 144. Foley, *Radical Representations,* 98–126, argues for the increasing complexity of the prolet lit. Rideout lists about twenty works that came out in the late 1930s that might be described as proletarian or radical and another forty or so after that (pp. 297–300). The *Partisan Review* was the center of attacks on the prolet cult during the late 1930s.

14 The Pells quotation is a chapter subheading from *Radical Visions,* 310. On the Western Writers Congress, see CM, box 13, and WWC, box 1 for documents. The Freeman quotation is from a letter to Floyd Dell, 7/1/51, FD, Freeman-Dell sect.

15 Jacoby, *The Last Intellectuals* (New York: Farrar, Straus and Giroux, 1987), 3–26 especially.

16 See Foley, *Radical Representations,* pt. 2.

17 Quotations are from ex. comm. minutes, 12/4/35, LAW, pt. 2; Cowley, *Dream,* 297; Taggard at the ex. comm. 12/11/35, and Trachtenberg at the ex. comm., 3/27/36, both in LAW, pt. 2. On CP unwillingness to expand the ex. comm., see Buckles to Hicks, 12/23/35, GH. On other proposals to encourage activity, see minutes, 3/27/36, LAW, pt. 2.

18 Quotations are from ex. comm. minutes, 3/27/36, LAW, pt. 2; Mary McCarthy, "My Confession," 82; "Moscow Offers an Olive Branch," N, 141 (8/7/35), 145.

19 Quotations are from "Moscow Offers," 145; Freeman to E. Browder, 8/5/37 (marked "not sent"), JF, box 151; Trachtenberg's motion to the ex. comm., 10/2/35, LAW, pt. 2. Beside the editorial cited above, see also "A People's Front for America," NR, 85 (1/8/36), 241; "The Week," NR, 83 (8/7/35), 345; "Toward a United Front," SF, 2 (1/36), 103–4.

20 Quotations are from ex. comm. minutes, 3/27/36, LAW, pt. 2, and memo fragment composed by Walter Lowenfels in JF, box 190.

21 Quotations are from "United Front," *Radical Religion,* 1 (winter 1935), 3, and CS, 5 (12/35), 2–3.

22 On the war, see Robert Rosenstone, *Crusade of the Left* (New York: Pegasus, 1969), or David T. Cattell, *Communism and the Spanish Civil War* (Berkeley: University of California Press, 1956).

23 Quotations are from Chamberlain, "*Was* It a Congress of American Writers," CS, 6 (8/37), 15; Quincy Howe, "Spain's Threat to America's Peace," CS, 5 (10/36), 11–14; Holmes to Norman Thomas, 1/7/37, JHH, cont. 184; cummings

to Cowley, 12/23/36, MC, incoming, original capitalization retained. Other
sources suggest Holmes was expelled from the Socialist Party because of his
position on Spain and other matters.

24   The dissidents' best expert on the war in Spain was Anita Brenner. See
her "Who's Who in Spain," N, 143 (8/15/36), 174–77. For a Trotskyist perspective, see Trotsky's own "The Lesson of Spain," SA, 2 (9/36), 1–2, or the Trotskyists' expert Felix Morrow, "How the Workers Can Win in Spain," SA, 2 (10/36),
6–8. See also "POUM and the Spanish Revolution," SA, 2 (12/36), 5–6.

25   Quotations are from Leigh White, "Barcelona Faces Front," N, 146
(3/5/38), 267; Joseph Lash to Nancy Bedford Jones, summer 1937, as quoted in
Robert Cohen, When the Old Left Was Young (New York: Oxford University
Press, 1993), 167; Freeman, Writer in a Changing World (New York: Equinox,
1937), 237. On the POUM, see Ralph Bates, "Forging Catalonian Unity," NM, 22
(1/26/37), 18–20, and Draper, "Behind the Lines in Spain," NM, 22 (1/26/37),
15–17. See also "Trotskyists Organize Anti-Soviet Campaign," SRT, 5 (2/37), 7.
Frank Warren, Liberalism and Communism, 134; Allen Guttman, The Wound
in the Heart (New York: Macmillan, 1962), 149; and R. Dan Richardson, Comintern Army (Lexington, University Press of Kentucky, 1982), 151–54, all agree
that Party reports coming out of Spain were often deliberately inaccurate.

26   On the International Brigade, see Richardson, Comintern Army, passim;
on the Lincoln Battalion, see Rosenstone, Crusade. Louis Fischer complained
about the International Brigade during his examination by Immigration and
Naturalization Service officers, 5/5/49, LF, box 2. Joseph Freeman commented
to Jack Friedman, fighting in Spain, "What a wonderful lot of organisers you
will be when you come back," 6/1/37, JF, box 180.

27   Quotations are from Josephson's diary, entry dated 8/27/36, as quoted in
David Shi, Matthew Josephson, Bourgeois Bohemian (New Haven: Yale University Press, 1981), 179; Frank to Louis Fischer, 10/24/38, LF, box 2; Fischer,
"On Madrid's Front Line," N, 143 (10/24/36), 470; Stewart, "Inside Spain," N,
143 (8/29/36), 235; "Uprising in Catalonia," N, 144 (5/15/37), 552.

28   Quotations are from Hellman in a 1968 interview with Fred Gardner in
Conversations with Lillian Hellman, ed. Jackson R. Bryer (Jackson: University
Press of Mississippi, 1986), 113; Fischer, Men and Politics (London: Cape,
1941), 386–401; Herbst's letter to Mary and Neal Daniels, 2/17/66, as quoted in
Langer, Herbst, x. William Alexander, Film on the Left (Princeton: Princeton University Press, 1981), 149–58; Virginia Carr, Dos Passos, 362–70; and
Wright, Hellman, 136, each give background on "The Spanish Earth." On
Fischer, see his examination by the Immigration and Naturalization Service
and his 1938 memos to David Amariglio in LF, box 2. HUAC, Communist Infiltration of the Hollywood Motion Picture Industry, vol. 2 (Washington, D.C.: Government Printing Office, 1951), 1881.

29   Quotations are from Dreiser, speech before the LAW, 9/15/38, LAW, pt. 8;
Strong to Roosevelt, 1/13/3[7], ER, box 1405; Cowley, "To Madrid, Part I," NR,
92 (8/25/37), 64; Carleton Beal, "Correspondence," SR, 3 (Summer 1937), 207.

30   Quotation is from LAW Bulletin, 4 (Summer 1938). On the size of the

268   organization, see LAW *Bulletin,* 1/37, 1. Walter Lowenfels to Freeman, n.d., JF, box 190, expressed the CPUSA perspective. On the manuscript auction, which raised $2,000, see the program, "Sale of Manuscripts and Letters," 3/25/38, LAW, pt. 7. Other lecture and fund-raising activities are described in LAW *Bulletins,* 10/36, 3/37, 4–5/37, and fall 1938. On the arms embargo, see the press release issued by LAW on 11/14/38, LAW, pt. 7.

31   Quotations are from ex. comm. minutes, 3/11/37, LAW, pt. 2, and Seaver in DW, 6/9/37, 7. Trachtenberg attended nine LAW meetings in 1935, eight in 1936, two in 1937, and no others; Gold attended once in 1935 and once in 1936, but never again; Hicks attended only once (in 1935); Lowenfels once in 1935 and five times in 1936. On keynote speakers, see minutes, 4/8/37; on resolutions, see "Report of 2nd LAW Congress," both in LAW, pts. 2 and 1. Newton Arvin's speech is in *The Writer in a Changing World,* 34–43. He, remember, refused to sign the 1935 Call for a congress. Gabriella Ferruggia correctly suggests that the two issues driving the 1937 Congress were "total freedom from party 'regimentation' . . . and a rigorous defense of the popular front strategy," "Organizing the 'Ivory Tower,' " 146.

32   Powell to Dos Passos, n.d., JDP, ser. 2, box 4. The concern that the conference would become too political was Cowley's, expressed in "Minutes" [either of the LAW's ex. comm. or conference planning subcommittee], 3/11/37, LAW, pt. 2. *Writer in a Changing World* was the official record of the 1937 conference.

33   Quotations are from De Silver to Dos Passos, n.d., JDP, ser. 2, box 1, and Donald Ogden Stewart, *By a Stroke of Luck* (New York: Paddington, 1975), 238. See also the Powell letter cited above.

34   Quotations from Ellen Blake to Hicks, 5/20/37, GH; Freeman to Carl Reeve, 5/29/37, JF, box 129; Freeman to Gold, 1/17/38, JF, box 152. See also Freeman to Rahv, 6/19/35, JF, box 155; Freeman to Earl Browder, 8/5/37 (marked "not sent"), JF, box 151; Rolfe Humphries to E. Merrill Root, 2/4/37, in *Poets, Poetics and Politics,* 136.

35   Folsom to Hicks, 7/27/38, GH. On Dreiser and the CPUSA's fight over his anti-Semitism, see Aaron, *Writers,* 293–96. On the Dreiser dinner, see LAW *Bulletin,* 5 (Fall 1938).

36   Quotation is cited in Richard W. Fox, *Niebuhr,* 173. LAW, pt. 8 contains letters from Benét, Saroyan, Frankfurter, Hurst, Canby, and Burt declining membership invitations. On Dell, see Folsom to Hicks, 12/2/37, GH. On the president, see FDR to V. W. Brooks, 4/23/38, and FDR's secretary to Brooks, 4/27/38, LAW, pt. 8.

37   Quotations are from Lovett, "For Peace and Democracy," NR, 93 (12/15/ 37, 164; ALPD, "Proceedings of the Fourth U.S. Congress against War," 16; "Peace or War?" *The Arbitrator,* 20 (9/38), 2; Baldwin to Lovett, 2/5/42, RML, box 1; Samuel Sillen, "Peace Grows 85 Percent," NM, 30 (1/24/39), 13. The membership figure is enormously misleading. It was produced by adding together the membership totals of the 1,023 affiliated organizations. Most of

those eight million members did not even know they belonged; since many
people also belonged to more than one affiliated organization, quite a few of the
names were duplicates. Herbert Solow, in an exposé of the organization, argued that its dues-paying membership was actually 20,000.

38   Anderson quotation is from a letter to LAW c. 11/36 in response to a
request that he chair a LAW meeting on Spain. On the Hollywood Anti-Nazi
League, see Ceplair and Englund, *The Inquisition,* 104–12. On Stewart, see his
By a Stroke. Diana Trilling recalled that in the NCDPP she had Anderson's permission to use "his signature as he saw fit," *Beginning,* 198.

39   Draper, "Life of the Party," 46.

FOUR   Left-wing Opposition to the People's Front, 1937–1938

1   Robert Conquest's *The Great Terror* (London: Macmillan, 1968) and Roy A.
Medeved's *Let History Judge,* ed. David Joravsky and Georges Haupt (New
York: Vintage, 1971) provide information on the trials and purges.

2   Quotations are from Schneider to Cowley, n.d., MC, incoming, and John
Garnett, "A Trial of Traitors," SRT, 7 (4/38), 6. Many other stories in SRT take
this same tone.

3   Hicks, *Part,* 144; Wechsler, *The Age of Suspicion* (New York: Random
House, 1953), 106; Freeman to Floyd Dell, 3/20/53, FD, Freeman-Dell sect.
Robert Bendiner, *Just around the Corner* (New York: Harper and Row, 1967),
100–101, also comments on Freeman's difficulty in assimilating the trials.
Note that all of these are recollections colored by time and changes in political
outlook. Yet, the sheer number of memoirs mentioning doubts suggests these
were fairly common feelings about the trials within Party circles.

4   Quotations are from K. Lapin to Joseph Freeman, 10/7/37, JF, box 151, and
Wechsler, *Age,* 106–7. On Kunitz, see Aaron, *Writers,* 369, who recounts a story
told to him by Freeman. On Freeman, see his letter to Dell, 6/28/51, FD,
Freeman-Dell sect.

5   Quotations are from Gold, "Notes on the Cultural Front," NM *Literary Supplement,* 25 (12/7/37), 3; John Hyde Preston, "May Day, 1938," *Direction,* 1
(5/38), 2; Bendiner evaluating "You Cannot Be a Liberal and Favor Trotsky,"
dated 12/24/36, JF, box 130.

6   Quotations are from Powell to Dos Passos, n.d., JDP, ser. 2, box 4; "The
Lessons of Barcelona," SRT, 6 (6/37), 5; Magil in *Writer in a Changing World,*
241; "The Editorial Jitters," NM, 26 (3/22/38), 10; Browder, *Writer in a Changing World,* 54.

7   Quotation is from Minor to Browder, 7/20/37, EB, reel 2. Frank's letter
appeared in NR, 91 (5/12/37), 39–40. His visit to Trotsky was in March 1937;
see Trotsky's memo, received in New York, 3/24/37, HS, box 11. Frank's side of
the story is in his *Memoirs,* 190–97. Curiously, Michael Blankfort also visited
Trotsky in Mexico and suffered no such attacks as Frank did.

270   8   Quotations are from Mumford, *My Works and Days* (New York: Harcourt, Brace, Jovanovich, 1979), 519, and Basso to Cowley, n.d., 1937 ("Sunday"), MC, incoming. See also Rolfe Humphries to Louise Bogan, 10/4/38, *Poets, Poetics and Politics,* 154, who noted that Frank *"commutes* in and out of the doghouse."

9   "The Fourth Moscow Trial," NR, 94 (3/9/38), 117.

10   Quotations are from Lewis Mumford to Herbert Solow, 2/20/37, HS, box 2; Herbst to Hicks, 9/21/37, as quoted in Langer, *Herbst,* 227; "Russian Politics in America," NR, 90 (2/17/37), 33. See also "The Russian Executions," NR, 81 (1/23/35), 292–93, and "Correspondence," NR, 94 (4/13/38), 306–7, a series of letters complaining of NR's inability to make a public statement on the trials.

11   Quotations are from Upton Sinclair in Sinclair and Eugene Lyons, *Terror in Russia?: Two Views* (New York: Richard Smith, 1938), 10; Duranty, "The Riddle of Russia," NR, 91 (7/14/37), 272; Anna Louise Strong, "The Terrorists' Trial," SRT, 5 (10/36), 9; "'Old Bolsheviks,' on Trial," N, 143 (8/22/36), 201.

12   Cowley, "Moscow Trial: 1938," NR, 95 (5/18/38), 50. The second half of his review was in the next issue, 5/25/38, 79. Cowley's recollections come from a letter to the author, 6/4/81.

13   Quotations are from "Moscow Loses Caste," NR, 94 (3/16/38), 151, and "'Old Bolsheviks,'" 201.

14   Quotations are from Cowley to author, 6/4/81; Alfred Kazin to Cowley, 5/6/42, MC, incoming; Cowley, "Echoes from Moscow 1937–38," *Southern Review,* 20 (Winter 1984), 3. Bliven's letter appeared in NR, 94 (3/30/38), 216–17.

15   Quotations are from William Henry Chamberlin, "Correspondence: the Moscow Trials," *Pacific Affairs,* 11 (9/38), 367; [Niebuhr], "The Moscow Trials," *Radical Religion,* 3 (Summer 1937), 1; Lyons, *Terror,* 39.

16   Quotations are from Niebuhr, "Russia and Karl Marx," N, 146 (5/7/38), 531; Rodman, "Trotsky in the Kremlin," CS, 6 (12/37), 19; Chamberlain, "It's Your State," CS, 7 (10/38), 9; "USSR and USA," CS, 6 (10/37), 5; Lyons, *Terror,* 18; Villard, "Issues: Russian," 729. A pamphlet in which John Dewey debated Trotsky over the trials was tellingly called *Their Morals and Ours: Marxist Versus Liberal Views on Morality.*

17   The first two quotations are from Dos Passos to Sinclair, 4/38, *Fourteenth Chronicle,* 516, and Dewey to Dos Passos, 6/12/37, JDP, Ser. 2, box 1. The third quotation is the title of an article by Dewey that appeared in CS, 6 (1/37), 10; my emphasis. The fourth is the title of Hays's 1939 book. The final quotation comes from a letter from Hamilton Basso to Malcolm Cowley, 8/12/37, MC, incoming.

18   Holmes to Baldwin, 12/30/37, JHH, cont. 185.

19   Quotations are from Villard to Holmes, 3/26/37, in Villard, *The Dilemmas of an Absolute Pacifist in Two World Wars,* ed. Anthony Gronowisz (New York: Garland, 1983), 465; Krutch as quoted in John Margolis, *Joseph Wood Krutch* (Knoxville: University of Tennessee Press, 1980), 115, 116; Dewey to Dos Passos, 6/12/37, JDP, ser. 2, box 1; Villard to Holmes, 3/26/37, in Villard, ibid., 465–66.

20   Wilson to Dos Passos, 1/11/35, JDP, ser. 2, box 4. Diana Trilling quotes from a long letter from her husband, Lionel Trilling, to Alan Brown (8/36) that she finds "puzzling" because of its tentative tone toward the trials. Her later political identity precludes her acknowledging that in 1935 and 1936 many proto-anti-Stalinists were not as staunchly anti-Stalinist as they would become later. See *Beginning*, 296–98.

21   Wilson to Cowley, 4/15/37, MC, incoming.

22   Ibid.

23   Cannon's perspective on the AWP's problems is in his *History*, 200–206. On the SP in the 1930s, see Frank Warren, *An Alternative Vision*, or David Shannon, *The Socialist Party of America*, 227–55. The Trotskyists emphasized that once the Militants split, they would be easy prey for the CPUSA. See Cannon, 194, and Shachtman's comments in *New Militant*, 5/16/36, 4. Given Norman Thomas's bitter feelings about the Madison Square Garden fight, fusion between the CPUSA and the Militants seemed unlikely.

24   Quotations are from George Novack, "A. J. [Muste] and American Trotskyism," *Liberation*, 12 (9–10/67), 23; Muste, "How the Cannon-Shachtman Group 'Builds' the Party," 7–8/35, SWP, reel 32; Lens, *Unrepentant Radical* (Boston: Beacon, 1980), 41; Muste, "Statement on the Attitude of the Workers Party to the Socialist Party and the Communist Party," Workers Party "Special" *Bulletin*, 1/10/36, 1, and *The Essays of Muste*, 169.

25   All quotations are from Cannon, *History*, 225, 226, and 241. See also Arne Swabeck's unpublished memoir, chap. 15.

26   Quotations are from Hook, *Out of Step*, 224. The initial announcement of the ACDLT appeared in *Socialist Appeal* 2 (12/36): 15–16. Other information comes from George Novack to the author, 10/12/80.

27   Quotations are from Kirchwey to George Novack, 2/9/37, as cited in Sara Alpern, *Freda Kirchwey* (Cambridge: Harvard University Press, 1987), 119; Hallgren to V. F. Calverton, 1/29/37, VFC, box 7; McCarthy to Farrell, 10/5/57, as cited in Brightman, *Writing Dangerously*, 131. On Adamic, see *My America*, 85. Another whose name appeared without permission was John Dos Passos. See Virginia Carr, *Dos Passos*, 360–61. Other membership controversies may be found in NYT, 3/5/38, 8 (Franz Boas), NR's letters to the editor, 90 (4/21/37), 325 (H. N. Brailsford), and NM's readers' forum, 22 (2/16/37), 21 (Lewis Gannett).

28   Quotations are from Trotsky's letter to the "comrades" on the ACDLT, n.d., in *Writings of Trotsky*, vol. 9 (New York: Pathfinder, 1970), 254; Dewey to Dos Passos, 6/12/37, JDP, ser. 2, box 1; Gruening to Cowley, 3/16/37, MC, incoming.

29   The first two quotations come from Novack's report to the SP's ex. comm., 5/8/37, ACDLT, item 7.23; the third is from an ACDLT news release, 5/7/37, ACDLT, item 7.22; the fourth is from Gus Tyler, "Socialist Discipline and Action!," *Socialist Review*, 6 (9/37), 23. See also the Minutes of the National Action Committee, 4/23/37, SP, reel 35, 2–3.

272 30 Quotations are from Hook, "My Running Debate with Einstein," *Commentary*, 74 (7/81), 38; Beard to John Dewey, 3/22/37, HS, box 11; Becker to Morrow, as quoted in Harold Kirker and Burleigh Taylor Wilkins, "Beard, Becker and the Trotsky Inquiry," *American Quarterly*, 13 (winter 1961), 523; Solow to Waldo Frank, 6/8/37, HS, box 1. Hook, "Memories of the Moscow Trials," *Commentary*, 77 (3/84), 59, his "Running Debate," 38, and Isaac Deutscher, *The Prophet Outcast* (London: Oxford University Press, 1963), 368–70, have the most complete lists of those who declined to be a part of the Commission of Inquiry.

31 Hook, "Memory of the Trials," 57.

32 Quotations are from Hook to the author, 9/18/80; Novack, "How the Moscow Trials Were Exposed," *Militant*, 41 (5/6/77), 20; Beals, "The Fewer Outsiders the Better," *Saturday Evening Post*, 209 (6/12/37), 74. Trotsky's *Writings of Trotsky*, vol. 9, contains at least seven letters to Trotskyists on the ACDLT. Solow to "Meg" [De Silver] noted that "Novack has proven useful too, although I too would not have favored sending him," 4/10/[37], HS, box 1. Dewey's report on the hearings was called "Truth Is on the March." When confronted in 1941 with a request from George Novack for access to its mailing list to send out a letter, the Union for Democratic Action hesitated to grant it, largely because of "experience with the Trotsky Defense Committee of several years ago." See James Loeb to Roger Baldwin, 11/8/41, ADA, ser. 1, no. 47.

33 Quotations are from Calverton to *Socialist Appeal*, 2/4/38, VFC, box 15, and Calverton to Beals, 4/24/38, VFC, box 1. Felix Morrow to the ACDLT's membership, 4/19/37, suggested that Beals was "if not directly, at least indirectly, under Stalinist influence," but not a GPU agent. ACDLT, item 7.19. Another Trotskyist, Albert Glotzer, however, believed Beals was linked to "Stalin and his secret police." See his *Trotsky* (Buffalo: Prometheus Books, 1989), 266–70. Eastman made the initial request to drop Beals, but thereafter Trotskyists did all of the pushing.

34 Quotations are from Meyer Schapiro to Bertram Wolfe, 11/27/37, BDW, box 63; Kazin to author, 5/7/81; Wilson to Dos Passos, 2/12/37, JDP, ser. 2, box 5 (talking about both Trotskyists and Stalinists); Bogan to Wilson, 2/10/37, in *What the Woman Lived*, 150–51; Wolfe to Schapiro, 11/27/37, BDW, box 63.

35 Quotations are from Schapiro to Wolfe, 11/26/37, BDW, box 63; Oak to Corliss Lamont, 3/3/38, LO, box 1; "The Moscow Trials," MM, 10 (3/37), 3.

36 Both stories come from "Symposium: Thirty Years Later: Memories of the First American Writers' Congress," *American Scholar*, 35 (Summer 1966), 509, 511.

37 Quotations are from McCarthy, "My Confession," 102–3, her *Intellectual Memoirs* (New York: Harcourt Brace Jovanovich, 1992), 58, her "Portrait of the Intellectual as a Yale Man," in *The Company She Keeps* (New York: Harcourt, Brace, 1942), 218–19; John Haynes Holmes to Corliss Lamont, 12/29/39, JHH, cont. 189; Bellow, "Writers, Intellectuals, Politics," *National Interest*, 31 (Spring 1993), 125.

38   Quotations are from Liston Oak, "Is Stalinism Bolshevism?" MM, 10
(3/38), 10. Calverton to Carleton Beals, 4/24/38, VFC, box 1.

39   Quotations are from Brenner, "Letters to the Editor: Calling for Protest,"
N, 145 (8/21/37), 206; "Beyond Franco and Stalin," MM, 10 (9/37), 2; Solow to
Lewis Mumford, 2/24/[37], HS, box 2.

40   Quotation is from Oak to Leonard Saunders, n.d., BDW, box 11. His story is
told briefly in a letter to Bertram Wolfe, 1/16/50, BDW, box 11, and before HUAC,
3/21/47, 72–74.

41   The Dos Passos story is told in his letter to the editors of NR, 7/39, *Fourteenth Chronicle,* 527–29, from which all quotations are taken. Dorothy Gal-
lagher, *All the Right Enemies* (New Brunswick: Rutgers University Press,
1988), 159, also reiterates the story of Tresca's warning to Dos Passos. Malcolm
Cowley to Edmund Wilson, 2/2/40, EW, expressed a typical progressive response to Dos Passos.

42   Quotations are from L. Trilling to Alan Brown, n.d., as cited in D. Trilling,
Beginning, 301; Brenner, "Who's Who," 174; Bogan to Zabel, 8/22/37, *What
the Woman Lived,* 161–62, and "Ripostes," PR, 5 (8–9/38), 77.

43   Quotations are from Solow, "Substitution at Left Tackle: Hemingway for
Dos Passos," PR, 4 (4/38), 62–64; Oak's "Dear Friend" letter, and Trilling, *Be-
ginning,* 180–81. Oak did eventually get a job with the WPA in the History
Section, allegedly through the intervention of another anti-Stalinist, Lewis
Corey. Dos Passos's novel was *The Adventures of a Young Man* (New York:
Harcourt, Brace, 1939). It was not well reviewed by the left press.

44   Quotations are from Rexroth to Bertram Wolfe, 11/13/39, BDW, box 12,
and Calverton in "Is State Capitalism Progressive?" MM, 10 (3/38), 3.

45   Quotations are from Rahv to Trotsky, 4/10/38, as quoted in Eric Homberger, *American Writers and Radical Politics* (London: Macmillan, 1986),
209–10; Rorty in NL, 6/24/39, 8; Herbert Solow to Lewis Mumford, 2/24/[37],
HS, box 2; Rexroth, ibid.

46   Quotations are from Rahv, "Trials of the Mind," PR, 4 (4/38), 5, and Oak to
Baldwin, 3/1/38, LO, box 1. On Kazin, see his letter to Cowley, 5/6/42, MC,
incoming. Diana Trilling's comments in note 43, above, support this position
also.

47   Oak to Lamont, 3/3/38, LO, box 1.

48   Quotations are from "Editorial Statement," PR, 4 (12/37), 3, and Freeman
to Herbst, 8/4/58, JF, box 112. Phillips recounted his version of the evolution of
the *Partisan Review* several times. See "On PR," in *The Little Magazine in
America,* ed. Elliot Anderson and Mary Kinzie (Yonkers: Pushcart Press, 1978),
133, and Phillips, "How *Partisan Review* Began," 42–46.

49   Quotations are from Freeman to Herbst, 8/4/58, JF, box 112; Gold's DW
column, 10/12/37, 7; "Falsely Labeled Goods," NM, 24 (9/14/37), 9–10; Herbst
to Hicks, 9/21/37, as cited in Langer, *Herbst,* 231; Herbst to Katherine Anne
Porter, 9/21/37, CAL.

50   Quotation is from "Editorial Statement," PR, 4 (12/37), 3. James Murphy's

274   *The Proletarian Moment* overstates the case against Phillips and Rahv for re-writing their own history, but he is right in suggesting that they did have political reasons for disassociating themselves from the prolet cult.

51   Quotations are from William Phillips, "*The Partisan Review* Then and Now," *Partisan Review*, 9, PR "Editorial Statement" cited above, 3, and Rahv in NL, 12/10/38, 8. The last four quotations all come from Rahv's "Two Years of Progress—From Waldo Frank to Donald Ogden Stewart," PR, 4 (2/38), 22.

52   Quotations are from Blackmur to Cowley, 11/5/38, MC, incoming; Cowley to Wilson, 10/31/38, EW; Rexroth to Cowley, n.d., MC, incoming; Cowley to Wilson, 10/31/38, ibid.

53   Quotations are from McCarthy's introduction to her *Theatre Chronicles* (New York: Farrar, Straus, 1963), viii. See also Blackmur to Zabel, 10/7/37, MDZ, incoming. Phillips and Rahv may not have been entirely wrong in some of their darker moments. Terry Cooney suggests in *The Rise of the New York Intellectuals,* 112–17, that there were many frictions between the PR faction and the more pro-CP intellectuals as, indeed, all the correspondence about PR to and from Cowley in the above note should suggest. "The Partisans" is Cowley's phrase from the letter to Wilson cited above.

54   Quotations are from Porter, "Correspondence," PR, 4 (3/38), 62; Wilson to Cowley, 10/20/38, MC, incoming; Rexroth to Cowley, n.d., MC, incoming; Herbst to Porter, 4/5/38, KAP, ser. 1, box 12. Trilling and Farrell, "Correspondence: *Partisan Review* Omnibus," NR, 97 (11/30/38), 103–4; Deutsch to PR, 4 (2/38), 64; Wolfe to PR, 11/14/38, BDW, box 11, all offer their support. Cowley's comments were "*Partisan Review,*" NR, 96 (10/19/38), 311–12, and "Red Ivory Tower," NR, 97 (11/9/38), 22–23.

55   Quotation is from Lamont to Lewis Corey, managing editor, 8/23/37, in the Lewis Corey papers, Columbia University, box 15. The Corey papers also contain a series of letters that show the publication's early range of contributors. On the *Marxist Quarterly,* also see Bertram D. Wolfe's deposition on Corey, 3/5/52, in BDW, box 78, and George Novack, "Radical Intellectuals in the 1930s," *International Socialist Review,* 29 (3–4/68), 30. Christopher Phelps, "*Science and Society* and the *Marxist Quarterly,*" *Science and Society,* 57 (fall 1993), 359–62, particularly emphasizes the independent nature of the journal.

56   Quotations are from Dahlberg as cited in Penkower, *The Federal Writers Project,* 191, and Ben Belitt to Morton Zabel, 7/18/38, MOZ, incoming. In the latter quotation Belitt refers specifically to the Federal Writers Project issue on poetry. On Rosenberg, see Jerre Mangione, *The Dream and the Deal* (New York: Avon, 1972), 248–50, and Penkower, ibid., 175–76. On Dahlberg, see Penkower, 191.

57   Quotations are from Hook to Schilpp, 6/12/39, and Schilpp to Hook, 6/19/39, both (as well as related correspondence) in JD, Hook-Dewey sect. On Macdonald, see Michael Wreszin, *A Rebel in Defense of Tradition: The Life and Politics of Dwight Macdonald* (New York: Basic Books, 1994), 60, and Brightman, *Writing Dangerously,* 143.

1   Hicks to Rovere, 12/28/38[?], RR, box 2.

2   Quotations are from Albert Glotzer, *Trotsky,* 253; Sidney Hook, "Liberalism and the Case of Leon Trotsky," *Southern Review,* 3 (autumn 1937), 267; ACDLT, *Bulletin,* 4 (2/19/37), 1; Taggard to Field and Wood, n.d., GT, box 16. Adamic, *My America,* 84–85, tells his tale. On Dupee, see Wald, *New York Intellectuals,* 86–87. Meyer Schapiro warned ACDLT members to be prepared for bad treatment by the CPUSA in a letter published in the above ACDLT *Bulletin,* p. 3.

3   Quotations are from Baldwin, "Recollections of a Life in Civil Liberties—II," *Civil Liberties Review,* 2 (Fall 1975), 25; Fischer, *Men and Politics,* 474; Strong as cited in a letter from W. H. Chamberlin to Eugene Lyons, 3/12/38, EL-O, pt. 2; Cowley, "A Sense of Guilt," 137. Contrary to what he said, Fischer did write on the trials; see his "Trotsky in the USSR," N, 144 (4/10/37), 404, and "Behind the Kirov Executions," pts. 1 and 2, N, 140 (5/8 and 5/15/35), 529–31 and 566–68. Malcolm Cowley's "Echoes from Moscow, 1937–1938," *Southern Review,* 20 (winter 1984), 1–11, provides a good sense of progressive thought processes vis-à-vis the trials.

4   Mumford to Solow, 2/25/37, HS, box 2.

5   Cowley, "A Sense of Guilt," 152.

6   Powell to Dos Passos, n.d., JDP, ser. 2, box 4.

7   Quotations are from "G" [Alexander Gumberg] to Raymond Robins, 12/21/37, RRO, box 28, and Kirchwey to Stewart, 7/28/39, FK. Schneider to Freeman, n.d., JF, box 157. On the twentieth anniversary of the Russian Revolution, see Bessie Beatty to Raymond Robins, 11/6/37, RRO, box 28.

8   All quotations are from Hindus to Freeman, 5/21/39, JF, box 153. Halper to Alexander Godin, 2/6/35, AH, box 6. "Censorship is an unpleasant word . . . yet we wonder if the *Nation* itself would not draw the line somewhere," NM stated after it published an ad for a book by Max Eastman, "A Question for the *Nation,*" NM, 30 (12/27/38), 12. See also "The Shape of Things," N, 147 (12/17/38), 651, and Bruce Bliven, "Readers' Forum," NM, 27 (4/12/38), 19.

9   The money for Spain was raised through a manuscript auction. In general, meetings were poorly attended during the summer and fall of 1938. On 8/10/38 and 9/21/38 only two board members attended at all. On Cowley, see Franklin Folsom to Joseph Freeman, n.d., JF, box 191. The request for public endorsement of the LAW came in the form of a questionnaire that had to be reissued because it was so poorly answered the first time around. See Folsom to LAW members, 5/24/38, copy in SA, incoming. *Writers Take Sides* (New York: LAW, 1938).

10   Quotations are from Carlisle to Malcolm Cowley, 1/27/37, MC, incoming; Report of the Chicago Chapter, 6/2/39, LAW, pt. 11; Folsom to Hicks, 1/25/38, GH. On the impact of Folsom on the LAW, see Casciato's "Citizen Writers," 180–81. On the failures of the various branches of the League, see New England

Meeting, 11/18/37, LAW, pt. 18; ex. comm. minutes 11/3/37 and 11/17/37, LAW, pt. 2; "Report of the Chicago Chapter," 6/2/39, LAW, pt. 11; Ethel Turner, "Report of the Northern California Branch to National Council," 5/11/38, LAW, pt. 17. On the radical nature of the Hollywood writers, see Matthew Josephson to Malcolm Cowley, 3/4/38, MC, incoming.

11   Quotations are from Folsom to Hicks, 4/26/38, Folsom to Hicks, 1/25/38, Folsom to Hicks, 1/25/38, "Plan for Literary Campaign to Be Undertaken by the League of American Writers," n.d., all in GH, and Rivers to Freeman, JF, box 156. On Adamic, see Folsom to Hicks, 1/25/38, GH; on Cowley, see Folsom to Freeman, n.d. (ca. late 1937), JF, box 191.

12   The description of Ken is from Gingrich, Nothing but People (New York: Crown, 1971), 138. On Ken, see Gingrich's HUAC testimony, 1938, 1222–24; Seldes, " 'Ken'—the Inside Story," N, 146 (4/30/38), 497–500; Seldes, Witness to a Century (New York: Ballantine Books, 1987), 328–32; Gingrich, ibid., 131–48. On Hemingway, see Kenneth S. Lynn, Hemingway (New York: Simon and Schuster, 1987), 452–53.

13   Quotations are from LAW Minutes, 5/25/38, LAW, pt. 2, and Levin, In Search, 128. It is likely that Folsom called a "special, small meeting" of the LAW's Party fraction in April 1938 to plot strategy against Gingrich. See Folsom to Granville Hicks, 4/26/38, GH.

14   Motion is from LAW ex. comm. minutes, 12/7/38, LAW, pt. 2. A letter from Joseph Freeman to Folsom, 12/6/38, JF, box 154, suggests that the motion was Cowley's doing. Folsom sent Freeman a notice of the meeting with a note that said "you may want to attend," JF, box 154. Frank's speech was "Civil War in Europe," 1/18/39, LAW, pt. 8.

15   The full story and all quotations come from "Ripostes," PR, 4 (1/38), 61–62.

16   ACDLT Bulletin, 4 (2/19/37), 2, lists nine resignations. On the ACLU, see press release, c. summer 1938, ACLU, reel 7, and Baldwin Affidavit, 12/31/38, ACLU, vol. 2064. The quotation comes from a penciled notation on a letter from Ralph Roeder to Anderson, 1/13/39, SA, incoming.

17   On LAW membership qualifications, see minutes, 5/16/35, and fragment c. 1935, LAW, pt. 2. A copy of the application blank is in LAW, pt. 7. Membership lists are in LAW, pt. 1, but none are very complete and should be augmented by the lists of people compiled in each Bulletin. On dues, see "Report of Credentials Committee," 6/39, LAW, pt. 11. FOIA files suggest that the Friends of the Soviet Union, allegedly inactive since the line change, and the American Committee for Friendship with the Soviet Union merged in 1938 to form the American Council on Soviet Relations, presumably for the same reasons LAW expanded. See FOIA files for FSU or SRT.

18   Quotation is from W. H. Auden to Nan Golden, 11/8/39, LAW, pt. 8. The executive committee's names are listed in a letter from Folsom, 12/30/38, LAW, pt. 2. Officers' names appeared on the letterhead of a letter from Folsom to Malcolm Cowley, 10/6/39, MC, incoming. Cowley marked "R" after several

names indicating that they resigned after the Nazi-Soviet Pact. After several
more, he has marked question marks. Those who remained, presumably very
close to the CPUSA, are only four of the original sixteen officers. On Sinclair, see
ex. comm. minutes, 9/4/40, LAW, pt. 2.

19   The full text and list of signatures is in DW, 8/14/39, 2. I count 165 names
on this letter and estimate that roughly 40 percent were Communists or very
strong front supporters. The group that approached the LAW ex. comm. included Dorothy Brewster, Dashiell Hammett, Mary Van Kleeck, and Maxwell
Stewart. The evening they met with the executive committee there were fifteen
board members present, nine of whom were Party members or close supporters. Minutes, 6/12/39, LAW, pt. 2. Frederick Prokosch was one who thought the
LAW initiated the letter. See his letter, n.d., LAW, pt. 8. Traditionally, when other
groups requested access to the LAW's mailing list, the LAW did the actual printing and the mailing to protect its membership.

20   The open letter appeared publicly just as news of the Nazi-Soviet Pact
reached American progressives, meaning that many probably regretted their
public association with a pro-Soviet document. Kirchwey, "Red Totalitarianism," N, 184 (5/27/39), 605–6; Kirchwey to Maxwell Stewart, 7/20/39, FK; "In
Reply to a Committee," NR, 100 (8/23/39), 63; Bliven to Malcolm Cowley,
7/18/38, MC, incoming. See also Fischer, *Men and Politics,* 566–67.

21   Quotations are from Herbst to Hicks, 9/21/37, CAL; "The Krivitsky Af-
fair," N, 149 (7/8/39), 32–33; "Yankee Communism," N, 146 (6/4/38), 632. On
Cowley and Krivitsky, see his letter to Edmund Wilson, 2/2/40, EW, and to
Louis Fischer, 6/28/39, LF, box 2. His own comments appeared in "Krivitsky,"
NR, 102 (1/22/40), 120–23.

22   Quotations are from board minutes, 11/28/38, ACLU, reel 7, and Arthur
Garfield Hays, telegram sent to Martin Dies, 8/22/39, ACLU, vol. 2076. Regarding the writ, see Jerome Britchey to Hays, 9/18/39, ACLU, vol. 2077. The ACLU
was so obsessed by the Dies committee that it collected two volumes of information relating to it and their own attempts to be heard and correct the record.
See ACLU, vols. 2076 and 2077.

23   Sinclair's affidavit, submitted 12/28/38, is in *Thirty Years of Treason,* ed.
Eric Bentley (New York: Viking, 1971), 48–51; quotation from p. 48.

24   Quotations are from "Soviet Democracy," N, 142 (6/17/36), 761–62;
Counts, *The Prospects of American Democracy* (New York: Day, 1938), 143;
Lerner, *It Is Later Than You Think* (New York: Viking, 1938; rev. ed., 1943), 79.
See also Lerner, ibid., 101–5, and Mumford, *Men,* esp. 46–51.

25   Quotations are from Brooks, "Personal Statement," *Direction,* 2 (5–6/39);
Brooks to Folsom, 12/17/38, LAW, pt. 8; Brooks to Taggard, 12/7/38, GT, box 3;
Taggard to Brooks, c. 12/38, GT, box 3. On packing the meeting, see Les Rivers to
Joseph Freeman, n.d., JF, box 156. Folsom to Hicks, 4/22/39, GH, contains Fol-
som's request about a response.

26   Quotations are from MacLeish to Malcolm Cowley, postcard postmarked
7/11/39, MC, incoming; Isidor Schneider, statement of policy draft, 7/17/39,

278   MC, incoming; LaFarge, statement draft, n.d., MC, incoming (my emphasis). The final statement, as read at the special LAW board meeting, 7/19/39, is virtually identical to LaFarge's statement, LAW, pt. 2.

27   The Cowley quotation is from "Symposium: Thirty Years Later," 513. The record of the congress is *Fighting Words,* ed. Donald Ogden Stewart (New York: Harcourt, Brace, 1940), which was published after the Nazi-Soviet Pact changed the League's line, meaning that the record has been somewhat altered in the process. The "Call" for the congress appeared in *Direction,* 2 (5–6/39), 1. On the idea of holding a congress in Hollywood, see LAW ex. comm. minutes, 9/6/39, LAW, pt. 2. Ferruggia, "Organizing the 'Ivory Tower,'" 155–56, sees the Third Congress as evidence of the LAW at its peak. As my analysis should suggest, I disagree.

28   Quotations are from Baldwin, "Recollections," *Civil Liberties Review,* 2 (fall 1975), 35, and Baldwin to James Loeb, 2/10/39, RB, box 7. A critical view of the organization is Merwin K. Hart, "Our Position Respecting Spain," *Vital Speeches,* 5 (1/1/39), 187–91. The incident also demonstrates the possible diversity of front groups.

29   Details and quotations are from Ceplair and Englund, *The Inquisition,* 121. The emphasis in the pledge is my own.

30   MacLeish, "Liberalism and the Anti-Fascist Front," 321–23.

31   Quotations are from Herbst, "The Starched Blue Sky of Spain," *Noble Savage,* 1 (1960), 79; Ernest Hemingway, "On the American Dead in Spain," reprinted in *New Masses Anthology,* 341; Michael Blankfort, interview with author, 1/23/82, and Milly [Bennett?] to Anna Louise Strong, n.d. (ca. 1939), ALS, box 1.

32   Quotations are from Josephine Herbst to Katherine Anne Porter, 4/5/38, KAP, ser. 1, box 12, and Strong to Granville Hicks, 9/29/39, ALS, box 4. On the LAW, see National Board minutes, 6/14/39, LAW, pt. 2. The fusion of the two Spanish war groups and FSU with the American Committee for Friendship with the Soviet Union might also be interpreted as the result of a decline in the number of active progressives in fronts, necessitating consolidation.

SIX   The Emergence of Extremism, 1939

1   Williams to Kenneth Rexroth, 6/4/37, KR, box 22.

2   See, for example, Lerner, *It Is Later,* 101–5; Hamilton Basso to Malcolm Cowley, 8/12/37, MC, incoming; Mumford, *Men Must Act,* 46–51, on the progressive side, or John Chamberlain in "Symposium: Can Democracy Survive?" MQ, 11 (summer 1939), 69, and Harry Elmer Barnes, "The Lessons of 1914 for 1939," MQ, 11 (summer 1939), 8–15, on the liberal side.

3   Diana Trilling noted that "between the founding of *Partisan Review* in 1937 and its issue of Summer 1939, on the eve of the outbreak of war in Europe, Nazism is not mentioned in the magazine. The word 'fascism' appears frequently but as an abstraction," *Beginning,* 293.

4   Cannon's version of these events is in his *History*, 246–52. Secondary versions include Shannon, *The Socialist Party*, 251–54; Warren, *Alternative*, 85; Myers, *Prophet's Army*, 123–25. Leon Trotsky advised his followers to leave the SP in a letter dated 6/15/37, in *Writings of Trotsky*, vol. 9, 334–35.

5   The first two quotations are from Carter and Burnham, "Amendment on the Soviet Union," in *Internal Bulletin of the Organizing Committee for the Socialist Party Convention*, 2 (11/37), 12, and Cannon to Trotsky, 12/16/37, in *The Struggle for a Proletarian Party*, ed. John G. Wright, reprint (New York: Pathfinder Press, 1972), 28. Burnham's amendment is in SWP *Bulletin*, 6 (1/38), in SWP, reel 32. The final quotations are from Manny Geltman, letter to author, 5/17/82. Geltman's brother, Max, was part of the expelled group. Trotsky's comments and his request for Burnham to come to Mexico are in his "Not a Workers' and Not a Bourgeois State" and letter to Cannon, 12/6/37, both in *The Writings of Leon Trotsky*, vol. 10, 60–71 and 87–88. Italian Trotskyists evolved a similar interpretation at about the same time, but Geltman discounted its influence on Carter's thought.

6   Quotations are from "Is State Capitalism Progressive?," MM, 10 (3/38), 2; "Shall We Defend the Socialist Emperor?" MQ, 11 (winter 1939), 2; Rahv, "Trials of the Mind," 6 (2 quotations); editor's notes to "Was the Bolshevik Revolution a Failure?" MQ, 11 (fall 1938), 5; Calverton to Scott Nearing, 3/21/38, VFC, box 11; "Is State Capitalism Progressive?," ibid., 2. Rahv's comments were strictly about the USSR; he did not, as Diana Trilling noted about the PR group more generally, have much to say about Nazism.

7   Quotations are from Nearing to Calverton, n.d. (ca. 1938), VFC, box 11; James Rorty in "Can Democracy Survive?" MQ, 11 (summer 1939), 77; Calverton in "Was the Bolshevik Revolution a Failure?," 4; Oak, ibid., 15; Hook in "Violence, For and Against: A Symposium on Marx, Stalin and Trotsky," CS, 7 (1/38), 23; Calverton to Nearing, 3/21/38, VFC, box 11; Bates in "Was the Bolshevik Revolution a Failure?," 8. There were differences among anti-Stalinists on these points. In general, Calverton and the *Modern Monthly* circle, Oak, and Max Eastman tended to see more connections between Stalinism and Leninism and the *Partisan Review* group fewer. On the last point in the paragraph, Malcolm Cowley suggested to Edmund Wilson in 1940 that Sidney Hook's political evolution in the 1930s involved a greater recognition of democracy. See Cowley to Wilson, 2/2/40, EW.

8   Quotations are from "Ripostes," PR, 4 (1/38), 62; Rahv, NL, 12/10/38, 8 (2 quotations); Trilling, *Beginning*, 294.

9   Quotations are from Calverton to Max Eastman, n.d., VFC, box 5, and Cooney, *New York Intellectuals*, 49. Several individuals singled out Cowley as someone who thought of himself as an arbiter of political correctness. On Phillips, see "What Happened in the 1930s?" in *A Sense of the Present* (New York: Chilmark Press, 1967), 204–12. See also his letter to Josephine Herbst, 11/5/37, as quoted in Langer, *Herbst*, 232, and his letter to Trotsky, 4/10/38, in Homberger, *American Writers*, 209–10. The *Partisan Review* group seemed particularly prone to this kind of thinking.

280   10   Quotations are from LaFollette to Wolfe, 7/19/39, BDW, box 9, and Solow, fragments of an article entitled "Stalin's Spy Scare." The deposition is dated 11/12/38, HS, box 5. There are also a series of letters between Solow and Chambers in HS, box 1.

11   The documents, including both letters of resignation, are in LAW, pt. 8.

12   The quotations are from board minutes, 6/14/39, and Becker to LAW, 6/29/39, both in LAW, pts. 2 and 8. Many other documents, including both manifestos and the replies Becker received from Brooks, Wilson, and Mumford, are in LAW, pt. 8.

13   The phrase is Becker's, from "The Pen, the Ax, and the Axis."

14   Peter J. Kuznick, *Beyond the Laboratory: Scientists as Political Activists in 1930s America* (Chicago: University of Chicago Press, 1987), 182–219, describes Boas's actions and the formation of the ACDIF in much more detail. The phrase "Jewish science" is from a German article in *Nature* and discussed on page 184. The final quotations are from NYT, 5/15/39, 13, and Hook, *Out of Step,* 257.

15   The first quotation is from Hook, *Out of Step,* 259; the second is from Lyons, *Red Decade,* 343. Hook also is the source of detail on the early League.

16   Quotations are from Van Kleeck to Roger Baldwin, 1/27/39, ACLU, vol. 2063, and "Editorial Statement," PR, 4 (12/37), 3. On the term *totalitarianism* see Thomas Maddux, "Red Fascism, Brown Bolshevism: The American Image of Totalitarianism in the 1930s," *The Historian,* 60 (11/77), 94; Lifka, "The Concept 'Totalitarianism,'" chap. 1, and Les K. Adler and Thomas G. Patterson, "Red Fascism: The Merger of Nazi Germany and Soviet Russia in the American Image of Totalitarianism, 1930s–1950s," *American Historical Review,* 75 (4/70), 1046–64.

17   League against Totalitarianism draft manifesto, in the Dwight Macdonald papers, Yale University, my emphasis.

18   Ibid.

19   Quotation is from Dewey to Boas, 5/15/39, JD, Hook-Dewey sect.; NYT, 5/15/39, 13.

20   Quotations are from Dewey to Boas, 5/15/39, JD, Hook-Dewey sect., and Boas's reply, in the same sequence of letters, 5/26/39. See also Dewey to Hook, 5/27/39. Kuznick, *Beyond the Lab,* 218–19, says Dewey rejected the proposed merger, but that does not jibe with the letters in the Dewey archive.

21   Quotations are from Kuznick, ibid., 216–17, and Hook to Sherwood Anderson, 5/27/39, SA, incoming. Hook, ironically, was possessed of far more of a national reputation than he ever led others to believe. As late as May 1939, *The Nation* would still publish his pieces, despite his complaints about cultural repression, and his dispute with Paul Schilpp over the inclusion of the McGill essay in the book on Dewey (see Chapter 4 herein) demonstrated his power.

22   Quotations are from Macdonald to Hook, 12/6/38, Macdonald papers; "Still Another Committee," NR, 99 (6/14/39), 144; League for Cultural Freedom and Socialism, "Statement," PR, 6 (Summer 1939), 125–27. Calverton and

James Rorty belonged to both organizations, suggesting that the relative positions of the two were not entirely clear to all.

23 Quotations are from Anderson to Franklin Folsom, 5/23/39, and Williams to Folsom, 5/20/39, both in LAW, pt. 8.

24 Quotations are from "Trotskyist Trap," 21; Hook to the NYT, 5/15/39; copy of the letter to the editors issued to all CCF members and as a press release in SA, incoming; Hook to Anderson, 4/21/39, SA, incoming; Kirchwey, "Red Totalitarianism," 605; Williams to Frank Trager, n.d., as cited in "Techniques of Disruption," CCF *Bulletin*, 1 (10/15/39), 3; "Liberty and Common Sense," NR, 99 (5/31/39), 89–90. Charges against Hook appeared in "Cultural Front," *Direction*, 2 (7–8/39), 18.

25 Quotations are from Kirchwey, "Red Totalitarianism," 605; "Liberty and Common Sense," 89; Kirchwey, ibid.

26 Quotations are from "Trotskyist Trap," 21; "Cultural Front," 18; "Techniques of Disruption," 2. The Muzzey incident was discussed at a CCF board meeting, 6/26/39, ACCF, box 2. I have no reason to doubt that the incident occurred except as recounted by Muzzey, but it is difficult to reconstruct a situation that would enable his letter to fall into Franklin Folsom's hands. Either he was extremely naive or wrote a legitimate letter of resignation that he regretted after he saw what the CPUSA did with it. The letter of resignation itself is more consistent with the latter thesis.

27 Quotations are from board of directors' minutes, 1/23/39, ACLU, reel 7; minutes of a special [national] committee meeting, 3/6/39, ACLU, reel 7; Baldwin to Harry F. Ward, 3/5/39, ACLU, vol. 2157. While the pamphlet title changed, the content of the pamphlet did not, and "totalitarianism" is never directly mentioned at all.

28 Quotations are from a special [national] committee meeting, 3/6/39, ACLU, reel 7; Van Kleeck to Rice, 3/27/39, and Rice to Van Kleeck, 3/28/39, both in MVK, box 36; Rice to Hays, 3/3/39, AGH, box 42; Van Kleeck to Rice, 3/27/39. On Baldwin's role, see his "A Memo on Elizabeth Gurley Flynn," 3/74, PL, box 1. He may well have learned the technique of quorum-plotting from the Communists, who, he later said, used it in the North American Committee for Spanish Democracy.

29 Van Kleeck to Rice, ibid.

SEVEN The Nazi-Soviet Pact and
the Breakup of the Intellectual People's Front, 1939–1940

1 Quotations are from Lamson, *Baldwin*, 201; Josephson, *Infidel*, 477 and 484; Cowley to Kenneth Burke, 10/14/39, MC, outgoing.

2 Magil, "Principles Stand: Tactics Change," NM, 32 (9/19/39), 11. On CPUSA reactions, see Maurice Isserman, *Which Side Were You On?* (Middletown, Conn.: Wesleyan University Press, 1982), 32–36.

3　Quotations are from "The Meaning of the Non-Aggression Pact," SRT, 8 (9/39), 6 (emphasis in original); "Chamberlain Goes Boom," B&W, 1 (9/39), 3; "Stalin's Munich," NR, 100 (8/30/39), 88; "Chamberlain Goes Boom," 3; Granville Hicks's diary entry, 8/24/39, cited in Levenson and Natterstad, *Hicks,* 119; Strong to E. Roosevelt, 8/24/39 and 8/30/39, both in ER, box 1528.

4　Quotations are from "Stalin's Munich," 88; "Why Did Russia Do It?" NR, 100 (9/6/39), 118; "What Stalin Has Lost," NR, 100 (9/27/39), 197–98; Mumford, notebook entry, 9/39, in *My Works and Days,* 386. See also "Red Star and Swastika," N, 149 (8/26/39), 212, and "The Mystery of Moscow," N, 149 (9/30/39), 309–10.

5　Quotations are from Freeman to Gessner, 8/24/39, JF, box 152; Rovere to Joe [North?], 9/17/39, RR, box 1; Hicks, "On Leaving the Communist Party," NR, 100 (10/4/39), 144–45. Browder confessed his doubts to Hicks. See *Part of the Truth,* 182–83. On CP policy, see Isserman, *Which Side,* 36–38.

6　Quotations are from Browder, message to American Communists, as cited in Jaffe, *Rise and Fall,* 44, and "War and Civil Liberties," B&W, 1 (10/39), 6. Note the use of the term *totalitarian* in the last source. On the Party's response, see Jaffe, 38–49, Klehr, *Heyday,* 388–409, and Coser and Howe, *American CP,* 387–95, keeping in mind that each is critical of the CPUSA. Ottanelli's *The Communist Party,* 159–96, and Isserman, *Which Side,* 39–43, offer a slightly different perspective.

7　The quotation is from Earl Browder's speech, DW, 9/13/39, 1. See also Gold, *The Hollow Men,* 99–102, or his "What Side Are You On?" NM, 33 (10/3/39), 17, or A. B. Magil's "Background of the Anti-Soviet War," NM, 33 (1/2/40), 9–12.

8　Quotations are from "War and Civil Liberties," 6; Strong to Eleanor Roosevelt, 9/21/39, ER, box 1528; Brown, "Fascism Afloat," NM, 33 (10/17/39), 19; "War and Civil Liberties," 6; "They're Not Confused," NM, 33 (10/3/39), 10.

9　Quotations are from "Communist Imperialism," NR, 100 (10/11/39); Sheean, "Brumaire: The Soviet Union as a Fascist State, II," NR, 101 (11/15/39), 105; "The Mystery of Moscow," N, 149 (9/23/39), 309; "Power Politics and People," NR, 101 (11/29/39), 155.

10　Quotations are from Rovere to Joe [North?] on 9/17/39 and 9/18/39 in RR, box 1. On Hicks, see *Part,* 182–83, or Levenson and Natterstad, *Hicks,* 120–23. Hicks decided to print his letter of resignation, cited above in note 5, because NM would not allow him to present an alternative view. On Davis, see his testimony before HUAC, 2/25/53, 27. Hicks to Joseph Freeman, 5/8/[41?], suggests that Hicks believed that his "innocence" was deliberately cultivated by the CP leadership. Schrecker, *No Ivory Tower,* 54, contends that the number of academics who left the Party over the Pact was small and most were friends of Hicks's. The number of intellectuals was somewhat larger than she suggests, and some of those who left were not close to Hicks. Mark Naison, "Remaking America: Communists and Liberals in the Popular Front," in *New Studies in the Politics and Culture of U.S. Communism,* ed. Brown et al., 63, shows how

different the level of cultural freedom was during the front period than before
or after.

11   Quotation is from LaFarge to Folsom, 11/3/39, LAW, pt. 8. Early resignations included Marvin Lowenthal's, Brooks's, MacLeish's, Richard Neuberger's, and Elmer Rice's. Mann's letter of resignation, n.d. (ca. 12/39) is in LAW, pt. 8. On the matter of the letterhead, see ex. comm., 12/4/39, LAW, pt. 2.

12   Sheean's comment is from a letter to Folsom, 10/9/39, LAW, pt. 8. The complete statement appeared in the League's *Bulletin,* 6 (11/39), 12. The ex. comm. discussed it on 10/4/39, 10/18/39, and 11/1/39, LAW, pt. 2.

13   Quotations are from "Stalin Spreads the War," NR, 101 (12/13/39), 218; Schuman, "Machiavelli Gone Mad," NR, 101 (12/27/39), 290; Kirchwey, "'By Fire and Sword,'" N, 149 (12/9/39), 640; Strong to Eleanor Roosevelt, 2/12/41, ER, box 1622.

14   Quotations are from "Brave Little Finland," B&W, 2 (1/40), 3, and Lillian Hellman, cited in Wright, *Hellman,* 161. See also Joseph Starobin, "War on the Soviet," NM, 33 (12/19/39), 3–7; "No Civilian Bombings," NM, 33 (12/12/39), 16; "The Soviet Union and Finland," SRT, 8 (12/39), 4, 6–8.

15   All quotations are from Bates, "Disaster in Finland," NR, 101 (12/13/39), 223–24.

16   Quotations are from LaFarge to Folsom, 11/3/39; Fearing to LAW, 10/27/39, Gregory to Folsom, 12/16/39, and Halper to Folsom, n.d., all in LAW, pt. 8. Curiously, LaFarge did not resign from the League and Fearing signed the statement. Of a total membership of 757, 392 people did not vote at all, 337 voted for the referendum, 24 voted against, and 4 had "special objections." Considering how well organized LAW Party writers were and how highly motivated the Party sympathizers tended to be, it is unlikely that many of the 392 members who did not vote would have voted for the statement. See ex. comm., 12/27/39, LAW, pt. 2. The description of the form letter is in ex. comm. minutes, 12/13/39, LAW, pt. 2. On the branches that closed, see ex. comm. minutes, 2/7/40, LAW, pt. 2.

17   Quotations are from Arvin to Cowley, 12/20/39, MC, incoming; Dunn, *Take Two* (New York: McGraw Hill, 1980), 113; ex. comm. minutes, 12/13/39, LAW, pt. 2; Cowley to Edmund Wilson, 2/2/40, EW. The financial situation is discussed in minutes for 11/8/39, 11/16/39, and 12/4/3; the antiwar activities on 12/13/39 and 4/30/40, all in LAW, pt. 2. Arvin's attitude in his letter to Cowley suggested that he was willing to give up: "I can certainly do no good by staying in."

18   Northern California League minutes, 1/19/40, LAW, pt. 17.

19   Hollywood minutes, 1/40 and 1/25/40, LAW, pt. 15. The word "large" was attached to the word "majority" in the margin, as though to emphasize it. Since both the first introduction of Gibney's resolution and the election of Stewart occurred at a meeting or meetings without minutes on file, I cannot say with absolute certainty that Gibney lost out because of his views.

20   Quotations are from Sam Grafton at an ex. comm. meeting, 4/17/40, LAW,

pt. 2; Eleanor Flexner, LAW minutes, 4/30/4, LAW, pt. 2; Odets in his diary, 5/15/40, *The Time Is Ripe* (New York: Grove, 1988), 155; LaFarge, amendment proposed in the 6/19/40 ex. comm. meeting, LAW, pt. 2, my emphasis. The discussion of the statement begins at the 4/30/40 meeting and continues through 7/8/40. The vote was 9 for and 17 against the LaFarge amendment, but 8 of the no votes were absentee. When the smoke cleared, three vice-presidents, two board members, and five representatives to the Exiled Writers Committee had to be elected to replace those who left.

21 Quotations are from Benjamin to Folsom, 3/7/40, cited in Casciato, "Citizen Writers," 214; LaFarge to Cowley, 7/17/40, MC, incoming; Cowley to Folsom, 7/29/40, LAW, pt. 8. I cannot confirm Cowley's assessment of the number of ex. comm. post-Pact resignations; however, I believe Cowley actually meant officers, as there is a piece of LAW letterhead in the Cowley papers with "r's" penciled in by the names of officers who resigned and question marks after other names. Cowley does make reference to the names on the letterhead in his letter of resignation.

22 Quotations are from Donald Ogden Stewart, *By a Stroke*, 256; Rexroth to Folsom, 5/12/41, KR, box 6; Smedley to Malcolm Cowley, 7/23/41, MC, incoming; Dos Passos to Fred Beal, 6/22/41, JDP, ser. 2, box 1.

23 Folsom, "Report for the Period between the Third and Fourth Congresses (1939–1941)," LAW, pt. 8. Alan Wald contends in "Culture and Commitment," 290, that the salient statistic regarding the League was that seven-eighths of the organization did not resign after the Pact. But only 35 percent of the members had actually paid their dues even before the Pact, so the question of what defined membership needs to be considered. I think it likely that more members resigned by allowing their memberships to fade or by not paying dues than by sitting down and writing letters of resignation. Only 18 (including 13 Party members) of the 118 who signed the public call for the 1941 congress signed the 1939 call. This suggests a fair amount of active member turnover.

24 All quotations and material are from Ceplair and Englund, *The Inquisition*, 146.

25 See Kuznick, *Beyond the Lab*, 221–25. I am not as familiar with the scientific community as Kuznick is. He does not portray the ACDIF as a typical front group, although I see many points of comparison. Marshall Hyatt, *Franz Boas: Social Activist* (Westport: Greenwood Press, 1990), 146–50, argues that Boas opposed the war (until Pearl Harbor) for traditional liberal reasons and did not like the CPUSA.

26 The first quotation is from "Save the American Student Union," as cited in Cohen, *When the Old Left Was Young*, 294. The second is from Cohen, 284. The details of the struggle are from Cohen, 280–98. Lash's version is in his testimony in HUAC, "Executive Hearings Made Public," 1/21/42, 2800.

27 Quotations are from ALPD resolution, cited in David Caute, *The Fellow Travelers* (New York: Macmillan, 1973), 189; Baldwin to William B. Spofford, 8/29/39, RB, box 7; Ward, as quoted in Alsond Smith, "Death of a League," NR,

102 (3/18/40), 373; Baldwin to ALPD National Executive Board, 9/18/39, RB, box 7; Baldwin to ALPD National Committee, 10/21/39, RB, box 7; Smith, ibid., 373.

28 Quotation is from Lash's diary, 11/4/39, as cited in Cohen, *When the Old Left,* 286. Details are from 286–87.

29 Quotations are from Ward before HUAC as cited in Goodman, *The Committee,* 72, and Board minutes, ACLU, 10/30/39, ACLU, reel 7. On Ward's testimony, see August Raymond Ogden, *The Dies Committee* (Washington, D.C.: Catholic University of America Press, 1945), 153–55.

30 Quotations are from Lerner to Malcolm Cowley, 10/19/39, MC, incoming, and Hicks, "New Directions on the Left," NR, 102 (6/17/40), 815. On the group, see Wechsler, *Age of Suspicion;* Josephson, *Infidel,* 480–81; Hicks, *Part,* 187; Hicks to Richard Rovere, 9/26/39, 10/3/39, 10/10/39, and 11/8/39, in RR, box 2. Members included Lerner, Hicks, Cowley, Wechsler, Josephson, Robert Lynd, Leo Huberman, Joseph Lash, and I. F. Stone. Levenson and Natterstad, *Hicks,* 130–33, emphasize the organizational quarrels between Lerner and Hicks, but most other sources see the anticommunist split as the more critical one.

31 Quotations are from Cowley to Wilson, 2/2/40, EW, and Cowley to Kenneth Burke, 8/23/40, MC, outgoing. Steven Biel sees Cowley "reaffirming the necessity of nonaffiliation," but Cowley seemed more distressed by the absence of honorable groups than appalled by the idea of joining them. See *Independent Intellectuals,* 222.

32 A. Redfield's cartoon, NM, 33 (11/28/39), 16–17, shows a group of intellectuals marching with a series of signs that read "Russia was okay until . . . the Pact, the Czar left, the 5 Year Plan, Trotzky left." Lash's testimony is in HUAC, "Executive Hearings Made Public," 1/21/42, 2800. The final quotation is from Lamson, *Baldwin,* 201. Gold, *The Hollow Men,* and V. J. Jerome, *Intellectuals and the War* (New York: Workers Library, 1940), are two blanket condemnations of progressives by CP intellectuals.

33 Quotations are from Mumford, "The Corruption of Liberalism," NR, 102 (4/29/40), 568; Baldwin in Lamson, *Baldwin,* 195; "Communist Imperialism," NR, 100 (10/11/39), 257–58; Kirchwey, "The Law and Mr. Dies," N, 149 (11/4/39), 486; Cowley to Edmund Wilson, 2/2/40, EW.

34 Quotations are from Brooks to Calverton, 12/29/39, VFC, box 2, and ACLU board minutes, 10/30/39, ACLU, reel 7. Kirchwey, "The Communists and Democracy," N, 149 (10/14/39), 400. On the ALPD, see Goodman, *The Committee,* 70–75. Virtually no one on the left defended Dies.

35 Quotations are from Cowley to Wilson, 2/2/40, EW; Cowley to Kenneth Burke, 1/9/41, MC, outgoing; Cowley to Wilson, 2/2/40 ("explanation . . ." and long quotation), EW; Kirchwey, N, 149 (10/14/39), 400; Robert Morss Lovett to Cowley, 4/2/40, MC, incoming (specifically referring to James T. Farrell). Cowley switched from being an editor at *The New Republic* to a regular contributor late in 1940.

36 Quotations are from Strong to Granville Hicks, 9/29/39, ALS, box 4; Mc-Williams, "Honorable in All Things," 90; Malcolm Cowley to J. V. Healy, 12/5/39, MC, outgoing; Campbell to Wolcott, 8/39, cited in Marion Meade, *Dorothy Parker* (New York: Villard Books, 1988), 297. On Stewart, see his *By a Stroke,* 248–57. On Hellman, see either Carl Rollyson, *Lillian Hellman* (New York: St. Martin's Press, 1988), 148–51, or Wright, *Hellman,* 160–61.

37 Quotations are from Hemingway to Edwin Rolfe, spring 1940, as cited in Cary Nelson and Jefferson Hendricks, *Edwin Rolfe* (Champaign-Urbana: University of Illinois Press, 1990), 90; Smedley to Cowley, 7/23/41 and 7/24/41, MC, incoming; Folsom to Fischer, 8/6/40, LAW, pt. 3; Lovett to Ickes, 4/30/41, RML, box 1; Folsom to Dashiell Hammett, 11/18/42, LAW, pt. 7. See FOIA files on the LAW as well.

38 Quotations are from Clifford Odets's diary entry dated 6/5/40, in *Time Is Ripe,* 179; McWilliams, *Education of McWilliams,* 93; Cowley to Wilson, 2/2/40, EW; Cowley to Kenneth Rexroth, 9/7/41, KR, box 4.

39 Quotation is from Odets diary entry, ibid. Harrison's essay appeared in NL, 11/11/39, 8.

40 Quotations are from James Wechsler, *Age,* 125; Frank, *Memoirs,* 189; Freeman to Dell, 2/14/52, FD, Freeman-Dell sect. The last source suggests that the break was very painful for Freeman, for in several very long letters to Dell he rehashed his breakup with the Party. Other views of Freeman include Kenneth Rexroth to Malcolm Cowley, n.d. (ca. 1940), MC, incoming; Lee Lowenfish, "Joseph Freeman," paper presented to the Organization of American Historians, 1980, 13–15 (my thanks to Lowenfish for providing me with a copy); Bloom, *Left Letters,* 71–110; Joseph Starobin, *American Communism in Crisis* (Cambridge: Harvard University Press, 1972), 253–54.

41 This conclusion, as revisionists like Foley and Murphy have shown, has become an established part of literary history.

42 Quotations are from Rovere, *Final Reports* (Garden City: Doubleday, 1984), 63, and Hicks, *Part,* 185. See Rovere's "On Joining the Socialist Party," SC, 1/27/40, 4. Levenson and Natterstad, *Hicks,* suggest that Hicks turned down a functionary position within the CP earlier so that he would not be financially connected with the Party. This was not an action that would have occurred to most younger intellectual recruits.

43 Freeman to Dell, 2/14/52, FD, Freeman-Dell sect.

44 The quotations are from Browder, lecture at the University of Illinois, "The American Communist Party in the 1930s," 3/9/66, EB, ser. 3, reel 154, 25, and Hicks, *Part,* 182. *The New Masses'* official comment on Hicks, relatively tame, was "Granville Hicks Resigns," NM, 33 (10/3/39), 21. Compare with a more anti-Stalinist report, SC, 10/7/40, 1. The details of Hicks's break with the Party are also in *Part,* 176–83.

45 The first quotation is cited in Isserman, *Which Side,* 55. The original lyric was "anti-fascist weather." The second quotation is from Davis's HUAC testimony, 2/25/53, 27.

46   Isserman, ibid., 55–73, talks about the difficulties the Party faced.
47   From *Whose Revolution? A Study of the Future Course of Liberalism in the United States,* ed. Irving DeWitt Talmadge (Westport: Hyperion, 1941; reprint, 1975), 169.
48   HUAC, spring 1942, 3146.
49   This will be covered in more depth in Chapter 9.

EIGHT   The Demise of Anti-Stalinism and the Emergence of Liberal Anticommunism, 1939–1940

1   Quotations are from Peter F. Drucker, "That Coming Nazi-Soviet Pact," the introduction by the editors, CS, 8 (3/39), 16, and Stolberg, NL, 9/16/39, 5.
2   Quotations are from Holmes as cited by Max Eastman in NL, 3/13/44, 11; Dewey, "What Hope for Civilization?," CS, 8 (12/39), 10. Warren, *Liberals,* 194–97, gives a good summary of the liberal response to the Pact.
3   Quotations are from "On Hating Russia," CS, 9 (1/40), 17, and CS, 9 (3/40), 16. On Holmes, see his letter to Roger William Riis, 12/6/39, JHH, cont. 187. Oswald Garrison Villard, one-time editor of *The Nation,* resigned from the periodical altogether in 1940 because of what he perceived as his replacement's (Freda Kirchwey) pro-war attitudes. See his letters to Kirchwey, 6/13/40, and Holmes, 6/28/40, in his *Dilemmas,* 596–97 and 599–602. Sponsors of the KAOWC included Bingham, Holmes, John Chamberlain, and Quincy Howe, along with the occasional progressive, and many anti-Stalinists. A list of sponsors is in RML, box 1.
4   Quotations are from Philip Rahv, "This Quarter," PR, 6 (Fall 1939), and "What Is Living and What Is Dead," PR, 7 (5–6/40), 175.
5   Quotations are from Max Eastman, *Reflections on the Failure of Socialism* (New York: Devin-Adair, 1955), 30; Wilson, *To the Finland Station* (Garden City: Doubleday, 1940), 196; Eastman, *Stalin's Russia and the Crisis in Socialism* (New York: Norton, 1940), 220. Wilson's book, Hook's *Reason, Social Myths, and Democracy* (New York: John Day, 1940), and Eastman's *Stalin's Russia* all appeared within a year of each other, arguing roughly the same thesis. See also Lewis Corey's series on Marxism in *The Nation,* "Marxism Reconsidered, Parts I, II, and III," 150 (2/17/40, 2/24/40, and 3/2/40), 245–48, 272–75, 305–7. I discuss the anti-Stalinists' disillusionment in more depth in my dissertation, "Toward the Beautiful Tomorrow" (UCLA, 1986), 94–100.
6   Quotations are from Dewey to Sidney Hook, 11/16/39, JD, Hook-Dewey sect., and CCF minutes, 11/27/39, ACCF, box 2. See also "A Clarifying Amendment," CCF *Bulletin,* 1 (10/15/39), 10, and the CCF's letter in SC, 1/20/40, 3.
7   Quotations are from Dewey to Hook, 9/13/39; Hook to Frank Trager, note on Dewey's draft dated 9/13/39, both in JD, Hook-Dewey sect.; CCF minutes, 9/11/39, ACCF, box 2. I have not been able to find a copy of Hook's draft, which might be contained in Sidney Hook's papers, not yet accessible. The CCF's

288 *Bulletin* noted that the letter netted six responses and two new members, hardly a phenomenal showing, but certainly not quite like Hook remembered it later. See *Out of Step*, 270.

8   Quotations are from "The Browder Case and Civil Liberties," CCF *Bulletin,* 2 (2/40), 11, and "Principles and Policies," CCF *Bulletin,* 2 (2/40), 3. Hook's later *Heresy, Yes—Conspiracy, No,* published by the CCF's successor, the American Committee for Cultural Freedom, in 1952 states his postwar position on the CPUSA.

9   Quotation is from Dewey, letter of resignation, 11/16/39, JD, Hook-Dewey sect. Although several versions of the letter appear in Dewey's files, I can find no reference to Dewey's resignation anywhere else. It is possible, therefore, that he changed his mind or that the organization conveniently omitted reference to his resignation in its publications for fear others would follow suit. Membership figures were cited in the minutes 9/11/39 and 11/27/39; Boas's response was reported on 10/1/39, ACCF, box 2.

10   See CCF statement regarding Dies in SC, 1/20/40, 3. On Ernst, see Jerold Simons, "Morris Ernst and Disclosure: One Liberal's Quest for a Solution to the Problem of Domestic Communism, 1939–1949," *Mid-America,* 71 (1/89), 23.

11   All quotations are from "Stalinist Outposts in the United States," report #2, 4/40, ACCF, box 2, except the comment about the legality of the report. It comes from a letter from Louis P. Goldberg to S. M. Levitas, 5/6/40, ACCF, box 2. "Project for an Information Bureau," CCF *Bulletin,* 1 (10/15/39), 11, describes the impetus for the report, and CCF minutes 2/12/40 fix Lundberg as its author. "Stalinist Outposts" was intended to be a series (the existing issue is labeled #2); but there is no copy of #1 in the Committee's papers.

12   See Chapter 9 for more details. See also Kutulas, " 'Totalitarianism' Transformed: The Mainstreaming of Anti-Communism, 1938–1941," *Mid-America* (forthcoming).

13   On ACLU factions, see Walker, *In Defense of Civil Liberties,* 101–3.

14   Baldwin to Alexander Hamilton Frey, 3/5/40, ACLU, vol. 2163.

15   Quotations are from Hook to Roger Baldwin, 9/27/39 and 10/18/39, both in ACLU, vol. 2064; Riis to Baldwin, 10/20/39, ACLU, vol. 2064; Thomas to O. K. Fraenkel, 12/19/39, ACLU, vol. 2063; Thomas, "Your World and Mine," SC, 12/16/39, reprinted in *The Trial of Elizabeth Gurley Flynn,* ed. Corliss Lamont (New York: Horizon, 1968), 150. See also Villard to Baldwin, OGV, box 119, and Ross to Baldwin, 12/6/39, ACLU, vol. 2064.

16   Quotations are from unsigned report on Thomas (presented 1/18/40), ACLU, vol. 2064. See also Fraenkel's comments to Thomas, 12/15/39, in the same volume.

17   Quotations are from De Silver to Thomas, 12/5/39, NT, reel 9; De Silver to Baldwin, 12/8/39, ACLU, vol. 2164; Elmer Rice to Baldwin, 1/12/40, ACLU, vol. 2162; Thomas to Osmond Fraenkel, 12/19/39, ACLU, vol. 2063. On the two investigations, see "Crisis in the Civil Liberties Union," minority report issued 6/12/40, ACLU, reel 93.

18 Quotations are from Gardner Jackson to the ACLU board of directors, 12/25/39, ACLU, vol. 2077; Jackson to Ward, 1/7/40, AGH, box 44; original draft report on Dies, 12/14/39, ACLU, vols. 30–32 (1948); Holmes to Baldwin, 1/3/40, AGH, box 44. Discussion of the Dies report occurred at board meetings on 12/26/39, 1/2/40, and 1/8/40. The committee consisted of Raymond Wise, Ernst, Riis, and Florina Lasker.

19 The resolution, Ward's ruling, and the second resolution are all in board minutes, 1/18/40; Van Kleeck's defeated resolution is in board minutes, 1/29/40, all in ACLU, reel 8.

20 Quotations are from "Crisis in the Civil Liberties Union" and Hays to Baldwin, 1/31/40, ACLU, reel 2164.

21 Holmes's statement upon being elected chairman, 2/26/40, board minutes, ACLU, reel 8.

22 Baldwin to Harry Elmer Barnes, 7/29/40, ACLU, vol. 12 (1975).

23 Quotations are from Baldwin to Holmes, 3/15/40, ACLU, vol. 2163, and Holmes to De Silver, 2/21/40, JHH, cont. 187. On the costs of the resolution and Flynn expulsion, see Lucille Milner, *Education of an American Liberal* (New York: Horizon, 1954), 266, and Holmes to John Finerty, 3/15/40, JHH, cont. 187.

24 Quotations are from Baldwin to Holmes, 3/15/40, ACLU, vol. 2163 (my emphasis); Holmes to Milner, 3/21/40, JHH, cont. 187; press release, 2/5/40, ACLU, reel 8; Holmes to Baldwin, 6/18/40, ACLU, vol. 12 (1975); Holmes to Baldwin, 3/19/40, ACLU, vol. 2162. On the Bingham matter, see letter to the members of the national committee, 6/40, Holmes to Baldwin, 6/15/40, Arthur Garfield Hays to Baldwin, 6/18/40, Baldwin to Milner, 6/7/40, and Milner to Baldwin, 6/7/40, all in ACLU, vol. 12 (1975).

25 Quotations are from Board minutes, 3/4/40, ACLU, reel 8, and William B. Spofford to Flynn, 5/9/40, MVK, box 19. Most of the documents, including a transcript of the proceedings and the votes, are in *The Trial of Flynn*. Holmes's apology, dated 5/9/40, is in JHH, cont. 187. Holmes to Flynn, 8/14/40 (written at Baldwin's urging) expressed his "personal regret" despite his belief that justice had been done her (ACLU, vol. 2162). On Baldwin and Flynn, see Rosalyn Fraad Baxandall's introduction to *Words on Fire: The Life and Writings of Elizabeth Gurley Flynn* (New York: Rutgers, 1978), 41, and Lamson, *Baldwin,* 236.

26 Quotations are from "Crisis in the Civil Liberties Union, ACLU, reel 93, 12; Holmes to Huebsch, 8/10/40, BH, cont. 9; Baldwin to Huebsch, 7/3/40, ACLU, vol. 2163. The resolution was tabled 10/7/40 and untabled and defeated 10/28/40, ACLU, vol. 2163.

27 The 1976 ACLU resolution is cited in Baxandall, *Words,* 42.

28 The opinion is Joseph Freeman's, as expressed to Floyd Dell, 6/3/51, FD, Dell-Freeman sect. Freeman was the ACLU's only Communist employee, serving as its publicity director in the 1920s. The ACLU's secretary, Lucille Milner, delivered exactly the same verdict on the Flynn matter in her *Education,* 261.

29 Quotations are from *Flynn's Sunday Worker* article, "I Am Expelled from

290   Civil Liberties!,'' entered as "trial" exhibit #6, Roger Riis's characterization of Flynn's perception of the ACLU board ("mercenary") at her "trial," Flynn in her defense, and Corliss Lamont's introduction, all in *Trial of Flynn*, 153, 150, 162, and 21; Isserman to the board, 2/28/40, AGH, box 44; Gardner Jackson, Walter Gellhorn, Sidney Schlesinger, Herbert Howe Bancroft, and John P. Davis to the ACLU executive committee, 12/14/39. Baldwin's denial is 12/16/39, ACLU, vol. 2077.

30   Quotations are from Norman Thomas to Osmond Fraenkel, 12/19/39, and Holmes to Richard Childs, 12/22/39, both in ACLU, vol. 2063. Steven Biel, *Independent Intellectuals*, 69–72, talks a little about the liberal commitment to expertise.

31   The first quotation is cited in William Eaton, *The American Federation of Teachers* (Carbondale: Southern Illinois University, 1975), 114; the other two are from Donald Axelrod, "How 'Red' Is the Teachers' Union?" CS, 9 (2/40), 22 and 21–22. See Eaton, 112–21, and Marjorie Murphy, *Blackboard Unions* (Ithaca: Cornell University Press, 1990), 165–66. On the earlier problems in Local 5, see David Berenberg, "Even Radicals Grown Old," MM, 9 (12/35), 370–72.

32   Wolfe to Rexroth, 10/23/39, BDW, box 12.

33   See Cohen, *When the Old Left*, 319.

34   Quotations are from Thomas R. Amlie to the Oshkosh *Northwestern*, 6/6/42, and Robert Bendiner, "Writers Division," UDA, 10/41, both in ADA, ser. 1, #4 and #303.

35   All quotations are from ADA. The first comes from an edited version of General Principles, 1/11/42 (ser. 1, #36), the second from the notes of the International Policy and Peace panel, 1/11/42 (ser. 1, #36), the third from a UDA press release, 6/25/41 (ser. 1, #138), the fourth from a memo on the organization of UDA local groups, summer 1941 (ser. 1, #138); the fifth is Frank Kingdon's description of the Dies committee's label in Kingdon to Joseph Starnes, 6/25/42 (ser. 1, #4), and the final two are from Freda Kirchwey and Bruce Bliven's remarks at "The Case against Martin Dies" forum, 7/28/42 (ser. 1, #55).

36   The quotation in from a letter to Hook, 5/17/41, that is cited in Edward S. Shapiro, "The Sidney Hook–Corliss Lamont Letters," *Continuity*, 12 (Fall 1988), 72.

37   The quotations are from Harrison in NL, 11/18/39, 8, and Kenneth Rexroth to Franklin Folsom, 5/12/41, KR, box 6.

38   Quotations are from Lyons in *Whose Revolution*, 133; Eastman, "Correspondence" [which *The New Republic* chose to subtitle "The Enjoyment of Yah-Yah"], NR, 100 (10/25/39), 344; Hook, "Unreconstructed Fellow Travelers," SC, 1/13/40, 2.

39   Often, in fact, other intellectuals believed extreme anticommunists were ready to make compromises to get ahead. Joseph Freeman, for example, noted of Eugene Lyons that he was "always ambitious to make money and a career for himself in conventional society." Freeman to Dell, 4/10/55, FD, Freeman-Dell

sect. Eastman's editorial position with *Readers' Digest* in the early 1940s prompted similar comments.

40   Quotations are from Lyons, *Red Decade,* chapter title; his "It Was Smart to Be a Red," *Saturday Evening Post,* 212 (12/9/39); Stolberg's New York *Tribune* article, 11/26/39, 1.

41   Davis, *Character Assassination* (New York: Philosophical Library, 1950), 159–74, 168.

42   Dos Passos to Louis Adamic, 6/18/40, as cited in Henry A. Christian, "Ten Letters to Louis Adamic," *Princeton University Library Chronicle,* 28 (Winter 1967), 92.

43   Lyons, "It Was Smart to Be a Red," 78 and 79.

44   Quotations are from Lyons, introduction to *The Red Decade,* 15; his statement, 10/24/41, EL-O, pt. 2; Holmes to Lyons, 11/12/41, JHH, cont. 195. See also Holmes to Lamont, 11/7/41, Holmes to Lyons, 11/7/41, and Holmes to Lyons, 11/19/41, JHH, cont. 195. Lyons did not expect his book to do well; see Lyons to Wesley Stout, 7/10/41, EL-H, box 4. A summary of the reviews of *The Red Decade* may be found in the 1941 volume of *Book Review Digest,* 570–71. Lamont does seem to have been a popular target for anticommunists.

45   Holmes to Lyons, 11/7/41, JHH, cont. 195.

46   Both quotations are from *Red Decade,* 402.

47   On Lovestone see HUAC Hearings, 12/2/39, 7097. On Grebanier, see NYT, 12/3/40, 1, 27 and 12/7/40, 19, and Schrecker, *No Ivory Tower,* 78, from which the quotation comes. On the Rapp-Coudert committee more generally, see Stephen Leberstein, "Purging the Profs," in *New Studies in the Politics and Culture of U.S. Communism,* ed. Brown et al., 91–122.

48   On Matthews and the disrepute in which others held him, see Bruce Bliven's remarks at "The Case against Martin Dies" forum, 7/28/42, ADA (ser. 1, #55). On Ernst, see Maurice Isserman, *Which Side,* 68, and Simons, "Ernst and Disclosure."

49   Howe, *Margin,* 77.

50   Trotsky, *In Defense of Marxism (Against the Petty-Bourgeois Opposition)* (New York: Pioneer, 1941), 19, 28, and 29.

51   Quotation is from Cannon to members of the national committee, 9/8/39, as cited in Cannon, *Struggle,* 86. I have pieced together this chronology from sometimes conflicting accounts by the two sides. Cannon's "Majority" version is in the introduction to Trotsky's *In Defense,* ix–x; Burnham's "Minority" version is in "War and the Bureaucratic Conservatism," 257–59, and Shachtman's "Report on the Russian Question," *Internal Bulletin,* 2 (11/14/39), 1a–23a, SWP, reel 15.

52   See Cannon to C. Charles, 12/1/39, to Joseph Hansen, 12/14/39, and to Bill Morgan, 12/15/39, all in Cannon, *Struggle,* 107–16.

53   All quotations are from "War and the Bureaucratic Conservatism," 266 and 290. See also Political Committee Minority, "The Judgment of Events," 3/22/40, IDSP, box 1.

292   54   Trotsky, "Petty Bourgeois Moralists and the Proletarian Party," *In Defense,* 166–69, and Cannon to Farrell Dobbs, 1/3/40, *Struggle,* 132.

55   Quotations are from Burnham, "Science and Style," in Trotsky, *In Defense,* 205; Trotsky, *Internal Bulletin,* 2 (12/20/39), 25, swp; Manny Geltman to author, 5/17/82.

56   This was the title of Trotsky's essay, "From a Scratch—to the Danger of Gangrene," ni, 6 (3/40), 51. Second quotation is from one of the April 1940 convention documents, in Cannon, *Struggle,* 241. Myer's *Prophet's,* 165, says the swp split half-half. Maurice Isserman, *If I Had a Hammer* (New York: Basic, 1987), 46, reports that of the approximately two thousand swp members, about eight hundred followed Burnham and Shachtman.

57   Quotations are from Isserman, ibid., 49, Burnham's letter of resignation, 5/21/40, and Trotsky, *In Defense,* 207. Burnham, *The Managerial Revolution* (New York: John Day, 1941).

58   Dwight Macdonald, *Memoirs of a Revolutionist* (New York: Farrar, Straus and Cudahy, 1957), 20.

59   On the Workers Party, see Howe, *Margin,* 80–89. On Shachtman and the Workers Party, see Isserman, *If,* 37–75.

60   On the Smith Act trials, see nyt, 12/2/41, 1. On the defense group, see Farrell to John Dos Passos, 7/25/41, jdp, ser. 2, box 1. On the swp and its intellectuals, see Wald, *New York,* 366–74.

NINE   The Legacy of the 1930s Intellectual Left

1   Hicks to Malcolm Cowley, 6/30/[41], mc, incoming, and Kirchwey, "Stalin's Choice," n, 158 (1/22/44), 89. See also Kirchwey, "The End of the Comintern," n, 156 (5/29/43), 762.

2   On the law in 1942, see Call for Writers-Win-the-War Congress, 11/3/42, and Franklin Folsom to Dashiell Hammett, 11/18/42, both in law, pt. 7. See also foia files on the League regarding its finances. The very fact that the government continued to investigate the law during the war suggests a changing climate of opinion.

3   See, for example, Freda Kirchwey, "The People's Offensive, n, 42 (10/11/41), 323, or Albert Rhys Williams, *The Russians: The Land, the People, Why They Fight* (New York: Harcourt, Brace, 1943). foia files on Friends of the Soviet Union show that *Soviet Russia Today's* 1942 circulation was 80,000, up from its Pact low of 18,000.

4   Bliven, "The Hang-Back Boys," nr, 110 (3/6/44), all quotations from 306.

5   The first quotation is from Dewey to nyt, 1/11/42, 7E; the rest are Oak's in nl, 11/6/43, 7.

6   The open letter, signed by sixty-six intellectuals, appeared in nl, 5/29/43, 2. The other quotation is from Hook, *Out of Step,* 313. O'Neill provides more detail in *A Better World,* 76–77.

7 Quotations are from Cowley to Burke, 6/28/42, MC, outgoing; Dies, as cited in Goodman, *The Committee*, 127; Cowley to Burke, 6/28/42, Brooks to Cowley, 3/13/42, Frankfurter to Cowley, 3/17/42, Kirchwey to Cowley, 2/13/42, and Gollumb to Cowley, 4/7/42, all in MC, incoming. Cowley later wrote about his experience in "A Personal Record," in *And I Worked*, 158. Natalie Robins, *Alien Ink* (New York: Morrow, 1992), 223–25, provides details about Cowley's dossier and informants.

8 Quotations are from "XXX," "Washington Gestapo, Part I," N, 157 (7/17/43), 65, and "The Washington Inquisition," NR, 108 (5/24/43), 684. On Schuman, see his testimony before Dies, HUAC, *Hearings*, spring 1943, 3091–92. On Mangione, see *Ethnic*, 293–94. On Herbst, see her story, "Yesterday's Road," *New American Review*, 3 (4/68), 84–104. Langer, *Herbst*, 248–58, also recounts the story and suggests that one of Herbst's informers was her old friend Katherine Anne Porter, something Robins confirms in *Alien Ink*, 230. On Lovett, see his *All Our Years*, 268–309.

9 Quotations are from Wald, *New York*, 5, and NL, 1/13/45, 16. Even the old *New Leader* angered Malcolm Cowley with its obsessive anti-Stalinism. See his letter to Edmund Wilson, 2/2/40, EW. On the *Partisan Review* during this period, see William Barrett, *The Truants* (Garden City: Doubleday, 1982). On *Politics*, see Michael Wreszin, *A Rebel in Defense of Tradition* or Stephen Whitfield, *A Critical American: The Politics of Dwight Macdonald* (Hamden, Conn.: Archon Books, 1984), 56. Robins, *Alien Ink*, 88–90 and 152, suggests the FBI kept files on both *Partisan Review* and *Politics*.

10 On the CPUSA during the war, see Isserman, *Which Side?* On the FBI, see Athan Theoharis and John Cox, *The Boss* (Philadelphia: Temple University Press, 1988). On Stewart and Winter, see Robins, *Alien Ink*, 93. On Hammett, see Diane Johnson, *Dashiell Hammett* (New York: Random House, 1983), 154–299.

11 On "Browderism," see Isserman, *Which Side?*, 186–243, or Jaffe, *Rise and Fall*, 53–85. I do not subscribe to what Ellen Schrecker calls "the self-destruction explanation" of the CPUSA's decline. External forces seriously weakened it during the late 1940s and 1950s. I am merely suggesting that the particular form the Party took after Browderism made anticommunists' tasks easier. See Schrecker, "McCarthyism and the Decline of American Communism, 1945–1960," in *New Studies in the Politics and Culture of U.S. Communism*, ed. Brown et al., 123–40.

12 The first three quotations are from Schneider, "Probing Writers' Problems," NM, 57 (10/23/45), 24, 24, and 25. The next six are from Maltz, "What Shall We Ask of Our Writers?" NM, 58 (2/12/46), 19, 19, 20, 20, 22, and 22. "The literary equivalent . . ." is from Nancy Lynn Schwartz, *The Hollywood Writers' Wars*, completed by Sheila Schwartz (New York: MacGraw Hill, 1982), 237. The condemnatory quotation is from a Michael Gold *Daily Worker* article cited in Ceplair and Englund, *Inquisition*, 234. The final quotation is from Maltz's oral history, "The Citizen Writer in Retrospect," 572. On the Hollywood versus

294 New York slant to the conflict, see Schwartz, ibid., 235–37, or Ceplair and Englund, ibid., 233–36. Maltz's retraction was "Moving Forward," NM, 59 (4/9/46), 8–10, 21–22.

13   The word is from the Maltz article.

14   I borrow this phrase and concept from Cary Nelson.

15   Quotations are from Schneider to Cowley, 8/29/46; MC; Endore to Schneider, 7/9/45, GE, box 78; Schneider to Endore, 8/7/45, GE, box 78.

16 . My argument is derived mainly from Schrecker's "McCarthyism and the Decline of American Communism." The term "separate world" is on page 124. For a different view, see Starobin, *American Communism in Crisis,* or David Shannon, *The Decline of American Communism* (New York: Harcourt Brace, 1959).

17   The best brief summary of the Wallace movement is Norman Markowitz's "Progressive Party" entry in *The Encyclopedia of the American Left,* ed. Mari Jo Buhle, Paul Buhle, and Dan Georgakas (Urbana: University of Illinois, 1992), 600–601. The characterization of Wallace is Reinhold Niebuhr's, as cited in Fox, *Niebuhr,* 236.

18   On Arendt, see Richard Pells, *The Liberal Mind in a Conservative Age* (New York: Harper, 1985), 83–96. Frank Warren's 1993 introduction to *Liberals and Communism* (p. xvii) talks about how much Arendt's analysis shaped his conceptualization of what might be called totalitarian liberalism.

19   Howe, "The New York Intellectuals," in *Decline of the New* (New York: Harcourt, Brace and World, 1963), 222.

20   On Americans for Democratic Action, see Steven M. Gillon, *Politics and Vision: The A.D.A. and American Liberalism, 1947–1985* (New York: Oxford University Press, 1987).

21   MacLeish to David Mearns, 8/4/58, in his *Letters,* 409.

22   Glazer, "Did We Go Too Far?" *National Interest,* 31 (Summer 1993), 137.

23   My source here is Brightman, *Writing Dangerously,* 305–11. The quotations are from 307, 309, and 306.

24   Quotations are from Macdonald, as interviewed by Diana Trilling, *Partisan Review,* 323; Brightman, *Writing Dangerously,* 323; Hook, *Out of Step,* 385. Hook, in "The Communist Peace Offensive," PR, 51 (1984), 692–711, shows a very different level of interaction than Brightman or the Macdonald interview do. Howard Fast, who chaired the session McCarthy and Macdonald attended, did not think they were invited, but also did not think they had much to say. See Fast, *Being Red* (Boston: Houghton Mifflin, 1990), 202.

25   Basic information on the organization may be found in Christopher Lasch, "The Cultural Cold War: A Short History of the Congress for Cultural Freedom," in *The Agony of the American Left* (New York: Random House, 1968), 78–114. I find Peter Coleman's *The Liberal Conspiracy* (New York: Free Press, 1989), which focuses on the components of the international Congress for Cultural Freedom, less useful on the ACCF than the above source, although it does show the contrast between the U.S. group and its counterparts in other countries.

26   Quotations are from Fowler Harper, cited in Victor Navasky, *Naming*
Names (New York: Viking, 1980), 56; Kristol's telegram to participants of the
ECLC's 1953 conference, a copy of which is in RN, box 1; Lasch, "Short History"
87; Paul Lehmann to the ACCF, as quoted in Mary Sterling McAuliffe, *Crisis on
the Left* (Amherst: University of Massachusetts Press, 1978), 117.

27   The first quotation is cited by Richard Rovere to Arthur Schlesinger,
3/30/52; the second is from Schlesinger to Sidney Hook, 4/1/52. John P. Diggins was kind enough to share with me these documents from his private files.

28   Quotations are from William Phillips, "Writing and Rewriting the Past,"
PR, 50 (1983), 169; a letter from Sol Stein to Sidney Hook, cited in McAuliffe,
Crisis, 125; James Rorty and Moshe Decter, *McCarthy and the Communists*
(Boston: Beacon, 1954), 125. Both O'Neill and McAuliffe provide more de-
tailed summaries of the ACCF's attitude vis-à-vis McCarthy, although the two
present rather different perspectives. Conservatives who resigned included
James Burnham and George Schuyler.

29   Quotations are from ACCF memo, 1/6/55, Farrell to Norman Jacobs of
ACCF, 8/28/56, Trilling to ACCF board, n.d. [8/30/56], all in BDW, boxes 78 and
84.

30   Quotations are from Roger Baldwin to Sol Stein, 7/12/54, RB, box 20, and
Glazer, "Did We?" 138.

31   Quotations are from Rovere to Schlesinger, 9/30/52, RR, box 32; McCarthy, "No News *or* What Killed the Dog," in *On the Contrary* (New York: Farrar,
Straus and Cudahy, 1961), 38; Trilling, "A Memorandum on the Hiss Case,"
Claremont Essays (London: Secker and Warburg, 1965), 68. On the assumption
of Hiss's guilt, see Kenneth O'Reilly, "Liberal Values, the Cold War, and American Intellectuals," *Beyond the Hiss Case,* ed. Athan Theoharis (Philadelphia:
Temple University Press, 1982).

32   Quotations are from McCarthy at the "In Defense of Free Culture" meeting, as cited in NL, 4/7/52, 4, and the ACCF's NYT statement, 1/5/53, cited in
Lasch's "Short History," 87.

33   Quotations are from Wolfe, deposition to the State of New York, 3/5/52,
BDW, box 78, and McCarthy, "Naming Names: The Arthur Miller Case," in *On
the Contrary,* 153.

34   Rovere, "J. B. Matthews—the Informer," N, 155 (10/3/42), 315.

35   The incidents are described in Navasky, *Naming Names,* 46 and 377. The
quotation is from page x.

36   "Reluctant" is from NL, 4/13/53, 21. The other quotations are from Hicks,
Part, 261; his *Where We Came Out* (New York: Viking, 1954), 4; his journal,
6/23/52, cited in Levenson and Natterstad, *Hicks,* 183; *Where,* 4; *Part,* 261.

37   Bertram Wolfe to Morris Fine, 5/1/52, as cited in *Breaking with Communism,* ed. Robert Hessen (Stanford: Hoover Institution Press, 1990), 79. On the
legitimacy of HUAC and similar agencies, see NL, 11/8/47, 3; Liston Oak to
George Novack, 10/4/48, LO, box 1; John Dos Passos to William Rose Benét,
1/12/48, *Fourteenth Chronicle,* 580; Oak in NL, 3/29/47, 2; revised draft copy

296   of the ACCF's "Is There New Light on the Lattimore Case," n.d. (ca. early 1955),
       BDW, box 78.

38   Quotations are from Rorty and Decter, *McCarthy*, 140; Coser, as cited in
Isserman, *If I Had a Hammer*, 96; Navasky, *Naming Names*, 77. On Kazan and
On the Waterfront, see Stephen J. Whitfield, *The Culture of the Cold War* (Bal-
timore: Johns Hopkins University Press, 1991), 107–13. I agree with Navasky's
characterization of the process of informing as a "ritual" whose symbolic significance was as a "degradation ceremony." See Navasky, 314–29.

39   Quotations are from Trilling, "Liberal Anti-Communism Revisited," 57;
Joseph Freeman describing the ACCF to Floyd Dell, 4/19/55, FD, Freeman-Dell
sect.; Chamberlin, "Exit Party-liner, Enter the AAC," NL, 6/17/50, 20; Hook,
"Breaking with the Communists," *Commentary*, 77 (2/84), 47; Hook to Corliss
Lamont, 6/22/66, as cited in Shapiro, "The Hook-Lamont letters," 89; Trilling
in NL, 4/28/52, 18; Hicks, "The PM Mind," NR, 112 (4/16/45), 516; Chamberlin,
NL, 6/17/50, 20.

40   Quotations are from "Submission to Moscow," NL, 10/12/46, world
events sect.; Dos Passos to HUAC, 1/22/53, and Dos Passos to the editors of the
NYT Book Review sect., 3/15/47, both in *Fourteenth Chronicle*, 601 and 578;
Eugene Lyons, "Liberals Fleeing the 'Terror,' but They Still Write," *Saturday
Evening Post*, 225 (9/27/52), 10; D. Trilling, "Liberal Anti-Communism," 57
and 47. Trilling has repeated her opinions in her more recent memoirs, *Beginning*, 182, although by her own admission the most limiting force in her life in
the 1930s was her psychological problems.

41   Quotations are from McCarthy, *Intellectual Memoirs*, 10, and Kazin to
Cowley, 5/6/42, MC, incoming.

42   Quotations are from Diana Trilling, "Liberal Anti-Communism," 46–48,
and Norman Mailer, as cited in Brightman, *Writing Dangerously*, 611.

43   Quotation is from Rahv to Morton Zabel, 10/10/50, MDZ, incoming. Diana
Trilling confirmed this assessment in *Beginning*, 306. Norman Podhoretz talks
about the influence of anticommunism on his generation in *Making It* (New
York: Harper and Row, 1967), 87–89. The survey was published in the *New
York Times Book Review*, 10/29/72, 1. One reason why it was so easy to deny
that they had achieved the status progressives seemed to have in the 1930s is
that, as Russell Jacoby suggested, the intellectual community became more
composed of specialists and more institutionalized. It was no longer possible
for most intellectuals to freelance.

44   Quotations are from Hook in "Our Country and Our Culture: A Sym-
posium," PR, 19 (May–June, 1952), 569, 574, and Macdonald, "I Chose the
West," *Memoirs*, 198. On the pro-American phenomenon more generally, see
Cooney, *Rise*, 261, Pells, *Liberal Mind*, 130–47, and Bloom, *Prodigal*, 181–84.

45   Quotations are from Macdonald, "Liberal Soap Opera," in *Memoirs*, 246–
47; Niebuhr, *The Children of Light, the Children of Darkness* (New York: Scribner's Sons, 1944); Schlesinger, *The Vital Center* (Boston: Houghton Mifflin,
1949), ix; Steven Gillon, *Politics and Vision*, x; Barrett, *Truants*, 122. On vital
center liberalism, see McAuliffe, *Crisis*, 66–72, or Pells, *The Liberal Mind*, 136.

46   Hook, "Our Country and Our Culture," 307. Curiously, Diana Trilling inverted his assessment, arguing that anticommunists were "not excluded . . . from the intellectual mainstream" until McCarthy tarnished their reputation with his extremism. Yet she is talking only about the postwar period. See *Beginning,* 343.

47   Quotations are from Josephson to Murray Kempton, 3/8/55, as cited in Shi, *Josephson,* 242, and Frank, "'Anti-Communist Peril': Rediscovering Our Roots," N, 178 (6/19/54), 519.

48   Baldwin, "Progressives and Communists," NR, 114 (6/17/46), 871. On Wallace, see Vincent Sheean's "Why I Will Not Vote for Henry Wallace," *Saturday Evening Post,* 221 (9/18/48), 23, 153, 155.

49   HUAC *Hearings,* 2/48, 214.

50   Freeman to Dell, 6/16/53, FD, Freeman-Dell sect.

51   Quotations are from Freeman to the committee, 11/27/40, copy in JF, box 5, and Lash to HUAC, "Executive Hearings Made Public," 1/21/42, 2790.

52   The first quotation is from Freeman to Dell, 4/15/53 and 4/30/53, FD, Freeman-Dell sect. Scott Nearing had a similar reaction to Hicks's comments; see Levenson and Natterstad, *Hicks,* 190. The other quotations are from Stone, "Must Americans Become Informers?" included in his *The Truman Era* (Boston: Little, Brown, 1953; new ed., New York: Vintage, 1973), 97; Cowley to Alan Barth, 8/10/49, MC, outgoing; Josephson, *Infidel,* 481; Hellman, *Scoundrel Time* (New York: Bantam, 1976), 39; Stone, "Whittaker Chambers: Martyrdom Lavishly Buttered," in *Truman Era,* 183.

53   Quotations are from Cowley to Kenneth Burke, 12/17/40, MC, outgoing; Cowley to Burke, 9/4/52, *Selected Correspondence of Burke and Cowley,* 307; Stone, "The Right to Travel: The ACLU's Split Personality," in *The Truman Era,* 103; Baldwin in Lamson, *Baldwin,* 264. On the ACCF, see McWilliams, *Education of McWilliams,* 154–56. On the ACLU, see "Time for Decision," N, 178 (2/12/54), 123–24.

54   Quotations are from ACLU board minutes, 10/19/53, ACLU, reel 13; John Finerty to Patrick Malin, 3/15/54, ACLU, reel 23; Lamont's statement to the board, 11/30/53, ACLU, reel 13; Malin to the board, 3/12/54, ACLU, reel 23. Walker, *In Defense,* is probably the best source on the ACLU during this period, although McAuliffe, *Crisis,* is also good. The proposal is in ACLU, reel 23. The suggestion that mere rewriting would correct the problem was raised, and approved, by the board on 11/2/53, ACLU, reel 13. Thomas's proposal was raised 10/14/53, ACLU, reel 23; his interim proposal was 3/15/54, ACLU, reel 13. Lamont told his story in a letter dated 1/22/53, ACLU, reel 23. The whole story, too long to tell here, is very reminiscent of the Flynn battle.

55   Quotations are from ECLC statement, cited in McAuliffe, ibid., 118; Cowley, "Gammon for Dinner," in *The Flower and the Leaf,* ed. Donald W. Faulkner (New York: Viking, 1985), 107; his "Sense of Guilt," 160; Josephson to Kenneth Burke, 4/1/47, cited in Shi, *Josephson,* 242.

56   Quotations are from Cowley, as cited in Robins, *Alien Ink,* 223; Baldwin to the UDA, n.d. (ca. 7/42), ADA, ser. 1, #55; Endore to McWilliams, 8/1/52, GE,

298   box 77. On Cowley, see also his letter to Kenneth Burke, 1/5/50 and 11/1/50, MC, incoming. Progressives who were observed by the government included Sherwood Anderson, Van Wyck Brooks, Cowley, Theodore Dreiser, Waldo Frank, Horace Gregory, Lillian Hellman, Ernest Hemingway, Josephine Herbst, Archibald MacLeish, F. O. Matthiessen, Lewis Mumford, Clifford Odets, Dorothy Parker, Theodore Roethke, Upton Sinclair, Nathaniel West, and William Carlos Williams.

Some Conclusions

1   Jumonville, *Critical,* 7.

2   Quotations are from Soule, *The Coming American Revolution,* 8; "No More Ivory Towers," NR, 99 (5/24/39), 59; Sheean, "Ivory Tower for Rent," NM, 31 (6/13/39), 8.

3   The first quotation is Bertram Wolfe's description of Morris R. Cohen, who particularly impressed him as a student. See his *A Life in Two Centuries* (New York: Stein and Day, 1981), 107. The second comes from Irving Howe in an interview with William Cain, *American Literary History,* 1 (Fall 1989), 563.

4   Halper to McFee, 9/23/35, AH, box 6.

5   Trilling, *The Middle of the Journey* (New York: Scribner's Sons, 1947). The book is a fictionalization of Whittaker Chambers's experiences. Eugene Lyons told of a similar encounter with progressive journalists whose eyes glazed over as he spoke about the Moscow trials because they were completely unable to assimilate or accept what he said. See the last section of *Assignment in Utopia.*

6   Phillips, "How PR Began," 42.

SELECTED BIBLIOGRAPHY

Published Letters

Breaking With Communism: The Intellectual Odyssey of Bertram D. Wolfe. Edited by Robert Hessen. Stanford: Hoover Institution Press, 1990.

Christian, Henry A. "Ten Letters to Louis Adamic." *Princeton University Library Chronicle* 28 (Winter 1967): 76–94.

Epitaphs of Our Times: The Letters of Edward Dahlberg. New York: Braziller, 1967.

The Fourteenth Chronicle: Letters and Diaries of John Dos Passos. Edited by Townsend Ludington. Boston: Gambit, 1973.

Letters of Archibald MacLeish, 1907 to 1982. Edited by R. H. Winnick. Boston: Houghton Mifflin, 1983.

Letters of Katherine Anne Porter. Edited by Isabel Bayley. New York: Atlantic Monthly Press, 1990.

Letters of Sherwood Anderson. Edited by Howard Mumford Jones. Boston: Little, Brown, 1953.

Letters of Theodore Dreiser. Edited by Robert Elias. 3 vols. Philadelphia: University of Pennsylvania Press, 1959.

Poets, Poetics and Politics: America's Literary Community Viewed From the Letters of Rolfe Humphries, 1910–1969. Edited by Richard Gillman and Michael Paul Novak. Lawrence: University Press of Kansas, 1992.

The Selected Correspondence of Kenneth Burke and Malcolm Cowley, 1915–1981. Edited by Paul Jay. New York: Viking, 1988.

300   *Selected Letters of Theodore Roethke.* Edited by Ralph J. Mills. Seattle: University of Washington Press, 1956.

Shapiro, Edward S. "The Sidney Hook–Corliss Lamont Letters." *Continuity* 12 (Fall 1988): 59–95.

The Van Wyck Brooks–Lewis Mumford Letters: The Record of a Literary Friendship, 1921–1963. Edited by Robert Spiller. New York: Dutton, 1970.

What the Woman Lived: Selected Letters of Louise Bogan, 1920–1970. Edited by Ruth Limmer. New York: Harcourt Brace Jovanovich, 1973.

Wilson, Edmund. *Letters on Literature and Politics, 1912–1972.* Edited by Elena Wilson. New York: Farrar, Straus, and Giroux, 1977.

Miscellaneous Primary Materials

American Writers Congress. Edited by Henry Hart. New York: International, 1935.

Baldwin, Roger. *Liberty Under the Soviets.* New York: Vanguard, 1928.

Bingham, Alfred. *Insurgent America.* New York: Harper and Brothers, 1935.

——. *Man's Estate.* New York: Norton, 1939.

Bishop, Hillman. *The American League Against War and Fascism.* Privately published, 1936.

Browder, Earl. *The Peoples' Front.* New York: International, 1938.

——. *What Is Communism?* New York: Workers' Library, 1936.

Burnham, James. *The Managerial Revolution.* New York: Day, 1941.

——. *The Peoples' Front: The New Betrayal.* New York: Pioneer, 1937.

Calverton, V. F. *For Revolution.* New York: Day, 1932.

Cannon, James P. *The Struggle for a Proletarian Party.* Edited by John G. Wright. Reprint. New York: Pathfinder, 1972.

Chamberlain, John. *Farewell to Reform.* New York: Liveright, 1932.

Chamberlin, William Henry. *Collectivism: A False Utopia.* New York: Macmillan, 1936.

——. *Russia's Iron Age.* Boston: Little, Brown, 1934.

——. *The Soviet Planned Economic Order.* Boston: World Peace Foundation, 1931.

Chase, Stuart. *A New Deal.* New York: Macmillan, 1932.

Commission of Inquiry into the Charges Made Against Leon Trotsky in the Moscow Trials. *The Case of Leon Trotsky.* New York: Harper and Brothers, 1937.

——. *Not Guilty.* New York: Harper and Brothers, 1938.

The Communist League of America, 1932–1934: James P. Cannon, Writing and Speeches. Edited by Fred Stanton and Michael Taber. New York: Monad, 1985.

Corey, Lewis. *The Crisis of the Middle Class.* New York: Covici, Friede, 1935.

——. *The Decline of American Capitalism.* New York: Covici, Friede, 1934.

Counts, George. *A Ford Crosses Soviet Russia*. Boston: Stratford, 1930.

——. *The Prospects of American Democracy*. New York: Day, 1938.

——. *The Soviet Challenge to America*. New York: Day, 1931.

Dewey, John. *Freedom and Culture*. New York: Putnam's Sons, 1939.

——. "The Future of Liberalism." *Journal of Philosophy* 22 (1935): 225–30.

——. *Impressions of Soviet Russia and the Revolutionary World*. New York: New Republic, 1929.

——. *Liberalism and Social Action*. New York: Putnam's Sons, 1935.

——. *Truth Is on the March: Reports and Remarks on the Trotsky Hearings in Mexico*. New York: American Committee for the Defense of Leon Trotsky, 1937.

Dreiser, Theodore. *Dreiser Looks at Russia*. New York: Liveright, 1928.

Duranty, Walter. *Russia Reported*. London: Victor Gollancz, 1934.

Eastman, Max. *Artists in Uniform*. New York: Knopf, 1934.

——. *The End of Socialism in Russia*. Boston: Little, Brown, 1937.

——. *The Last Stand of Dialectic Materialism: A Study of Sidney Hook's Marxism*. New York: Polemic, 1934.

——. *Marx and Lenin: The Science of Revolution*. New York: Albert and Charles Boni, 1927.

——. *Marxism: Is It Science?* London: Allen and Unwin, 1941.

——. *Reflections on the Failure of Socialism*. New York: Devin-Adair, 1955.

——. *Since Lenin Died*. London: Labour Publishing, 1925.

——. *Stalin's Russia and the Crisis in Socialism*. New York: Norton, 1940.

Eddy, Sherwood. *The Challenge of Russia*. New York: Farrar and Rinehart, 1931.

——. *Russia Today*. London: Allen and Unwin, 1934.

Farrell, James T. *A Note on Literary Criticism*. New York: Vanguard, 1936.

Fischer, Louis. *Soviet Journey*. New York: Smith and Haas, 1935.

——. *The Soviets in World Affairs*. 2 vols. New York: Cape and Smith, 1930.

——. *Stalin and Hitler*. New York: *Nation*, 1940.

——. *The War in Spain*. New York: *Nation*, 1937.

The Founding of the Socialist Workers Party: Minutes and Resolutions, 1938–39. New York: Monad, 1982.

Frank, Waldo. *In Russia*. New York: Scribner's Sons, 1932.

——. *In the American Jungle*. New York: Farrar and Rinehart, 1937.

Gold, Michael. *Change the World!* New York: International, 1936.

——. *The Hollow Men*. New York: International, 1941.

Granville Hicks in the New Masses. Edited by Jack Alan Robbins. Port Washington: Kennikat Press, 1974.

Hallgren, Mauritz. *Seeds of Revolt*. New York: Knopf, 1933.

——. *Why I Resigned From the Trotsky Defense Committee*. New York: International, 1937.

Hays, Arthur Garfield. *Democracy Works*. New York: Random House, 1939.

Hazlitt, Henry. *Instead of Dictatorship*. New York: Day, 1933.

302 Hicks, Granville. *I Like America*. New York: Modern Age, 1938.

Hindus, Maurice. *The Great Offensive*. New York: Smith and Haas, 1933.

———. *Humanity Uprooted*. New York: Cape and Smith, 1929.

———. *Red Bread*. New York: Cape and Smith, 1931.

Hook, Sidney. "Communism and the Intellectuals." *American Mercury* 68 (2/49): 133–44.

———. "Lillian Hellman's *Scoundrel Time*." *Encounter* 48 (2/77): 82–91.

———. *Reason, Social Myths, and Democracy*. New York: Day, 1940.

———. *Toward the Understanding of Karl Marx*. New York: Day, 1933.

Howe, Irving. *Leon Trotsky*. New York: Viking, 1978.

Kallen, Horace. *A Free Society*. New York: Ballou, 1934.

———. *Individualism*. New York: Liveright, 1933.

Krivitsky, W. G. *In Stalin's Secret Service*. New York: Harper and Brothers, 1939.

Krutch, Joseph Wood. *Was Europe a Success?* New York: Farrar and Rinehart, 1932.

Lamont, Corliss. *The Story of Soviet Progress*. New York: *Soviet Russia Today*, 1938.

———. *You Might Like Socialism*. New York: Modern Age, 1939.

Lamont, Corliss, and Margaret Lamont. *Russia Day By Day*. New York: Covici, Friede, 1933.

League of American Writers. *Fighting Words*. Edited by Donald Ogden Stewart. New York: Harcourt, Brace, 1940.

———. *The Writer in a Changing World*. New York: Equinox, 1937.

League of Professional Groups for Foster and Ford. *Culture and the Crisis*. New York: League of Professional Groups for Foster and Ford, 1932.

The Left Opposition in the U.S., 1928–1931. New York: Monad, 1981.

Lerner, Max. *Ideas Are Weapons*. New York: Viking, 1939.

———. *It Is Later Than You Think*. New York: Viking, 1938; rev. ed., 1943.

Lyons, Eugene. *The Red Decade*. Reprint. New Rochelle: Arlington House, 1970.

The Meaning of Marx: A Symposium. New York: Farrar and Rinehart, 1934.

Mike Gold: A Literary Anthology. Edited by Michael Folsom. New York: International, 1972.

Morrow, Felix. *Revolution and Counter-Revolution in Spain [including] The Civil War in Spain*. New York: Pathfinder, 1938.

Mumford, Lewis. *Men Must Act*. New York: Harcourt, Brace, 1939.

The New Russia: Between the First and Second Five Year Plans. Edited by Jerome Davis. New York: Day, 1933.

Niebuhr, Reinhold. *The Children of Light and the Children of Darkness*. New York: Scribner's Sons, 1944.

———. "The Liberal Illusion." *Christian Century* 56 (4/26/39): 542–44.

———. *Moral Man and Immoral Society*. New York: Scribner's Sons, 1936.

———. *Reflections on the End of an Era*. New York: Scribner's Sons, 1936.

Olgin, M. J. *Trotskyism: Counter-Revolution in Disguise.* New York: Workers Library, 1935.

A Practical Program For America. Edited by Henry Hazlitt. New York: Books For Libraries Press, 1932.

Proletarian Literature in the United States. New York: International, 1935.

Rahv, Philip. *Essays on Literature and Politics, 1932–1972.* Edited by Arabel J. Porter and Andrew J. Dvosin. Boston: Houghton Mifflin, 1978.

Rorty, James. *Where Life is Better.* New York: Reynal and Hitchcock, 1936.

Rorty, James, and Moshe Decter. *McCarthy and the Communists.* Boston: Beacon, 1954.

Schlesinger, Arthur M., Jr. *The Vital Center.* Boston: Houghton Mifflin, 1949.

Shachtman, Max. *Behind the Moscow Trial.* New York: Pioneer, 1936.

——. *Genesis of Trotskyism: The First Ten Years of the Left Opposition.* 2d. ed. Privately published, 1973.

——. *The History and Principles of the Left Opposition.* New York: Pioneer, 1933. New ed. London: New Park Publications, 1974.

Sheean, Vincent. *Not Peace But a Sword.* New York: Doubleday, Duran, 1939.

Sinclair, Upton and Eugene Lyons. *Terror in Russia? Two Views.* New York: Smith, 1938.

The Socialist Workers Party in World War II. Edited by Les Evans. New York: Pathfinder, 1975.

Soule, George. *The Coming American Revolution.* New York: Macmillan, 1934.

——. *The Future of Liberty.* New York: Macmillan, 1936.

——. *A Planned Society.* New York: Macmillan, 1932.

Stalin, Joseph. *The New Russian Policy.* Foreword by George Counts. New York: Day, 1931.

Stolberg, Benjamin, and Warren Jay Vinton. *The Economic Consequences of the New Deal.* New York: Harcourt, Brace, 1935.

Stork, A. "Mr. Calverton and His Friends: Some Notes on Literary Trotskyism in America." *International Literature* 3 (7/34): 97–124.

Strong, Anna Louise. *Dictatorship and Democracy in the Soviet Union.* New York: International, 1934.

——. *The Soviets Conquer Wheat.* New York: Henry Holt, 1931.

——. *The Soviets Expected It.* New York: Dial, 1941.

——. *Spain in Arms, 1937.* New York: Henry Holt, 1937.

——. *The Stalin Era.* Altadena: Today's Press, 1956.

——. *This Soviet World.* New York: Henry Holt, 1936.

Their Morals and Ours: Marxist Versus Liberal Views on Morality. Reprint. New York: Merit, 1966.

Thompson, Dorothy. *The New Russia.* New York: Henry Holt, 1928.

"Totalitarian Liberalism." *Politics* 2 (8/45): 254–64.

Toward an American Revolutionary Labor Movement: Statement of Programmatic Orientation by the American Workers Party. New York: Provisional Organizing Committee of the AWP, 1934.

304 *The Trial of Elizabeth Gurley Flynn.* Edited by Corliss Lamont. New York: Horizon, 1968.

Trilling, Diana. *Claremont Essays.* London: Secker and Warburg, 1965.

Trilling, Lionel. *Speaking of Literature and Society.* Edited by Diana Trilling. New York: Harcourt, Brace, Jovanovich, 1980.

Trotsky, Leon. *In Defense of Marxism (Against the Petty Bourgeois Opposition).* New York: Pioneer, 1942.

——. *In Defense of the Soviet Union.* New York: Pioneer, 1937.

——. *I Stake My Life: Trotsky's Address to the New York Hippodrome Meeting.* Introduced by Max Shachtman. New York: Pioneer, 1937.

——. *The Real Situation in Russia.* Translated by Max Eastman. London: Allen and Unwin, 1928.

——. *The Revolution Betrayed.* New York: Pathfinder, 1937; new ed., 1972.

Villard, Oswald Garrison. *The Dilemmas of an Absolute Pacifist in Two World Wars.* Edited by Anthony Gronowisz. New York: Garland, 1983.

Ward, Harry F. *Democracy and Social Change.* New York: Modern Age, 1940.

——. *In Place of Profit.* New York: Scribner's Sons, 1933.

Wechsler, James. *Revolt on the Campus.* New York: Covici, Friede, 1935.

Wilson, Edmund. *The American Jitters.* New York: Scribner's Sons, 1932.

——. *To the Finland Station.* Garden City: Doubleday, 1940.

Winter, Ella. *Red Virtue.* New York: Harcourt, Brace, 1933.

Wolfe, Bertram D. *Civil War in Spain.* New York: Workers' Age [1937].

Writers Take Sides. New York: League of American Writers, 1938.

Writings of Leon Trotsky, 1930–31. New York: Pathfinder, 1973.

Writings of Leon Trotsky, 1932. New York: Pathfinder, 1973.

Writings of Leon Trotsky, 1932–33. New York: Pathfinder, 1972.

Writings of Leon Trotsky, 1936–37. Edited by Naomi Allen and George Breitman. New York: Pathfinder, 1970.

Writings of Leon Trotsky, 1937–1938. New York: Pathfinder, 1970.

Writings of Leon Trotsky, Supplement, 1934–1940. New York: Pathfinder, 1979.

Memoirs

Adamic, Louis. *My America.* New York: Harper and Brothers, 1938.

As We Saw the Thirties: Essays on Social and Political Movements of a Decade. Edited by Rita James Simon. Urbana: University of Illinois Press, 1967.

Baldwin, Roger. "Recollections of a Life in Civil Liberties—II: Russia, Communism, and the United Fronts, 1920–1940." *Civil Liberties Review* 2 (Fall 1975): 10–40.

Barrett, William. *The Truants.* Garden City: Anchor Press/Doubleday, 1982.

Bellow, Saul. "Writers, Intellectuals, Politics: Mainly Reminiscence." *National Interest* 31 (Spring 1993): 124–34.

Bendiner, Robert. *Just Around the Corner: A Highly Selective History of the* 305
Thirties. New York: Harper and Row, 1967.

Bliven, Bruce. *Five Million Words Later: An Autobiography*. New York: Day,
1970.

Bogan, Louise. *Journey Around My Room*. Edited by Ruth Limmer. New York:
Viking, 1980.

Brooks, Van Wyck. *An Autobiography*. New York: Dutton, 1965.

——. *From the Shadow of the Mountains*. New York: Dutton, 1961.

Cannon, James P. *The History of American Trotskyism*. New York: Pioneer,
1944.

Carlson, Oliver. "Recollections of American Trotskyist Leaders," *Studies in
Comparative Communism* 10 (Spring/Summer 1977): 161–65.

Chamberlain, John. *A Life With the Printed Word*. Chicago: Regnery Gateway,
1982.

Chamberlin, William Henry. *The Confessions of an Individualist*. New York:
Macmillan, 1940.

——. *The Evolution of a Conservative*. Chicago: Regnery, 1959.

Chambers, Whittaker. *Witness*. New York: Random House, 1952.

Cole, Lester. *Hollywood Red*. Palo Alto: Ramparts, 1981.

Corey, Esther. "Lewis Corey (Louis C. Fraina), 1892–1953: *A Bibliography With
Autobiographical Notes.*" *Labor History* 4 (Spring 1963): 103–131.

Cowley, Malcolm. *And I Worked at the Writer's Trade*. New York: Viking, 1963.

——. *The Dream of the Golden Mountains*. New York: Viking, 1964.

——. "Echoes From Moscow, 1937–1938." *Southern Review* 20 (Winter 1984):
1–11.

——. *Exile's Return*. Revised ed. New York: Viking, 1962.

——. "1935: The Year of the Congress." *Southern Review* 15 (4/79): 273–87.

——. "A Remembrance of the Red Romance." *Esquire* 61 (3–4/64): 124–130
and 78–80.

Crichton, Kyle [Robert Forsythe]. *Total Recoil*. Garden City: Doubleday, 1960.

Dahlberg, Edward. *The Confessions of Edward Dahlberg*. New York: Braziller,
1971.

Davis, Hope Hale. "A Memoir: Looking Back at My Years in the Party." *New
Leader* 63 (2/11/80): 10–18.

David, Jerome. *A Life Adventure for Peace*. New York: Citadel, 1967.

Dos Passos, John. *The Best Times*. New York: New American Library, 1966.

——. *Journeys Between Wars*. New York: Harcourt, Brace, 1938.

Dunne, Philip. *Take Two*. New York: McGraw-Hill, 1980.

Duranty, Walter. *I Write as I Please*. New York: Halcyon House, 1935.

Eastman, Max. *Enjoyment of Living*. New York: Harper and Brothers, 1948.

——. *Love and Revolution*. New York: Random House, 1964.

Eddy, Sherwood. *A Pilgrimage of Ideas*. New York: Farrar and Rinehart, 1934.

Farrell, James T. "Dewey in Mexico." *Reflections at Fifty and Other Essays*.
New York: Vanguard, 1954.

306 ——. "A Memoir on Leon Trotsky." *University of Kansas City Review* 23 (Summer 1957): 293–98.

Fast, Howard. *Being Red.* Boston: Houghton Mifflin, 1990.

——. *The Naked God: The Writer and the Communist Party.* New York: Praeger, 1957.

Fischer, Louis. *Men and Politics.* London: Cape, 1941.

Frank, Waldo. *Memoirs.* Edited by Alan Trachtenberg. Amherst: University of Massachusetts Press, 1973.

Freeman, Joseph. *An American Testament.* New York: Octagon, 1936.

Glotzer, Albert. *Trotsky: Memoir and Critique.* Buffalo: Prometheus, 1989.

The God That Failed. Edited by Richard Crossman. 1949. Reprint. New York: Harper and Brothers, 1954.

Gregory, Horace. *The House on Jefferson Street: A Cycle of Memoirs.* New York: Holt, Rinehart and Winston, 1971.

Hellman, Lillian. *Scoundrel Time.* New York: Bantam, 1976.

Herbst, Josephine. "The Starched Blue Sky of Spain." *The Noble Savage* 1 (1960): 76–117.

——. "Yesterday's Road." *New American Review* 3 (4/68): 84–104.

Hicks, Granville. *Part of the Truth.* New York: Harcourt, Brace, and World, 1965.

——. *Where We Came Out.* New York: Viking, 1954.

Holmes, John Haynes. *I Speak For Myself.* New York: Harper and Brothers, 1959.

Hook, Sidney. "Breaking With the Communists—A Memoir." *Commentary* 77 (2/84): 47–53.

——. "Memories of the Moscow Trials." *Commentary* 77 (3/84): 57–63.

——. *Out of Step.* New York: Harper & Row, 1987.

Howe, Irving. *A Margin of Hope.* New York: Harcourt, Brace, Jovanovich, 1982.

——. "A Memoir of the Thirties." In *Steady Work,* 349–64. New York: Harcourt, Brace and World, 1954.

James P. Cannon as We Knew Him. New York: Pathfinder, 1976.

Josephson, Matthew. *Infidel in the Temple: A Memoir of the Nineteen-Thirties.* New York: Knopf, 1967.

Kazin, Alfred. *Starting Out in the Thirties.* Boston: Little, Brown, 1962. New ed. Ithaca: Cornell University Press, 1989.

Kent, Rockwell. *It's Me O Lord.* New York: Dodd, Mead, 1955.

Kristol, Irving. *Reflections of a Neoconservative.* New York: Basic, 1983.

Krutch, Joseph Wood. *More Lives Than One.* New York: William Sloane Associates, 1962.

Lamont, Corliss. *Yes To Life: Memoirs of Corliss Lamont.* New York: Horizon, 1981.

Lens, Sidney. *Unrepentant Radical.* Boston: Beacon, 1980.

Levin, Meyer. *In Search: An Autobiography.* New York: Horizon, 1950.

"Liberal Anti-Communism Revisited: A Symposium." *Commentary* 44 (9/67): 31–79.

Lovett, Robert Morss. *All Our Years.* New York: Viking, 1948.

Lyons, Eugene. *Assignment in Utopia.* New York: Harcourt, Brace, 1937.

———. *Moscow Carrousel.* New York: Knopf, 1935.

McCarthy, Mary. *Intellectual Memoirs.* New York: Harcourt, Brace, Jovanovich, 1992.

———. *On the Contrary.* New York: Farrar, Straus and Cudahy, 1961.

Macdonald, Dwight. *Memoirs of a Revolutionist.* New York: Farrar, Straus and Cudahy, 1957.

McWilliams, Carey. *The Education of Carey McWilliams.* New York: Simon and Schuster, 1978.

Mangione, Jerre. *An Ethnic at Large.* New York: Putnam's Sons, 1978.

Matthews, J. B. *Odyssey of a Fellow Traveler.* Privately published, 1938.

Mumford, Lewis. *My Works and Days.* New York: Harcourt, Brace, Jovanovich, 1979.

North, Joseph. *No Men Are Strangers.* New York: International, 1958.

Novack, George. "A.J. [Muste] and American Trotskyism." *Liberation* 12 (9–10/67): 21–24.

———. "How the Moscow Trials Were Exposed: A Memoir of the Dewey Commission." *The Militant* 41 (5/6/77): 13–14, 20–21.

Phillips, William. "How *Partisan Review* Began." *Commentary* 62 (12/76): 42–44.

———. "*Partisan Review*" Then and Now." *Partisan Review* 51 (1984): 491–93.

Podhoretz, Norman. *Making It.* Harper and Row, 1967.

Rexroth, Kenneth. *Excerpts From a Life.* Santa Barbara: Conjunctions, 1981.

Rice, Elmer. *Minority Report: An Autobiography.* New York: Simon and Schuster, 1963.

Richmond, Al. *A Long View From the Left.* Boston: Houghton Mifflin, 1973.

Roskolenko, Harry. *When I Was Last on Cherry Street.* New York: Stein and Day, 1965.

Rovere, Richard. *Arrivals and Departures.* New York: Macmillan, 1976.

———. *Final Reports.* Garden City: Doubleday, 1984.

Seaver, Edwin. *So Far So Good: Recollections of a Life in Publishing.* Westport: Lawrence Hill, 1986.

Seldes, George. *Tell the Truth and Run.* New York: Greenberg, 1953.

Sheean, Vincent. *Personal History.* New York: Modern Library, 1939.

Stewart, Donald Ogden. *By a Stroke of Luck.* New York: Paddington, 1975.

"Symposium: Thirty Years Later: Memories of the First American Writers' Congress." *American Scholar* 35 (Summer 1966): 495–516.

The Time Is Ripe: The 1940 Journal of Clifford Odets. New York: Grove, 1988.

Trilling, Diana. *The Beginning of the Journey.* New York: Harcourt, Brace, 1993.

Trilling, Lionel. "Young in the Thirties." *Commentary* 41 (5/66): 43–51.

Villard, Oswald Garrison. *Fighting Years.* New York: Harcourt, Brace, 1939.

Whose Revolution? A Study of the Future Course of Liberalism in the United States. Edited by Irving DeWitt Talmadge. Westport: Hyperion, 1941; reprint, 1975.

308   Winter, Ella. *And Not To Yield: An Autobiography.* New York: Harcourt, Brace and World, 1963.

Wolfe, Bernard. *Memoirs of a Not Altogether Shy Pornographer.* Garden City: Doubleday, 1972.

Wolfe, Bertram D. *A Life in Two Centuries.* New York: Stein and Day, 1981.

Wright, Richard. *American Hunger.* New York: Harper and Row, 1944; new ed., 1977.

Fiction

Brooks, Van Wyck. *Opinions of Oliver Allston.* New York: Dutton, 1941.

Dos Passos, John. *Adventures of a Young Man.* New York: Harcourt, Brace, 1939.

Farrell, James T. "Tom Carroll." In *Judith and Other Stories.* Garden City: Doubleday, 1973.

Freeman, Joseph. *Never Call Retreat.* New York: Farrar and Rinehart, 1943.

Gold, Michael. *Jews Without Money.* New York: Liveright, 1930.

Harrison, Charles Yale. *Meet Me On the Barricades.* New York: Scribner's Sons, 1938.

Lawson, John Howard. *Blockade [The River is Blue].* Screenplay written for Walter Wanger Productions, 1938.

McCarthy, Mary. "Portrait of the Intellectual as a Yale Man." In *The Company She Keeps.* New York: Harcourt, Brace, 1942.

———. *The Group.* New York: Harcourt, Brace and World, 1954.

Rodman, Selden. *The Revolutionists: A Tragedy in Three Acts.* New York: Duell, Sloan and Pearce, 1942.

Roskolenko, Harry. *The Terrorized.* Englewood Cliffs: Prentice Hall, 1967.

Schneider, Isidor. *The Judas Time.* New York: Dial, 1946.

Trilling, Lionel. *The Middle of the Journey.* New York: Scribner's Sons, 1947.

Wolfe, Bernard. *The Great Prince Died.* New York: Scribner's Sons, 1959.

Secondary Sources

Aaron, Daniel. "Some Reflections on Communism and the Jewish Writer." In *The Ghetto and Beyond,* edited by Peter Rose, 253–69. New York: Random House, 1969.

———. *Writers on the Left.* New York: Harcourt, Brace and World, 1961.

Abbott, Philip. *Leftward Ho! V. F. Calverton and American Radicalism.* Westport: Greenwood, 1993.

Adler, Les K., and Thomas G. Paterson. "Red Fascism: The Merger of Nazi Germany and Soviet Russia in the American Image of Totalitarianism, 1930's–1950's." *American Historical Review* 75 (4/70): 1046–64.

Alexander, Robert J. *The Right Opposition: The Lovestoneites and the International Communist Opposition of the 1930s.* Westport: Greenwood, 1981.   309

The American Radical Press, 1880–1960. Edited by Joseph R. Conlin. 2 vols. Westport: Greenwood, 1975.

Bell, Daniel. *Marxian Socialism in the United States.* Princeton: Princeton University Press, 1967.

Benson, Frederick R. *Writers in Arms: The Literary Impact of the Spanish Civil War.* New York: New York University Press, 1967.

Biel, Steven. *Independent Intellectuals in the United States, 1910–1945.* New York: New York University Press, 1992.

Biographical Dictionary of the American Left. Edited by Bernard K. Johnpoll and Harvey Klehr. Westport: Greenwood, 1986.

Blake, Casey Nelson. *Beloved Community: The Cultural Criticism of Randolph Bourne, Van Wyck Brooks, Waldo Frank and Lewis Mumford.* Chapel Hill: University of North Carolina Press, 1990.

Bloom, Alexander. *Prodigal Sons: The New York Intellectuals and Their World.* New York: Oxford University Press, 1986.

Bloom, James D. *Left Letters: The Culture Wars of Mike Gold and Joseph Freeman.* New York: Columbia University Press, 1992.

Bottomore, T. B. *Critics of Society: Radical Thought in North America.* New York: Random House, 1966.

Brightman, Carol. *Writing Dangerously: Mary McCarthy and Her World.* New York: Clarkson Potter, 1992.

Brown, Deming. *Soviet Attitudes Toward American Writing.* Princeton: Princeton University Press, 1962.

Caute, David. *The Fellow Travellers.* New York: Macmillan, 1973.

——. *The Great Fear.* New York: Simon and Schuster, 1978.

Ceplair, Larry, and Steven Englund. *The Inquisition in Hollywood.* Garden City: Anchor Press/Doubleday, 1980.

Cohen, Robert. *When the Old Left Was Young: Student Radicals and America's First Mass Student Movement, 1929–1941.* New York: Oxford University Press, 1993.

Coleman, Peter. *The Liberal Conspiracy: The Congress For Cultural Freedom and the Struggle for the Mind of Postwar Europe.* New York: Free Press, 1989.

"The Communist Party: An Exchange." *New York Review of Books* 30 (4/14/83): 50–51.

Conquest, Robert. *The Great Terror.* London: Macmillan, 1968.

Cooney, Terry A. *The Rise of the New York Intellectuals.* Madison: University of Wisconsin Press, 1986.

Deutscher, Isaac. *The Prophet Outcast: Trotsky, 1929–1940.* London: Oxford University Press, 1963.

——. *Stalin.* 2d ed. New York: Oxford University Press, 1966.

Diggins, John P. *The American Left in the Twentieth Century.* New York: Harcourt, Brace, Jovanovich, 1973.

310 ——. "The *New Republic* and Its Times." *New Republic* 191 (12/84) : 23–73.

——. *The Rise and Fall of the American Left.* New York: Norton, 1992.

——. *Up from Communism.* New York: Harper and Row, 1975.

Draper, Theodore. *American Communism and Soviet Russia.* New York: Viking, 1960.

——. "American Communism Revisited." *New York Review of Books* 32 (5/9/85): 32–37.

——. "The Life of the Party." *New York Review of Books* 41 (1/13/94): 45–51.

——. "The Popular Front Revisited." *New York Review of Books* 32 (5/30/85): 44–50.

——. *The Roots of American Communism.* New York: Viking, 1957.

Dykhuizen, George. *The Life and Mind of John Dewey.* Carbondale: Southern Illinois University Press, 1973.

Eaton, William Edward. *The American Federation of Teachers.* Carbondale: Southern Illinois University Press, 1975.

Encyclopedia of the American Left. Edited by Mari Jo Buhle, Paul Buhle, and Dan Georgakas. Urbana: University of Illinois Press, 1992.

Felix, David. *Protest: Sacco–Vanzetti and the Intellectuals.* Bloomington: Indiana University Press, 1965.

Feuer, Lewis. "American Travelers to the Soviet Union 1917–32." *American Quarterly* 14 (Summer 1962): 119–49.

Foley, Barbara. *Radical Representations: Politics and Form in U.S. Proletarian Fiction, 1929–1941.* Durham: Duke University Press, 1993.

Fox, Richard Wrightman. *Reinhold Niebuhr.* New York: Pantheon, 1985.

Geismar, Maxwell. *Writers in Crisis: The American Novel Between Two Wars.* Boston: Houghton Mifflin, 1942.

G[e]nizi, Haim. "*The Modern Quarterly:* 1923–1940: An Independent Radical Magazine." *Labor History* 15 (Spring 1974): 199–215.

Gerstle, Gary. "Mission From Moscow: American Communism in the 1930s." *Reviews in American History* 12 (12/84): 559–66.

Gilbert, James Burkhart. *Writers and Partisans: A History of Literary Radicalism in America.* New York: Wiley and Sons, 1968.

Goldwater, Walter. *Radical Periodicals in America, 1890–1950.* New Haven: Yale University Press, 1964.

Gordon, Max. "The Communist Party of the 1930s and the New Left." *Socialist Revolution* 6 (1–3/76): 11–66.

Guttmann, Allen. *The Jewish Writer in America.* New York: Oxford, 1971.

——. *The Wound in the Heart: America and the Spanish Civil War.* New York: Macmillan, 1962.

Harrison, Helen A. "John Reed Club Artists and the New Deal." *Prospects* (1980): 241–68.

Hollander, Paul. *Political Pilgrims.* New York: Oxford University Press, 1981.

Hollinger, David. "Ethnic Diversity, Cosmopolitanism and the Emergence of the American Liberal Intelligentsia." *American Quarterly* 27 (5/75): 133–51.

Homberger, Eric. *American Writers and Radical Politics, 1900–39*. London: 311
Macmillan, 1986.
——. "Proletarian Literature and the John Reed Clubs, 1929–1935." *Journal of American Studies* 13 (8/79): 221–44.
Hoopes, James. *Van Wyck Brooks: In Search of American Culture*. Amherst: University of Massachusetts Press, 1977.
Howe, Irving, and Lewis Coser. *The American Communist Party*. Boston: Beacon, 1957.
Isserman, Maurice. *If I Had a Hammer . . . The Death of the Old Left and the Birth of the New Left*. New York: Basic, 1987.
——. "The 1956 Generation: An Alternative Approach to the History of American Communism." *Radical America* 14 (3–4/80): 43–51.
——. *Which Side Were You On? The American Communist Party During the Second World War*. Middletown, Conn.: Wesleyan University Press, 1982.
Jacoby, Russell. *The Last Intellectuals*. New York: Basic, 1987.
Jaffe, Philip. *The Rise and Fall of American Communism*. New York: Horizon Press, 1975.
Jumonville, Neil. *Critical Crossings: The New York Intellectuals in Postwar America*. Berkeley: University of California Press, 1991.
Kalaidjian, Walter. *American Culture Between the Wars: Revisionary Modernism and Postmodern Critique*. New York: Columbia University Press, 1993.
Kazin, Alfred. "The Jew As Modern Writer." In *The Ghetto and Beyond*, edited by Peter I. Rose, 421–32. New York: Random House, 1969.
Klehr, Harvey. *The Heyday of American Communism*. New York: Basic, 1984.
——. "Leninism and Lovestoneism." *Studies in Comparative Communism* 7 (Spring/Summer 1974): 3–20.
Kovel, Joel. *Red Hunting in the Promised Land: Anti-Communism and the Making of America*. New York: Basic, 1994.
Kuznick, Peter. *Beyond the Laboratory: Scientists as Political Activists in 1930s America*. Chicago: University of Chicago Press, 1987.
Lamson, Peggy. *Roger Baldwin*. Boston: Houghton Mifflin, 1976.
Langer, Elinor. *Josephine Herbst*. Boston: Little, Brown, 1983.
Lasch, Christopher. *The Agony of the American Left*. New York: Knopf, 1969.
Lawson, R. Alan. *The Failure of Independent Liberalism, 1930–1941*. New York: Putnam's Sons, 1971.
Levanson, Leah, and Jerry Natterstad. *Granville Hicks: The Intellectual in Mass Society*. Philadelphia: Temple University Press, 1993.
Liebman, Arthur. *Jews and the Left*. New York: Wiley and Sons, 1979.
Ludington, Townsend. *John Dos Passos: A Twentieth Century Odyssey*. New York: Dutton, 1980.
McAuliffe, Mary Sperling. *Crisis on the Left: Cold War Politics and American Liberals, 1947–1954*. Amherst: University of Massachusetts Press, 1978.
Margulies, Sylvia R. *The Pilgrimage to Russia: The Soviet Union and the Treatment of Foreigners, 1924–1937*. Madison: University of Wisconsin Press, 1968.

312   Murphy, James F. *The Proletarian Moment: The Controversy Over Leftism in Literature*. Urbana: University of Illinois Press, 1991.

Murphy, Marjorie. *Blackboard Unions: The AFT and the NEA, 1900–1980*. Ithaca: Cornell University Press, 1990.

Myers, Constance Ashton. *The Prophet's Army: Trotskyists in America, 1928–1941*. Westport: Greenwood Press, 1977.

——. " 'We Were a Little Hipped on the Subject of Trotsky': Literary Trotskyists in the 1930s." In *Cultural Politics: Radical Moments in Modern History*, edited by Jerold M. Starr, 153–72. New York: Praeger, 1985.

Naison, Mark. "Communism From the Top Down." *Radical History Review* 32 (3/85): 97–101.

——. "Richard Wright and the Communist Party." *Radical America* 13 (1–2/79): 60–63.

Navasky, Victor. *Naming Names*. New York: Viking, 1980.

Nelson, Cary. *Repression and Recovery: Modern American Poetry and the Politics of Cultural Memory, 1910–1945*. Madison: University of Wisconsin Press, 1989.

New Studies in the Politics and Culture of U.S. Communism. Edited by Michael E. Brown, Randy Martin, Frank Rosengarten, and George Snedeker. New York: Monthly Review, 1993.

O'Neill, William L. *A Better World: The Great Schism: Stalinism and American Intellectuals*. New York: Simon and Schuster, 1982.

Pells, Richard H. *Radical Visions and American Dreams: Culture and Social Thought in the Depression Years*. New York: Harper and Row, 1973.

Penkower, Monty Noam. *The Federal Writers' Project*. Urbana: University of Illinois Press, 1977.

Rabinowitz, Paula. *Labor and Desire: Women's Revolutionary Fiction in Depression America*. Chapel Hill: University of North Carolina Press, 1991.

"Revisiting American Communism: An Exchange." *New York Review of Books* 32 (8/15/85): 40–44.

Rideout, Walter B. *The Radical Novel in the United States, 1900–1954*. Cambridge: Harvard University Press, 1956.

Robbins, Jack Alan. *The Birth of American Trotskyism, 1927–1929*. Privately published, 1973.

Robins, Natalie. *Alien Ink: The FBI's War on Freedom of Expression*. New York: Morrow, 1992.

Rollyson, Carl. *Lillian Hellman*. New York: St. Martin's Press, 1988.

Schrecker, Ellen W. *No Ivory Tower: McCarthyism and the Universities*. New York: Oxford University Press, 1986.

Schwartz, Lawrence. *Marxism and Culture*. Port Washington: Kennikat Press, 1980.

Schwartz, Nancy Lynn. *The Hollywood Writers' Wars*. Completed by Sheila Schwartz. New York: McGraw-Hill, 1982.

Shannon, David A. *The Decline of American Communism*. New York: Harcourt, Brace, 1959.

——. *The Socialist Party of America.* New York: Macmillan, 1955.

Shi, David. *Matthew Josephson, Bourgeois Bohemian.* New Haven: Yale University Press, 1981.

Starobin, Joseph R. *American Communism in Crisis, 1943–1957.* Cambridge: Harvard University Press, 1972.

Strong, Tracy B., and Helene Keyssar. *Right in Her Soul: The Life of Anna Louise Strong.* New York: Random House, 1983.

Wald, Alan M. *James T. Farrell.* New York: New York University Press, 1978.

——. *The New York Intellectuals.* Chapel Hill: University of North Carolina Press, 1987.

——. *The Revolutionary Imagination: The Poetry and Politics of John Wheelwright and Sherry Mangan.* Chapel Hill: University of North Carolina Press, 1983.

Walker, Samuel. *In Defense of American Liberties: A History of the ACLU.* New York: Oxford University Press, 1990.

Waltzer, Kenneth. "The New History of American Communism." *Reviews in American History* 11 (6/83): 259–67.

Warren, Frank A. *An Alternative Vision: The Socialist Party in the 1930s.* Bloomington: Indiana University Press, 1974.

——. *Liberals and Communism: The "Red Decade" Revisited.* Bloomington: Indiana University Press, 1966.

Weinstein, James. *Ambiguous Legacy: The Left in American Politics.* New York: New Viewpoints, 1975.

——. *The Decline of Socialism in America, 1912–1925.* New York: Monthly Review Press, 1967.

Westbrook, Robert B. *John Dewey and American Democracy.* Ithaca: Cornell University Press, 1991.

Whitfield, Stephen. *A Critical American: The Politics of Dwight Macdonald.* Hamden, Conn.: Archon Books, 1984.

——. "Totalitarianism in American Historical Writing." *Continuity* 12 (Fall 1988): 39–58.

Wilcox, Leonard. *V. F. Calverton: Radical in the American Grain.* Philadelphia: Temple University Press, 1992.

Wreszin, Michael. *A Rebel in Defense of Tradition: The Life and Politics of Dwight Macdonald.* New York: Basic, 1994.

Wright, William. *Lillian Hellman: The Image, The Woman.* New York: Simon and Schuster, 1986.

Dissertations

Bicker, Robert Joseph. "Granville Hicks as an American Marxist Critic." Ph.D. diss., University of Illinois at Urbana-Champaign, 1973.

Brogna, John J. "Michael Gold: Critic and Playwright." Ph.D. diss., University of Georgia, 1982.

314   Buhle, Paul M. "Louis C. Fraina, 1892–1953." MA thesis, University of Connecticut, 1968.

Bulkin, Eleanor. "Malcolm Cowley: A Study of His Literary, Social, and Political Thought to 1940." Ph.D. diss., New York University, 1973.

Burnett, James Thomas. "American Trotskyism and the Russian Question." Ph.D. diss., University of California at Berkeley, 1968.

Casciato, Arthur Domenic. "Citizen Writers: A History of the League of American Writers, 1935–1942." Ph.D. diss., University of Virginia, 1986.

Clecak, Peter E. "Marxism and American Literary Criticism." Ph.D. diss., Stanford University, 1964.

Dvosin, Andrew James. "Literature in a Political World: The Career and Writings of Philip Rahv." Ph.D. diss., New York University, 1977.

G[e]nizi, Haim. "V. F. Calverton: Independent Radical." Ph.D. diss., City University of New York, 1968.

Kinney, Sister Honora Margaret. "The Independents: A Study of the Non-Communist Left in the United States, 1919–1929." Ph.D. diss., Syracuse University, 1973.

Lifka, Thomas E. "The Concept 'Totalitarianism' and American Foreign Policy, 1933–1949." Ph.D. diss., Harvard University, 1973.

Long, Terry L. "The Radical Criticism of Granville Hicks in the 1930s." Ph.D. diss., Ohio State University, 1971.

Lowenfish, Lee E. "American Radicals and Soviet Russia, 1917–1940." Ph.D. diss., University of Wisconsin, 1968.

Peck, David R. "The Development of an American Marxist Literary Criticism: The Monthly *New Masses*." Ph.D. diss., Temple University, 1968.

Poole, Thomas Ray. " 'Counter-Trial': Leon Trotsky on the Soviet Purge Trials." Ph.D. diss., University of Massachusetts, 1974.

Rozakis, Laurie. "How the Division Within the Liberal Community Was Reflected in the *Nation,* 1930–1950." Ph.D. diss., SUNY Stonybrook, 1984.

Sanders, David Scott, Jr. "Pattern of Rejection: Three American Novelists and the Communist Literary Line, 1919–1949." Ph.D. diss., University of California at Los Angeles, 1956.

Wolfe, Thomas Kennerly. "The League of American Writers." Ph.D. diss., Yale University, 1956.

Index

About the Author

Judy Kutulas is
Assistant Professor
of History at St. Olaf
College, Northfield,
Minnesota.

Library of Congress Cataloging-in-Publication Data

Kutulas, Judy, 1953–

The long war : the intellectual people's

front and anti-Stalinism, 1930–1940 / Judy Kutulas.

p.   cm.   Includes bibliographical references (p.   )

and index.

ISBN 0-8223-1526-2 (cloth). —

ISBN 0-8223-1524-6 (paper)

1. United States—Intellectual life—20th century.

2. Intellectuals—United States—Political activity—

History—20th century.   3. Communism—United States.

4. Right and left (Political science)   I. Title.

E169.1.K835   1995   320.5'31'097309043—dc20

94-26407   CIP